Cruising Guide
to Coastal
North Carolina

OTHER BOOKS BY CLAIBORNE S. YOUNG

*Cruising Guide to Coastal South Carolina and Georgia*
*Cruising Guide to Eastern Florida*
*Cruising Guide to the Northern Gulf Coast*
*Cruising Guide to Western Florida*

Please remember that bottom configurations, channel conditions, aids to navigation, and almost all on-the-water navigational data is subject to change at any time. While I have been careful to provide firsthand verification of all navigational information, on-the-water conditions may very well be quite different by the time of your cruise. Failure to follow current on-the-water reality, even when it differs from the instructions contained in this guide, can result in expensive and dangerous incidents. Unlike wending your way down an interstate highway, taking a waterborne cruise always has the potential of becoming an adventure. I have worked hard to help minimize your risk, but there are potential hazards in any cruising situation, for which captains, navigators, and crew are solely responsible.

John F. Blair, Publisher, makes no guarantee as to the accuracy or reliability of the information contained within this guidebook and will not accept any liability for injuries or damages caused to the reader by following this data.

**THE AUTHOR**

Claiborne Young also publishes a *free* quarterly newsletter called *The Salty Southeast*. This newlsetter updates new marinas, bridge schedules, changes in aids to navigation, and other timely cruising information. If you are interested in receiving this free newsletter write:

**Watermark Publishing**
**P.O. Box 67**
**Elon College, North Carolina 27244-0067**

# Cruising Guide to Coastal North Carolina

by Claiborne S. Young

John F. Blair, Publisher
Winston-Salem, North Carolina

Fourth Edition, 1997

DESIGNED BY DEBRA LONG HAMPTON
MAP DESIGN BY KERRY HORNE
COMPOSED BY CAROL DEAKIN
COVER PHOTOGRAPH BY BERNARD CARPENTER
INTERIOR PHOTOGRAPHY BY THE AUTHOR UNLESS OTHERWISE NOTED

*The paper in this book meets the guidelines for permanence
and durability of the Commitee on Production Guidelines for
Book Longevity of the Council on Library Resources.*

Library of Congress Cataloging-in-Publication-Data

Young, Claiborne S. (Claiborne Sellars), 1951–
    Cruising guide to coastal North Carolina / by Claiborne S. Young.—4th ed.
        p.      cm.
    Includes index.
    ISBN 0-89587-204-8 (alk. paper)
    1. Boats and boating—North Carolina—Guidebooks.
2. Intracoastal waterways—North Carolina—Guidebooks.
3. North Carolina—Guidebooks.
I. Title.
GV776.N74Y68     1997
797.1'09756—dc21        97-44541

This book is dedicated to
my Mother and Father
who taught me
the love of boating
and to Karen
my faithful, first-rate first mate

# Contents

# Acknowledgments

First and foremost, I would like to thank my first-rate first mate, Karen Ann, without whose experienced assistance as a researcher, navigator, photographer, and partner this book would not have been possible.

I extend a special thanks to my other research assistants, John Horne, Kerry Horne, Carol Deakin, and Earle Williams.

To my good friends Andy Lightbourne, Pete Driscoll, Jet Matthews, Penny Leary Smith, and Jerry Outlaw, I offer a heartfelt thanks for their many hours of proofreading, their good advice, and their enthusiasm. Thanks also to Barbara Huffman for all her ideas and aid in getting the guide off the ground and her help with the early chapters. To Faythe Brooks goes a warm thanks for her tireless efforts to read my unreadable handwriting and keep up with my impossible typing schedule.

I gratefully acknowledge the research assistance given by Chris Bean and the Edenton Historical Society, the North Carolina Mariners Museum, the Dredging Division of the Corps of Engineers, and the staff of May Memorial Library of Burlington, North Carolina.

Thanks also to Ken Markel and Bruce, John, Susan, Paul, and Renée Fetzer for their help in keeping my vessels ready for research, for their encouragement, and for helping to make boating fun.

Special thanks goes to the staff of Cape Hatteras National Seashore and to the Coast Guard personnel at Ocracoke for their invaluable aid in securing the use of the Cape Hatteras and Ocracoke Lighthouses for photographic platforms. Thanks also goes to the people at Hatteras Fishing Center for the trusting loan of a car when I needed it and, finally, to the people of Currituck County for all the information they provided on Currituck Banks.

I also make grateful acknowledgment to *The State* magazine for permission to quote from articles it has published. The quotation on page is from "Weapomeiock," by Bill Sharpe, which appeared in *The State* on July 3, 1954.

# Introduction

I envy the boaters and sailors who have not yet experienced the delights of the North Carolina coast. The state has the largest area of inland waters on the East Coast, and shoreline enough for years of exploration. Much of the shore remains undeveloped and retains its natural character. What a treat it is to anchor for the first time in a cove miles from civilization and to see the incredible array of stars in the clear coastal sky. Such anchorages give the boater an opportunity to feel something akin to what the early settlers must have felt when they first explored this storied coastline.

Out-of-the-way anchorages are often surprisingly near coastal cities and towns where cruisers can enjoy life ashore. Edenton, Washington, Oriental, New Bern, Morehead City, Beaufort, and Wrightsville Beach are major centers of pleasure boating known to all who have traversed the Intracoastal Waterway in North Carolina; but the cruising boater will also find marinas near many lesser-known towns, or even hidden behind a bend in a creek or river in the middle of nowhere.

Vast areas of North Carolina's waters have been largely ignored by cruisers, partly because boaters have not had easy access to the reliable and detailed information needed to fully take advantage of this splendid cruising potential. I have tried to satisfy that need with this guide. I have paid special attention to facilities and anchorages, as well as general navigational information. To add value and pleasure to your cruise, I have included accounts of coastal history, legends and folklore, and current information on shoreside attractions.

One of the great delights in cruising North Carolina waters is the many fine restaurants found along the coast. Within the body of this guide, you will find reviews of many dining spots convenient to dockside. Unless you happen to dislike all forms of seafood, coastal dining will never be an unpleasant experience. The Tar Heel State is justly famous for its fried seafood. For those with a landlubber palate, I have also mentioned some of the many coastal restaurants that specialize in exotic sandwiches and beef dishes. One particularly popular inn offers a smorgasbord with more than eighty selections.

Although this guide will not detail the many sport-fishing opportunities of the North Carolina coast, it is worth noting that fishing is very popular on both inland and ocean waters. One of the largest charter fleets on the East Coast is to be found at Morehead City. Other impressive sport-fisherman fleets are based at Hatteras and at Oregon Inlet. These intrepid craft regularly ply the coastal waters for any catch from billfish to king mackerel.

A familiarity with the coast of North Carolina requires some knowledge of both the geography and the history of the region. The tides, winds, and rivers have blessed (some might say cursed) the state with a unique geographical feature known as the Outer Banks. The narrow, long sandspits of the banks block off the Atlantic Ocean and enclose four large sounds: Currituck, Albemarle, Pamlico, and Core. Albemarle Sound is the largest freshwater sound in America. It is served by eight principal rivers, all navigable by the pleasure boater. Except for Chesapeake Bay, Pamlico Sound is the largest essentially landlocked coastal water in the United States. While parts of Pamlico are shallow and treacherous, much of it is readily navigable. Among a host of lesser streams, three major rivers—the Neuse, the Pamlico, and the Cape Fear—are navigable for considerable lengths and provide excellent cruising.

The Outer Banks protect the sounds from the more violent effects of ocean storms, but their shifting sands keep the waters in constant flux. Much of the history of the Tar Heel coast is the story of the rise and fall of the various inlets. If a once-deep inlet shoaled, then the community built around that cut died. If a new and deep inlet was opened by storm, new commercial ventures sprang up in response to the natural phenomenon.

Edenton, Manteo, Hatteras, Ocracoke, New Bern, Bath, Beaufort, Southport, and Wilmington are just some of the well-preserved coastal cities that have enduring pride in their historical heritage, especially their place in the history of colonial times and the Civil War. It is often forgotten that the Carolina coast was the first area in North America to be settled by English colonists. The 400th anniversary of Sir Walter Raleigh's Roanoke colonies was celebrated in North Carolina from 1984 to 1987.

For many years, North Carolina coastal communities existed in a state of near isolation. Overland travel was difficult and often dangerous. The sea lanes were the region's main communication with the outside world. The fruits of this isolation include a tradition of storytelling and a large body of folk tales and legends that have been handed down from generation to generation. Through these tales, the unique character of the coastal native can be understood and appreciated.

Some of the Eastern Seaboard's most treacherous offshore waters are to be found on the North Carolina coast. Cape Hatteras, with its adjoining Diamond Shoals, has long been known as the Graveyard of the Atlantic. Cape Lookout was once given the dubious title of "*Promontorium tremendum*" by early explorers.

Soon after the Revolutionary War, the fledgling American government began to address the problem of marine safety by the erection of lighthouses along the Outer Banks and southern coastal area. Many lighthouses have come and gone since those early days, but today, five major lights remain in operation on the banks. Two lighthouses, Cape Hatteras and Cape Lookout, are threatened by erosion of the beaches and may not survive many more years. The cruising boater should not miss the chance to view these monuments from an age of the sea now long departed.

As the lighthouses came to the North Carolina coast for the safety of offshore mariners, so came the Lifesaving Service. In the nineteenth century, lifesaving stations were established all along the Outer Banks. The bravery and courage of the early lifesaving crews is still remembered with pride and honor. Several of the old stations still stand, and a few continue in operation under the United States Coast Guard.

Cruising captains visiting North Carolina from other climes will find the state's waters very different from those of Chesapeake Bay, Long Island Sound, or even Charleston Harbor. North Carolina's waters are much shallower than their northern or southern counterparts. While most are certainly deep enough for the pleasure boater, there are many sandbars, shoals, and other obstructions that can readily bring the unwary cruiser to grief. Consequently, the science of navigation must be actively practiced by those cruising Tar Heel waters.

On the plus side, there is a noticeable absence of swift tidal currents along much of the North Carolina coastline. There are exceptions, however, particularly along the southerly part of the state's coast, so stay alert.

This guide is not a navigational primer, and I am assuming that you have a working knowledge of piloting and coastal navigation. If you don't, you should acquire these skills before tackling North Carolina's coastal waters.

Even the most experienced skipper will find it prudent to have certain safety instruments aboard. The shallow depths and changeable nature of the state's waters make a reliable depth sounder an absolute necessity. I prefer the digital or video variety for their easily recognized information. However, no matter what type of sounder you have, it won't do any good unless it is carefully watched. An error in navigation can quickly result in a hard grounding, sometimes out of sight of land; a reliable and closely watched sounder is the only valid insurance against such an occurrence.

The smart boater will also equip his craft with a log. It is often just as important to know how far you have gone as to know what course you are on. Many boaters used to deeper waters may find this an unusual recommendation, but remember this: In North Carolina, you must practice navigation, not just play at it. A log is an integral part of any serious navigator's arsenal of aids.

On the other hand, I do not feel that it is absolutely necessary for boaters in Tar Heel waters to have Loran C or GPS. Of course, if you plan to cruise offshore, Loran C or the newer, more flashy GPS would be most beneficial, but it is not a make-or-break consideration for inland passage-making. Of course, one of these electronic marvels might be welcome while cruising long legs between aids to navigation on Pamlico Sound, but good coastal navigation will see you safely through as well.

Inland waters in North Carolina exhibit a wave pattern quite different from those of deeper waters. The consistently shallow depths can result in short but steep waves in high winds. Onboard motion is very different from that given by deep-water swells. If bad weather threatens, it is better to wait out the storm rather than have the fillings jarred out of your teeth. The Pamlico and Albemarle Sounds are particularly susceptible to such conditions. However, with winds less than 15 knots, cruising conditions, particularly under sail, are generally delightful.

As a general rule, power craft of less than 25 feet and sailcraft under 20 feet should take great care before venturing on the open waters of Pamlico and Albemarle sounds. Happily, most rivers and creeks offer sheltered cruising for smaller craft.

In North Carolina waters, it is sometimes necessary to follow narrow, improved channels. For this reason, it is extremely important to watch for lateral leeway. The unwary navigator can quickly be set aground by a crosswind or current even when he thinks he is headed just where he should be going. Watch your stern as well as your forward course. By looking back, you can quickly tell if you are being swept sideways.

Aids to navigation along the North Carolina coast are reliable and well maintained. The vast majority are placed exactly where they should be to warn of shallow water. It is rare, except in the vicinity of inlets, that an aid is moved. While you should, of course, have the most up-to-date charts, studies of older maps reveal that many coastal aids to navigation are still where they were a decade ago.

Ice damage is not a problem on Tar Heel waters, and the boater from the North will find many more daybeacons and far fewer buoys than he might expect.

In this guide, lighted daybeacons are always called "flashing daybeacons." I feel this is a more descriptive term than the officially correct "light" or the more colloquial "flasher." Also, to avoid confusion, daybeacons without lights are always referred to as "unlighted daybeacons." Similarly, lighted buoys are called "flashing buoys."

The maps contained within this guide are placed to help locate marinas, anchorages, and other geographic points of interest. They are *not* meant to be used for navigation. Be sure to have the latest NOAA charts aboard for this crucial purpose.

Autumn is the ideal season for cruising North Carolina waters. From about the tenth of September to the first of November, coastal weather is usually at its best, with only a few stormy exceptions. There is generally just enough of a breeze for a good sail, but not too much wind to kick up a nasty chop. October is also the driest month in the state. Often, good weather persists until December. Unless a hurricane threatens to roar up from the tropics, fall cruising along the Tar Heel coastline is usually a genuine delight.

Summer is also a good boating season, though temperatures and humidity during July and August can be uncomfortable. Summer calms can leave sailcraft plodding along under auxiliary power, but this condition usually lasts only a few days. Afternoon thunderstorms can also be a problem, but generally, summer cruising of the Tar Heel coast is a pleasurable experience.

From about March 15 to the middle of May, cruising conditions range from good to simply awful. There are bright, shining days with light winds which seem born in paradise. The trouble is that the next day may be overcast and cool with 40-knot gales. Spring cruising should be planned with a ready ear to the weather forecast.

Most North Carolina pleasure boating ends by the latter part of December and resumes as early as March 1. However, some hearty souls cruise the state's waters year-round. Certainly, the commercial fisherman is not daunted by the North Carolina winter.

With three exceptions, inlets along the coast should be considered hazardous; channels can shift overnight! Generally, cruisers should seek local knowledge before attempting any of these capricious cuts. Aids to navigation at most North Carolina inlets are seldom charted because they are frequently shifted to mark the ever-changing sands.

The three exceptions to this rule of unreliability are Beaufort, Masonboro, and Cape Fear inlets. All three are carefully maintained, deep, and well marked. Aids to navigation in the Beaufort and Cape Fear Inlets are clearly charted. A stone jetty facilitates navigation of the Masonboro cut.

By now, after having read all my warnings about shallow water, you may have some concerns if you pilot a sailcraft with a fixed keel.

Happily, by practicing basic navigation, sailors whose craft draw less than 6 feet can safely cruise all major North Carolina bodies of water except the Currituck and Core Sounds. While shallow-water areas exist and in some sections are numerous, it is reasonably easy to avoid such hazards if you pay attention to what you are doing. I have personally checked every sidewater for the latest depth information, but remember, bottom configurations do change, and you should exercise caution at all times when venturing into new waters.

I hope this introduction has served to inform you of the nature and diversity of North Carolina waters. It is all too rare for the present-day boater to discover a coastline that has so many necessary facilities but still retains so much of its verdant natural character. All of us are very fortunate that North Carolina's waters fulfill these requirements. I take pride in being able to help my fellow boaters discover the North Carolina coast. Steeped in history and tradition, blessed by a benevolent climate, and peopled by some of the most friendly souls on this good earth, the Tar Heel coast beckons.

Good boating!

# Cruising Guide
to Coastal
North Carolina

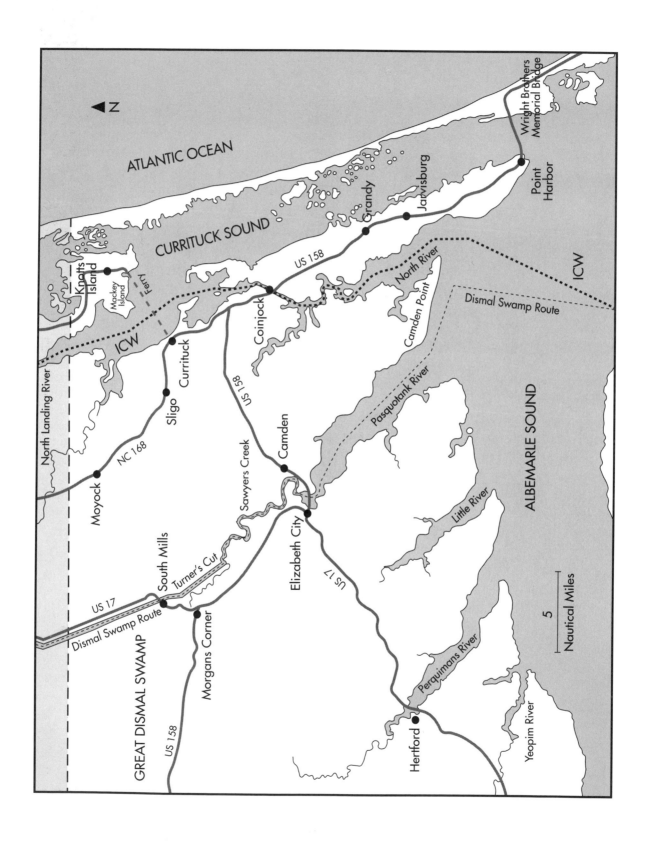

# Approaches to Albemarle Sound

## Charts

You will only need one NOAA chart for navigation of either the Dismal Swamp or Virginia–North Carolina Cut routes:

**12206** covers both passages from Norfolk, Virginia, to Albemarle Sound

Cruising boaters have a choice of two inland routes moving south from Virginia into North Carolina's waters. A few miles south of Norfolk, the Intracoastal Waterway splits into two separate passages, each with its own distinctive character. The Dismal Swamp leg of the ICW is a must for boaters who are not in a hurry and who wish to enjoy a backwater cruising experience well off the beaten path. The Virginia–North Carolina Cut, although lacking the unique natural scenery of the Dismal Swamp passage, offers reliable cruising ground and good facilities for almost any pleasure craft. This channel is heavily used, and your passage will probably be shared with several other vessels.

## DISMAL SWAMP ROUTE

The Dismal Swamp ICW passage cuts through the heart of the great swamp that straddles the North Carolina–Virginia state line. Part of the route is composed of the long Dismal Swamp Canal, which is situated between two locks, one at Deep Creek, Virginia, and the other in the small North Carolina village of South Mills. Both locks raise or lower cruising craft about 8 feet, and care must be taken when mooring to the lock walls. The locks currently operate four times a day, and skippers must take this schedule into consideration when planning their voyage.

A distance of 13 nautical miles separates the Deep Creek lock and the North Carolina state line, and an additional run of 6.8 nautical miles leads visiting cruisers to the South Mills lock.

Below South Mills, the ICW follows the wild, almost swampy northern headwaters of the Pasquotank River for 14.5 nautical miles to Elizabeth City. Beginning as a narrow, swampy stream, the river enlarges into a significant body of water by the time it reaches Elizabeth City. The only full-service facilities catering to cruising boaters on the Dismal Swamp passage are found here.

If you find yourself in need of mechanical repairs on the Dismal Swamp Canal, call Bob Baker at Fox Marine Services (919-331-1417). This independent mechanic will be glad to drive to the welcome center's docks (see below) or wherever you have managed to tie off along the canal. Baker has a deserved reputation for thorough and friendly service.

Farther south past Elizabeth City, the ICW follows the ever-broadening waters of the lower Pasquotank to Albemarle Sound. Surprisingly, the southern portion of the river offers only a single possibility for overnight anchorage.

Anchorages are all but nonexistent on the Dismal Swamp Canal itself. Several overnight havens offer good shelter on the Pasquotank north of Elizabeth City, particularly for vessels under 40 feet in length.

*Early morning on Dismal Swamp Canal*

Due to its width, the Dismal Swamp Canal is not particularly recommended for craft over 50 feet in length or those drawing more than 5½ feet. Generally, minimum depths on the canal run 6½ feet, though drought conditions occasionally lower these soundings. In times of plentiful rainfall, the canal offers greater depths, sometimes running to as much as 8 or 9 feet.

The Dismal Swamp passage is definitely a treat for those interested in natural scenery. The canal allows a magnificent view of the swampy terrain, still for the most part in its natural state. Tall cypress trees with garlands of gray moss stand against a backdrop of steamy, coffee-colored water. Cruisers will likely encounter little traffic along the way, and the isolation can make for a unique cruising experience.

Unfortunately, this wild backwater character can occasionally cause problems. Floating logs and partially submerged snags are sometimes found along the canal and the northern Pasquotank. Corps of Engineers boats regularly check the channel for obstructions, but boaters should still be on the lookout for these hazards. For safety's sake, it is generally a good idea to proceed slowly along the northern (canal) portion of the route.

Several years ago, the Dismal Swamp Canal had more than its share of problems. A few dry summer seasons lowered water levels so much that the canal was closed for long stretches at a time. The water level in the canal is controlled by the depth of Lake Drummond in Virginia. If droughts lower the lake's waters below a safe depth, the canal must remain closed until conditions improve. Coastal congressmen also faced the mammoth task of generating the necessary funding to keep the locks and bridges along the canal operating. This entire situation is now much improved, with far more stable funding and generally consistent operating times.

As of this writing, the canal is usually open year-round, weather conditions permitting. The locks at both Deep Creek and South Mills operate at 8:30 A.M., 11:00 A.M., 1:30 P.M., and 3:30 P.M. During winter, the canal is sometimes closed for maintenance. Call the Corps of Engi-

neers' Waterway office in Great Bridge, Virginia (804-547-2109), or the Dismal Swamp Canal Welcome Center (919-771-8333) ahead of time to check on the latest canal conditions, particularly during the winter months.

### Dismal Swamp Route History

By the late 18th century, it was apparent that northeastern North Carolina badly needed a ready outlet for its produce. Overland routes were primitive at best, and the long passage south down Pamlico Sound to Ocracoke Inlet was expensive and dangerous. In 1786, commissioners were appointed from North Carolina and Virginia to study the linkage of Albemarle Sound and Chesapeake Bay by a canal running through the Dismal Swamp. In 1790, both states passed the necessary legislation for the establishment of the Dismal Swamp Canal Company. One of the first subscribers was none other than George Washington. As far as this writer has been able to learn, there is no truth to the tradition that Washington conducted the original survey for the canal. He was involved in the project, but his contribution seems to have been moral and financial.

Construction began in 1793. By 1796, funds were temporarily exhausted, but a portion of the canal was completed, and a good road connected the northern and southern works. Until 1812, shallow-draft barges would journey as far north or south as possible, at which point their cargo would be unloaded onto wagons; these goods would, in turn, be reloaded on other craft waiting at the opposite end of the road. With the British blockade of the coastline during the War of 1812, the federal government awoke to the canal's potential for safely transporting goods north and south. Necessary funds were appropriated, and the project was finally completed in 1814.

The original canal was woefully inadequate for its purpose. It was too small and shallow for vessels that were large enough to safely ply Albemarle and Pamlico Sounds. Even with the canal's disadvantages, however, the initial heavy traffic demonstrated the need for a more easily navigable waterway. More money was advanced by the federal government, and a loan was procured from Virginia. By 1828, the canal had been completely rebuilt. The new stream averaged 40 feet in width and could accommodate vessels drawing 4½ feet.

About this time, Alexander Macomb, the chief federal engineer, put forward a plan for the construction of an "inland waterway" from Norfolk to Beaufort. Nothing was done at the time, but Macomb planted a seed that would one day grow into the Intracoastal Waterway.

Even with the improvements, passage on the Dismal Swamp Canal was often fraught with delays. The five stone locks gave continual trouble, and vessels were frequently delayed for several days while repairs were made. By 1859, the Albemarle and Chesapeake Canal (the present-day North Carolina–Virginia route) opened. This new cut was mostly free of locks and delays and eventually lured away most commercial traffic. The Dismal Swamp route fell on hard times.

Still, there were those who believed in the older channel. Through private investment, the entire canal was again rebuilt between 1895 and 1899. The new passage was wider and deeper and had only two locks. Because of these improvements, the Dismal Swamp Canal regained commercial dominance over its rival. However, in 1913, the federal government purchased the Albemarle and Chesapeake Canal as part of the new Intracoastal Waterway. The Dismal Swamp Canal could not compete with the new toll-free passage, and the older route was little used until 1929, when it also was purchased by federal authorities and incorporated into the ICW.

## Great Dismal Swamp

The Great Dismal Swamp stretches from southeastern Virginia into northeastern North Carolina, beginning about 4 miles south of Suffolk, Virginia, and extending to Elizabeth City, North Carolina. Today, it covers 600 square miles, but it was formerly more than six times as large. Over the years, many drainage projects have reclaimed much of the land as highly productive farming areas.

Most of the swamp is a morass of acidic, coffee-colored water, peat bogs, and large patches of rushes known as the "green sea." Some drier tracts are dense timberland that yields valuable quantities of cypress, gum, and pine. Lake Drummond, 6 miles long and 3 miles wide, sits at the center of the great swamp. It was discovered in 1677 by William Drummond, North Carolina's first colonial governor.

Since earliest colonial times, the swamp has had a sinister reputation. William Byrd surveyed the area while establishing the dividing line between North Carolina and Virginia in 1728. It was he who first attached the label *dismal* to the swamp. Later, George Washington acquired a goodly portion of the swamp and had his slaves dig its first small canal in 1763.

Though vastly reduced in size, the Dismal Swamp still lives up to its name. Few will ever forget a trip through the magnificent Great Dismal.

## Welcome Center (Standard Mile 28)

In 1989, North Carolina opened an on-the-water welcome center overlooking the Dismal Swamp Canal. This facility is the best thing to happen to the old canal since its last rebuilding. The center's director, Penny Leary Smith, is a prominent, vocal proponent of the Dismal Swamp Canal. She has worked long and hard to successfully promote this notable passage. Penny is one of the most knowledgeable people about conditions and points of interest in northeastern North Carolina that you will ever come across. If you are in need of any information, seek out Penny or one of her fine staff at the welcome center.

The Dismal Swamp Canal Welcome Center is the only state-sponsored facility in the United States welcoming both automobile and boating visitors. The center guards the canal's eastern banks 5 miles north of the South Mills lock, a short jog south of the North Carolina–Virginia line. Passing boaters are welcome to moor their vessels free of charge either temporarily or overnight to the 150-foot fixed wooden-face dock. Freshwater connections are available, though power connections are not. Average dockside depths are the usual 6½ feet. Overnighters can make use of the on-site restrooms, though there are no showers; there is also an adjacent cookout area. Many brochures and maps are available at the center, including information about the ICW passage both north and south of the Dismal.

Expansion plans are now completed to enlarge the Dismal Swamp Canal Welcome Center to almost twice its original size. Most of the old structure has been given over to extended restroom facilities, while the welcoming desk has been moved to the new portion of the building. A cartop boaters' access (for canoes and other very small craft) is also in the offing. It's nice to see that our tax money does something really useful now and then!

The on-site staff monitors VHF channel 16 and stands ready to assist any visiting cruiser. From Memorial Day to October 31, the center is open seven days a week from 9 A.M. to 5 P.M. Between November 1 and Memorial Day, it is open from Tuesday through Saturday.

Similarly, cars traveling on U.S. 17, which parallels the canal in this area, can stop for the same information. With the demise several years ago of the ICW Welcome Station in Fernandina Beach, Florida, North Carolina can now lay claim to one of the most unique facilities on the entire Waterway.

**Dismal Swamp Canal Welcome Center  (919) 771-8333**

Approach depth: 6½–8 feet (typical)
Dockside depth: 6½ feet (typical)
Accepts transients: yes
Fixed wooden-face dock: yes
Dockside water connections: yes
Shoreside restrooms: yes

### South Mills (Standard Mile 32.5)

After cruising under a high-rise span and then through a low-level swing bridge, visiting boaters will pass through the tiny village of South Mills for a short distance before reaching the lock. Don't blink, or you might miss the town.

South Mills was once, believe it or else, an important port, as it sat astride the Dismal Swamp Canal in the stream's days of prolific commerce. Today, the community has shrunk to a tiny village which does not even appear on many state maps.

There used to be a motel in South Mills with a dock to which visiting cruisers could tie if they missed a lock opening. That facility is now long closed, and the dock is overgrown and dilapidated.

Boaters who miss a lock opening can tie to a bulkhead or a group of pilings just north of the lock gate. A similar complex of pilings is found south of the lock and can be used by northbound craft for the same purpose. Given the sheltered, little-trafficked nature of the narrow canal, this spot usually makes an acceptable overnight or temporary berth. No power or water connections or any other marine facilities are available. You may be able to dinghy ashore, but be diplomatic and don't trespass. A healthy walk of about a mile will lead you to a grocery store. Ask the lock master for directions.

### Turner's Cut

South of the South Mills lock, the ICW briefly follows another man-made canal known as Turner's Cut on its way to the northern Pasquotank River. Not far from the lock's exit, a wayward branch of the cut leads back north to an active timber-barge loading facility. Although the arm holds 9 to 11 feet of water, there is not really enough swinging room for anchorage. Additionally, any barge loading or unloading would make this body of water an undesirable haven for pleasure craft.

### Upper Pasquotank River (Standard Mile 37)

Upon leaving Turner's Cut, most cruising craft will cut east and south on the Pasquotank River as they cruise toward Elizabeth City. However, the uppermost reaches of the river, abandoned by the ICW, cut sharply southwest from the Pasquotank–Turner's Cut intersection. These waters hold 7- to 13-foot soundings for several hundred yards upstream, but there is only enough room for craft as large as 32 feet to swing comfortably on the anchor. Slightly larger vessels might still be able to anchor by employing a Bahamian-style mooring to minimize swinging room. If your boat fits these size requirements, give this potential overnight stop a look. The shores are completely in their natural state, and the protection from inclement weather is almost up to hurricane-safe proportions.

If you choose to anchor here, consider breaking out the dinghy and exploring the point of land separating the upper Pasquotank from Turner's Cut. During on-site research, I found that someone had cleared a small space on this point and even provided an idyllic park bench overlooking the water.

## Goat Island Anchorage
## (Standard Mile 43.5)

Goat Island bisects the Pasquotank southeast of unlighted daybeacon #13 and the charted location of "Shipyard Ldg." The ICW continues down the northeastern branch, but the southwestern leg can serve as an excellent and attractive overnight anchorage for most craft drawing less than 5 feet. Protection is good from all winds and should prove adequate even for a heavy blow. Both shores are heavily wooded and mostly undeveloped, though one or two private homes peep out of the wooded banks here and there. Swinging room should be sufficient for boats up to 45 feet.

The waters abeam of the island's northwestern and southeastern points hold 5- to 6-foot depths, but behind the main body of land, soundings deepen to between 6 and 10 feet.

Fellow cruisers have reported that the bottom is foul with stumps and other debris, though I myself did not encounter this problem. Set an anchor trip line for maximum safety.

## Sawyers Creek (Standard Mile 46.5)

Sawyers Creek cuts into the Pasquotank's

*Southern entrance to South Mills lock*

northeastern shore near the charted location of Camden, just above the railway swing bridge. This stream provides good anchorage for craft less than 33 feet in length that draw no more than 5 feet. An unmarked channel flowing through the creek's mouth holds 6-foot depths, but you have to identify it correctly or you could end up in 4½ feet of water. Soundings ranging from 6 to 13 feet can be expected a bit farther upstream.

The roomiest anchor-down spot is found just past the tricky entrance. Here, boats up to 32 feet can anchor in 8 feet of water and be protected from all winds. The surrounding shores are mostly natural and make for a pleasing backdrop.

### Railroad Bridge Anchorage (Standard Mile 47)

An unnamed creek makes into the Pasquotank's southeastern banks 0.3 nautical mile southwest of the charted railroad bridge near Camden. This sidewater offers the best overnight anchorage on the northern Pasquotank. It boasts minimum depths of 8 to 10 feet and affords plenty of swinging room for boats up to 50 feet. Two lovely homes overlook the stream's northeastern shores, adding to the anchorage's appeal. Protection is sufficient for any winds short of a hurricane.

### Pasquotank River Yacht Club (Standard Mile 50)

South of flashing daybeacon #9, passing cruisers will observe the fixed wooden piers of Pasquotank River Yacht Club along the river's southerly banks. This club normally does not

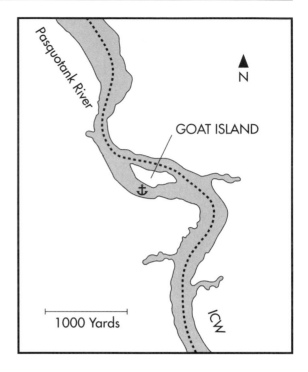

offer reciprocal privileges. Minimum entrance depths are 6 feet, with 4½ to 6 feet of water dockside.

### Elizabeth City (Standard Mile 50.5)

West of flashing daybeacon #9, you will quickly spy the Elizabeth City waterfront overlooking the banks of a hairpin turn in the Pasquotank River. Since this guide first appeared in the early 1980s, the pleasure-boating climate in Elizabeth City has undergone a radical change for the better. To quote Fred Fearing, the unofficial leader of Elizabeth City's boat-welcoming committee, "Hospitality is our first name." This motto really says it all! As has been true for many years, the town offers the only full-service marine facilities on the entire Dismal Swamp route.

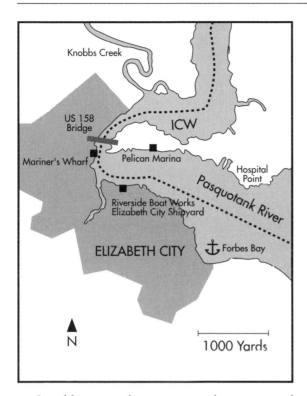

In addition to the commercial marinas and boatyards that have always been available, this industrious community has built its own town docks, to which visiting cruisers are welcome to tie for 48 hours free of charge. Back in 1985, Willard Scott, the famous television weather forecaster, visited Elizabeth City for several days. He was so impressed with the wonderful hospitality in the community that he donated an electric golf cart to help in the town's welcoming efforts. Now, before visiting cruisers can even coil their lines, Fred or one of his fellow volunteers will usually appear in the "Rose Buddie" golf cart and present the female members of the crew with a bouquet of roses; they also give everyone pamphlets describing Elizabeth City's nearby historic district and the surrounding

region's fascinating history. Free local newspapers are available, and the community volunteers have established a program with the local library whereby boaters can swap their used paperbacks for similar publications. If more than five vessels are docked at the town slips on any given night, the industrious volunteers throw a wine-and-cheese party (with chips and dip) at the adjacent parking lot. A local company even donates free dog and cat food to visiting boaters who have a "Fido" or "Meow" aboard. Boaters needing a ride to the local supermarkets, laundromats, or other shoreside facilities can be sure of receiving the transportation they need from Fred and company.

It's difficult to overstate the enthusiasm Elizabeth City has for developing a rapport with cruising boaters. In all my travels, I have never before encountered such a well-organized and successful program. Boaters are highly encouraged to include Elizabeth City in their cruising plans and experience this unusually gracious climate for themselves.

Cruisers lucky enough to moor on the Elizabeth City waterfront are only a short walk from the downtown historic district. If you have not already gotten one from the local volunteers, you can find tour maps at the chamber of commerce. Ask any local citizen for directions.

One historic attraction of particular note is the Museum of the Albemarle (1116 U.S. 17 South, 919-335-1453). This most fascinating point of interest gives visitors insight into the rich heritage of the region. The museum's current location is too far for easy walking from the town docks and marina, but plans are in the works to move this attraction to the downtown district. While a completion date for this fortunate move could not be determined at the time of this writing, the museum will be far more accessible to cruising visitors when the change of venue is accomplished.

As you might imagine, many restaurants, grocery stores, laundromats, and other shoreside businesses are within walking distance of the town slips and local marinas. Even if you should need a service that lies a bit too far for walking, you can almost always obtain a ride from one of the friendly locals. Taxis are also available from Winslow Taxi Service (919-335-7180).

Cruisers seeking to restock their galleys should set sail for White and Bright Food Center (315 South Road Street, 919-338-6385). This is a small, community-minded grocery story that is located within two long blocks of the city docks. Several locals have informed this writer that the meat department here is first-class. Just next door to White and Bright, fresh veggies are usually available at Sunshine Produce. Similarly, Colonial Cleaners and Laundromat (300 West Ehringhaus Street, 919-335-2797) can be reached via a three-block jaunt from the town docks.

The city docks themselves, known as Mariner's Wharf, line the western banks just south of the U.S. 158 bascule bridge. This facility is comprised of fixed wooden finger piers leading out from a concrete sea wall. Twin-screw power craft will almost certainly want to dock stern-first for maximum convenience. Less maneuverable craft can decide on their docking procedure as the tide and wind dictate. At worst, it's only a minor inconvenience to successfully negotiate the trip ashore.

Fifteen boats can be comfortably accommodated at Mariner's Wharf, while a few extras can be squeezed in by rafting up. If you find the slips full, anchorage is permitted on the river beside the piers. A shoreside dinghy dock facilitates an easy trip ashore for those swinging on the hook. Dockside depths run in the 12-foot-plus range, so most any craft can pull alongside with no fear of finding the bottom.

Unfortunately, no power connections are available. Several water taps allow boaters to refill their tanks. Fuel can be purchased at nearby Pelican Marina. Several bicycles are kept dockside for the use of boaters. A small picnic and outdoor barbecue area further enhances the facility's attractiveness.

**Mariner's Wharf**
**(919) 338-3981**

   Approach depth: 10–20 feet
   Dockside depth: 12+ feet
   Accepts transients: yes
   Fixed wooden finger piers: yes
   Dockside water connections: yes
   Restaurants: several nearby

## Elizabeth City Restaurants

Come dinnertime, cruisers fortunate enough to coil their lines in Elizabeth City have several excellent choices. Comstock's, also known as Stalk's (115 South Water Street, 919-335-5833), is found within a few steps of the town docks. This establishment reminds me of the lunch counter at the neighborhood drugstore of my younger years. Stalk's is open for breakfast and lunch and continues to serve until 7 P.M. The sandwiches are first-rate, and the chocolate milk shakes are memorable.

*Public slips at Mariner's Wharf*

The Colonial Restaurant (418 East Colonial Avenue, 919-335-0212) is within a three-block walk of the town docks. Serving three meals a day, this dining spot is characterized by down-home, Southern-style cuisine that is somewhat plain but undeniably tasty.

If you have a yearning for the best hamburger in town, track your way to Thumper's Downtown Bar and Grill (200 North Poindexter Street, 919-333-1775). Veteran Elizabeth City visitors will recognize this address as the old location of Mulligan's Grille.

For those seeking Elizabeth City's high point in dining, Mulligan's Waterfront Grille (919-331-2431) is now located within sight of the town docks at The Waterworks (see below). This superb dining spot serves wonderful seafood, beef dishes, and sandwiches. I was very taken with my crabmeat casserole, as were my dinner companions with their grilled fish and sautéed scallops. Do yourself a huge favor and give Mulligan's your most serious gastronomical attention.

## The Waterworks

Since the last edition of this guide, a new waterside development known as The Waterworks has opened just south (downstream) of the Mariner's Wharf piers. This combination dining and retail complex is housed in a renovated 30,000-square-foot building which was once a waterfront warehouse. Besides serving as the home of Mulligan's Waterfront Grille (see above), it also offers a book shop, a coffee shop, and a wine, gourmet food, and gift store.

Visiting cruisers will most certainly want to make the acquaintance of Carolina Espresso (919-338-4040). Beside offering the "best coffee on the ICW," the manager is happy to allow cruisers to use his business address (400 South Water Street, Suite 105, Elizabeth City, N.C. 27909) as a mail drop. Patrons are also encouraged to make use of the coffee shop's "public computer," which is connected to the Internet. Be sure to check out the ICW-Net at http://www.icw-net.com. This is a great source of Internet information for those cruising along the coastline of North (and South) Carolina.

Elizabeth City Milling Company (919-338-4040) carries a modest but interesting collection of wines and packaged gourmet foods. Check it out and carry your selection of Chardonnay or Merlot back to the galley.

## Elizabeth City Lodgings

If it's time to take a break from the live-aboard routine, there are at least two lodging opportunities worthy of any Elizabeth City visitor's attention.

The Culpepper House Inn (609 West Main Street, 919-335-1993) is located in one of the city's most impressive brick Colonial-style houses, built in 1935 by the prominent Culpepper family. The furnishings and decor are exquisite. Some rooms feature "soaking tubs," fireplaces, and king-size beds. This writer's stays at the Culpepper have always been a pure delight. New owners Julia and Robert Russell are glad to pick up cruising visitors at any of the nearby docks and return them to their boat after their stay.

Elizabeth City Bed and Breakfast (108 East Fearing Street, 919-338-2177) is owned and operated by Joe and Darla Semonich, one of the most charming couples with whom it has ever been my privilege to spend a night. Few know more about Elizabeth City than these two. The inn is an unpretentious, cozy affair, which any bed-and-breakfast aficionado will appreciate. Don't miss Joe's breakfasts—he's a legendary cook. Evening meals (open to the public) are served Wednesday through Friday; reservations are suggested. Dockside pickup and delivery service for guests is also in the offing from this establishment.

## Other Elizabeth City Facilities and Restaurants

Located just next door to Mariner's Wharf and The Waterworks, Riverside Boat Works and Elizabeth City Shipyard continue under the same ownership along the river's southern banks. Unfortunately, transient dockage at this facility cannot be recommended, even though overnighters are readily accepted. The poor condition of the fixed wooden piers at the time of this writing would make a visit to this complex downright hazardous.

On the other hand, both full-service mechanical and below-the-waterline repairs are offered. The firm's travel-lift is rated at 60 tons.

**Riverside Boat Works
(919) 335-2118
Elizabeth City Shipyard
(919) 335-0171**

Approach depth: 10-15 feet
Dockside depth: 6½-11 feet
Accepts transients: yes (see account above)
Fixed wooden piers: yes
Dockside power connections: 30 & 50 amps
Dockside water connections: yes
Mechanical repairs: extensive
Below-waterline repairs: extensive
Ship's store: parts only
Restaurants: several nearby

Friendly Pelican Marina guards the Pasquotank's northern banks opposite Elizabeth City Shipyard, where chart 12206 shows good depths extending almost to shore. This top-notch facility offers excellent transient dockage at fixed wooden piers, with water and both 30- and 50-amp power connections. Dockside depths at the outer slips run 7 to 8½ feet; typical soundings of 5 feet may be expected at the innermost berths. Shoreside showers, waste pumpout service, gasoline, diesel fuel, and an expansive ship's store are all on-site. Some limited mechanical repairs to gasoline engines are offered. The Marina Restaurant (919-335-7307) is immediately adjacent to Pelican Marina. By all accounts, the food is quite good. This dining spot is now open Tuesday through Saturday during the evenings only and Sunday for lunch and dinner. For this writer's money, if you choose to bypass the free Mariner's Wharf docks, then by all means set your course for Pelican Marina.

> **Pelican Marina**
> **(919) 335-5108**
>
> Approach depth: 12-15 feet
> Dockside depth: 7½-8 feet (outer slips)
> 5-6 feet (inner slips)
> Accepts transients: yes
> Fixed wooden piers: yes
> Dockside power connections: 30 & 50 amps
> Dockside water connections: yes
> Showers: yes
> Waste pump-out: yes
> Gasoline: yes
> Diesel fuel: yes
> Mechanical repairs: limited
> Ship's store: extensive
> Restaurant: next door

## Elizabeth City History

Elizabeth City has always been a river town, and waterborne commerce continues to be important. The community's central position along the Dismal Swamp passage solidified its trading position: goods could flow north to the Chesapeake or south to the Albemarle region. Bill Sharpe, in *A New Geography of North Carolina*, comments, "For many years it [Elizabeth City] has been the social and economic center of a sizable territory. . . . One had to go beyond this area to Norfolk to the north to match Elizabeth City."

Early records indicate that trading vessels were calling in the region by 1722. The community was originally known as "the Narrows of the Pasquotank" and was first incorporated as Reading. The name was changed to Elizabeth Town in 1793, six years before the town

became the seat of Pasquotank County. The name was finally changed to Elizabeth City in 1801.

For many years, Elizabeth City was the seafood center of coastal North Carolina. More than a dozen oyster canneries once lined the town's shore. One old story suggests that the transplanting of oysters from the Pasquotank to Chesapeake Bay led to that region's lucrative oystering industry.

Many years ago, Charles Luther Graves wrote an enchanting song about the Pasquotank area. The last verse is as follows:

Ye wee frog folk of the Pasquotank,
May your race dwell long on its reedy bank,
May you chart always the same old notes,
In the same white vests and bright green coats,
May you always sing, fry bacon, fry bacon,
The song of plenty, of herrings and bacon;
May the tide creep cool 'neath the netted roots,
Down under the roots, down under the roots,
And the stream move quiet and happy and deep,
Move happy and deep, knee deep, knee deep.

## Forbes Bay (Standard Mile 53)

The only anchorage worthy of consideration by cruising-size craft on the Pasquotank River south of Elizabeth City is on the broad stream's southwestern banks northwest of flashing daybeacon #7. Forbes Bay offers plenty of swinging room and 6- to 8-foot depths. There is good shelter from southwestern and western winds and fair protection from northwestern and southeastern breezes. Strong blows from the north or northeast call for another strategy. Along the bay's northwestern banks, set amidst light to moderate residential development, is a large brick structure which once served as a hospital.

The best spot to drop the hook is on the waters of the bay's mid-width at least 150 yards from shore. Closer in, depths rise sharply.

## Blimp Factory

Southeast of flashing daybeacon #5, look toward the southwestern banks and you will immediately catch sight of a huge rooftop sitting back from the shore; its location is noted on chart 12206. This immense structure was built during World War II for the manufacture of dirigibles. In times past, boaters could actually catch sight of two mammoth buildings at this location. The larger of the two—one of the biggest wooden structures in the world—burned in spectacular fashion during 1995; at that time, it still served as a blimp factory, while the smaller of the two structures was leased to a furniture company. Now, the blimp plant has been moved to the surviving building, and dirigibles are once again being constructed in Elizabeth City. If you're lucky, you may spot one of the mammoth balloons being tested as you pass.

# DISMAL SWAMP ROUTE NAVIGATION

Cruisers traveling south on the ICW via the Dismal Swamp Canal will cross into North Carolina 2.6 nautical miles south of the charted Lake Drummond feeder ditch. The small loop shown on chart 12206 occupying the canal's western banks just south of the state line is overgrown and shoal. Don't attempt to enter.

The canal continues nearly south in an arrow-straight passage to the lock at the tiny village of South Mills. There are no markers, anchorages, or side trips between the border and South Mills. Remember to keep a sharp watch for floating debris.

**South Mills**   After passing under a high-rise highway bridge with 65 feet of vertical clearance, you will sight the South Mills swing bridge dead ahead. This span has a closed vertical clearance of only 4 feet, but it does open in conjunction with the South Mills lock. The lock attendant also doubles as the bridge operator. Please allow adequate time for him (or her) to switch positions as you approach either the bridge or the lock.

Soon, the narrow canal meets the northern entrance of the South Mills lock. At the time of this writing, both locks on the Dismal Swamp route opened at 8:30 A.M., 11:00 A.M., 1:30 P.M., and 3:30 P.M. pretty much year-round. The wise mariner will call the Corps of Engineers' office at Great Bridge, Virginia (804-547-2109), or the Dismal Swamp Canal Welcome Center (919-771-8333) for the latest schedule information.

**Turner's Cut**   Once through the South Mills lock, boaters will find themselves in Turner's Cut, a narrow ribbon of water quite similar to the Dismal Swamp Canal. Depths continue good (8 to 13 feet), but snags and flotsam are sometimes encountered. The cut runs generally southeast for 3.7 nautical miles before emptying into the northern Pasquotank River.

Not far from the lock's exit, a side branch of the cut leads back north to a barge-loading dock. You can carefully explore this cut along its centerline amid typical 7- to 8-foot depths, but be on watch for any barges entering or leaving the offshoot. There is not really enough room for cruising-size craft to anchor.

These same timber barges are a cause for concern if you happen to meet or overtake one of them while transiting Turner's Cut or the upper reaches of the Pasquotank River. The channel is a bit narrow along these stretches. It can tax your piloting skills more than a little to stay in the channel while avoiding the barges and tugboats. Slow down and proceed with maximum caution if you should be unlucky enough to meet one of these ponderous monsters of the Waterway.

Some 1.1 nautical miles southeast of South Mills, the cut passes through a small settlement. No Wake signs are posted and enforced along this stretch.

### Northern Pasquotank River

Soon, the ICW passes into the northern headwaters of the Pasquotank River. The route remains narrow for several miles, but unlike Turner's Cut and the Dismal Swamp Canal, the channel winds first one way and then another. There are no markers for the first 4.5 nautical miles, and this stretch is tricky to run after dark.

After sighting the Pasquotank's first aid to navigation, those studying chart 12206 will immediately note that marker colors are suddenly reversed from the normal ICW pattern. The Pasquotank River channel takes precedence over the ICW. As you are now going downstream (south), take green beacons to your starboard side and red markers to port. This color scheme continues south to Albemarle Sound.

Once the river begins to widen south of unlighted daybeacon #19, cruising boaters can anchor in light to moderate wind conditions most anywhere along the way. Good depths run almost to shore in many places. Simply cruise away from the marked channel before dropping the hook to avoid any barge traffic which might happen along. Be sure to show an anchor light.

**On the ICW**   As the Waterway enters the northerly waters of the Pasquotank River from Turner's Cut, the channel takes a sharp turn to the east. To the southwest, you might choose to enter the upper portion of the river, abandoned by the ICW.

**Upper Pasquotank River**   Stick to the centerline as you enter the upper limits of the Pasquotank River southwest of the Turner's Cut Intersection. Good depths continue along the mid-width until the stream cuts sharply to the northwest. Discontinue your explorations before reaching this turn.

### On the ICW and Pasquotank River

Cruising south and southeast from Turner's Cut on the Pasquotank River, visiting boaters will finally sight unlighted daybeacon #19 near the charted location of Lambs Corner. Daybeacon #19 is the first marker on the North Carolina portion of the Dismal Swamp route. After so long a time without any aids, #19 is a welcome sight. Be sure to pass it fairly close to its northeasterly side to avoid some submerged pilings abutting the northeasterly shore.

From #19, the ICW passes through one of the

few shoal-prone stretches on the Pasquotank River. Point to pass between unlighted daybeacons #17 and #18. Continue downstream by passing unlighted daybeacon #16 to its southwesterly side and unlighted daybeacon #15 to its northeasterly quarter. South of #15, unlighted daybeacon #13 marks a sheltered overnight anchorage.

**Goat Island**    Enter the stream flowing behind (southwest of) Goat Island on the mid-width of its northwestern or southeastern entrance. Depths at both entrances run to 5 feet but improve to 6- and 10-foot soundings on the stream's interior reaches. Stick to the centerline and drop the hook at any point that meets your fancy.

**On the ICW**    No markers are found south and southeast of Goat Island until just before the waters lying about Elizabeth City. The river continues to be consistently deep and begins to widen. Just southeast of Standard Mile 45, passing cruisers will note a large hospital on the southwestern shoreline. Don't attempt to enter the small, charted canal leading to the hospital. Depths are more than suspect.

Sawyers Creek, just north of the charted railroad bridge near the small village of Camden, is a good anchorage consideration.

**Sawyers Creek**    When entering Sawyers Creek, favor the northwestern (port-side) shores heavily. A shoal occupies the mid-width of the stream's mouth and seems to be building toward the entrance's southeastern banks as well. Once inside the mouth, work your way back to the centerline. Drop anchor soon after passing through the entrance for maximum swinging room.

**On the ICW**    Study chart 12206 for a moment and notice the unnamed creek southeast of Sawyers Creek. Boaters might be lured into this errant offshoot by a sign at the stream's mouth advertising gasoline and other supplies. Don't attempt to enter unless your craft can stand consistent 3½-foot depths. The small marina advertised on the sign is associated with a trailer park and caters almost exclusively to small, shallow-draft powerboats.

Chart 12206 lists the horizontal clearance of the manually operated railroad bridge beyond Sawyers Creek as 42 feet. To me, the span seems much narrower. Proceed with caution, particularly in high winds. The railway bridge is almost always open unless a train is due. Should you find it closed, you'll certainly have to wait, as the closed vertical clearance is a mere 3 feet.

**Railroad Bridge Anchorage**    Soon after you leave the charted railway bridge behind, an unnamed creek offering good overnight anchorage will come abeam to the southeast. Enter this stream anywhere within shouting distance of its mid-width. While staying at least 25 yards or more from the low-level highway bridge blocking the stream's southeasterly tip, select any likely spot to drop the hook.

**On the ICW**    From the railroad bridge, the ICW flows through several sharp turns on its way to Elizabeth City. The Waterway follows a wide and deep but mostly unmarked passage to the town waterfront. Be sure to pass well southeast of flashing daybeacon #9, the single aid to navigation north of the U.S. 158 bridge. No additional anchorages are to be found north of Elizabeth City.

Southeast of flashing daybeacon #9, sharp-eyed cruisers may note a large metal building and a single dock in the small cove noted on chart 12206 as "trees in water." This facility is known as City Marina. Its primary business is dry-stack storage of small power craft. A lack of other marine services and approach depths of only 4 feet or less render City Marina uninteresting for cruising-size craft.

Cruisers will spot the docks of Pasquotank River Yacht Club just downstream from City Marina on the southern banks. The club's piers lie almost opposite flashing daybeacon #9.

Dismal Swamp route veterans may be surprised to note the absence of the old concrete grain elevators which once lined the northern shoreline just above the highway bridge. These venerable structures were demolished to make room for a complex of riverfront townhouses.

As you begin your approach to the highway span, look again to the north and northwest for a quick glimpse of some lovely old whitewashed homes lining Poindexter Street just above the riverbank.

The Elizabeth City–U.S. 158 twin bascule bridge has an official closed vertical clearance of only 2 feet, but it looked to this author as if a vessel requiring as much as 6 or 7 feet of clearance could make it through.

The U.S. 158 span currently opens on demand. After passing under the bridge, the Pasquotank River curls around to the east and southeast, while the town's waterfront opens out on both banks.

### Elizabeth City
Passing cruisers will spot the Mariner's Wharf public slips on the western shore soon after leaving the highway bridge in

their wake. To continue downstream, set course to pass unlighted daybeacon #8 to its southwestern side. Do not drift north or northeast of #8. A large collection of old pilings and other underwater debris stretches out from the northern banks to #8. These hazards also run east for a bit along the northern banks.

Look south after passing #8 and you will see a large, motley collection of boatyards and docks. This series of piers comprises Riverside Boat Works and Elizabeth City Shipyard. Not far downstream from #8, Pelican Marina guards the northern banks.

### Southern Pasquotank River
South and southeast of Elizabeth City, the Pasquotank quickly widens as it moves toward its intersection with Albemarle Sound. Surprisingly, the lower river offers only one overnight anchorage. For the most part, ICW navigation between Elizabeth City and Albemarle Sound is quite simple. The stream remains deep and free of shoals almost to its banks. However, even on the wide southern Pasquotank, snags and floating debris can be encountered. Keep a sharp watch.

*Old Elizabeth City grain elevator*

Flashing daybeacon #7 is the first aid to navigation south of Elizabeth City. Come abeam of #7 well to its northeasterly side. Shoal water lies southwest and southeast of #7.

Before you reach #7, the southern Pasquotank's only sheltered overnight anchorage will come abeam to the southwest.

**Forbes Bay**   As you begin to enter Forbes Bay, use your binoculars to pick out the charted pilings occupying the middle of the bay's mouth. Pass either to the northwest or southeast of these obstructions. After leaving the piles behind, cruise back to the mid-width. Drop the hook before approaching to within 150 yards of the southwestern shoreline.

**On the ICW**   From a position abeam of flashing daybeacon #7, set course to eventually come abeam of flashing daybeacon #5A and then flashing daybeacon #5 well to their northeasterly sides.

Do not approach #5A or #5 closely. They guard shoal water to the southwest.

Point to come abeam of flashing daybeacon #4, near Miller Point, by several hundred yards to its southwesterly side. As you approach #4, the broad mouth of Newbegun Creek will come abeam to the southwest. Don't be tempted! The stream is quite shoal, with 1- to 4-foot depths at the mouth. What a shame! Newbegun Creek leads to some of the few unspoiled, first-growth cypress-tree stands left in coastal North Carolina. Those of you with *shallow*-draft dinghies, take note!

From #4, navigation remains quite straightforward all the way southeast to the unnumbered 30-foot flashing daybeacon west-northwest of Camden Point. This beacon marks the intersection of the Pasquotank River and Albemarle Sound. Continued ICW navigation across the mighty Albemarle is presented in the next chapter.

# VIRGINIA-NORTH CAROLINA CUT

Many pleasure and commercial boaters follow the Virginia–North Carolina Cut, officially called the Albemarle and Chesapeake Canal, south from Virginia's waters. This portion of the Waterway is deep, reliable, and well marked. As an additional bonus, it does not include any locks on the North Carolina portion of its passage. There is one lock at Great Bridge, Virginia, but it raises or lowers passing craft only a few inches. This lock generally operates on the hour and is not nearly as restrictive as its counterparts on the Dismal Swamp route.

Cruising captains following the North Carolina cut enter Tar Heel waters near the southern mouth of the North Landing River. The channel then follows a dredged cut through the northern headwaters of Currituck Sound until it enters a short canal on the southern shores of Coinjock Bay. The small village of Coinjock sits on the banks of the canal and offers full services for cruising skippers.

Below Coinjock, the ICW soon flows into the northern headwaters of the North River, where a well-marked passage leads south down this substantial stream to Albemarle Sound. This noble river offers several sheltered and isolated anchorages.

### Virginia–North Carolina Cut History

Before the Dismal Swamp Canal was rebuilt in 1899, the lengthy and numerous delays in its passage led many people to believe that a new, more easily traveled cut should be built between Albemarle Sound and Chesapeake Bay. As early as 1807, federal engineers suggested that two canals be dredged, one to connect the Elizabeth and North Landing Rivers and the other to connect Currituck Sound and the North River. Public support for the project grew, and in 1854, legislation was passed to organize the Albemarle and Chesapeake Canal Company. Actual construction began in 1855. Eventually, seven new steam dredges were employed in the canal's excavation. The project was completed in 1859. Additional improvements were made following the Civil War, and the new cut became for a time the primary conduit of commercial water traffic for northeastern North Carolina.

As plans went forward for the federally maintained Intracoastal Waterway from Norfolk to Miami in the early 20th century, the United States government decided to purchase the Albemarle and Chesapeake Canal rather than the Dismal Swamp cut as the northernmost link of the Waterway. It was correctly perceived that the former would be easier to maintain and would allow freer travel than the Dismal Swamp route.

### Currituck Sound

The Waterway crosses Currituck Sound for only a short distance before it ducks into Coinjock Bay near flashing daybeacon #105. The waters of Currituck Sound outside the friendly confines of the ICW are uniformly shallow. Currituck is the only major North Carolina coastal water that lacks any sort of channel traversing its length. Much of the sound is choked by weeds, and except for the ICW channel, these waters are generally avoided by cruising captains. Even the small skiffs that frequent Currituck Sound for its excellent bass fishing and waterfowl hunting have been known to find the bottom.

### Currituck Sound Side Channels

Near the midpoint of the ICW's trek through Currituck Sound, two narrow channels lead east and west from flashing daybeacon #95. Both cuts are used on a regular basis by a small ferry that crosses the sound from the mainland village of Currituck to Knotts Island. While the beginning of the western route holds minimum 6-foot depths, 4 feet of water can be expected as you approach flashing daybeacon #3 near the mainland shore. No facilities for cruising craft are available at Currituck. Similarly, the channel to the east leads only to a small ferry dock on Knotts Island, which also has no berths or facilities. It is a good idea to bypass both arms of the channel.

*Midway Marina–Coinjock*

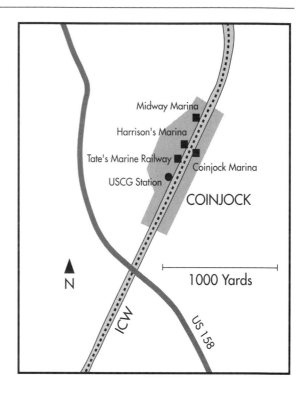

## Coinjock (Standard Mile 50)

Situated almost midway between Great Bridge and Belhaven, Coinjock is an ideal spot to spend an evening of peace and security before continuing your voyage. The marinas of the village are popular stopovers for northbound and southbound pleasure craft.

Taxi service to and from the Norfolk, Virginia, airports is now available in Coinjock. Cruisers can arrange to leave their boats here for a time while flying home to see who's minding the store. A Coast Guard station is also located along the Waterway at Coinjock. If bad weather threatens, the station's personnel may be able to inform you of current conditions on the often-rough Albemarle Sound.

All three Coinjock marinas offer dockage facing directly onto the ICW north of the fixed bridge. While this stretch of the ICW is a no-wake zone, it is still a wise practice to set out your largest fenders.

Midway Marina and Motel is the newest and northernmost of Coinjock's facilities. Its two ranks of docks guard the western banks south-southwest of flashing daybeacon #123.

As the owner of Midway Marina put it, "We're the new kids on the block, and we have to try harder." Well, they certainly do try hard, and the results are impressive. Originally, Midway Marina put up all transients at a long, fixed wooden-face dock which fronts directly onto the Waterway. A second dock just to the north is now in place as well, and even more pier space is planned for the future.

As you may have guessed by now, the aggressive Midway Marina management is eager to greet transients of both the sail and power persuasions. Average dockside depths run 7 to 9 feet. Fresh water and 30- and 50-amp power connections are readily available, as are dockside cable-television and telephone hookups. The marina offers gasoline and diesel fuel and waste pump-out service. The extra-nice on-site ship's and variety store stocks a selection of frozen meats and seafood. Ultraclean showers and a laundromat are close at hand. Mechanical repairs for both diesel and gasoline engines can be arranged by Midway with independent contractors. For those who want to take a break from the live-aboard routine, Midway Marina maintains four large, well-appointed rooms atop the marina store. These "efficiencies" include a kitchenette as well as a nice view of the Waterway. Future plans call for the construction of a swimming pool that will, of course, be open to all visiting cruisers.

Midway Marina can normally provide courtesy transportation to nearby restaurants and grocery stores. Ask the dockmaster for help.

If by now you have gained the impression that Midway Marina deserves your most serious consideration, you are on the right track. It almost goes without saying that this facility adds greatly to the already impressive marine services in this tiny village.

**Midway Marina
(919) 453-3625**

  Approach depth: 12+ feet
  Dockside depth: 7-10 feet
  Accepts transients: yes
  Fixed wooden piers: yes
  Dockside power connections: 30 & 50 amps
  Dockside water connections: yes
  Showers: yes
  Laundromat: yes
  Waste pump-out: yes
  Gasoline: yes
  Diesel fuel: yes
  Mechanical repairs: independent contractors
  Ship's & variety store: extensive
  Restaurant: nearby

Coinjock Marina, located on the ICW's eastern banks, is one of the friendliest facilities in all of North Carolina. You cannot visit here for more than five minutes without gaining the impression that the staff cares intensely about its visitors' comfort and welfare. Just about every amenity and service you might ever desire is close at hand, including a superb restaurant.

Coinjock Marina welcomes cruising powerboaters and sailors to its extensive fixed wooden-face dock, which features water and 30- and 50-amp power connections. Minimum dockside soundings are in the 8-foot range. Diesel fuel and gasoline are readily available, as is waste pump-out. Mechanical repairs can be arranged through independent technicians. Showers and a laundromat are located just behind the docks. Coinjock Marina has one of the nicest and most extensive ship's and variety stores I have ever reviewed. A large selection of frozen and fresh meats is stocked, including homemade country sausage.

A boaters' lounge is provided under the same roof as the ship's store. It features a color

*Coinjock Marina and Restaurant*

television, a pool table, complimentary pop-corn, and a paperback exchange library.

And if all these impressive features aren't enough, Coinjock Marina can also lay claim to its own first-class restaurant specializing in fresh fried seafood and a 32-ounce prime rib. I highly recommend the combination seafood platter. The crab cakes are also worthy of note.

How's that for full service?

**Coinjock Marina
(919) 453-3271**

Approach depth: 12-15 feet
Dockside depth: 8 feet (minimum)
Accepts transients: yes
Fixed wooden piers: yes
Dockside power connections: 30 & 50 amps
Dockside water connections: yes
Showers: yes
Laundromat: yes
Waste pump-out: yes
Gasoline: yes
Diesel fuel: yes
Mechanical repairs: independent contractors
Ship's & variety store: extensive
Restaurant: on-site

Harrison's Marina, directly across the canal from Coinjock Marina, offers gasoline, diesel fuel, and plentiful overnight dockage at a fixed wooden pier with all power and water connections. An on-site ship's and variety store offers basic food items, ice, charts, and marine supplies. Some low-key showers are available. Harrison's also provides free transportation to Coinjock restaurants. Numerous conversations with fellow cruisers have led me to believe that Harrison's is a power-craft-oriented marina.

Just south of Harrison's Marina, Tate's

**Harrison's Marina
(919) 453-2631**

Approach depth: 12-15 feet
Dockside depth: 7-8 feet (minimum)
Accepts transients: yes
Fixed wooden piers: yes
Dockside power connections: 30 & 50 amps
Dockside water connections: yes
Showers: yes
Gasoline: yes
Diesel fuel: yes
Ship's & variety store: yes
Restaurant: nearby

Marine Railway (919-453-3281) offers complete repair service and haul-outs via a 60-ton travel-lift. Tate's is the only facility of its kind between the Virginia line and Belhaven. If you need mechanical or below-the-waterline repairs, you'd better stop here.

## North River

South of Coinjock, the ICW flows smoothly south down the broad and deep track of the North River. This noble stream offers a number of snug overnight stops for shallow-draft vessels far from the most remote vestiges of civilization. A few of these are now a bit tricky, so read the information below carefully.

It is particularly fortunate that the North River offers several secure overnight stops. As we will discover in the next chapter, Albemarle Sound, which lies across the Waterway's path directly to the south, is often more than a little rough. If foul weather is in the offing, it is ever so nice to wait for fair breezes and while away the hours in one of the North River's fine havens. Of course, you might also choose to coil the lines at one of Coinjock's excellent marinas.

### Upper North River (Standard Mile 52.5)

The upper reaches of the North River, abandoned by the Waterway west of the gap between the ICW's unlighted daybeacons #129 and #132, are an anchorage consideration for adventurous captains piloting boats of less than 40 feet that draw 4 feet or preferably less. The entrance channel skirts the western shores south of #132 and then turns into the upper portion of the river, paralleling its southern banks. Be sure to read the upper North River navigational section presented later in this chapter *before* attempting entry. Minimum depths run between 5 and 5½ feet *if* you can keep to the unmarked channel.

After negotiating the difficult entrance, visiting cruisers will find themselves in an attractive, rather broad body of water with good protection from southerly winds and fair shelter from moderate northerly breezes. Strong easterly or westerly blows raise a most uncomfortable chop. Consider dropping the hook on the upper North River just west of charted Green Island Creek's westerly entrance point, where chart 12206 shows its "4" dividing line. The surrounding shoreline is delightfully undeveloped.

### ICW Anchorage (Standard Mile 54)

Another anchorage along the North River's northerly stretch lies between unlighted daybeacons #134 and #137. Here, 6- to 8-foot depths abut the undeveloped westerly banks and run almost to shore. This spot is exposed to the wake of all passing vessels, but in light to moderate winds or even stronger breezes from the west, vessels of almost any size should not be too uncomfortable. Strong northerly blows clearly call for another strategy.

### Buck Island (Standard Mile 56)

The waters lying about the northern shores of Buck Island southwest of flashing daybeacon #149 make an ideal spot to drop the hook. Good depths of 5 to 8 feet are held quite close to the island's northern shoreline as far west as flashing daybeacon #153. The body of all-natural Buck Island shelters the waters from southern and southwestern breezes, but strong northern and northeastern winds can make for a bumpy evening. There should be enough swinging room to amply accommodate a 48-footer.

Some other guides warn cruisers of stakes and crab pots when entering the northern Buck Island anchorage, but this writer's on-site research in 1997 did not reveal any such hazards. Things may be different when you visit, however, so be alert.

With northern, northeastern, or northwestern winds in the offing, you might also choose to anchor off the southern shores of Buck Island in 5- and 6-foot depths east of flashing daybeacon #155. There is enough elbow room for even the largest pleasure craft. This spot is decidedly uncomfortable in southern winds of any magnitude.

Northeast of flashing daybeacon #157, the unnamed creek to the east of Buck Island leads to charted Goose Pond. It offers yet another anchorage for craft as large as 45 feet drawing 4 feet or less. Minimum 5-foot depths hold until the creek swings to the north and heads for

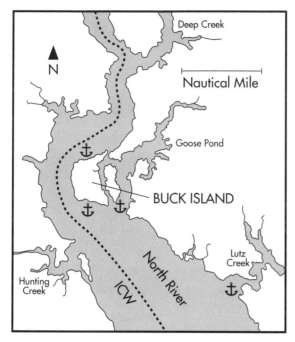

shallow Goose Pond. There is good protection from all but southerly winds.

All these anchorages border on shores which are entirely in their natural state. Each haven can provide a safe and peaceful sanctuary for the night, depending on the quarter from which the fickle wind blows.

## Lutz Creek (Standard Mile 59)

Lutz Creek makes into the North River's eastern shore east of flashing daybeacon #159. Depths on this stream have deteriorated during the last several years. The soundings pictured on chart 12206 are no longer accurate.

The western mouth of Lutz Creek plays host to a small, charted marsh island which is now barely visible to the on-the-water visitor. Depths upstream of this small landmass have now shoaled to 4-foot levels.

On the other hand, it is possible to anchor

to the north-northwest of the small island in 6-foot depths with good shelter from all but westerly and southwesterly winds. Cruising boaters will find enough room for craft up to 36 feet. The creek's shoreline is completely undeveloped.

## Broad Creek (Standard Mile 61)

Broad Creek (one of many bodies of water in North Carolina bearing this moniker) is still the best anchorage on the North River, even though soundings are not quite as deep as they once were. This magnificent stream cuts into the North River's western shoreline opposite flashing daybeacon #164. Minimum depths of 6 to 8 feet hold into the stream's interior reaches but fall off much sooner than a study of chart 12206 would indicate.

Broad Creek offers superb protection from all airs, and the heavily wooded shores are absolutely virgin. The entire stream boasts a tangible air of isolation. The banks beckon to be explored and fished by dinghy.

Broad Creek can be a bit difficult to locate. Consult the navigational information below for hints on how to avoid this potential problem.

Consider anchoring shortly after entering the creek's interior reaches, as the stream swings sharply north. Here, you will find 5½- to 9-foot soundings, good protection from all winds, and the luscious shores described above. Passage farther upstream (to the north) is no longer recommended.

Even if you usually frequent marinas and seldom anchor-off, consider dropping the hook in Broad Creek for an evening you will not soon forget. Your cruising experience will be far richer for the effort.

# VIRGINIA–NORTH CAROLINA CUT NAVIGATION

Navigation of the ICW along the North Carolina–Virginia route from the Virginia state line to Albemarle Sound is generally straightforward. The Waterway channel is its usual well-marked self.

The passage across Currituck Sound can be a bit dicey. A sharp chop can sometimes develop, and portions of the channel are bounded by protective underwater stakes. Shoaling is an occasional

*Shoreline of Broad Creek*

problem between maintenance dredgings.

There is nothing unusual about the sheltered landcut leading past Coinjock. The channel running down the North River to Albemarle Sound is generally a delight unless the wind really gets its dander up. In general, this is a good place to take your time and enjoy the sights.

**On the ICW**   South of flashing daybeacon #61, the ICW soon passes into North Carolina's waters as the Waterway follows the North Landing River southward. Much of the marked passage from here to Coinjock across Currituck Sound is bordered by long pickets of submerged pilings that help guard the channel from shoaling. These areas are clearly shown on chart 12206. Be careful not to let a beam wind ease you out of the channel onto the stakes.

The Waterway remains quite straightforward until unlighted daybeacon #76. Here, Tull Bay comes abeam to the west and Back Creek to the east. Tull Bay, which serves as an entrance to the mostly deep Northwest River, is itself unmarked and shoal. Depths of 3 and 4 feet are all too common. Cruising captains are advised to bypass Tull Bay and the Northwest River.

The approach to Back Creek holds 5-foot minimum depths, but 4-foot readings are soon encountered on the creek's interior section. The stream's mouth is wide, offering little shelter for overnight anchorage. Back Creek, like Tull Bay, is best avoided.

**Currituck Sound**   After passing between unlighted daybeacon #86 and flashing daybeacon #87, the ICW cuts to the southeast and flows into the northern headwaters of Currituck Sound. Over the past several years, the Currituck Sound

section of the ICW has suffered more than its share of shoaling. Be on guard for signs posted by the Corps of Engineers warning of new encroachments by the surrounding shallows. Boats drawing 6 feet or less can usually depend on the Corps' frequent dredging to see them safely through.

As you cruise past Bell Island near flashing daybeacon #105, look to the west, where you will see several beautiful homes nestled among the tall pines. At flashing daybeacon #116, the Waterway briefly follows a short landcut across Long Point into the southern reaches of Coinjock Bay. As you start through the canal, look west to catch sight of some interesting masonry ruins. These bricks were once part of a lighthouse oil depot. Loads of this light-giving substance were once dispatched by boat from this location to lighthouses from Corolla to Ocracoke.

The Waterway continues its southerly trek until it enters Coinjock Canal south of unlighted daybeacon #122 (misidentified on the 6/3/95 edition of chart 12206 as #22). This man-made cut holds consistent depths of 10 to 15 feet and presents no navigational difficulties. About halfway to the canal's southerly exit, the small village of Coinjock is bisected by the ICW.

**Coinjock**   Cruising south into Coinjock, you will first spy Midway Marina guarding the western shoreline, followed by Coinjock Marina on the eastern shores and Harrison's Marina to the west. South of Harrison's, Tate's Marine Railway also occupies the western shores. Be sure to maintain idle speed when cruising past all the marinas.

Immediately southwest of the village waterfront, Waterway cruisers will pass under a fixed high-rise bridge with 65 feet of vertical clearance.

**On the ICW**   South of the Coinjock span, the Waterway continues following a sheltered canal for 1.4 nautical miles before entering the headwaters of the North River at flashing daybeacon #125. Stick strictly to the marked channel as you make your entrance into the North River. North of unlighted daybeacon #132, shoal water lines the dredged cut to the east and west. Keep chart 12206 close at hand to resolve any questions that arise.

**Upper North River**   Between flashing daybeacon #128 and unlighted daybeacon #132, you will pass the upper reaches of the North River (abandoned by the ICW) west of your course. Please remember that this is an anchorage only for wild-eyed captains who are ready to risk a little adventure. Be on the lookout for crab pots when entering this haven.

Don't attempt to enter the upper North River by leaving the ICW between #128 and #132. Instead, continue south on the ICW until you are at least 300 yards south of #132. Then turn toward the western banks. After approaching to within 100 yards or so of this shoreline, turn sharply north and run parallel to this shore until the eastern entrance point of Green Island Creek comes abeam west of your track.

You should then turn to the west-northwest and enter the upper reaches of the North River by favoring its southerly banks. As you cruise a bit farther to the west, keep a sharp watch for a small patch of grass, sticks, and old stumps north of Green Island Creek's westerly entrance point. Set course to pass at least 75 yards north of this obstruction and continue into the river's midsection, still favoring the southerly banks slightly. Discontinue your upriver explorations before

passing through the area depicted on chart 12206 as dividing line #4.

**Waterway Anchorage**   The North River's next anchorage is located along the western shore between unlighted daybeacons #134 and #137. For best depths, depart the ICW abeam of (or slightly south of) flashing daybeacon #135 and cut in toward the western banks. Feel your way along carefully with the sounder. Be sure to stay north of the charted pilings which you will sight to the south. Also, be sure to avoid the charted submerged piles just to the north abutting the western shoreline. Drop the hook before approaching to within less than 100 yards of the western banks.

**On the ICW**   Don't attempt to enter Deep Creek east of flashing daybeacon #143. Contrary to its name, the stream holds 3-foot depths at its mouth.

**Buck Island**   To reach the anchorage adjacent to the island's northern shore, set course from flashing daybeacon #149 toward the small, charted stream to the south, which leads to shallow Goose Pond. Expect 5- to 8-foot depths past #149 and all along the northern shoreline. Some 50 yards short of the small creek's mouth, swing to the west (starboard), pointing toward flashing daybeacon #153. Pick a spot before coming abeam of the western point of Buck Island. As you are traversing this channel, be on the lookout for crab pots.

Cruisers choosing to drop anchor south of Buck Island should depart the Waterway 25 yards south-southeast of flashing daybeacon #155. Set course to the east-northeast and drop anchor as you approach to within 100 yards of Buck Island's southerly banks.

If you choose to spend the night on the un-named creek east of Buck Island which leads to charted Goose Pond, set course from flashing daybeacon #157 toward the stream's large mouth. Depths run 5½ to 8 feet at the approach but quickly decline to 5 feet past the entrance, as the creek begins a swing to the north. Don't cruise any farther upstream, as 3- and 4-foot depths are soon encountered.

**On the ICW**    From flashing daybeacon #149 to flashing daybeacon #159, the ICW continues its easy passage down the North River. To the east of #159, another possible anchorage will come abeam.

*Sunrise over North River*

**Lutz Creek**    Set course from flashing daybeacon #159 to the center portion of the creek's entrance. Take care to avoid the finger of shallow water extending from the sharp point northwest of the stream's entrance, clearly shown on chart 12206. Point to come abeam of the small, charted island to its north-northwesterly side. You can anchor here. On the water, this small landmass appears as nothing more than a little grass and several lumps of mud. Do not attempt to cruise upstream past the island. Farther to the east, depths have now shoaled to 4 feet or less.

Deeper-draft boats might wisely consider dropping the hook a bit west of the small island, thereby ensuring that the shallow upstream waters are kept at a good distance.

**On the ICW**    It is a short trek downriver from flashing daybeacon #159 to the gap between un-lighted daybeacon #163 and flashing daybeacon #164. West of #164 is the North River's finest anchorage.

**Broad Creek**    Carefully set course from flashing daybeacon #164 for what appears to be the northern portion of the large bay leading to Broad Creek. As you track your way west on the bay, watch for an uncharted, **U**-shaped dump buoy. Pass this errant marker by 50 to 100 yards to its southern side.

Watch carefully for Broad Creek's mouth to the north as you approach the rear (westerly end) of the large bay leading to the creek. Don't be fooled by Little Broad Creek to the south. This small body of water holds only 4- to 5-foot depths and does not offer much protection.

The entrance to Broad Creek is partially hidden by a sharp point that will be passed north of your course. The stream then takes a sharp turn to the north.

After spotting the entrance, swing sharply north and enter the creek, favoring the eastern banks ever so slightly. Drop anchor before the first charted baylike offshoot comes abeam on the western shoreline. Contrary to what chart 12206 would lead you to believe, 4-foot depths are all too common on the waters adjacent to this sidewater and farther upstream.

**On the ICW**   From flashing daybeacon #164, the ICW continues south for 4.6 nautical miles down a well-marked channel until it intersects Albemarle Sound at flashing daybeacon #173. As described in the next chapter, Albemarle Sound can be the roughest section of the entire Waterway. If bad weather threatens, retreat to one of the North River anchorages or one of the Coinjock marinas and wait for fair breezes.

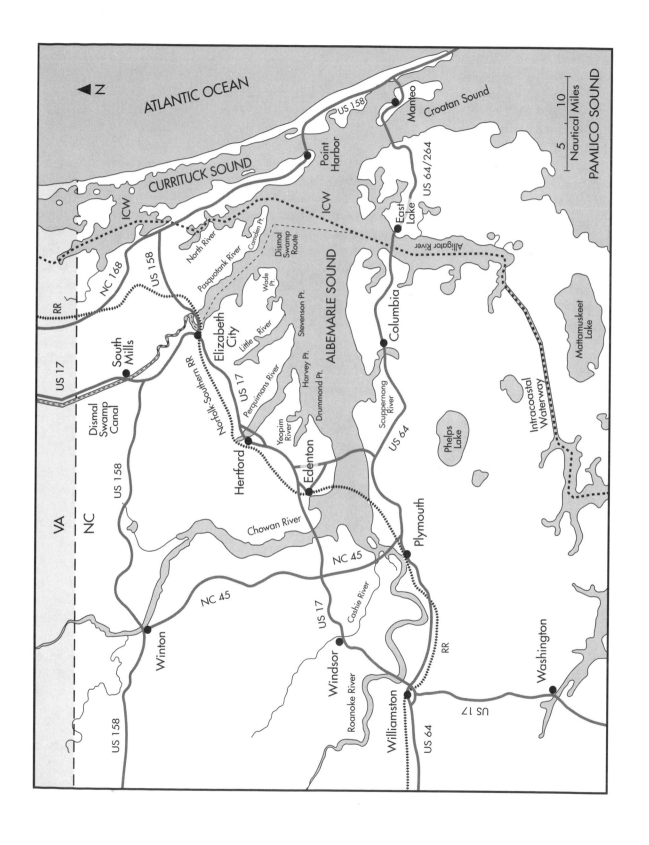

# The Albemarle Sound

Albemarle Sound is the largest freshwater sound in the United States. Writing for *The State* magazine in 1954, Bill Sharpe described Albemarle Sound thus:

Were a marine architect to set up an ideal location for a new colony, he might first round up thousands of acres of level agricultural and timber lands. . . . In the middle of the land he would place an inland sea completely sheltered from oceanic disturbance. . . . The sea would be long (say 60 miles) so as to tap a maximum territory, but fairly narrow. . . . To facilitate its crossing it would taper as it progressed inland. It would generally be approachable by dry shores and would have deep water connections with the outside world. . . . At frequent intervals there would be large rivers pouring into the sea from every direction. These would keep it fresh . . . and provide fish with spawning grounds. . . . It would merely cost wishing to give this body of water a beautiful forested shoreline and all needed then would be to drench it with sunshine, history and romance. Around its coast would be planted small towns, comfortable, prosperous, well kept and hospitable. This precisely is Albemarle Sound, a brilliant gem.

## Charts

You will need two charts for successful navigation of Albemarle Sound and its adjoining rivers:

**12205** is necessary for general navigation of Albemarle Sound and all its streams except the North, Pasquotank, and Alligator Rivers

**11553** follows the ICW route across Albemarle Sound and up the Alligator River

Sharpe's description may be romantic, but it is essentially correct. There is perhaps no other major body of water in North Carolina that has been so consistently overlooked by cruising boaters. This is largely because Albemarle Sound has the dubious reputation of having the roughest inland waters on the eastern seaboard. It is quite true that winds from most any quarter tend to funnel up or down the sound's entire length. This long wind fetch, coupled with the Albemarle's shallow depths, can quickly form violent seas that can daunt the heartiest captain and crew. *Always* consult the latest weather forecast before venturing on the sound's wide waters.

Those who are put off by the often rough conditions of the sound need not bypass the numerous cruising opportunities of the Albemarle's many rivers. All but the Alligator and the Chowan are very sheltered, and it takes a hard blow indeed to stir their waters into a menacing froth. Nine major rivers and several smaller streams, all of which are now readily navigable, serve Albemarle Sound. Taken as a whole, the Albemarle's rivers comprise the largest group of cruising opportunities in North Carolina.

Albemarle Sound is 51 nautical miles in length from its mouth at the intersection of Currituck and Croatan Sounds to its headwaters east of the great Chowan River. The sound is 11.5 nautical miles wide near its mouth, but it narrows consistently as it stretches west, tapering to a width of 4 nautical miles at its narrowest span just east of Edenton. The sound is deep and well marked for navigation. Unlike other North Carolina sounds, the Albemarle is mostly free of shoals. Generally, cruising captains can take a welcome break from their constant vigil over the depth sounder.

The Albemarle's rivers and creeks afford many sheltered overnight anchorages. Often, cruisers can anchor far from the most remote vestige of civilization. A night spent under the stars here may lead one to believe that this is what cruising is all about.

Facilities for pleasure craft on Albemarle Sound and its rivers have improved greatly during the past several years. A new marina (with, for the first time, a clearly marked channel) now beckons cruisers on the shores of the beautiful Yeopim River. A large, friendly full-service marina welcomes visiting boaters at Edenton, and a few additional slips are available at the town docks. A small facility is located on Rockyhock Creek, a sidewater of the Chowan River, but you won't find much in the way of services for visiting cruisers at this location. Pleasure craft can also tie to either the newly built (but shallow) town piers or the older, deeper (but poorly maintained) city docks at Plymouth on the Roanoke River. A new and rather interesting marina is now located on Mackeys Creek, while two facilities welcome cruising boaters near the town of Columbia on the Scuppernong River. Another particularly well-placed marina offers fuel and transient dockage near the Alligator River bridge immediately adjacent to the path of the southward-running ICW. This collection of marina facilities is a great improvement over what cruising skippers found but a few short years ago on the wide Albemarle and its nine rivers.

The freshwater shoreside foliage of the Albemarle is very different from that of its saltwater counterpart, Pamlico Sound. Marsh grass gives way here to cypress and hardwoods. The farmlands surrounding Albemarle Sound are extremely rich. All sorts of crops grow readily from the dark black loam. The produce of the Albemarle region has long been the economic mainstay of northeastern North Carolina.

## Albemarle Region History

The northern shore of Albemarle Sound was the first region of North Carolina permanently settled by English colonists. Some settlers fled Virginia seeking freedom of religion; others came for less honorable reasons, fleeing indentured service or financial responsibility. In 1657, the Comberford map showed a single structure, Batts House, on the tongue of land between the Roanoke and Chowan Rivers. Settlement spread east down the wide Chowan until the river's mouth was finally reached. There, about 1710, the colonists established a town that eventually was named Edenton, after Royal Governor Charles Eden. It was for a short time the state capital.

The city of Edenton has been the center of the Albemarle region since colonial times. Today, the town jealously guards its rich past. Many fine old homes and public buildings have been preserved and restored. The Edenton Historical Society is a very active organization that strives to enhance the town's rich heritage. Visiting Edenton is a genuine delight for all who make this charming community a port of call.

As the settlement of the district spread during colonial times, many beautiful plantations sprang up along the shores of Albemarle Sound, as well as on the Chowan and Roanoke Rivers. The Albemarle region was peopled by very special men and women who valued their rights and liberty as only those who have wrested their livelihood from a wilderness can. The area nurtured many of the great leaders of North Carolina. Joseph Hewes, signer of the Declaration of Independence, and James Iredell, United States Supreme Court justice, were but two of the many distinguished men of early America who called the Albemarle region home.

So intense were the region's patriots that long before the Revolution they were known as "the iron men of Albemarle." During the war with England, the Albemarle served as part of a vital supply line of the patriot cause. Stealthy blockade runners entered through Ocracoke Inlet and deposited their cargo in the warehouses of Edenton.

In the 19th century, much of the state's population began to shift to the Piedmont, and the Albemarle region gradually lost its political importance. Agriculture and commercial fishing became the mainstays of the local economy. Albemarle Sound was first bridged by a railroad span in 1910. This major accomplishment, followed by a trans-Albemarle highway bridge in 1938, finally relieved the isolation of northeastern North Carolina.

The history of the Albemarle region is long and colorful; only a smattering of the story can be presented here. For more information, consult the section on Chowan County in Bill Sharpe's *New Geography of North Carolina*. Even better is Inglis Fletcher's group of historical novels known collectively as the "Carolina series." Many of these novels deal with the early history of the Albemarle region.

# WEST ON ALBEMARLE SOUND

For those who cruise west on Albemarle Sound to visit the region's many attractions, flashing daybeacon #2, south of Reed Point, will probably be the first objective. If you entered the Albemarle by the Dismal Swamp route and the Pasquotank River, set course to #2 from the un-numbered, 30-foot flashing daybeacon marking the Pasquotank's southern foot. This is a long run of 12.5 nautical miles. Be careful to avoid any slippage to the north. Excessive leeway could land the hapless boater in the shallows near Flatty Creek and Stevenson Point.

If you entered the sound by way of the Virginia–North Carolina Cut and the North River, set course for #2, south of Reed Point, from either flashing daybeacon #173 or flashing daybeacon #N. Both of these latter aids are located south of the North River's southerly genesis. Some 16 nautical miles separate #2 from either #173 or #N. Fortunately, the entire run is through open water and presents no difficulty.

From #2, two excellent sidewater opportunities on the Albemarle's northern shore present themselves.

## LITTLE RIVER

The Little River is one of the Albemarle's smaller offshoots, but it still offers several miles of interesting cruising for skippers whose craft can stand some 4- to 5-foot depths. Unlike most of its sister streams, the Little has some shoals extending fairly far out into the main body from the shoreline. None of these problem patches is marked, but caution and good navigation may help you bypass them. The entrance is also surrounded by some shoal water, but there is a broad channel with one navigational aid.

Most of the Little River's shoreline is heavily wooded and undeveloped. As is the case with most of the Albemarle's rivers, the banks are lined by cypress trees trailing beards of gray moss. The boater who travels on the Little River will certainly enjoy waters that few pleasure boaters have known.

The northern reaches of the Little River border the small village of Nixonton. This commu-nity was once the seat of Pasquotank County. When Elizabeth City became the county seat, Nixonton apparently "lost heart." Only a few homes and buildings remain, and there are no facilities for cruising boaters here or anywhere else on the Little River.

Craft drawing 4½ feet or less will find good anchorage on the Little River. Moving upstream, you might first consider Deep Creek, which makes into the southwesterly banks. Minimum 5-foot depths hold along the centerline for several hundred yards upstream, and swinging room is adequate for a 36-footer. Deep Creek offers excellent shelter from all but particularly strong northeasterly blows. Be sure to read the navigational account of Deep Creek below before deciding to cruise this body of water.

Hall Creek splits off from the upper Little River's eastern shores. This rather petite stream offers 5-foot minimum depths and enough swinging room for craft under 30 feet. The anchorage is quite protected and completely undeveloped. Hall Creek eventually leads to a launch area, but the channel winds too much for large cruising vessels to safely proceed so far upstream.

The extreme upper reaches of the Little River past the Hall Creek intersection make an almost ideal overnight stop for vessels as large as 36 feet. You must negotiate one tricky spot with 5-foot depths to get there, but otherwise, the upper Little River supports minimum 6- to 7-foot depths, with many deeper soundings in evidence. The banks are crowded with cypress and other hardwoods. Protection is so good that the upper Little River might even make a good hurricane "hidey-hole." One of the best places to drop the hook is near a lovely private residence along the starboard shoreline.

## LITTLE RIVER NAVIGATION

From flashing daybeacon #2, set course for unlighted daybeacon #1 east of Stevenson Point. Using chart 12205, carefully set a new course from #1 to avoid the shallow water on the entrance's western quadrant. Also, be on guard against the finger of shallow water extending into the main stream from Mill Point to the northeast. If you successfully avoid the surrounding shoals, minimum entrance depths are 6 feet. Once past Mill Point, stick to the mid-width for 7-foot minimum depths as far upstream as Long Point.

Southeast of Long Point, the main channel is pinched between shallow water extending northeast from Durant Neck and a smaller patch of shoals near Long Point to the northeast. Favor the river's northeastern shore, but don't approach Long Point too closely. If depths fall below 7 feet, your course is encroaching on the shallows. Slow down and assess the situation before you reach grounding depths.

Upstream, the channel again narrows between Deep Creek and Trueblood Points. Very shallow water extends out from shore for quite a distance between the two points. Cruise carefully through the river's centerline and avoid both points of land.

Just past the constricted channel, deep water again opens out almost from shore to shore. Deep Creek, the river's first good opportunity for anchorage, will come abeam to the southwest.

*Deep Creek*   Favor the northwestern (starboard) shores when entering. Do not cruise toward the port banks to read a sign you may see there; it tells of a small-craft marina farther upstream, inaccessible to cruising-size craft. Depths of 5 feet can be held upstream on Deep Creek until just before you come abeam of a small baylike area to port bordered by several private residences. Drop anchor somewhere between the stream's entrance and this offshoot.

*On Little River*   North of Deep Creek, the Little River flows towards Nixonton. As you approach the small community, favor its shoreline. As chart 12205 clearly shows, a patch of shallow water extends outward from the southwestern banks. Cautious boaters may wish to discontinue their cruise on the Little River abeam of Nixonton, but devil-may-care skippers whose craft draw 4 feet or less can still find several isolated cruising opportunities not far upriver.

Stick to the mid-width until the quickly narrowing stream takes a sharp jog to the east and rounds a sharp point. Favor the starboard shore when rounding this point. By following this procedure, 5-foot depths can be expected. The port shore at the turn is very shallow and must not be approached.

Past the sharp bend, cruise back to the mid-width. Depths deepen to 7-foot minimums and reach 11-foot readings in a few spots. Soon, Hall Creek will come abeam to starboard.

**Hall Creek**   Favor the port shore when entering, but don't approach the shoreline too closely. You will encounter minimum depths of 5 feet at the creek's mouth. The water deepens to as much as 11 feet farther upstream. Don't cruise past the stream's first sharp turn to the south. There, the channel begins to wind and conditions become unsafe for large vessels.

**Upper Little River**   The best anchorage on the Little River is on the stream's narrow northern reaches. Simply keep to the midline and drop the hook at any place that looks good to your weary eyes.

# PERQUIMANS RIVER

The Perquimans River is a lovely, gentle stream usually seen by only a few fishermen plying the waters in their small craft. It has just about everything cruisers could ask for except marina facilities. The river is deep almost to its shoreline and offers no particular navigational difficulties. It takes a heavy blow to raise a rough chop on the Perquimans. Generally, wave conditions are ideal for large pleasure craft. The river boasts at least three good anchorages, one of which is sufficient for even long-legged craft in heavy weather.

The banks are lined with untouched belts of cypress and other hardwood trees, broken here and there by picturesque homes and farms. The old river town of Hertford is perched on the banks of the upper Perquimans. Although the village does not have any marinas for cruising craft, there is plenty of room to anchor and dinghy ashore.

Sailcraft skippers should note, however, that you must be able to clear a 33-foot fixed bridge to reach the Hertford waterfront and the best Perquimans anchorages. Boaters choosing to anchor just southeast (downstream) of the fixed span will discover that a long dinghy ride is necessary to reach Hertford.

## Sutton Creek

Sutton Creek cuts the Perquimans River's northeastern banks northwest of charted White Hat Landing. This stream's lower reaches can provide adequate overnight anchorage for craft drawing 4 feet or less in all but strong southwestern breezes. Winds from this quarter blow directly into the creek's mouth and make for a decidedly uncomfortable evening. Minimum depths of 4½ to 5 feet can be expected at the entrance (if you successfully avoid the unmarked shallows) and on the initial interior reaches, but 4-foot depths are found farther upstream. Semisubmerged snags are

*Dock of "1812 on the Perquimans"*

very much in evidence and call for more than the usual caution. The creek's shores are flanked by a handsome collection of dense cypress trees.

For best depths, drop anchor in the wide southwesterly portion of the creek short of its second point on the southeasterly banks. Past this point of land, the stream narrows and depths begin to rise.

### 1812 on the Perquimans

The Perquimans River's newest facility for boaters, albeit one for small cruising craft, lies along the river's northeasterly banks just southeast of the charted "Platform PA" about 1.8 nautical miles southeast of the fixed highway span. Industrious owners have renovated one of the river's historic homes and opened it as the "1812 on the Perquimans Bed and Breakfast Inn" (919-426-1812). For boaters, they have also built a small dock nestled amid the cypress trees along the shoreline.

Approach depths run between 5½ and 6

feet, while 4½ to 5 feet of water can be expected dockside. The pier can probably accommodate one 30-footer, but it is not really appropriate for larger vessels. If you dock, you can walk to shore from the pier and up a steep flight of steps, then gaze across a long field pierced by a dirt road. The large house in the distance is "1812 on the Perquimans." Advance arrangements with the friendly innkeepers are highly recommended.

### Hertford and Associated Anchorages

Hertford is truly one of the great cruising finds on Albemarle Sound. Visiting cruisers sighting the village waterfront for the first time will be struck by the many lush green lawns stretching down to the river. This verdant grass borders a host of houses dating from antebellum and even Revolutionary War times. Such visual attractions are a good clue to the town's genteel, laid-back character. Until now, few cruisers have taken advantage of this unique port of call.

Hertford is tucked far upstream at a bend in the river where the Perquimans transforms itself from a wide river to a narrow track. Positioned well off the ICW, the village has remained delightfully undiscovered by cruising boaters and tourists alike. As a boy, I spent many a happy day casting for largemouth bass near the shores of Hertford on the tranquil Perquimans. It is only fair to say that I am more than a little prejudiced when discussing the town's charm.

While Hertford does not boast any marina facilities, boaters who can clear the 33-foot fixed bridge spanning the river southeast of town will find superb overnight anchorage adjacent to the city waterfront. First, you must negotiate a swing bridge with 7 feet of closed vertical clearance;

this bridge leads into the Perquimans River's protected upper reaches. The span opens on demand from April 1 to September 30 from 8 A.M. to midnight but remains closed during the early-morning hours. From October 1 through March 31, the span opens on signal from 10 A.M. to 10 P.M. First-time visitors should be sure to read the Hertford navigational information presented later in this chapter before attempting these waters.

After leaving the swing bridge behind, you will spot the city's launching ramps and a newly renovated park on the southerly banks. Boats as large as 40 feet can drop anchor in 8 feet of water abeam of this fine facility, though the ramps and park shouldn't be approached too closely by deep-draft vessels. It's then only a quick dinghy trip ashore to experience the town's subtle charms.

For maximum protection, continue tracking your way upstream until the river passes through a hairpin turn to the north. The long, straight stretch of water which opens out before you is an idyllic haven with tons of elbow room. The cautious mariner can maintain minimum depths of 7 to 10 feet. Most of the shores are completely undisturbed by the hand of man, though a few attractive homes gaze benignly over the narrowing river here and there. Protection should be adequate for all winds under 35 knots.

Wherever you choose to anchor, break out the dinghy as soon as the lines are coiled and head for the municipal launching park. There, you can usually find a spot to tie off while visiting the downtown district. Your first stop should be the local chamber of commerce (919-426-5657), housed in the white wooden building just behind the newly renovated park. There, you can obtain brochures

and other information about the town and the surrounding county. Then, if it's lunchtime, stroll to the downtown area and ask anyone to point out Frankie's Hertford Café (127 North Church Street, 919-426-5593). If you are the type of cruiser who enjoys good home-cooked meals in a 1950s setting, you will be delighted to find this cafe. After lunch, take some time to stroll around the quiet, lovely town. The downtown business district has remained virtually unchanged for the last 50 years. Don't miss the corner Hertford Hardware Store (103 North Church Street, 919-426-5211), a town institution for many a year; in my younger days, I could often be found perusing the fishing lures at this venerable firm. Also, be sure to check out the new Bibliopath Bookshop (146 North Church Street, 919-426-8186) for a surprisingly complete selection of current and used volumes. Unfortunately, I must report that the popular bakery in downtown Hertford is now closed. For those looking to restock their galleys, a six-block (approximately 0.4-mile) walk west on

*Hertford Waterfront and Swing Bridge*

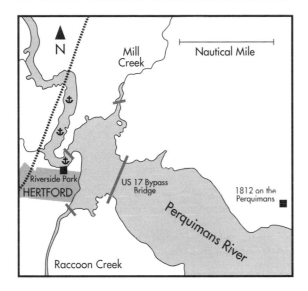

Grubb Street (S.R. 1110) from the municipal launching ramp will lead you to a Bi-Rite supermarket. You will spot the Little Mint hamburger shop along this stretch as well.

Of course, a visit to Hertford wouldn't be complete without a walk along Front Street, which fronts on the Perquimans River one block east of Church Street (U.S. 17 Business). Some of the town's finest homes can be viewed by fortunate visitors strolling at their leisure along this tranquil lane.

Another Hertford attraction is the Newbold-White House, one of the oldest surviving homes in North Carolina. Unfortunately, this historic site is located too far away for walking. You will need to hitch a ride with a friendly local to visit this historic structure.

Hertford now boasts a second shoreside lodging facility in addition to "1812 on the Perquimans," described above. The Beechtree Inn (919-426-7815) is a rustic establishment with three separate guest cottages. It is set on a se-

cluded, wooded lot with 14 pre–Civil War buildings which have been moved here for protection and restoration. A full country breakfast is served to inn guests only. The cheerful owners are glad to pick up and return cruising visitors either from the Hertford municipal launching area or nearby Albemarle Plantation Marina (see below).

If you are the type of cruiser who enjoys only large, full-service marinas with nearby restaurants serving mesquite-grilled fish, then Hertford is probably not for you. But if you, like me, thrive on the peace and quiet of a lovely, close-knit river town that time seems to have forgotten, Hertford should definitely be included in your cruising itinerary.

### Hertford History

In 1661, George Durant purchased land from Chief Kilcacanin of the Yeopim Indians. This acquisition in what was to become Perquimans County was the first deed of its type in North Carolina. Settlement of the region went forward but was impeded by a severe drought in 1667 and a hurricane in 1668. By 1696, some 70 families were settled around the Perquimans River. In 1732, a courthouse was built near Phelps Point, and a town began to grow around it. Incorporated as Hertford in 1758, the town became the seat of Perquimans County.

The Perquimans district ardently supported the patriot cause during the Revolutionary War. One of its citizens, General William Skinner, was the hero of the Battle of Great Bridge in Virginia. Hertford was shelled during the Civil War, but the bombardment resulted in only one casualty. Progress after the war was impeded by the region's lack of overland transportation. Until 1917, it

*Downtown Hertford*

was necessary to travel by water to Norfolk, Virginia, to reach Raleigh. Finally, in 1925, the completion of U.S. 17 lifted Perquimans out of its long era of isolation.

Long before U.S. 17 became a reality, however, the citizens of Hertford found a way to bridge the Perquimans River near their settlement. In 1780, they engaged the services of a Mr. Perry, who used empty whiskey barrels to construct a pontoon bridge between Phelps and Newby Points. A detachable section could be floated aside to allow passage of river craft. During the Civil War, the Hertford Confederates surprised a detachment of Yankee soldiers attempting to use the pontoon bridge. The crafty citizens removed the pegs from the detachable span's hinges. When the Union troops tried to march into town, they marched instead into the river.

This interesting structure survived until 1885, when it was replaced by a wood-and-steel bridge. The popular ballad "Carolina Moon" is said to have been composed while the songwriter watched the Perquimans by moonlight from the 1885 bridge. Proof of this contention remains elusive, but it is easy to imagine the artist's fascination as he watched the moon play upon the beautiful stream.

In 1928, the state replaced the 1885 structure with a modern concrete-and-steel bridge. Even this span is unique. For reasons that remain obscure, the bridge forms an **S** pattern. It is thought that the Perquimans Bridge is the largest **S**-type bridge in the world.

Bathed in the glow of the "Carolina moon," the lovely Perquimans River sits poised to receive far more cruising visitors than it has hosted in the past. I hope that the above account will encourage boaters to take advantage of these all but undiscovered waters.

## PERQUIMANS RIVER NAVIGATION

Successful entry into the Perquimans River calls for minimal navigation. Set course from flashing daybeacon #2 to come abeam of flashing daybeacon #5 (east of Harvey Point) by 200 yards to its easterly side. Don't mistake unlighted daybeacon #3 (south of Harvey Point) for #5. Use your binoculars to make the correct identification.

From #5, continue upstream on the Perquimans River's mid-width. Near Blount Point, unlighted daybeacon #7 clearly marks a small patch of shoal water, as does flashing daybeacon #8 near Grassy Point. Obviously, you should pass #7 well to its

*Diving from the Perquimans River Bridge*

northeasterly side and #8 well to its southwesterly quarter.

Watch the northeastern banks 2 nautical miles after passing #8 and you will see the entrance to Sutton Creek, the first possibility for sheltered anchorage on the Perquimans.

**Sutton Creek**    For best depths, enter Sutton Creek by favoring its southeastern (starboard) shores slightly. Watch carefully for snags and floating debris as you cruise through the stream's entrance and into its inner reaches. Expect some 4½- to 5-foot soundings in the creek. Discontinue your upstream explorations *before* coming abeam of the second point on the southeastern banks. Farther upstream, depths deteriorate quickly to 4 feet or less.

**On the Perquimans**    From a position abeam of Sutton Creek, it's a scenic cruise upriver to the fixed highway bridge southeast of Hertford. Vertical clearance at the pass-through is only 33 feet, so many tall sailcraft will be forced to anchor near the lee shore and take a long dinghy ride to Hertford. Northwest of the high-rise, two bays open out to port and starboard. Neither is good for anchorage. The starboard (northeasterly) branch, known locally as the "Thousand Islands," maintains only 4-foot depths and is littered with underwater obstructions. The port (southwesterly) cut, which eventually leads to charted Raccoon Creek, holds 5-foot depths at its wide mouth but drops off to 4 feet or less before narrowing enough for good protection.

To continue upstream to the Hertford swing bridge, set course to pass unlighted daybeacons #9 and #11 to their fairly immediate northerly sides. Depths of 8 feet or more can be expected here,

but south of the two aids, shoal water extends outward from the shore. From #11, point to pass through the swinging span of the Hertford Bridge. The bridge has a closed vertical clearance of only 7 feet but opens on demand from 8 A.M. until midnight between April 1 and September 30. From October 1 through March 31, it opens on signal from 10 A.M. to 10 P.M. After you pass through the bridge, the charming Hertford waterfront will come abeam to port.

**Hertford**    Favor the starboard shore once through the Hertford Bridge. Depths of 8 feet can be expected here. The port shore, which fronts onto some private residences and the Hertford launching park, carries only 4½ feet of water.

**Upper Perquimans River**    Follow the narrowing stream until it flows through a hairpin turn to the north. After you come out of the turn, a long, straight stretch of water will open out before you. For best depths, favor the westerly banks slightly as you cruise upstream.

From the sharp turn to the railroad bridge about a mile upstream, typical depths range from 7 to 20 feet. These waters are quite sheltered and offer an excellent spot to anchor.

A small railroad bridge with a vertical clearance of only 3 feet blocks travel farther upstream for all but the smallest craft. Consider a quick trip through by dinghy, however, for some beautiful natural scenery and excellent bass fishing.

**On the Albemarle**    From flashing daybeacon #2 on Albemarle Sound, cruisers have a choice of at least three destinations to the west.

To continue toward the westerly waters of Albemarle Sound and Edenton, set course for flashing daybeacon #3 north of Laurel Point. This is a run of 9.7 nautical miles through open, often choppy water. Watch carefully for leeway and pay attention to your compass. Come abeam of #3 by as much as 1 nautical mile to its northerly side.

The Yeopim River, located on the sound's northern shore, can be reached by setting course for unlighted daybeacon #2A at the stream's mouth. Come abeam of #2A well to its southern side, and do not approach the aid closely. Make sure to read the detailed Yeopim River Navigation section below before proceeding farther.

The Scuppernong River, a delightful tributary making into the Albemarle's southern shoreline, can be entered by setting course for flashing daybeacon #1 on Bull Bay. Come abeam of #1 by at least 1 nautical mile to its northwestern side. The Scuppernong will be reviewed later in the chapter.

## YEOPIM RIVER

The mouth of the Yeopim River cuts into the northern shores of Albemarle Sound a short hop west of the Perquimans River's entrance. The Yeopim is the smallest and shallowest of the major streams feeding into Albemarle Sound. Until recently, it was also the hardest to enter safely. In earlier editions of this guide, this writer was reluctant to recommend the Yeopim River to all but the boldest captains. That situation has now changed dramatically for the better with the opening of Albemarle Plantation Marina on the northern shores of adjacent Yeopim Creek. The good folks at this fine facility have marked a channel leading into the creek and river which usually holds at least 5 feet of depth. An additional marker or two would be nice, but by exercising the usual caution, skippers piloting boats drawing 5 feet (or preferably just a little less) can now explore these largely undeveloped streams with reasonable confidence.

Actually, most of the entrance channel is even deeper, but the outer portion of the cut passes over what was once an island. Believe it or else, in the 18th century, Batts Grave Island was located at the mouth of what is today the Yeopim River. According to some historians, this isle was the location of the first house built in North Carolina by European immigrants. Batts Grave has now completely eroded into the surrounding waters, raising depths significantly. As late as five years ago, it was still possible to see a few (at that time charted) stumps rising above the water and marking the island's former location. Today, even those scant markers are gone. Fortunately, as noted above, the newly marked channel allows visiting cruisers to pass over this hazard with 5 feet of water under their keels.

Of course, as with all of the Albemarle's streams, the Yeopim is subject to wind tides. Prolonged blows from the north, west, or northwest can lower water levels further. Usually, this is not a problem. The marked channel is normally quite passable.

Those cruisers who enjoy leaving the crowd far behind will want to check out the upstream reaches of the Yeopim River. Depart the marked channel at unlighted daybeacon #6. While depths can drop to 5 (or occasionally 4½) feet as you work your way upstream to Bethel and Middleton Creeks, most boats drawing 4½ feet or less will

*Middleton Creek shoreline*

be able to find their way to some superb overnight anchorages. Be sure to read the navigational account of the Yeopim presented in the next section of this chapter before attempting first-time entry; you will discover several tricks to help you keep to the best depths.

The residential community of Snug Harbor is located on the northern shores of the Yeopim River not far from its entrance. While the village's homes make pleasant viewing from the water, no facilities are available for large cruising craft. Two small marinas with depths of 3 feet or less sell gasoline and a few variety-store items to local outboarders and fishermen. Otherwise, the stream's shoreline is dotted by private homes but remains mostly undeveloped, heavily wooded, and absolutely magnificent.

Upstream on the Yeopim River, depths begin to shoal a bit. Most minimum soundings are in the 5-foot region, but a 4½-foot reading can sneak in from time to time. Eventually, the river dead-ends into a **T**-like section. The stream striking to the north is known (and charted) as Bethel Creek, while the southwestward-running body of water goes under the name of Middleton Creek.

Cruising boaters who thrive on exploring waters off the beaten track will find a visit to Middleton Creek a fascinating experience. This stream is not recommended for craft larger than 36 feet or those drawing more than 4½ feet, as there are some 5-foot depths along the way and a few unmarked shoals to avoid. If your boat fits these size and draft requirements, however, the risk just might be justified. The creek's shores are covered by a virgin growth of tall cypress, hardwoods, and scattered pine. A night on Middleton Creek is an evening spent about as far from the trappings of civilization as one is liable to get in this day. In spite of the navigational challenges necessary to get here, and always remembering the size and draft requirements outlined above, I cannot recommend this anchorage too highly.

Probably the best spot to drop the hook is between Middleton Creek's entrance from the Yeopim and its first sharp turn to starboard. For best depths, favor the port-side banks slightly. Large craft might want to consider a Bahamian-style mooring to minimize swinging room.

Bethel Creek is also visually attractive, but depths of 3 feet or even less relegate this stream to dinghy explorations. If you are up for a long dinghy ride, you can cruise upstream on Bethel Creek and find your way to Angler's Cove Restaurant (919-426-7294) in the tiny village of Bethel. Here, you can moor your dinghy temporarily to an old but serviceable dock a scant 100 feet from the restaurant. The locals swear by the seafood! Angler's Cove is open from 5 P.M. to 9 P.M. Monday through Thursday and from 5 P.M. to 10 P.M. Friday and Saturday. The restaurant is closed on Sunday.

## Yeopim Creek and
## Albemarle Plantation Marina

Once upon a time, Yeopim Creek was at best a good place for shallow-draft boats to drop anchor for an evening or two. That has changed decidedly for the better with the construction of Albemarle Plantation flanking the northern shores of the creek's entrance. This tasteful and attractive development is composed of private homes set on large, wooded lots, with a few condos thrown in here and there. There is also an 18-hole golf course on-site; a few of the holes border attractively on the waters of Albemarle Sound. A large clubhouse with a dining room, a pool, and a separate pool house also overlook the Albemarle. This writer may just consider an extended stay at this excellent complex at some future date. It is really that nice.

For those of us of the cruising persuasion, the construction of Albemarle Plantation Marina is an even greater boon. Cruisers will quickly spy the facility's fixed wooden piers to the north as they come abeam of unlighted daybeacon #8, the aid to navigation farthest upstream on Yeopim Creek. The passage from #8 to the marina's piers can be just a little tricky for first-timers. Read the navigational write-up below and you should not have any problems.

Albemarle Plantation Marina is an absolutely first-rate operation with a super staff. Boaters arriving at the pier will find 6 feet of water at the outer slips and 4½-foot depths on the innermost berths. Transients are gladly accepted. All slips feature freshwater and 30- and 50-amp power hookups. Cable-television and optional telephone connections are available as well. Waste pump-out service is offered. Transient visitors are afforded full guest privileges at the nearby clubhouse and dining room (currently open Tuesday through Thursday for lunch and Thursday through Saturday during the evenings), the pool, the pool house, the golf course, and the tennis courts. If you need to take a break from the live-aboard routine for a few days, condo rentals are also in the offing.

Future plans call for the construction of an on-site ship's and variety store plus an adjacent yacht-club building complete with showers and a laundromat. If these services are crucial to your cruising needs, call ahead of time to ascertain whether they are now in place.

Thanks to the marking of its reliable entrance channel and the availability of excellent transient facilities, Albemarle Plantation Marina has almost single-handedly transformed the Yeopim River and Yeopim Creek into a prime cruising destination.

### Albemarle Plantation Marina
### (919) 426-4037

Approach depth: 5-11 feet
Dockside depth: 6 feet (outer and
              middle slips)
4½-5 feet (innermost berths)
Accepts transients: yes
Fixed wooden piers: yes
Dockside power connections: 30 & 50 amps
Dockside freshwater connections: yes
Waste pump-out: yes
Restaurant: nearby

For those who prefer to anchor-off rather than coil their lines, the waters of Yeopim Creek west and north of Albemarle Plantation are yet another prime consideration. Depths of 5 feet or better extend as far north as the correctly charted

4-foot soundings. West of the marina, the waters are wide enough to accommodate a 45-footer nicely. Farther upstream, the creek turns sharply to the north and becomes a bit narrower, but boats as large as 40 feet should still have enough elbow room. The shores are dotted with attractive homes. While there is certainly more development here than along the untouched banks of Middleton Creek, this is still a good gunkhole. Shallow-draft vessels which can safely accommodate 4 feet of water can continue upstream into another totally natural paradise of tall cypress and other trees. It doesn't get much better than this.

## YEOPIM RIVER NAVIGATION

As indicated above, successful navigation of the Yeopim River and Yeopim Creek requires paying close attention to business. While the newly marked entrance channel is ever so helpful in facilitating safe transit of the combined streams' mouth, there are still plenty of shoals waiting to trap the unwary.

To enter the Yeopim River from the open waters of Albemarle Sound, find your way to a point abeam of flashing daybeacon #1 by 20 yards to your port side. Look to the northwest and identify unlighted daybeacons #2 and #3. Point for the gap between these two markers.

Once between #2 and #3, set course to come abeam of the next upstream aid, flashing daybeacon #5, by 20 yards to your port side. Between #1 and #5, visiting cruisers will discover the shallowest depths on the Yeopim entrance channel. Soundings of 5 feet are entirely possible along this stretch.

Abeam of flashing daybeacon #5, use your binoculars to help pick out unlighted daybeacon #6. There is a long gap between #5 and #6, and first-timers may need a moment to locate #6. Swing a bit to port after leaving #5 in your wake and point to come abeam of #6 by 20 yards to your starboard side.

Unlighted daybeacon #6 is a strategically placed aid to navigation. Cruisers planning to explore the upstream limits of the Yeopim River and Middleton Creek should depart the marked cut at this point, while those making for Albemarle Plantation and Yeopim Creek will follow an entirely different course. Let's first turn our attention to the river, then review the channel leading to the creek and the marina.

*Upstream on Yeopim River*   From a position abeam of unlighted daybeacon #6, cut sharply west and point for the mid-width of the river's upstream passage. Be sure to avoid the point of land separating the Yeopim River and Yeopim Creek. A large shoal is building southeast from this promontory.

As you cruise upstream (generally west and northwest) on the Yeopim River, the attractive resort community of Snug Harbor will come abeam to the north. Depths seem to run around 6 to 7 feet along this portion of the river. Just past Snug Harbor, look to port and you will see a beautiful home nestled on the river's southern shore. As this house comes abeam, depths deteriorate to 5- and 6-foot readings. Farther upstream, you will spy a small-craft marina along the northern shoreline. Approach depths of only 3 to 4 feet render this facility useless for most cruising-size vessels.

Just past the small marina, depths begin to fall off to 5 feet, possibly 4½ feet in a few spots. Cruisers bound upstream for Middleton Creek should continue scrupulously following the river's centerline. Keep a sharp watch for snags and floating debris, particularly semisunken logs and tree branches.

Eventually, the Yeopim River dead-ends into a **T**-shaped intersection at the combined mouth of Bethel and Middleton Creeks. Don't attempt to enter Bethel Creek to the north, as depths of 3 feet or less are soon encountered. Middleton Creek to the southwest, on the other hand, offers minimum depths of 4½ to 5 feet, with most of the stream holding much more water.

**Middleton Creek**   Enter Middleton Creek by turning sharply to port and favoring the port point and shoreline as you enter the stream. After cruising upstream 50 to 75 yards, swing back to the creek's mid-width. You will note some 5-foot readings for the first 30 yards or so, but depths soon increase significantly, typically to between 6 and 9 feet.

As Middleton Creek flows to the southwest, depths alternate between deeper soundings and 5-foot readings. Eventually, the stream takes a sharp jog to starboard and begins to narrow considerably. Be careful to come about while there is still room to maneuver.

Your best bet for overnight anchorage is on the waters between Middleton Creek's entrance and the creek's first sharp turn to starboard, mentioned above. Select a spot with sufficient swinging room and prepare for an evening of peace and solitude.

**Yeopim Creek**   Cruisers bound upstream on Yeopim Creek to Albemarle Plantation Marina or an anchorage on the creek should continue following the marked cut from unlighted daybeacon #6, where this review of the Yeopim River's upstream limits began. From #6, point to come abeam of unlighted daybeacon #8 by 20 yards to your starboard side.

Unlighted daybeacon #8 is the marker farthest upstream on Yeopim Creek. Another aid to navigation between #8 and the marina would be nice, but you can keep to good water by following the simple procedure outlined below.

For best depths, don't cut directly from your position abeam of unlighted daybeacon #8 to the Albemarle Plantation docks. Shallow water lines the eastern side of the stream along this stretch. Instead, set your course from #8 as if you were headed for the next private dock along the northern shoreline immediately upstream of the marina's piers. When the marina docks come abeam to starboard, you can then turn safely into the dockage basin.

Also, don't forget to carefully avoid the point of land lying between Yeopim Creek and the Yeopim River. As mentioned above, a shoal is building outward from this point.

Captains continuing upstream on Yeopim Creek will continue to find good depths for at least 100 yards past the stream's first sharp turn to the north. Eventually, soundings start to rise, reaching 4½-foot levels as the creek works its way into totally undeveloped country. Craft drawing 4 feet or more should anchor well short of this shallow water.

**On the Albemarle**   From flashing daybeacon #3, set course west for the central pass-through of

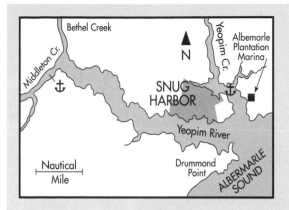

the new 65-foot high-rise highway bridge spanning Albemarle Sound from north to south. Along the way, you will pass unlighted daybeacon #4 well north of your course. Be sure to stay south of #4. This aid marks shoal water building out from Bluff Point to the north.

Past the high-rise, a distance of 4.1 nautical miles separates cruisers from the former location of the Albemarle's long railroad bridge. This span has now been removed, but its location is still noted on the current edition of chart 12205. Point to pass between flashing daybeacons #6 and #7 to avoid any leftover underwater obstructions.

The charted power lines just east of the old railway span have an official clearance of 94 feet over the marked channel and 54 feet elsewhere. Some reports place these lines at a bit less than charted levels, but I know for a fact that a sailcraft with a 70-foot mast made it underneath in the channel without difficulty.

Set course for flashing daybeacon #CR, located 2 nautical miles farther to the west. Three distinct cruising possibilities are available from #CR. To the north, the historic city of Edenton offers excellent facilities and fascinating shoreside activities. To the west, the mighty Chowan River has many miles of excellent cruising and imposing scenery. To the southwest is the entrance to the Roanoke River and its several auxiliary streams. The cruising opportunities of Edenton will first be reviewed, followed by those of the Chowan and Roanoke Rivers.

## EDENTON

Edenton is one of coastal North Carolina's loveliest communities. One of the state's oldest towns, it has a rich historical heritage that is still very much in evidence. An active local historical society has labored diligently to restore many old homes. These beautiful residences are perhaps the city's star attraction. They tell of that exciting era when the state's early citizens fought for liberty and independence. Some of the restored homes are the one-time dwellings of famous North Carolinians; several are open to the public, and others are well worth viewing from the outside. Stop by the Edenton Visitor's Center (108 North Broad Street, 919-482-2637). There, you can buy an inexpensive pamphlet that will guide you on a spectacular 1.5-mile walking tour. Guided tours are now available as well and are highly recommended by this writer. These sojourns include the famous Cupola House (1758), St. Paul's Episcopal Church (1736), the Barker House (1786), and the James Iredell House (1773). "Living History Days" are sometimes in the offing at this latter attraction. During these times, visitors can observe cooking, quilting, broom making, and other 18th-century activities being demonstrated by local volunteers.

Edenton is clearly the spot to visit on Albemarle Sound. The town's historical heritage and good facilities make a stay not only interesting but convenient as well.

## Edenton Marinas and Facilities

To the cruising captain's good fortune, Edenton has excellent facilities. At the northern extreme of the entrance cut, north of unlighted daybeacon #8, a small town dock offers limited facilities. One or two boats as large as 36 feet might be able to fit at the fixed wooden piers. Depths alongside run 7 to 10 feet. A few power and water connections are available, but no fuel or other services are to be had. This spot is convenient to the nearby visitor center and the downtown area. However, fresh winds, particularly from the southern quarter, can raise a very uncomfortable chop at the piers. If bad weather is remotely possible, you would be better off coiling your lines elsewhere.

For all the town dock's convenience, most cruising boaters wisely choose to berth at Edenton Marina on Pembroke Creek. The marina's entrance breaks the creek's northeasterly shore northwest of unlighted daybeacon #6 at the upstream limits of the Pembroke Creek channel. Edenton Marina is a friendly full-service facility that welcomes transient boaters with improved fixed wooden slips and piers. Water connections are available, and 30-amp power connections are offered at most slips. The almost fully enclosed dockage basin is well protected from inclement weather. Entrance depths from Pembroke Creek run 6½ to 7 feet, with average 6-foot soundings dockside. Gasoline, diesel fuel, mechanical repairs, waste pump-out, and below-the-waterline repairs are all readily available. Edenton Marina's travel-lift is rated at a 10-ton capacity. Ultraclean shoreside showers, a washer and dryer, and an unusually roomy boaters' lounge with color television, full kitchen facilities, and a paperback exchange library are all located on-site in a building which once served as a fish hatchery. Surprisingly enough, this large structure was moved across Pembroke Creek to its present location. The unusual furniture in the boaters' lounge (including, would you believe, an organ) once served a local pharmacy. A ship's store adjacent to the docks is also offered.

The marina's owner will sometimes loan his personal vehicle as a courtesy car for a trip to the grocery store or the downtown business district. Otherwise, taxis are readily available; call Charlie's Taxi Service at 919-482-3423. Rental cars are available from Albemarle Ford (919-482-2144). An IGA grocery store is located within

*Barker House–Edenton*

walking distance of the marina along U.S. 17 Business. Those up for a 1-mile walk can hike to the downtown business and historic district during fair weather.

### Edenton Marina
### (919) 482-7421

Approach depth: 6½–8 feet
Dockside depth: 6 feet
Accepts transients: yes
Fixed wooden piers: yes
Dockside power connections: 30 & 50 amps
Dockside water connections: yes
Showers: yes
Laundromat: yes
Waste pump-out: yes
Gasoline: yes
Diesel fuel: yes
Mechanical repairs: yes
Below-waterline repairs: yes
Ship's store: yes
Restaurant: nearby (see below)

## Edenton Dining

In times past, a two-block walk from Edenton Marina led visitors to Mrs. Boswell's Restaurant. Unfortunately, this Edenton institution closed in 1992, and several other dining establishments have failed to catch on at this location. I now enthusiastically advise hungry cruisers to head to the downtown district (just behind the town docks) for a visit to the Dram Tree Restaurant (110–112 West Water Street, 919-482-2711). This wonderful dining spot is located in a venerable brick building which once served as the headquarters for a local soft-drink bottling company and later housed an antique shop. Lunch is served Wednesday through Sunday from 11:30 A.M. to 2:00 P.M. The evening meal is offered seven days a week from 5:00 P.M. to 9:00 P.M.

Give the baked salmon and shrimp a try. You won't be sorry!

For a more down-home lunch experience, give either Mitchener's Drug Store (301 South Broad Street, 919-482-3711) or Blount Drugs (323 South Broad Street, 919-482-2127) a try. You will be almost sure that you've stepped back into the 1950s.

## Edenton Lodging

For those who wish to spend a night or two with solid ground under their feet, Edenton offers a host of motels, motor courts, and lovely inns. In recent years, the town has sprouted a crop of first-class bed-and-breakfast inns. Virtually all of these establishments are worth the notice of any visitor.

One hostelry of particular note is the Lord Proprietor's Inn (300 North Broad Street, 919-482-3641). Located in the heart of the downtown historic district, this inn has one of the most beautifully restored interiors that I have had the privilege of seeing. It is a great place to take a break from wind and wave. The Lord Proprietor's offers a Modified American Plan for its guests. By all accounts, the evening meals are wonderful. The inn is glad to provide courtesy transportation from Edenton Marina.

Another lodging spot of note is the Captain's Quarters Inn (202 West Queen Street, 919-482-8945). The innkeepers, Bill and Phyllis Pepper, are dyed-in-the-wool sailors, and those who arrive by water are in for a special welcome. All guests are spoiled with afternoon tea, which includes homemade goodies, lemonade, wine, and cheese. The Sunday-morning buffet breakfasts are super. Bill and Phyllis also offer charter cruises on

Albemarle Sound aboard their sailcraft, *Sandpiper*. I cannot recommend the Captain's Quarters too highly!

### Edenton Anchorages

Some local sailcraft are regularly berthed at mooring buoys north of unlighted daybeacon #4. There is room for visiting craft as large as 45 feet to anchor, but be warned that depths run as shallow as 4½ feet. Protection is more than adequate for all but strong easterly winds. The northerly banks are overlooked by a pleasing assortment of local homes.

For this writer's money, Edenton's best anchorage is upstream of unlighted daybeacon #6. From #6 to the charted low-level fixed bridge, craft as large as 42 feet will find an ideal spot to spend a night of peace and security. If you avoid a bit of shallow water along the northeasterly banks, you can expect 6½-foot minimum depths. A stately house guards the southerly shoreline, while the entrance to Edenton Marina is to the northeast. This is a great spot to ride out heavy weather before venturing back out on the broad Albemarle Sound.

*Edenton Marina*

### Edenton History

By 1658, colonists were filtering into the Albemarle region from Jamestown, Virginia. Many were fugitives, and the area was known for a time as Rogues Harbor. By 1710, however, the settlements had taken on importance, and a local capital was established at the confluence of Albemarle Sound and Queen Anne and Pembroke Creeks on the site of an old Indian village. The town was first known as the Port of Roanoke and later as Queen Anne's Town; it was incorporated as Edenton in 1772.

The village's first home was built in 1714 by Edward Moseley, surveyor of the colony. By 1730, there were 60 homes. By 1777, there were 165 residences. An early visitor noted that "within the vicinity of Edenton there was in proportion to its population a greater number of men eminent for ability, virtue and erudition than in any other part of America."

Before the Revolution, Edenton was a thriving community. Established as an official port of entry and later as provincial capital, the town bustled with commerce and politics. One local shipping enterprise and shipyard was owned by Joseph Hewes, who would one day affix his signature to the Declaration of Independence. In 1771, some 142 ships were said to have cleared the port.

During this time, the famous Cupola House was built near the Edenton waterfront. Its cupola was used as a lookout to identify the various ships entering the harbor. This revered residence still stands and is open to the public in restored form. It is readily visible to boaters cruising north down the entrance channel.

On October 25, 1774, an event later known

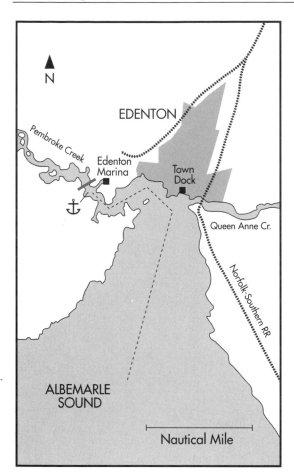

as the Edenton Tea Party took place in the home of Elizabeth King. About 50 patriotic Edenton ladies met and agreed to give up drinking English tea to protest the British tax on the much-loved brew. Legend tells that a concoction of dried mulberry leaves was drunk at the party.

Edenton was largely spared the pain of battle during the Revolution, though the town was briefly shelled twice. About this time, Captain William Boritz delivered 45 Swiss-made cannons to the port. The captain had been promised 100 pounds of tobacco for each cannon. Not having enough leaf in the Edenton warehouses, North Carolina officials desperately looked for more. His patience at an end, Boritz dumped 23 of the cannons into the bay and sailed away. Several of the old pieces, rescued from the waters, now guard the waterfront east of the Barker House.

Following the war with England, North Carolina's political activities shifted from the coast to the interior. Commercial fishing and agriculture grew to be Edenton's principal industries. Even before the Revolution, Richard Brownrigg had introduced commercial herring fishing into the area. A major development in commercial fishing in the Albemarle came in 1869. A German immigrant, John P. Hettrick, introduced the pound net. With the net and just a helper or two, all who were inclined could join in the commercial fishing game. In 1890, one individual, Tom Holly, made the astounding catch of 1,000,000 herring in one night. While the net was certainly a boon for fishermen, many cruising boaters would just as soon Hettrick had stayed in Germany.

### Edenton Tale

For many, many years, a stately cypress tree stood in the midst of Edenton's harbor. No one is entirely sure just how long the tree was there, but legend suggests it was standing long before the first English colonists set foot in the Albemarle region. Somehow, a curious custom grew up around the tree. Whenever a ship of trade called at Edenton, it was almost obligatory for the master to place a bottle of the best Jamaican rum in a hollow place in the trunk. Whenever a ship left for foreign parts, the vessel would stop at the tree and all hands would drink to a safe voyage. Thus it was that the old cypress became known as the Dram Tree. Ships whose crews failed to drink of the Dram Tree or, even worse, failed to place a bottle there when entering port were doomed to disaster. Many are the tales of ill-fated vessels that met violent storms or were becalmed in the doldrums. The tree survived until the spring of 1918, when a tremendous ice floe vanquished the landmark to the sound's waters.

## EDENTON NAVIGATION

To enter Edenton's harbor, set course from flashing daybeacon #CR to come abeam of flashing daybeacon #2 (which marks the southern foot of the Edenton channel) to its westerly side. Be careful not to mistake the red-and-green warning beacon to the west, obscurely marked on chart 12205, for #2. From #2, point to pass all red, even-numbered aids to navigation to your starboard side and all green markers to port. Pass flashing daybeacon #4 and unlighted daybeacon #6 to their fairly immediate western sides. Come abeam of unlighted daybeacon #8 to its western side. Between #2 and #8, minimum depths of 8 feet can be expected.

At #8, look toward shore and you will see the handsome Barker House. You will also see the Edenton town docks. If you choose to berth here, simply cruise straight into the piers. Depths continue good, typically between 7 and 11 feet.

From #8, most pleasure traffic turns west to Pembroke Creek, the site of Edenton Marina. The well-marked channel holds minimum 6-foot depths, with typical 7- and 8-foot soundings. To enter the cut, set course to come abeam of unlighted daybeacon #1 to its fairly immediate northeasterly side. Continue on course, pointing to come abeam of unlighted daybeacon #3 to its northerly side. Set a new course to come abeam

of and pass unlighted daybeacon #4 to its immediate southerly side.

Between #3 and #4, look to starboard and you will notice an interesting white house with a large beacon on its right-hand gable. This structure is an old lighthouse which once sat atop a collection of pilings at the mouth of the Roanoke River. It was saved by a salvage specialist from Edenton, who moved it to the present location.

If you choose to make use of the anchorage north of #4, cruise carefully off the channel and feel your way along with the sounder. Remember that some 4½-foot depths can be expected in this haven.

From #4, continue on course to pass unlighted daybeacon #6 to its immediate southerly side. Between #4 and #6, a large assortment of sunken barges and cranes lines the southerly flank of the channel. Past #6, stick to the creek's mid-width. Look again to port and you will see a beautiful home with a broad expanse of green grass extending to the water's edge.

Do not attempt to enter the south-running offshoot of Pembroke Creek east of the just-discussed house. Depths immediately drop to 4 feet or less.

Northwest of #6, Pembroke Creek holds 6-foot depths all the way to the low highway bridge, which blocks further cruising for all but small craft.

Favor the southwestern (port-side) shores slightly for best depths.

Past #6, you will soon encounter the entrance

to Edenton Marina on the northeastern shoreline. A small stream leads northeast to the facility's docks.

## CHOWAN RIVER

The Chowan River is the largest of the Albemarle's streams. It is also another of the undiscovered cruising opportunities of the North Carolina coast. Seldom will visiting skippers encounter another pleasure craft of any size on the mighty Chowan.

The Chowan is for the most part a delight to navigate. Only a few shoals are to be found between the river's mouth and the village of Winton. The Chowan is well marked, but snags and fishing stakes abound. These obstructions pretty much limit pleasure craft to daylight cruising.

The Chowan has one small marina on Rockyhock Creek, but at the time of this writing, no services for transient cruisers were available. There was once an inn, restaurant, and marina complex located on the Chowan at Winton, but that structure has been torn down and is now but a distant memory. Several reliable anchorages are found along the Chowan River. Most have good depths and excellent protection.

The Chowan's scenery is truly magnificent. In some sections, high earthen cliffs occasionally topped by beautiful homes overlook the river. Much of the shore is in its natural state, but there is more development here than on any of the Albemarle's other rivers. I strongly recommend that you include this impressive stream in your cruising plans.

### Chowan Legend

Many ghost stories are set along the North Carolina coast, but there is perhaps no more pitiful tale than "The Beckoning Hands," as related by Charles Harry Whedbee in *Outer Banks Mysteries and Seaside Stories*. The tale begins with the construction of a beautiful stone house on a high bluff overlooking the Chowan River. The builder was none other than an infamous pirate. He perceived that his new home would be a secure hiding place, since it commanded a wide view both up and down the great river. It seems that the pirate had a young wife who did not approve of his lawless ways. Soon after the house was finished, she and her daughter moved to Charleston, where they lived until the buccaneer's death.

Even as the magnificent edifice was being built, the pirate became the unhappy recipient of a strange curse. Legend tells that he kidnapped the only son of an old hag from Nags Head who was rumored to be a witch. It was not long before the boy was killed in another attack by the pirates. The old woman cursed the pirate and said that since she would never have grandchildren, neither would he.

Following the brigand's death, his widow and her lovely daughter, Caroline, moved back to the house. In a few years, Caroline became engaged, and the ceremony was set for the bride's home. As the service was about to begin, Caroline appeared atop the great stairs and coyly beckoned her groom to come catch her if he could. Taking to the innocent game, he bounded up the stairs, but his bride was nowhere to be found. That was the last anyone saw of Caroline as a living being. Her grief-stricken mother soon moved away, and the house was closed for many years.

Before long, it began to be whispered that the old home was haunted. Children reported seeing a ghostly visage flitting from window to window on New Year's Eve, always beckoning with white hands. The stone mansion became known as "the House of the Beckoning Hands."

The mystery remained unsolved until modern times. A famous ghost hunter finally undertook to lay the matter to rest. While awaiting the apparition on New Year's Eve, he fell asleep and had a strange dream. In his dream, he saw the long-ago wedding day. After Caroline beckoned to her groom, the investigator saw her run down the upstairs hall and trip over her wedding gown. As she put out her hands for support, a portion of the wall gave way, tipped her through, and then snapped back into place. Caroline was entombed alive in a secret room!

Startled awake by the intensity of his dream, the investigator ran upstairs. Sure enough, the wall opened just as he had seen in his sleep. He beheld the pitiful figure of a small skeleton still anointed by a bit of bridal lace.

The remains were given a Christian burial. Perhaps Caroline's spirit was at last laid to rest.

## Salmon Creek

Salmon Creek, near the mouth of the Chowan well southwest of flashing daybeacon #2, makes a fair overnight anchorage, but water levels have shoaled on this stream during the last several years. Minimum depths of 6 feet can now be expected only as far as the second point of land making in from the southerly banks. Past this point, soundings drop off to 4 feet or sometimes considerably less.

Consider setting the hook just short of the second southern entrance point, where there is plenty of swinging room for boats up to 42 feet in length and fair protection from all but eastern and northeastern winds. There is a large industrial plant on the creek's southern shore, but the rest of the banks are undeveloped.

## Cypress Point Marina

Cypress Point Marina is a small facility perched on the upper reaches of Rockyhock Creek east of the Chowan's flashing daybeacon #3. A newly marked entrance channel now carries minimum 5- to 6-foot soundings. I have always found the docks unattended here during several visits over the last five years. It seems as if no transient services are available. If this situation should change, visitors to Cypress Point will find fixed wooden piers with power and water connections.

## Keel Creek

Keel Creek opens its broad mouth on the Chowan's western banks northwest of unlighted daybeacon #7. This stream boasts fair anchorage for craft as large as 36 feet that draw 3½ feet or less. The creek's mouth is surrounded by numerous snags, making entry hazardous in high winds or low light. Otherwise, the stream holds 5-foot minimum depths and affords good protection from all winds. Both shores are wooded and virtually untouched.

Probably the best spot to anchor is in the body of the creek's first sharp jog to port. Consider dropping the hook here for excellent protection.

### Holiday Island Channels

North of flashing daybeacon #12, the mighty Chowan River is bisected by Holiday Island, a large but undeveloped body of land and marsh. The marked channel continues down the westerly fork, but the easterly arm also holds minimum 10-foot depths if you avoid one unmarked shoal. In light winds or moderate westerly breezes, cruisers can anchor behind (east of) Holiday Island, but there is insufficient protection from anything approaching heavy weather.

### Bennetts Creek

If you could design the perfect overnight anchorage, you would certainly include depths of 9 feet or better, excellent protection from all winds, attractive shores in their natural state, an easy approach, and plenty of swinging room. All these qualities are found on Bennetts Creek north of flashing daybeacon #13 (northwest of Holiday Island). The stream is without a doubt one of the best anchorages on all the Albemarle's rivers.

While it eventually becomes much too narrow and shallow for cruising-size craft, Bennetts Creek leads to beautiful Merchants Millpond State Park in remote Gates County. This magnificent, swampy, and somehow mysterious cypress pond is drawing more visitors every year. Canoeists sometimes make the long trek from Merchants Millpond via Bennetts Creek all the way to the mighty Chowan.

## CHOWAN RIVER NAVIGATION

The entrance to the Chowan River is bounded on the northeast by Reedy Point and on the southwest by Black Walnut Point. To enter the river, set course from flashing daybeacon #CR to come abeam of flashing daybeacon #2 west of Reedy Point by 300 yards to its southwesterly side. Once you are abeam of #2, the Chowan's first sidewater will come abeam to the southwest.

*Salmon Creek*   Set course from #2 for the mid-width of the stream's entrance. Continue holding scrupulously to the midline as you work your way upstream. Watch to port (south) for a sharp point

of land located just east of the "Avoca" notation on chart 12205. Don't cruise upstream past this promontory. Depths quickly decline to 4 feet or less. Instead, drop anchor along the creek's centerline between the first and second points stretching out from the southerly shoreline.

*On the Chowan*   From flashing daybeacon #2, set course for the central pass-through of the Edenhouse Bridge. The swinging span has a closed vertical clearance of only 4 feet, but it does open on demand. Look to the west as you are cruising through the span. The point of land on the western banks was once the site of Edenhouse, home of several Royal governors during North Carolina's colonial period.

Once the bridge is in your wake, set a new course to come abeam of flashing daybeacon #3, east of Hermitage Wharf, by several hundred yards to its easterly side. From #3, Cypress Point Marina is accessible to the east.

**Cypress Point**  Cypress Point Marina does not currently offer any transient services. If you choose to visit anyway, point to enter the mid-width of the large cove leading to Rockyhock Creek well east of flashing daybeacon #3. Be careful to avoid the finger of shallow water extending out from the northern point (clearly shown on chart 12205), as well as several groups of pound-net stakes which flank the marked channel. Keep a sharp watch for some small, privately maintained red and green daybeacons outlining the marina channel. As you would expect, take all red markers to your starboard side and green beacons to port. After curling around the northern shores of a small island which divides the creek, you will

*Cypress Trees on Chowan River*

eventually sight the marina's dockage basin ahead. Take your time and watch the sounder.

### On the Chowan
From a position abeam of flashing daybeacon #3, follow the river's mid-width, pointing to bring flashing daybeacon #5 abeam to its easterly side. Between #3 and #5, watch the westerly shoreline and you will see some of the Chowan's high earthen cliffs. As you approach #5, be on guard against fishing stakes. Many of these hazards are found east and north of #5.

To continue upstream, consider setting course for unlighted daybeacon #7. This aid can be passed on either side, but its color indicates that the preferred passage is east of the marker. Depths are not a problem here, but many snags and stakes litter the waters. Northwest of #7, Keel Creek, on the western shore, presents another opportunity for anchorage.

### Keel Creek
Approach the stream's entrance on its mid-width. Take your time and keep a sharp watch for snags and partially submerged logs. Expect approach depths of 5½ to 11 feet. The soundings fall off to one area of 5-foot readings just past the mouth. Soon, depths increase again to 6 and 8 feet. Follow the creek until it takes a sharp jog to port. Consider anchoring here for excellent protection. Don't cruise farther upstream unless your craft draws less than 3 feet.

### On the Chowan
Set course from unlighted daybeacon #7 to come abeam of unlighted daybeacon #10 to its westerly side. Along the way, you will pass flashing daybeacon #9 west of your course. From #10, another short run will lead you to flashing daybeacon #12. Northeast of #12, Holiday Island divides the Chowan River.

### Holiday Island Channels
The marked Chowan River channel passes west of Holiday Island, but the eastern arm holds 8 to 10 feet on its mid-width. Take care to avoid the correctly charted pilings abutting the eastern banks behind Holiday Island. To rejoin the main channel, simply avoid Holiday Island's northern tip and cruise west to flashing daybeacon #13.

Catherine Creek strikes off to the northeast near the northern extreme of the cut behind Holiday Island. There is a channel in the stream, but it is an unmarked, twisting snake. Wise captains will bypass Catherine Creek.

To follow the main channel west of Holiday Island, set course from #12 to come abeam of flashing daybeacon #13 to its fairly immediate easterly side. North of #13, cruisers have access to the Chowan's best anchorage, Bennetts Creek.

### Bennetts Creek
Simply strike a course for the creek's mid-width and drop the hook in a likely spot. Approach depths of 9 feet increase to 13-foot readings on the stream's interior reaches. Good soundings continue well upstream.

### On the Chowan
From flashing daybeacon #13, the Chowan continues deep, well marked, and easy to follow all the way to the Winton Bridge. No further sidewaters accessible to cruising craft are to be found between #13 and Winton. This account ends at Winton, but the Chowan continues unobstructed for many miles. Adventurous skippers may consider the upper Chowan, but they would be well advised to proceed with caution and avoid hurrying.

# ROANOKE RIVER

The Roanoke River is the narrowest of the major streams entering Albemarle Sound, but it is well marked and has minimum 8-foot depths as far upstream as Plymouth. Auxiliary streams including the Eastmost, Middle, and Cashie Rivers provide additional cruising opportunities for those who can clear some fairly low fixed bridges.

Facilities have recently improved on the Roanoke. Cruising boaters that can clear the 50-foot fixed Roanoke River–N.C. 45 bridge can now tie to some new but rather shallow town docks at Plymouth, 5 nautical miles upstream. The older, deeper docks are still there but remain in poor condition. No other marine services are available on the Roanoke.

Plymouth is the only town on this section of the Roanoke. Elsewhere on the river, the banks are mainly in their natural state. There is only one secluded anchorage possibility on the Roanoke itself, behind an island upstream from Plymouth, but the auxiliary rivers do offer some good spots for power craft.

Frankly, compared to the other Albemarle streams, the Roanoke River is a bit plain. However, the several tributaries are excellent opportunities for adventurous skippers. The Roanoke River has been of vital commercial importance to coastal North Carolina in the past. If you have the time, consider a cruise of the Roanoke to view this once-great artery of commercial traffic.

## Plymouth

Plymouth is a small but thriving coastal city that looks to both agriculture and modern industry for its livelihood. The town waterfront flanks the southerly shoreline well upstream of flashing daybeacon #17. Within the past several years, the town of Plymouth has constructed some new piers along the river's southerly flank immediately behind the Port O' Plymouth–Roanoke River Museum (see below). This structure can be recognized from the water by the several railroad cars and the red caboose on the museum grounds. Unfortunately, depths at these low-level fixed wooden piers are more than suspect. This writer sounded a mere 4 feet on the outermost sections of the slips, with a bare 2 to 3 feet near the inner portion of the docks. These depths limit this facility's usefulness to most cruising boaters, and even shallow-draft vessels will want to dock bow-in to avoid the 2- to 3-foot waters nearer shore. If you are able to stand these soundings, some 15-amp power hookups are available; water connections are not offered. The slips have obviously been designed for boats 30 feet or (preferably) smaller.

The dilapidated face docks that were for many years the only overnight space for pleasure craft on the Plymouth waterfront are still available. They are located along the Roanoke's southern banks a bit farther upstream (southwest) of the newer piers described above. Depths are much better here, typically 7 feet or more, but this facility will never win any maintenance awards. In fact, the so-called docks are really just a few pilings set out from a wooden bulkhead. Only a single power connection (which requires a very long shore power cord) is available, and no water hookups are in the offing. The Plymouth Police Department is located in the brick building just behind these docks.

The downtown Plymouth business district is readily accessible by foot from either the new or old docks. Begin your tour at the Port O' Plymouth–Roanoke River Museum (210 West Water Street, 919-793-1377), located just behind the new Plymouth city docks. This attraction gives visitors a good overview of Plymouth's and the Roanoke River's rich history. It is normally open Tuesday through Saturday from 8 A.M. to 5 P.M. year-round. During the summer months, local volunteers often open this attraction on Sunday afternoons as well.

After visiting the museum, stroll west on Water Street for about three blocks to discover J & C Hardware Store (201 West Water Street, 919-793-2464), located on the north side of the street.

If you are in need of provisions while docked in Plymouth, you will need to undertake a significant hike of about 1.5 miles to U.S. 64; try walking south on Washington Street. Here you will find a drugstore, a supermarket, and several fast-food restaurants.

## Plymouth History

Plymouth was probably settled around 1720. Its strategic position on the Roanoke River quickly gave rise to trade. The town was named a "port of delivery" in 1790 and a "port of entry" in 1808. By 1843, it was not unusual for 50 or more boats to be docked along the riverfront. That same year, however, a visiting vessel spread yellow fever into the community, and the town's population was reduced to 300 citizens.

During the Civil War, Plymouth was occupied by Union forces in 1862. Two years later, the Confederate ironclad ram *Albemarle* steamed confidently down the Roanoke and obliterated the small occupying Union fleet. A synchronized land attack routed the Federal defenders, and Plymouth temporarily returned to the Confederacy. But then a Union soldier stealthily rowed to the *Albemarle* by night and attached a bomb to the vessel. The *Albemarle* was destroyed, and a renewed attack by Union troops recaptured Plymouth in a few days.

Only 11 buildings were reportedly left standing after the war. However, the town was gradually rebuilt as the naval-stores trade grew. Plymouth was given a new mainstay of commerce in 1930 with the construction of a nearby pulp plant. Today, the pulp mill is a massive operation, and Plymouth's future appears bright, even if the smell of progress is not always sweet.

## Roanoke River Anchorage

West of Plymouth, the Roanoke is soon divided by a long, undeveloped, oval-shaped island. The main channel borders the island's southern quarter and soon meets up with the large pulp mill described above. The northern cut holds 6- to 8-foot depths behind the island and is an excellent spot to drop the hook, provided you can stand the smell. There is enough swinging room for a 34-footer abeam of the island's eastern reaches but a bit less farther upstream. Protection should be adequate for all winds short of a full gale.

## The Three Streams

The three small auxiliary rivers to the west of the Roanoke present some off-the-beaten-path

*Plymouth Pulp Mill*

cruising opportunities for adventurous skippers. To enter these waters, you must be able to clear several fixed spans with only 16 feet of vertical clearance. As you might expect, all three streams hold the ever-present threat of fishing stakes and partially submerged snags. Because they are so narrow, none of the three streams is recommended for craft over 36 feet in length. Otherwise, depths are consistently 5½ feet or better, and opportunities for sheltered anchorage abound. If you enjoy getting away from it all (and can clear the bridges), these are excellent cruising grounds.

The Eastmost River maintains minimum 6-foot depths until it meets up with the shallow waters of Bachelor Bay to the northeast. This sheltered river with a beautifully natural shoreline makes an ideal anchorage for boats as large as 32 feet.

The Middle River is, in my opinion, the most interesting of all the Roanoke's sidewaters. The shores are heavily wooded, undeveloped, and quite lovely indeed. Additionally, it is possible to enter the Middle River from the Roanoke River above

the paper plant, thereby avoiding the low bridges. Adventurous sailors might consider such an exploration, but they should be forewarned that the intersection of the two streams is flanked by stumps and a whole collection of semifloating debris. Some 5½-foot depths also guard the two rivers' intersection.

Minimum depths on the Middle River are 7 feet except for its intersection with the Roanoke River, but again, there are many, many fishing stakes to avoid. Don't even think about trying to cruise this waterway after dark! Anchorage opportunities are numerous, and protection is sufficient even for heavy blows. Vessels up to 36 feet should find enough room for a comfortable stay on the hook.

I will not attempt to select from the many possible overnight stops on the Middle River. The river widens and narrows as it works its way southwest toward an intersection with the Roanoke River. Select a likely spot with enough elbow room for your vessel and settle down amidst the virgin shores for an evening you will not soon forget.

The Cashie River is the least appealing of the Roanoke's three auxiliary streams. Minimum depths of 8 feet can be held for only a short distance southwest of the Roanoke Bridge before unmarked shoals are encountered.

Southwest of the Roanoke Bridge, Grennell Creek opens out on the Cashie's southern bank. This small creek carries 6 to 7 feet of water but is too small to provide sufficient swinging room for craft over 28 feet.

Otherwise, the Cashie River consists of open water without any sheltered spots for setting the hook. The stream's shoreline is mostly untouched but not as attractive as that of the Middle and

Eastmost Rivers. All in all, the Cashie should probably be bypassed, but for those captains who want to see it all, a short navigational summary is included.

# ROANOKE RIVER NAVIGATION

Enter the Roanoke River only by the marked channel beginning at flashing daybeacon #1 north of Albemarle Beach. Don't attempt to enter the Eastmost River or the Cashie River from Bachelor Bay, where the channel is narrow, winding, and unmarked. Stay strictly to the marked entrance cut. Outside the channel, depths quickly rise to grounding levels.

Set course from flashing daybeacon #CR to come abeam of #1 to its northerly side. From #1, set a new course to pass unlighted daybeacon #2 to its southerly side and come abeam of flashing daybeacon #3 to its fairly immediate northerly side. From #3, point to come between unlighted daybeacon #5 to your port side and flashing daybeacon #6 to starboard. As you approach the gap between #5 and #6, be on the watch for several particularly sinister snags flanking the channel.

From a position between #5 and #6, swing to the southwest and point to pass a short distance east of unlighted daybeacon #8 and flashing daybeacon #10.

From this point, the main body of the Roanoke River swings generally south and southwest on its way to the Plymouth waterfront. Remember the good old "red-right-returning" rule, and take all red markers to your starboard side and all green aids to port.

Between flashing daybeacons #13 and #14, you will pass the mouth of Conaby Creek south of your course. Avoid this small stream. Depths of 3 feet or less are encountered at the entrance.

Southwest of flashing daybeacon #15, you will soon spot the Roanoke River–N.C. 45 bridge. This fixed span has 50 feet of vertical clearance. Upstream of the bridge, a side channel leads northwest to the Eastmost, Middle, and Cashie Rivers. This chapter will first follow the Roanoke to a point west of Plymouth, then review the three auxiliary streams.

Between the Roanoke Bridge and Plymouth, only one aid, flashing daybeacon #17, is encountered. Stick to the mid-width and continue to watch carefully for stakes and snags.

Soon, you will see several large tanks and stacks to port, followed by an old barge-loading facility on the southern shore. Several derelict craft are half-sunk in the river. Just west of the old docks, the Plymouth waterfront will come abeam to the south.

*Roanoke River Anchorage*    Above Plymouth, the Roanoke is soon divided by a long, oval-shaped island. The main channel continues along the island's southerly quarter and borders the pulp mill. The northerly cut holds 6-foot minimum depths behind the island and makes an excellent spot to drop the hook.

The two branches rejoin at the island's westerly tip, where the southwesterly mouth of the Middle River makes into the Roanoke's northerly shore. This guide's coverage of the Roanoke ends here, but the river remains fairly deep for many miles upstream.

***The Three Streams***   All three auxiliary rivers can be reached by using the thoroughfare located on the northwestern quarter of the Roanoke Bridge. The cut-through holds 5½- to 7-foot depths but is spanned by a portion of the bridge with only 16 feet of vertical clearance. Any craft that cannot clear this height must forgo cruising all the sidewaters except the Middle River, which can be entered from the Roanoke west of Plymouth.

To enter, cruise past the Roanoke Bridge's central pass-through for 50 yards, then curl around 180 degrees to starboard. Head for the mid-width of the passage on the river's northwestern shore, which passes back under the bridge. Be careful to avoid the several snags that litter the thoroughfare near the span. Once through, you will be cruising on the narrow but mostly deep waters of the Eastmost River.

***Eastmost River***   If you wish to anchor, select a spot with sufficient swinging room and drop the hook. Don't attempt to enter Bachelor Bay through the northeastern mouth of the Eastmost

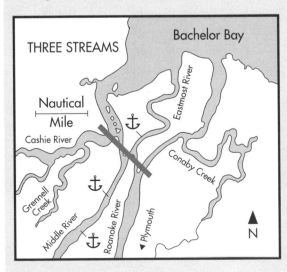

River. Depths near the entrance fall off to 3 feet.

Soon after passing through the Roanoke Bridge on the Eastmost, you will see a small cove to port. This stream provides entrance into the Middle River.

***Middle River***   Follow the mid-width of the port-side cove from the Eastmost River until you again pass under the Roanoke Bridge. Bear to port and enter the mid-width of the Middle River. As you pass out into the stream, your course will be flanked by groups of fish stakes both to port and starboard. Point to pass between these hazards.

Stick to the mid-width as you cruise upstream on the Middle River. You can expect depths of 7 to 25 feet. After traveling 2 nautical miles, you will spy a small island dividing the stream. Pass the island to its northwestern side *only*. Do not attempt the southeastern passage. It is choked with growth and debris and is barely discernible from the main shoreline.

Upstream of the island, the Middle River narrows, but good depths continue for several miles until the channel reaches a junction with the Roanoke River. The intersection of the Middle and Roanoke Rivers is bordered on both sides by snags and stumps. Pick a path between the two clumps of debris. You will encounter minimum depths of 5½ to 6 feet until you reach the deeper waters of the Roanoke.

***Cashie River***   To enter the Cashie River, follow the same cove from the Eastmost as you would to enter the Middle River. But instead of swinging to port once you are under the bridge, turn to starboard. Soon, you will again cross under the Roanoke Bridge while cruising to the north. Depths on these waters run from 8 to 25 feet.

North of the fixed span, several islands comprise the western banks. These undeveloped bodies of land separate your present course from the main upstream track of the Cashie River. Don't attempt to take a shortcut by cruising between the islands. Continue north until you can curve around the tip of the northernmost island. Then point toward the mid-width of the northwesternmost span of the Roanoke Bridge. As you pass through the bridge for the third time, depths fall off to between 8 and 10 feet.

Don't attempt to cruise upstream past the Cashie's intersection with Grennell Creek. Unmarked shoals with 4 feet of water or less will soon block your path.

***On the Albemarle***    To cruise east on Albemarle Sound from the Roanoke River, set course from flashing daybeacon #1, at the northeastern entrance of the Roanoke channel, toward the charted position of the now-defunct Albemarle railroad bridge. Just before you reach the bridge's former position, Mackeys Creek will come abeam on the southern shore.

## MACKEYS CREEK

Mackeys Creek cuts the southern shore of Albemarle Sound a short hop west of the charted position of the now-removed Albemarle railway bridge. This stream was once the home of Mackey's Ferry, which plied the sound from 1734 until 1938. The opening of the Albemarle's first highway bridge finally spelled the end of this historical operation. Today, this long-ignored stream boasts a new marina that beckons cruising captains to explore.

The outer (northwesterly) entrance to the Mackeys Creek entrance channel is marked by flashing daybeacon #1 and unlighted daybeacon #2. Minimum depths of 6 feet can be expected, while soundings improve to 8 or more feet on the stream's interior reaches. Navigators should be forewarned that the entrance cut is flanked by the partially submerged remnants of twin wooden breakwaters that once protected the channel. Once you reach the creek's interior, you will leave these potential hazards behind.

A bit farther upstream, Mackeys Creek was once crossed by a low-level railroad bridge which limited access farther upstream to very small power craft. Happily, this obstruction has been completely removed, and the charted power lines have been raised to a clearance of 85 feet.

In 1996, a new owner, Harry Enoch, took over the small fish-processing center upstream in the tiny village of Mackeys Creek. He also undertook the construction of Mackeys Marina. This interesting facility sports new wooden-decked floating piers set amidst a sheltered portion of the creek. Depths alongside run 9 feet or better. Plans call for expanding the 49 slips to a considerably larger number. The existing slips are probably most appropriate for boats 38 feet and smaller, but vessels up to 65 feet can be accommodated at several face docks. Transients are eagerly accepted, and visitors will discover freshwater and 15-amp power connections at every berth. The old on-site net house has been converted to a nice boaters' lounge complete with showers and a washer-dryer combination. Gasoline, diesel fuel, and waste pump-out are all readily available, as is an adjacent ship's store. The friendly owners can usually arrange motorized transportation into the nearby town of Roper (about 6 miles away) so guests can reprovision at the local supermarket. As you might expect, there is nothing in the way of a restaurant in Mackeys Ferry, so be ready to spend a little time in the galley.

All in all, this writer was very taken with this new, albeit smaller, facility. If you are looking for glitzy nightlife, forget it, but if you want a good, solid marina set amidst one of the least-discovered places on the North Carolina coastline, then by all means give Mackeys Marina a try.

**Mackeys Marina**
**(919) 793-5031**

Approach depth: 6-20 feet
Dockside depth: 8+ feet
Accepts transients: yes
Floating wooden piers: yes
Dockside power connections: 15 amps
Dockside water connections: yes
Showers: yes
Laundromat: yes
Waste pump-out: yes
Gasoline: yes
Diesel fuel: yes
Ship's store: yes

## MACKEYS CREEK NAVIGATION

Point to come between flashing daybeacon #1 and unlighted daybeacon #2. Carefully set course to the southeast, pointing toward the entrance's mid-width. Take care to avoid the old wooden piles and debris on both sides of the channel. Once you are through the mouth, hold to the centerline as you work your way upstream to Mackeys Marina. The docks will come up on the starboard banks after you round a bend in the stream.

*On the Albemarle*  To safely bypass the old position of the Albemarle railroad bridge, point to pass between flashing daybeacons #6 and #7. This course should help you avoid any leftover underwater obstructions.

To continue east on the Albemarle, set a new course for the central pass-through of the fixed high-rise span connecting Sandy and Leonards Points. Once through, set a new course for flashing daybeacon #3, north of Laurel Point. Come abeam of #3 well to its northerly side. From #3, you may choose to enter the delightful Scuppernong River on the Albemarle's southerly shore.

# SCUPPERNONG RIVER

Early explorers were so enchanted with the beauty of this river that they named it "Hearts Delight." It is a very lovely body of water indeed. Narrower than its sister streams to the north, the Scuppernong is lined by heavily wooded shores. Old, gnarled cypress trees with their trailing beards of gray moss majestically guard the banks. Here and there, a few picturesque homes break the landscape.

Tradition claims that the river is the birthplace of the Scuppernong grape. Early visitors are said to have carried clippings of the vine back to Roanoke Island, from which grew the "Mother Vineyard."

Columbia, a river town founded in 1792 and originally named Shallop's Landing, is located at the upstream cruising limit for large pleasure craft. According to Bill Sharpe in *A New Geography of North Carolina*, a visitor to Columbia was walking down the town's main street when he noticed that everyone seemed to be carrying a fishing pole. The stranger began to feel uneasy. He went to the sheriff's office and asked, "Is it a law in this town that everybody has to carry a fishing pole?" The deputy replied, "Well, I wouldn't exactly call it a law; but you might say it was the rule." This is a typical down-east tale if I have ever heard one. It embodies the spirit of this little town and emphasizes how good the fishing can be on the wide, lazy Scuppernong River.

The Scuppernong holds minimum 7-foot depths to Columbia. The dredged entrance channel from Bull Bay is well marked, as is the remainder of the river.

Two private marinas and new town docks are accessible to cruising craft in Columbia. Good anchorages litter the river between its mouth and the town. To say the least, there are more than a few points of interest to delight skippers on this fortunate stream.

## Scuppernong Anchorages

The Scuppernong River offers visiting cruisers many overnight anchorages. This is the sort of water where boaters can almost pick a spot at will. Those who want a little more direction might consider the havens described below.

Moving upstream from the river's entrance, cruisers might consider the waters west of flashing daybeacon #4, tucked behind (to the north of) the adjacent point. This haven offers protection from southern, southwestern, and southeastern winds. Depths of 7 to 9 feet can be expected short of the correctly charted 3-foot shallows to the west. There is ample elbow room for almost any size vessel, and the shores are completely natural.

With strong northeasterly winds in the offing, cautious cruisers can take shelter adjacent to the riverbanks northeast of the gap between flashing daybeacon #4 and unlighted daybeacon #5. Minimum depths of 6 feet run to within 100 yards of shore, and 5-foot soundings can be carried even closer to the banks. Again, swinging room and the adjacent scenery are all that any pleasure boater could ask for.

Another spot worth a look is southwest of flashing daybeacon #7, hard by the entrance canal leading to Sawyers Marina. While there are some surrounding shallows to avoid, minimum depths of 5 to 6 feet can be held well into the charted cove. Be sure to read the navigational information describing this anchorage before attempting first-time entry.

Finally, those who like to pitch the hook just a bit closer to civilization might try the 8- to 9-foot waters abutting the Scuppernong River's northeastern banks just upstream of flashing daybeacon #10. This anchorage is within sight of the Columbia waterfront and is protected enough for heavy weather.

## Scuppernong River Facilities

If you prefer coiling your lines at marina docks, you will also find much to attract you on the Scuppernong River. Moving upstream from the Albemarle intersection, you will first come to the entrance to Sawyers Marina (International Yachting Center) south of flashing daybeacon #7.

Several years ago, a German cruising family, the Dietrichs, purchased the poorly maintained Columbia facility called Sawyers Marina. Since that time, the new owners have worked long and hard to make their marina one of the best operations of its type on the North Carolina coast. In addition to offering the expected dockage and boatyard services, the Dietrichs have formed the International Yachting Center. Under the auspices of this firm, the Dietrichs import fine European sailboats and powerboats and offer them for sale at competitive prices.

For some years after the new owners took over

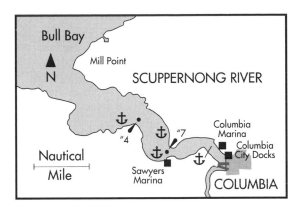

Sawyers Marina, there was a persistent problem with shallow water. Happily, that difficulty has now been remedied by dredging. Skippers of fixed-keel sailcraft can count on depths of 6½ feet, with many soundings in the 7-foot range in the entrance canal. Dockside depths have improved to 8 and 8½ feet. The marina owns its own dredge, so there is good reason to believe that these depths will be maintained.

Transient boaters are gladly accepted for overnight or temporary dockage at fixed wooden piers with water and 30- and 50-amp power connections. The dockage basin is quite well protected from foul weather. Gasoline, diesel fuel, waste pump-out services, and clean showers are offered, as is an unusually well-stocked ship's store that carries many spare parts.

Sawyers Marina offers complete mechanical repairs for both gasoline and diesel power plants. Haul-outs are accomplished by two cranes rated at 18 and 20 tons.

Sentells Restaurant (919-796-5006) is located within easy walking distance just behind the Sawyers Marina dockage basin. It serves three meals a day. This writer found the food here acceptable but a bit on the plain side. A motel is adjacent to the restaurant, a convenient arrangement for those wanting to spend a night or two ashore. Transportation is available to a new restaurant in downtown Columbia, Harley's Raw Bar and Grill, described below.

All in all, Sawyers Marina offers just about any service a mariner might ever desire. Visiting cruisers should give this facility a long look before moving on. Stop by if for no other reason than to see the unique European craft displayed for sale.

**Sawyers Marina
(International Yachting Center)
(919) 796-0435**

Approach depth: 6½–15 feet
Dockside depth: 8-8½ feet
Accepts transients: yes
Fixed wooden piers: yes
Dockside power connections: 30 & 50 amps
Dockside water connections: yes
Showers: yes
Waste pump-out: yes
Gasoline: yes
Diesel fuel: yes
Mechanical repairs: yes
Below-waterline repairs: yes
Ship's store: yes
Restaurant: nearby

Columbia Marina, just north of the town bridge, guards the eastern banks and is easily spotted from the water. This marina has one slip available for transients. Most of its berths are occupied by permanent residents. Thirty-amp power connections and water hookups are available at the fixed wooden piers. Downtown Columbia is only a few steps away. If you plan to berth at Columbia Marina, it is a good idea to call ahead to check on dockage availability.

**Columbia Marina
(919) 796-8561**

Approach depth: 8–15 feet
Dockside depth: 7–10 feet (outer slips)
    5–6 feet (inner berths)
Accepts transients: one slip
Fixed wooden piers: yes
Dockside power connections: 30 amps
Dockside water connections: yes
Showers: yes
Laundromat: yes
Restaurants: several nearby

Since 1995, the town of Columbia has constructed a series of low-level fixed wooden piers along the downtown waterfront, which flanks the river's eastern shore just downstream (north) of the fixed bridge. Visiting cruisers are welcome to tie to these docks on a first-come, first-served basis. The downtown area, with its visitor center, grocery store, and restaurant, is only a few convenient steps away. Depths alongside the piers run around 6 to 6½ feet. Neither power connections nor fuel is to be had, but there is a single freshwater hookup. Waste pump-out service is available through the town hall, located just behind the city piers. All in all, this is a free, convenient dockage facility for small cruising craft (up to 36 feet) that do not have an im-

**Columbia City Docks
(919) 796-2781**

Approach depth: 8-11 feet
Dockside depth: 6-6½ feet
Accepts transients: yes
Fixed wooden piers: yes
Waste pump-out: yes
Restaurant: nearby

mediate need for power hookups.

## Columbia and the Tyrrell County Visitors Center

Those who have not had the opportunity to visit Columbia during the past several years will discover big changes for the better. Perhaps the most significant addition is the visitor center overlooking the Scuppernong's eastern banks just south (upstream) of the fixed U.S. 64 bridge. The Tyrrell County Visitors Center (203 Ludington Drive, 919-796-0723) is dedicated to the preservation and understanding of the coastal North Carolina wetlands, with which the country surrounding Columbia is so richly endowed. The center features a 0.75-mile raised boardwalk interpretive nature trail which allows visitors a close look at a typical wetland. Complete with explanatory signs and an outdoor classroom, this trail is highly recommended for any who have an interest in coastal ecology.

The center also supplies kayaks for those adventurous souls who want to explore the upstream reaches of the Scuppernong River. As you might imagine, this waterway leads to a host of undeveloped wetlands.

Just behind the visitor center, cruisers can restock their larders at the Foodway grocery story, currently the only store of its type in Columbia. It's only a quick step from the town docks or Columbia Marina but a bit farther from Sawyers Marina. Ask the marina staff there for help with transportation.

For those interested in the history of Columbia, the visitor center provides a informative pamphlet entitled, "Columbia on the Scuppernong—Walking Tour." With this booklet in hand,

cruises can stroll downtown Columbia and identify 20 historical structures whose dates of origin range from the late 19th to the early 20th century.

A new restaurant in downtown Columbia, Harley's Raw Bar and Grill (203 Main Street, 919-796-1818) is open for lunch and dinner. Harley's is only a very short step from the town docks. I recently had the opportunity to sample the lunchtime fare at this new dining attraction, and both I and my companions were very taken with our crabmeat quiche. We think you will be similarly delighted.

If you'd like a good cup of coffee or a cappuccino, don't miss the Columbia Pharmacy (214 Main Street, 919-796-2421).

Heart's Delight Bed-and-Breakfast Inn (919-796-1778) is a first-class shoreside accommodation. Complimentary transportation to and from Sawyers Marina, Columbia Marina, and the city docks is available with advance arrangements. This homey establishment, housed in a large homeplace dating from 1908, boasts three warmly furnished guest rooms, as well as a full country breakfast. This writer found Heart's Delight an absolutely charming, totally unpretentious hostelry with very friendly innkeepers. It is recommended without reservation.

Visiting cruisers with an artistic bent will want to beat a path to Pocosin Arts (919-796-2787), located on the corner of Main and Water Streets. Housed on the second floor of a historic downtown building (next door to Harley's Raw Bar and Grill), this attraction features a display gallery, a gift shop, a sale gallery, and a large educational space. The proprietor, Feather Phillips, told this writer that her mission is to "expand understanding of the relationship between people and place, culture and environment through the production of traditional arts." Pocosin Arts is truly one of the finest establishments of its kind in eastern North Carolina.

If your waterborne travels bring you to Columbia during the second weekend in October, a lucky star is shining on your cruise. Visitors on this fortunate weekend can participate in the Scuppernong River Festival, an extravaganza of arts, craft, drama, music, fireworks, and food.

Clearly, with the advent of the town docks, a second restaurant, and the new Tyrrell County Visitors Center, Columbia can lay claim to a far larger share of many cruisers' attention than was true in years past. This writer suggests you heed its call.

## SCUPPERNONG RIVER NAVIGATION

To enter the Scuppernong River from Albemarle Sound, set course to come abeam of the entrance's outer channel marker, flashing day-beacon #1, to its fairly immediate westerly side. Once abeam of #1, adjust your course to the southeast and point to pass unlighted daybeacons #2 and #2A to their immediate northeasterly sides. The current edition of chart 12205 still shows unlighted nun buoy #2 on this portion of the channel, but on-site observation revealed that this aid has been replaced by unlighted daybeacon #2.

For best depths, pass #2 and #2A rather closely. By following this procedure, you can expect minimum 7- to 8-foot soundings. Any slippage to the northeast can land you in 4½- to 5-foot depths.

From #2A, continue on the same course, pointing to come abeam of flashing daybeacon #3 to its fairly immediate southwesterly side. Upstream of #3, the channel becomes quite wide and holds 8 feet or better all the way to Columbia. Set course from #3 to come abeam of flashing daybeacon #4 to its northerly side. These two beacons are 1.5 nautical miles apart, and you must watch carefully to catch sight of #4. Upriver from #4, be on guard for partially submerged snags and fishing stakes.

If you choose to anchor in the lee of the point west of flashing daybeacon #4, depart the main channel 100 yards northwest of #4. Cruise carefully north of the point of land, keeping 50 yards offshore. Be safe! Drop anchor well before reaching the charted shallows to the west.

Don't attempt to cruise into the rear of this cove, even though you may see sailcraft moored here. These are local craft whose skippers know how to follow the unmarked channel through the surrounding shoals.

Continuing upriver on the Scuppernong, set a new course from #4 to come abeam of and pass unlighted daybeacon #5 to its western side. Between #4 and #5, you can break off to the northeast and drop anchor as described earlier. For best

*Sawyers Marina–Scuppernong River*

depths, do not approach to within less than 50 yards of shore.

**On to Sawyers Marina**   From #5, continue on the same course, pointing to come abeam of flashing daybeacon #7 by 15 yards to its western side. At #7, the river takes a sharp bend to the east. Point to pass the next upriver aid to navigation, unlighted daybeacon #8, to its northern side. South of #7, the first facility on the Scuppernong and yet another possible anchorage will come abeam.

**Sawyers Marina and Adjacent Anchorage**   The canal leading to Sawyers Marina is located on the river's southern shore south of flashing daybeacon #7. Several privately maintained markers will lead you through the entrance. Obviously, you should take red aids to your starboard side and green markers to port. Cruise directly from #7 for the centerline of the marked entrance. Stick to the mid-width. Depths outside the marked channel are more than suspect and littered with under-

water debris. Soon, you will begin cruising upstream on a small canal. Maintain a track along the midline until the entrance to the marina's dockage basin opens up on the port shore.

Boaters choosing to anchor on the deep water southwest of flashing daybeacon #7 should abandon the main river channel just northwest of #7. Cruise carefully into the cove that opens out to the west-southwest, favoring the southern (port-side) banks slightly. Drop anchor well short of the shallows flanking the cove's southwestern shore.

**On the Scuppernong**   From #8, simply follow the river's mid-width as the Scuppernong winds its way toward Columbia. You will pass flashing daybeacon #10 to its northerly side along the way. Keep a sharp watch for snags and fishing stakes on both shores. As you approach Columbia Bridge, the town waterfront will come abeam to port. Just short of the span, you will see Columbia Marina and the new town docks, also to port.

**On the Albemarle**   Back on the sound, set course from flashing daybeacon #3 for flashing daybeacon #F well north of Mill Point. From #F, point for flashing daybeacon #1 well north of Lewis Point. It is a lengthy run of 12.4 nautical miles between the two aids. Be careful to prevent any southerly drift, as it might carry you into a United States Air Force target area near the southerly bank. From #1, set a new course for flashing daybeacon #1AR northeast of Long Shoal Point. This aid marks the entrance to the Alligator River and the ICW route south of Albemarle Sound.

# THE ICW, ALBEMARLE SOUND, AND ALLIGATOR RIVER

The Albemarle Sound section of the ICW is considered the roughest section of the entire Waterway. This charge is not without foundation. The prevailing winds tend to blow up or down the Albemarle's entire length, giving rise to rough, sometimes dangerous conditions. Pick your time of crossing carefully, and keep a ready ear for the current weather forecast.

On the southern portion of the Albemarle passage, the two ICW routes from the north rejoin. From here to the South Carolina line, the Waterway never again splits. The ICW across Albemarle Sound is well marked by a series of four flashing daybeacons placed 3 nautical miles apart. Often, the markers cannot be seen from the ones preceding them. Careful compass or GPS courses should therefore be followed between aids to navigation.

Once across Albemarle Sound, the ICW ducks into the northern mouth of the Alligator River. The Alligator is certainly one of the Albemarle's most impressive rivers. As part of the Waterway, it is quite well marked. Beautiful shores of dense, virgin cypress trees and deep swamp line the stream's broad waters. The river can produce a healthy chop, though not as steep as on the Albemarle. Several good anchorages are found along the Alligator's shoreline. There is one good marina on the river which welcomes transient boaters.

After a 21-nautical-mile cruise upstream, the ICW leaves the Alligator River and enters an 18-nautical-mile canal that connects the Waterway to the headwaters of the Pungo River, an auxiliary water of the Pamlico River. The Alli-

gator River–Pungo River Canal is straight, deep, and easily traversed. There is almost no development along its banks.

The lower Alligator River, abandoned by the Waterway, offers some cruising possibilities for wild-eyed captains. The channel twists a bit and is unmarked, but it is accessible to craft that draw 4 feet or less.

### Little Alligator River (Standard Mile 82)

The Little Alligator River makes into its larger sister's western shoreline west of flashing daybeacon #10. For those willing to brave its unmarked entrance channel, this stream offers good anchorage and superior protection from all but strong northern and northwestern blows. The Little Alligator is a particularly good spot for northbound boaters to wait out rough conditions on the Albemarle. Minimum entrance depths are 6 to 7 feet, but the unmarked channel must be carefully followed. The shoreline is completely in its natural state.

The best spot to anchor is on the waters of the large cove sandwiched between Mill Point and the unnamed point north of charted Sandy Point. After rounding the unnamed promontory, you will sight an old semisunken vessel to the south-southwest, set back into the body of the cove formed between the two points. By staying 50 to 75 yards off the southeasterly banks, you can maintain 6-foot depths to a point just short of the old derelict. Soundings in the 5-foot range are held abeam of the sunken vessel and for a short distance deeper into the cove. I suggest anchoring 50 yards northeast of the wreck.

## East and South Lakes (Standard Mile 82)

East and South Lakes, abutting the Alligator's eastern shore east of flashing daybeacon #10, offer another overnight anchorage consideration. A narrow, unmarked entrance channel heads a list of less-than-ideal qualities. If you can avoid the surrounding shallows, 7- to 8-foot depths can be maintained, but a navigational error could land you in 3-foot soundings. With these difficulties in mind, the waters of the twin lakes are not recommended for craft larger than 38 feet or those drawing more than 4½ feet.

East Lake is much shallower than shown on charts 12205 and 12204 and is choked with underwater weeds that can quickly foul props and intakes. It should probably be bypassed by cruising-size craft.

By avoiding the correctly charted shallows, cautious navigators can maintain minimum depths of 5 to 7 feet into South Lake. Underwater weeds seem to be mercifully absent. In eastern or northeastern winds, try anchoring in the lee of the second cove indenting the northeastern banks southeast of charted Boranges Point. Expect 5- to 6-foot depths on these waters and enough swinging room for 38-footers.

In strong southerlies, captains piloting vessels up to 38 feet might also consider anchoring on the mouth of Broad Creek west of Boranges Point. Soundings of 6 feet or so hold for only 30 yards upstream. Past this point, water levels drop off to 4½ feet or less.

On the plus side, the shorelines of both East and South Lakes exhibit the Alligator's magnificently undeveloped character. This is yet another Albemarle anchorage with a backwater feeling, a place far removed from the trappings of civilization.

By all accounts, the lakes and their entrance from the Alligator River call for good coastal navigation. If you choose to enter, take your time, identify all important landmarks, and watch the sounder carefully.

## Alligator River Marina (Standard Mile 84)

After decades without any pleasure-craft facilities, the Alligator River now boasts a friendly marina catering to transient craft. Alligator River Marina guards the westerly shore just north of the swing bridge south-southwest of flashing daybeacon #12. This facility's position is indeed fortunate for cruising boaters. Those heading north can wait out bad weather on the sound in a well-sheltered marina. Southbound cruisers can cross the Albemarle late in the day without having to worry with the long run south to Belhaven, site of the next southerly facilities. Additionally, with winds of 40 knots or more in the offing, the Alligator River swing bridge often will not open. Southbound craft can wait out the blow snugly ensconced in one of the marina's well-sheltered berths.

Alligator River Marina is the only fueling stop on the ICW between Coinjock (or Elizabeth City) and Belhaven. If past experience is any indication, this marina is destined to become a very popular stopover. Consider calling well ahead of time for dockage reservations.

At the time of this writing, the marina's marked entrance channel carried 7 feet of water, but that depth is subject to change. The friendly marina owners are usually quick to dredge if soundings begin to rise toward a bothersome level. As a matter of fact, maintenance dredging was accomplished during the spring of 1997. Dockside depths are an impressive 7 to 8 feet. For maximum safety, skippers of deep-draft vessels (6 feet or more) should call the marina ahead of time to check on the latest channel conditions.

Transients of any type or size are welcome at the facility's modern fixed wooden piers. Alligator River Marina is currently constructing a long face dock on the southern flank of the protected basin's outer reaches. When it is completed, skippers will be able to tie their lines to this new pier, fuel up, and remain in place for the night.

As you would expect, the latest power and water connections are in evidence. Some new 100-amp connections will become available when the face dock described above is completed. Gasoline, diesel fuel, waste pump-out service, and mechanical repairs via independent contractors are also readily available. A new on-site building houses ultraclean showers and a laundromat.

A well-stocked variety store with a diner that serves breakfast and lunch is located adjacent to the slips. All in all, except for haul-out repairs, Alligator River Marina provides an impressive array of services in a very advantageous location.

**Alligator River Marina
(919) 796-0333**

Approach depth: 7 feet
Dockside depth: 7–8 feet
Accepts transients: yes
Fixed wooden piers: yes
Dockside power connections: 30, 50, & 100 amps
Dockside water connections: yes
Showers: yes
Laundromat: yes
Waste pump-out: yes
Gasoline: yes
Diesel fuel: yes
Mechanical repairs: independent contractors
Variety store: yes
Diner: on-site

## Second Creek Anchorage (Standard Mile 88)

West of flashing daybeacon #18, the wide mouth of mostly shallow Second Creek opens out on the Alligator's westerly shoreline. Courtesy of Alligator River Marina's management, this writer learned that cautious skippers can pilot their way through 6-foot depths to the waters just south of Second Creek's first north-side entrance point and drop anchor amid similar soundings. On-site research confirmed these depths.

This spot is well sheltered from northern and northwestern blows and provides fair shelter in northeastern winds. Strong breezes from the south or east clearly call for another anchorage. Swinging room is adequate for boats up to 45 feet, and the adjacent banks carry on the Alligator's tradition of virgin shorelines.

If you arrive at the Alligator River swing bridge only to discover that it refuses to open because of strong northerly winds, this anchorage is a prime candidate for waiting out the foul weather.

## Milltail Creek (Standard Mile 88)

Milltail Creek is a rarely cruised stream that should be entered only by adventurous captains piloting craft of 30 feet or less which draw no more than 3½ feet. If you can meet these requirements and are willing to take a chance, your reward will be some of the most beautiful and isolated scenery on the North Carolina coast.

The creek's hard-to-find mouth lies well east of the Alligator's flashing daybeacon #18. It holds 6-foot minimum depths. Both sides of the entrance channel are littered with snags and stumps. Obviously, this passage calls for supreme caution. Upstream of the entrance, depths increase to 8 feet or more for quite a distance. This lower portion of the creek is too narrow for anchorage, but the primitive banks are absolutely magnificent. They give modern boaters a feeling akin to what must have been experienced by the early explorers who first charted Tar Heel waters. Eventually, you will encounter a patch of 4- to 5-foot depths near the remnants of Buffalo City, a small village wiped out by a yellow-fever epidemic many years ago. Past the old site, Milltail Creek deepens and becomes, for a time, a broad stream. Here, adventurous captains can anchor in as primitive and far-removed a place as they are ever likely to find.

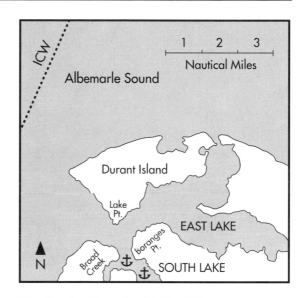

## The Straits (Standard Mile 95)

The creek known as "The Straits" flanks the river's western shore west of flashing daybeacon #26. This body of water has a tricky, unmarked entrance littered with snags, semisubmerged stumps, and other underwater debris. It is possible to avoid all these hazards and hold 6-foot depths into the creek's mouth, but it's not the easiest task a navigator will ever face. The entire shoreline of The Straits is an undisturbed cypress swamp backed by hardwoods.

If you successfully negotiate the entrance, you can use The Straits as an overnight anchorage. Depths on the interior waters hold very respectable 8- to 19-foot levels, but there are numerous unmarked shoals to worry about.

In all but strong southerly winds, your best bet for overnight anchorage is just short of the creek's first sharp bend to the west, where chart 11553 correctly notes a sounding of 13 feet. Here, there is enough room for a 38-foot craft to swing comfortably.

With fresh southerly breezes in the offing, you might also consider dropping the hook in the body of the creek's first westerly turn. Swinging room is skimpier, and depths of 20 feet or more call for a lot of anchor rode to maintain a proper six-to-one scope.

Upstream of this anchorage, The Straits eventually leads to a large, almost untouched body of water known as "The Frying Pan." Unfortunately, you must cruise through 3-foot depths to reach the deeper waters of The Frying Pan. Obviously, exploration of these waters is the province of small, shallow-draft powerboats. Rumor has it that bass fishing in The Frying Pan can be spectacular.

While The Straits is certainly one of the most protected anchorages along the mighty Alligator, its winding, obstruction-strewn entrance channel calls for more than the usual caution. Entry in stormy conditions or low light is strictly not recommended.

### Point Anchorages

Southwest of flashing daybeacon #37, the ICW and the Alligator River take a sharp swing to the west. The river finally begins to narrow as it rushes to an intersection with the Alligator River–Pungo River Canal.

Deep water surrounds three points of land lying between the westward turn and the canal's entrance. All three of these spots can be used for overnight anchorage in light winds or when prevailing breezes are blowing across the adjacent shoreline.

Just east of unlighted daybeacon #43, a small patch of deep water east of Deep Point (Standard Mile 102.5) offers anchorage. Good depths of 6 to 10 feet run almost to shore off the point's

*Alligator River shoreline*

eastern quarter. Avoid Deep Point itself, as it is surrounded by partially submerged piles. Craft up to 40 feet should discover sufficient elbow room. The shores are completely undeveloped. There is good protection from southern and western winds.

You might also choose to anchor north of flashing daybeacon #46 (Standard Mile 103) amid 6 to 7 feet of water. Protection is only sufficient for light airs and moderate northerly winds.

West of unlighted daybeacon #49, the ICW begins its approach to the Alligator River–

Pungo River Canal. One last light-air anchorage is available before the long man-made cut. Depths of 7 to 10 feet can be held south of Tuckahoe Point (Standard Mile 104.5) on the river's northern shore. There is ample swinging room and fair protection from northern winds. Otherwise, this anchorage is rather open.

### Upper Alligator River (Standard Mile 104.5)

The upper portion of the Alligator River, abandoned by the ICW, is not for everyone. The initial portion of the channel is unmarked and winding. Because of the uncertain depths, this portion of the river is definitely not recommended for craft over 36 feet and those which draw more than 4 feet. Don't attempt to follow the lower Alligator back to the Waterway canal. Though the stream does eventually rejoin the ICW south of Fairfield Bridge, it becomes so narrow as to be perilous for all but very small boats.

For those who relish the feeling that every turn of the screw or puff of air carries them farther from civilization, the lower Alligator River is one of the great cruising finds of Albemarle Sound. Below Cherry Ridge Landing, the stream becomes uniformly deep and well protected. Any boater who drops his hook here can be assured of an undisturbed evening.

In the past, some Waterway veterans have anchored off Point Lookout just upstream of the ICW's exodus from the Alligator River via the canal. While this haven still holds 7 to 9 feet of water and affords fair protection from northeastern winds, you must pass through a portion of the unmarked upper Alligator channel to reach it. The same cautions noted above for the lower Alligator apply to this anchorage as well.

### Alligator River–Pungo River Canal (Standard Mile 105)

From flashing daybeacon #54, the Alligator River–Pungo River Canal knifes generally southwest for 18 nautical miles. The canal is mostly unmarked but deep, though reports of shoaling have cropped up during the last several years. This is cattle country, and you may spy some herds as you cruise along.

## ALBEMARLE SOUND – ALLIGATOR RIVER NAVIGATION

The ICW passage across Albemarle Sound can be a teeth-rattling experience. More often than not, these waters are rough. It probably won't be long before you learn firsthand why Albemarle Sound is known as the roughest body of water on the ICW.

For those who followed the Virginia–North Carolina Cut, passage of the Albemarle begins at flashing daybeacon #173, which marks the North River's southern mouth. From #173, set course for flashing daybeacon #N. Continue on the same course past #N to flashing daybeacon #AS near the midpoint of the Albemarle. Remember that these markers may not be visible from the previous markers' positions, so run careful compass courses between daybeacons.

If your choice was the Dismal Swamp route, your cruise across Albemarle Sound will begin at the unnumbered 30-foot flashing daybeacon marking the southern reaches of the Pasquotank River. Set course from the 30-foot aid to flashing daybeacon #AS. It is a run of 6.2 nautical miles between the two aids.

**South to the Alligator**   From flashing daybeacon #AS, set course for flashing daybeacon #S. The same track will lead you past flashing daybeacon #1AR, located well west of Sound Point, and flashing daybeacon #3. Pass both aids to their westerly sides. From #3, point to eventually come between unlighted daybeacon #7 and flashing daybeacon #8. As you approach these two markers, you will begin to enter the Alligator's broad waters.

Be careful to avoid the shoal water east of #3, marked as "middle ground" on chart 11553, and the equally dangerous shallows east of Long Shoal Point near #8. Favor #7 when passing. Past these narrows, the Alligator becomes generally deep and easily navigated. From a position between #7 and #8, continue on course, pointing to come abeam

*Alligator River Bridge*

of flashing daybeacon #10 to its easterly side. At #10, two possibilities for anchorage—the Little Alligator River and East and South Lakes—will come abeam.

**Little Alligator River**   You will need chart 12205 for navigating the inner reaches of the Little Alligator River. Set course from flashing daybeacon #10 to come abeam of the sharp point on the entrance's southern quarter by 75 yards to your port side. As you approach the point, use your binoculars to pick out a small, uncharted island with two or three stunted trees. This island lies north of the point. *Be sure* to pass at least 30 yards *north* of this small landmass.

Once past the point, curl around to the southwest and enter the cove east of Mill Point by favoring its southeasterly (port-side) banks. Don't approach the shoreline too closely, as depths begin to fall.

Cruising into the cove's interior, you will spy a large, partially sunken boat 100 yards from shore. Depths of 6 feet can be expected from the entrance to a position abeam of the old wreck. They then fall to 5 feet past the sunken ship. Pick a spot just short of the derelict and set the hook.

**East and South Lakes**   Use chart 12205 for navigation in and around East and South Lakes. From the ICW's flashing daybeacon #10, set a careful compass course for the charted channel south of Lake Point. As you pass between Briery Hall and Lake Points, favor the northern shore a bit. Even by following this procedure, it's all too easy to wander into depths of 6 feet or slightly less.

Past Lake Point, begin to slowly bend your course to the south, pointing to eventually come abeam of Boranges Point by 50 yards to your port side. Continue cruising upstream until the northeastern shore's second cove comes abeam. Carefully feel your way in, but drop the hook before getting too close to the banks.

If you decide to anchor at the mouth of Broad Creek, cruise from a position abeam of Boranges Point into the wide mouth of Broad Creek. It's easy to see where this latter stream got its name. Be sure to anchor within 30 yards of the creek's mouth. Farther upstream, depths rise markedly.

**South on the Alligator**   From flashing daybeacon #10, it is a straight run to the central pass-through of the Alligator River Bridge. Be sure to pass flashing daybeacon #12 to its fairly immediate easterly side along the way. Sandy Point Shoal lies well east of #12, and a rather gross navigational error could land you in 5-foot depths.

Just north of the span, boaters can choose to turn west and visit well-positioned Alligator River Marina. Leave the ICW 50 yards short of the bridge and strike a course through the charted deep water for the entrance channel, which you will spy on the western banks. Recently, this cut was newly marked with unlighted daybeacons #1 and #3. You should pass to the fairly immediate northern sides of both these aids to navigation. Daybeacons #5 and #6 mark the entrance between the twin arms of a protective breakwater. Obviously, you will want to pass directly between #5 and #6. Continue holding to the channel's centerline as you cruise dead ahead into the protected harbor. The new fuel dock will soon come up to port.

The Alligator River Bridge has a closed vertical clearance of 14 feet, but it does open on demand, weather conditions permitting. As noted earlier in this chapter, the bridge often remains closed when winds exceed 40 knots. With strong blows in the offing, northbound and southbound ICW cruisers must retire to an appropriate anchorage (or to Alligator River Marina, in the case of southbound boaters) to wait for fair weather.

South of the span, the channel continues deep and well marked to flashing daybeacon #18. At #18, two adjacent bodies of water are accessible.

**Second Creek Anchorage**    Entrance into Second Creek calls for attention to navigational detail, as most of the stream is quite shallow. Set course from flashing daybeacon #18 for a position 150 yards south of the *first* north-side entrance point, just inside Second Creek's easterly mouth. Do not make a closer approach to shore or continue cruising west unless your craft can stand 3-foot depths.

**Milltail Creek**    Some 2.5 miles east of #18 lies Milltail Creek. The entrance is not easily seen from the Alligator. It is almost mandatory to run a compass course from #18 to find the mouth. As you near the shoreline, slow down and use your binoculars to pick out the creek's mouth. Make your approach from a position slightly south of the entrance. Watch for several pilings and one decrepit aid to navigation, unlighted daybeacon #8. These informal markers outline both sides of the channel. Both sides play host to an array of sunken stumps and other debris. Stick strictly to the indifferently marked entrance channel.

Past the tricky entrance, the stream continues narrow but uniformly deep for many pleasant miles. The only vestige of civilization to be seen is one lonely cabin on the port shore, now almost falling down.

After several miles, the stream takes a sharp turn to starboard. At this point, depths temporarily decrease to 4- and 5-foot soundings. Continue cruising on the mid-width around the curve and into the creek's upper reaches. Watch to port and you will see a few pilings, all that is left of Buffalo City.

Past Buffalo City, the creek begins to widen appreciably and soon takes another turn to starboard. Depths improve to better than 7 feet at this second turn. Anchor anywhere you choose on these waters. Protection is good, and the holding ground is thick mud.

Eventually, the creek narrows to a small stream. Though still deep, it does not afford enough swinging room for most craft.

**On the ICW**    From flashing daybeacon #18 to flashing daybeacon #26, the Waterway continues arrow-straight and well marked. No sidewaters are to be found between #18 and #26. However, at #26, a potential anchorage will come abeam to the west.

**The Straits**    Set course from #26 to avoid the large patch of shallows southeast of Catfish Point. It is a good idea to initially head for the unnamed sharp point of land due south of Catfish Point. Some 0.1 to 0.2 nautical mile before reaching the unnamed point, swing sharply to the north-northwest and point to pass into the mid-width of the entrance to The Straits, keeping Catfish Point to your starboard side. By following this procedure, you should be able to hold minimum depths of 6 feet if you successfully avoid the submerged debris. All hands should be on the lookout for the many snags, stakes, and stumps that litter the waters south of Catfish Point.

In the creek's inner section, depths increase markedly, typically to between 8 and 20 feet. The stream soon takes a turn to the west. Hold to the mid-width as you round the bend, and don't cut the corner.

Those truly adventurous souls who decide to cruise farther upstream should favor the starboard shore between the westerly turn and Lyons Point. Minimum depths of 8 feet can be held until you come abeam of the eastern tip of the small island marked "foul" on chart 11553. Past Lyons Point, begin to favor the port shore. Here, the deep water runs next to a large series of old pilings.

Discontinue your cruise of The Straits abeam of the small island. The large body of water beyond, known as "The Frying Pan," is quite shallow on its eastern reaches.

**On the ICW**   South of flashing daybeacon #26, the ICW remains well outlined and easily followed. Don't attempt to enter Grapevine Bay west of unlighted daybeacon #30. It is too shallow and exposed to warrant consideration as an anchorage.

Southwest of flashing daybeacon #37, the ICW follows the Alligator River through a sharp westerly turn. Point to come abeam of flashing daybeacon #39 to its northerly side. Continue cruising west by setting course to come abeam of and pass unlighted daybeacon #41 to its northerly quarter. West of #39, the Alligator begins to narrow, and rough water is seldom a problem.

South of #39, an indifferently marked channel holding minimum depths of 5 to 6 feet provides access to a man-made canal on the river's southern shore. This deep cut eventually leads to a barge-loading facility for Lux Farms, one of the so-called super farms of eastern North Carolina. There are no facilities for visiting boaters here, nor is there enough room to anchor.

West of unlighted daybeacon #41, successful navigation of the Waterway route continues to be an elementary matter, but out-of-channel depths begin to deteriorate. Stick to the marked cut. Just

east of unlighted daybeacon #43, a small patch of deep water east of Deep Point can serve as an anchorage. Avoid Deep Point itself, as it is surrounded by partially submerged piles.

West-southwest of unlighted daybeacon #49, the ICW begins its approach to the Alligator River–Pungo River Canal. One last light-air anchorage is available before you enter the long man-made cut. Depths of 7 to 10 feet can be held south of Tuckahoe Point on the river's northern shore. Don't cruise too close to the point or attempt to approach the northern banks.

To enter the canal, pass unlighted daybeacon #52 to its southerly side. Soon, you will spy flashing daybeacon #54, which marks the northwesterly side of the canal's mouth. Most cruising boaters will continue their journey down the Alligator-Pungo cut. However, the lower Alligator River offers some isolated cruising opportunities for wild-eyed skippers. For these hardy souls, a brief discussion of the lower Alligator is now presented. Coverage of the ICW will resume later in this chapter.

**Upper Alligator River**   Abandon the Waterway 0.4 nautical mile after passing unlighted daybeacon #49. Set a new course to come abeam of charted Point Lookout by 50 yards to its southwesterly side.

To continue upstream, begin using the Alligator River Extension section of chart 11553. Follow the river around Point Lookout as it passes through a sharp northerly bend. Set a new course to come abeam of Piney Point fairly close to its northeasterly side, then cruise through yet another sharp turn, this time to the west. Begin favoring the starboard shore until you come abeam of Bennett Point, then cruise toward the westerly shore and, keeping 25 yards off the banks, follow the shoreline until the river takes another sharp turn to the west. As you follow the river around this westerly turn, watch to starboard and you will see a few pilings on the northerly shore. This is apparently all that is left of Cherry Ridge Landing.

Above the old landing, the upper Alligator River becomes uniformly deep and well protected. You can drop the hook anywhere and feel secure from wind and wave. Upstream, the river soon forks. Follow the port branch, but don't travel too far, as the stream soon narrows drastically.

**Alligator River–Pungo River Canal**    From flashing daybeacon #54 to the Wilkerson Bridge, the ICW's passage down the Alligator River–Pungo River Canal knifes generally southwest for 18 nautical miles. The canal is mostly unmarked but deep, though some reports of shoaling along the canal's shoreline have cropped up during the last several years. Stick strictly to the mid-width. When passing another vessel, slow down and squeeze as close together as possible without risk of collision. Be on the alert for signs placed by the Corps of Engineers warning of new shoals. Usually, however, the Corps' frequent dredging clears away such obstructions in a few months.

The Fairfield swing bridge crosses the channel 7.6 nautical miles southwest of the canal's Alligator River entrance. This span has a closed vertical clearance of 7 feet. Fortunately, it opens on demand. Fairfield Canal makes into the Waterway's southerly shore just east of the bridge. Don't attempt to enter, as depths are uncertain.

The fixed, high-rise Wilkerson Bridge marks the southerly boundary of the canal. This span has a clearance of 64 feet (*not* 65 feet). Continued southerly navigation of the ICW can be found in chapter 5.

*Old derelict on Little Alligator River*

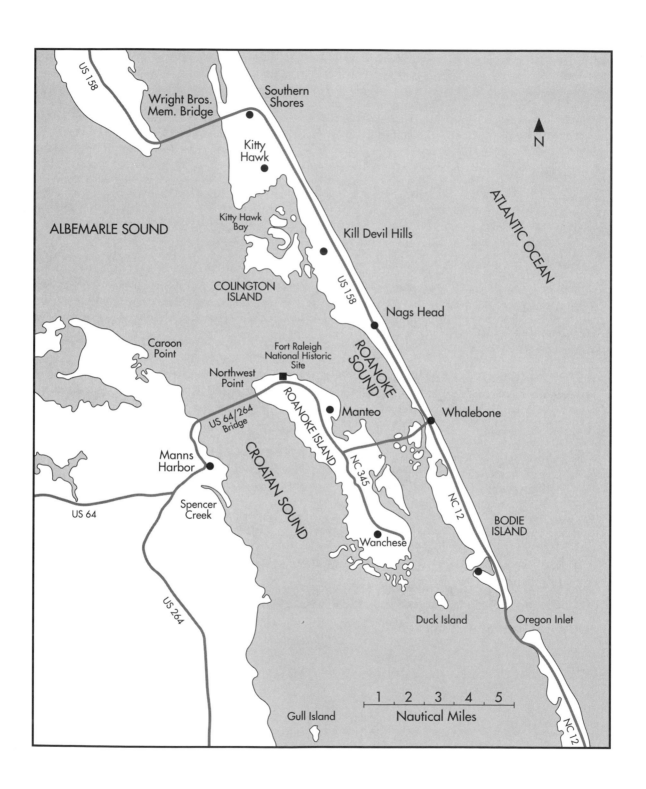

# The Croatan and Roanoke Sounds

Croatan and Roanoke Sounds span the gap between the freshwater Albemarle region and the northern headwaters of Pamlico Sound. Croatan Sound is bordered to the west by the North Carolina mainland and to the east by Roanoke Island. Roanoke Sound lies between Roanoke Island to the west and the Outer Banks to the east. Both bodies of water are generally hospitable to cruising vessels and are not crowded by other pleasure craft.

The ICW was originally planned to pass through Croatan Sound, but that proposal was abandoned in favor of the Alligator River–Pungo River route. For this reason more than any other, the twin sounds have never known heavy pleasure-boating traffic. However, both bodies of water are well marked and quite navigable. Croatan Sound offers several anchorages, while Roanoke Sound boasts good facilities at Manteo and near Oregon Inlet. Why not explore the twin sounds? Some beautiful, open, and little-used waters will be the reward.

## Charts

You will need two NOAA charts for navigation of Croatan and Roanoke Sounds:

**12204** covers the approach to the two sounds from Pamlico Sound and gives general navigational data on the Croatan and Roanoke Sounds

**12205** presents detailed scales of the Croatan and Roanoke Sounds, as well as of the Old House Channel

# CROATAN AND ROANOKE SOUNDS HISTORY

Since the time of early English colonization on Roanoke Island, a fascinating change in the natural character of both sounds has come about. In colonial times, what we know today as Croatan Sound was a wide marsh penetrated by a single shallow ditch. The main deepwater channel ran through Roanoke Sound from old Roanoke Inlet, which cut through the Outer Banks east of Roanoke Island.

Between 1780 and approximately 1810, the old inlet shoaled and eventually closed. Apparently, the huge drainage of the Albemarle's nine rivers was then diverted southward through the marshy area. This large volume of fresh water scoured out the one-time shallow bottom, leaving the wide and deep water that is today called Croatan Sound. Conversely, the once-deep Roanoke Sound has shoaled to 3- and 4-foot depths.

Over the years, considerable interest has been displayed in artificially reopening old Roanoke Inlet as a ready artery of commerce. One plan of note called for the building of dikes across the southern feet of Croatan and Roanoke Sounds to divert the Albemarle's drainage through the man-made cut. This plan may have worked, but adequate funds were never appropriated, and the ambitious project was not attempted.

## The Lost Colony

The history of Roanoke and Croatan Sounds is inextricably interwoven with the fabled Lost Colony of Sir Walter Raleigh. Volumes have been written, and probably will yet be written, on this mysterious chapter in American history.

In the late 16th century, England began an attempt to expand its influence into the New World. Sir Walter Raleigh, trusted counselor of Queen Elizabeth I, sent out an expedition in 1584 under Philip Amadas and Arthur Barlowe. In a search for appropriate sites of future colonization, they first touched the North Carolina coast in the vicinity of Hatteras and then moved north to what may have been Roanoke Inlet. The eventual report which the two explorers presented to Raleigh spoke of a land of plenty peopled by friendly and benevolent Indians.

So encouraged was Sir Walter by this handsome account that he launched a colonization party of 600 men under Sir Richard Grenville in April 1585. Landfall was made near Ocracoke Inlet, but the expedition eventually moved north to Roanoke Island. A settlement, Fort Raleigh, was soon constructed on the island's northern tip. In late August, Grenville returned to England, leaving 107 men under the leadership of Ralph Lane. A professional soldier, Lane apparently had no qualms about stealing supplies from the nearby Indians. The deterioration in relations was climaxed by an English raid on the main village of the Roanoke Indians and the murder of their chief.

In June 1586, Sir Francis Drake appeared off Roanoke Island and offered his aid. Perhaps goaded by the worsening situation with the Indians, Lane decided to abandon the colony. Just a few weeks later, Grenville dropped anchor nearby with three ships loaded with supplies. Finding the colonists gone, he left 15 men as a holding force and sailed again for England.

Following Lane's return to England, Sir Walter Raleigh began to prepare his most ambitious effort. A large group of men, women, and children under the governorship of John White set sail for the New World in early May 1587 and arrived at Roanoke Island in July. The plan was to retrieve the 15 men left there and move on to the southern shore of Chesapeake Bay.

Here is the first mystery of Raleigh's colony: Why didn't the colonists, after finding that the holding force had been slaughtered by mainland Indians, continue their voyage northward? Traditional accounts claim that the expedition's pilot, Simon Fernandez, refused to sail to the Chesapeake. Dr. David B. Quinn, perhaps the greatest authority on the Lost Colony, insists that the majority did indeed travel overland to the southern shore of the Chesapeake, where they were later massacred by the Powhatan Indians.

For whatever reason, at least some of the colonists reoccupied the fort built by Lane. For a time, all was well. The settlement was refurbished, crops were planted, and Virginia Dare, the first English child born in America, was delivered of Eleanor Dare on August 18. It soon became apparent, however, that not enough supplies had been sent to meet the colonists' needs before the settlement could become self-sufficient. On August 27, John White left for England to procure the needed goods.

Upon his arrival in England, White found the entire country preparing to meet the threat of the great Spanish Armada. Not even a small ship could be spared for the Roanoke colony. Finally, following Drake's brilliant victory over the Spanish, a relief force was dispatched in late August 1590, almost two years after White's return to England. The Roanoke Island fort was found abandoned. The only clue to the colony's fate was the word *Croatoan*, the Indian name for Hatteras, inscribed on a tree. Storms prevented further search, and the small fleet returned to England, leaving behind perhaps the most enduring mystery of American history.

Many theories have been advanced to explain the disappearance of the Lost Colony. Some have claimed that hostile Indians killed the inhabitants, but no bodies were found by the relief force. Charles Harry Whedbee has advanced the idea that the colonists migrated westward to the portion of the mainland separating Croatan Sound from the Alligator River. In his fascinating tale "Beechland" in *Legends of the Outer Banks*, Whedbee presents intriguing evidence to support his claim. The most plausible theory, however, argues that the Roanoke Island colonists traveled south to modern-day Hatteras and lived there with the friendly Croatan Indians.

The Lost Colony is remembered by an outdoor drama presented nightly during the summer months on the northern tip of Roanoke Island. This long-loved play has provided training for some fine actors, including Andy Griffith. It is fitting that the bravery and courage of those first English colonists are so well remembered.

From 1984 to 1987, Roanoke Island celebrated

the 400th anniversary of the Roanoke colonies. As an integral part of this celebration, a faithful replica of the *Elizabeth*, one of the ships that brought the members of the Lost Colony to the New World, was built in downtown Manteo. The craft was then ensconced in an innovative theme park on Ice Plant Island, just across Doughs Creek from the Manteo waterfront. Today, cruising visitors can visit the *Elizabeth II* by foot from the town docks.

## The Legend of Virginia Dare

Many tall tales have evolved concerning the Lost Colony. Virginia Dare is the subject of a particularly poignant story which has many variations. According to the legend, there was an attack by hostile Indians on the Roanoke colonists. Chief Manteo, returning from a fishing expedition, saw the raid in progress. By using a secret tunnel, he was able to lead all the inhabitants safely to nearby canoes. An all-night trip down the Pamlico brought the group to Manteo's village at Hatteras. There, the colonists were accepted into the tribe as brothers and sisters.

The fair-skinned, blond Virginia Dare was from the beginning a wonder to the Indians. As she grew in stature and years, many braves paid court for her hand in marriage. The fair girl loved all the people, both Indians and white, but was not yet ready to choose a mate.

Chico, the tribal medicine man, was greatly smitten by the maiden's charms. Though Virginia was kind to him, it was clear that Chico's ardor was not being returned. Finally, in a fit of passion, he vowed that if she would not marry him, she would have no man. Calling upon the power of the sea nymphs, Chico lured Virginia to Roanoke Island. Stepping ashore, she assumed the form of a snow-white deer.

Soon, it was whispered that a white doe was the leader of all the deer of Roanoke Island. Wherever the remarkable creature went, all others followed. Many great hunters tried to slay the mystical creature, but no arrow seemed to find a mark. As time went by, the white doe became a legend as well as a challenge.

Finally, a great hunt was organized, and all the young braves of noble blood vowed their efforts. Many prizes and honors were to be awarded the victor. Young Wanchese, son of Chief Wanchese, who had traveled to England, had a silver-tipped arrow presented to his father by Queen Elizabeth. He believed it had magical powers and would bring him the quarry he sought.

As fate would have it, Wanchese did indeed sight the snow-white doe. Taking careful aim, he loosed his deadly missile. The silver tip succeeded where all others had failed, and the deer fell to the ground. The young brave rushed forward to claim his prize, but all joy fled as he heard the deer whisper with her last breath, faint but clear, the words "Virginia Dare."

Fanciful it may be, but this tale has survived in one form or another since the earliest recorded history of North Carolina.

# EAST TO THE CROATAN SOUND– ROANOKE SOUND AREA

To cruise east on Albemarle Sound to the northerly waters of Roanoke and Croatan Sounds, set course from flashing daybeacon #AS (found along the ICW's north-to-south passage across Albemarle Sound) for flashing daybeacon #MG (at the Albemarle's eastern mouth). It is a run of 7.1 nautical miles through open water between #AS and #MG. From #MG, Croatan Sound lies to the south and Roanoke Sound to the southeast.

Boaters studying chart 12205 might conclude that the waters adjoining the banks to the east of Albemarle Sound offer three cruising opportunities. However, Colington Island, Kitty Hawk Bay, and Southern Shores pose serious navigational problems. The cruising skipper would do well to avoid all three areas.

*Colington Island*    Colington Island, the first portion of the Outer Banks to support permanent English settlement, is today served by a channel that holds 5-foot depths. The harbor is private.

Blount Bay, off the island's eastern banks, has a few facilities for small craft, but 3- and 4-foot depths render it inaccessible to most cruising vessels. Colington Island, unfortunately, has very little to offer the pleasure boater cruising in a large craft.

*Kitty Hawk Bay*    Kitty Hawk Bay has an indifferently marked channel leading east from Long Point into its interior reaches. Small craft use the cut regularly, but 4-foot depths are encountered, making the channel too shallow for many cruising craft. There is a small marina at Avalon Beach on the bay's southern arm, but no transient facilities are available. The water is too open for effective protection, so overnight anchorage is not a practical possibility.

*Southern Shores*    A short cruise north on the southern foot of Currituck Sound through the Wright Brothers Memorial Bridge, a fixed span with a vertical clearance of 35 feet, carries visiting cruisers to a short, shallow channel leading to the exclusive Southern Shores resort development. The poorly marked passage north on the Currituck maintains 5- to 6-foot depths, but the Southern Shores channel has only 4 to 5 feet of water. This cut does not lead to any real facilities—at the channel's eastern tip, only a small ramp area is to be found. Unless you are one of the fortunate few who owns a home in this beautiful and heavily wooded development, the region is best bypassed.

# CROATAN SOUND

Croatan Sound is wide, deep, and easily navigated. If it were not for one obstacle, it would be a simple matter to traverse the sound's entire length. Unfortunately, the Croatan is bridged by a fixed span with 43 feet of vertical clearance. Sailcraft that can't clear this height must opt for the Roanoke Sound passage.

Croatan Sound is a beautiful body of water. Both shores are only lightly developed, the mainland banks exhibiting numerous forests. On a bright, clear day with both shores visible,

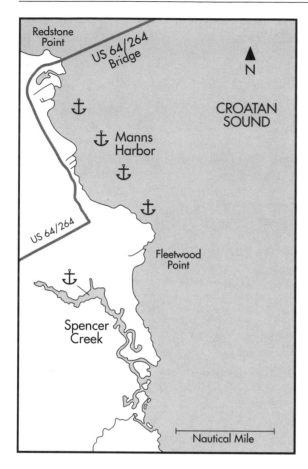

passage of the Croatan is indeed pleasing to the eye.

Currently, there are no facilities on Croatan Sound catering specifically to pleasure craft. The old marina at Manns Harbor has been in and out of business over the past several years, and even should it resume operations, the entrance channel is so shoal that even outboard craft can find the bottom at low tide.

Croatan Sound does offer several anchorages, one of which has enough shelter for heavy weather.

## Croatan Anchorages

Southeast of the fixed Croatan Sound Bridge, a large cove shown as "Manns Hbr" (Manns Harbor Bay) on chart 12205 indents the southwestern shoreline. Southeast of flashing daybeacon #1, the outer portion of the bay can serve as an overnight anchorage in light winds. There is virtually no protection from stronger breezes, except perhaps from the southwest. Depths run 5 to 7 feet, and there is ample room for vessels up to 50 feet.

Better shelter is found on the waters northwest of Fleetwood Point. Minimum depths of 5 to 6 feet run to within 200 yards of the point's northwesterly quarter. There is some shelter from southerly, westerly, and southwesterly breezes but virtually no protection from winds blowing down or across the sound.

## Spencer Creek

Spencer Creek empties into the southwestern waters of Croatan Sound well southwest of flashing daybeacon #8. This stream is heavily used by large commercial craft cruising to and departing from a North Carolina ferry repair center near the creek's upstream cruising limits. The channel is deep and carefully maintained to the repair yard. Minimum 5- to 8-foot depths can be maintained as far as this facility's piers. Boats as large as 34 feet can anchor on the creek just above the docks in depths of 5 to 8 feet. This spot affords superb shelter from foul weather. With the exception of the state service center, the surrounding shores are composed of undeveloped marsh grass.

# CROATAN SOUND NAVIGATION

The northern entrance of Croatan Sound is bounded by Reeds Point to the west and Northwest Point, on Roanoke Island, to the east. To enter the sound, set course from flashing daybeacon #MG, at the eastern mouth of Albemarle Sound, for flashing daybeacon #3, northeast of Reeds Point. This is a run of 3.8 nautical miles through open water. Along the way, you will pass unlighted daybeacon #2, which marks the shoals of Peter Mashoes Creek west of your course.

Don't attempt to enter Mashoes Creek, as depths of 3 feet are soon encountered. It is unfortunate that the stream's depth does not permit entry by cruising craft, as the nearby village of Mashoes is still one of the most isolated communities in North Carolina.

From #3, set course for the central pass-through of the fixed Croatan Sound Bridge, passing unlighted daybeacon #3A to its southwesterly side along the way. The fixed bridge has a vertical clearance of 43 feet. Sailcraft that cannot clear this gap must use the Roanoke–Old House Channel route to reach Pamlico Sound.

After leaving the fixed span in your wake, look to the southwest and you may catch sight of the two charted flashing daybeacons, #1 and #2. These aids to navigation mark the location of Manns Harbor Marina. This facility's entrance channel is *very* shoal. Do not attempt to enter.

Come abeam of flashing daybeacon #4 to its northeasterly quarter. Southwest of #4, two fair anchorages beckon.

***Manns Harbor Bay*** Southeast of flashing daybeacon #1, the outer portion of Manns Harbor Bay can serve as an overnight anchorage. Don't attempt to enter either of the two small, charted canals southwest of flashing daybeacon #1; both lead only to small private docks, and depths quickly fall off to 4 feet or less.

If winds are light and you choose to anchor in Manns Harbor, cruise southwest from flashing daybeacon #4. As you approach to within 0.2 nautical mile of the southwestern banks, begin feeling your way along with the sounder. When depths drop below 6 feet, you are beginning to impinge on the large shelf of shallow water abutting the shoreline. Retreat to the northeast a bit and throw out the hook.

To anchor behind Fleetwood Point, set a careful compass course from #4 for the waters off the point's northwestern flank. Good depths hold to within 200 yards of shore. A closer approach will land you in 4- to 5-foot depths.

***On the Sound*** From flashing daybeacon #4, set course for flashing daybeacon #6, which marks the sound's mid-width. Depths are not a concern between the bridge and the Croatan's southern foot. Consider setting course from #6 for flashing daybeacon #8. At #8, Spencer Creek comes abeam to the southwest.

***Spencer Creek*** From flashing daybeacon #8, set course to come abeam of flashing daybeacon #2 by 25 yards to its southeasterly side. From #2, use your binoculars to locate unlighted daybeacon #3, which marks the creek's entrance. Set a new course to come abeam of #3 to your port side.

Stay at least 10 yards away from #3—some shoal water seems to be building around this aid to navigation. Depths between #2 and #3 run 7 to 10 feet, dropping off to 6 and 7 feet at the stream's mouth.

Once inside the entrance, stick to the mid-width and don't be tempted to try any of the small side streams or bays. They are *all* quite shallow. The creek itself holds depths of 7 to 13 feet. Track your way upstream until you spy the ferry repair docks. Continue for 25 yards past the uppermost pier and anchor on the stream's midline. Don't cruise farther upstream, as depths quickly fall off.

**On the Sound**  From flashing daybeacon #8, it is a straightforward run of 1.7 nautical miles to flashing daybeacon #10. From #10, set course for the 42-foot flashing daybeacon #RM at the foot of Croatan Sound. Along the way, an unlighted and unnumbered warning beacon to the west marks underwater rocks. Don't approach #RM too closely, as it is surrounded by submerged pipes. Pass the marker well to its northeasterly side. From #RM, continuing your cruise to the south will carry you into vast Pamlico Sound. This body of water is covered in the next chapter.

## ROANOKE SOUND

Roanoke Sound is consistently shallow. Fortunately, a well-marked man-made channel allows passage to the interesting ports of Manteo and Wanchese on eastern Roanoke Island. This same cut provides access to Oregon Inlet, located at the Roanoke's southern foot. The inlet offers unreliable access to the open sea and is the subject of intense local controversy. Hardly a month seems to pass without some unfortunate shrimp trawler finding the bottom.

The Roanoke Sound channel currently carries minimum depths of 7 feet, with typical soundings of 8 to 15 feet, but caution is required to keep to these depths. In places—particularly the stretch between Shallowbag Bay and the Wanchese Harbor channel—the sound cut is a bit winding, and there are not as many aids to navigation along the way as one might wish. Obviously, the difficult sections of the channel require careful navigation and a steady eye on the sounder.

Roanoke Sound boasts notable facilities and attractions for cruising boaters. In addition to Manteo's many offerings, there are two marinas on the Roanoke Sound channel and a full-service boatyard in Wanchese Harbor.

The thriving village of Manteo is perched on the western shores of Shallowbag Bay, which makes into the western reaches of Roanoke Sound a few miles south of the sound's northern mouth. Manteo boasts excellent facilities catering specifically to the transient boater.

Because of its shallow depths, Roanoke Sound is virtually devoid of any sheltered overnight anchorages.

This region presents some fascinating scenery. As one enters the northern headwaters of Roanoke Sound, huge sand dunes are visible to port. These mammoth sand piles are known collectively as Jockey's Ridge. Many legends have been spun about these dunes. Today, the entire area is a state park. South of Jockey's Ridge, the Roanoke's banks are low and sandy. Near Oregon Inlet, the black-and-white, horizontally banded Bodie Island Lighthouse watches benignly over the sound.

## Manteo

Since this guide's original publication, the community of Manteo has undergone more changes than any other municipality in coastal North Carolina. Cruising boaters who have not visited this vibrant town within the last eight years will hardly recognize the waterfront or the downtown district. A huge condo/retail complex now overlooks the Manteo waterfront, rubbing shoulders with a deluxe three-story inn. The city docks have been completely rebuilt. Interesting shops, restaurants, and shoreside businesses of all descriptions, housed in new classical-style buildings, eagerly await the visiting cruiser. A bridge now stretches across Doughs Creek to a new park on Ice Plant Island, where the *Elizabeth II* calmly guards the creek's waters. What is really so striking about all this change, however, is the careful management of the development. All of the new construction has been painstakingly designed to harmonize with the town's unique architectural character. The result has been an unequivocal success, with cruisers profiting immensely.

Manteo is served by a reliable channel that leads from the principal Roanoke Sound passage through Shallowbag Bay to the town waterfront. This cut carries minimum depths of 7 feet, with soundings of 8 to 10 feet the norm. The old city docks near the municipal water plant are no longer in use, though you will still spy the unused piers to port as you enter Doughs Creek.

## Manteo Facilities

The Manteo town docks gaze proudly over the southwestern shores of Doughs Creek northwest of unlighted daybeacon #6. This first-rate municipal facility, now leased to a private management firm, is known as Manteo Waterfront Marina. The dockmaster here is very responsive to the needs of visiting cruisers. I recommend this marina highly!

Manteo Waterfront Marina features numerous transient berths at the latest wooden fixed-pier construction. Impressive dockside soundings of 8 to 10 feet are enough for even long-legged vessels. As you would expect, all power and water connections are found dockside. The marina features ultraclean showers and a complete laundromat. Gasoline and diesel fuel can sometimes be delivered by way of fuel trucks, but no dockside fuel pumps are available. Waste pump-out service can be arranged through a local sewage contractor. Marina patrons will now find a ship's and variety store in the dockmaster's office complex; this store offers NOAA charts. Mechanical repairs can be arranged through independent technicians.

The nearest grocery store, Food-A-Rama (919-473-2924), is approximately 0.25 mile from the marina piers. The local post office has been moved recently from its former downtown location to a spot near the grocery market. Many find it a pleasant walk to these facilities, but if you are not up to this hike, the dockmaster can usually help with courtesy transportation or car rentals. A host of restaurants and other

*Manteo Waterfront Marina*

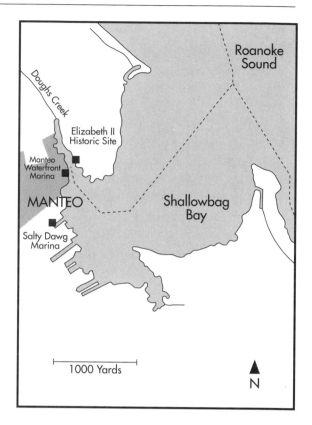

shoreside businesses (see below) is within a few steps of the dockage complex.

The amenities at Manteo Waterfront Marina are complemented by colorful landscaping set against idyllic Doughs Creek. Seldom will visiting cruisers find such an attractive spot to coil the lines and rest from their travels. A prominent gazebo pier just southeast of the principal slips can be used as a lunch stop or simply as a great place to watch the evening light fade from the waters.

**Manteo Waterfront Marina**
**(919) 473-3320**

Approach depth: 7–9 feet
Dockside depth: 8–10 feet
Accepts transients: yes
Fixed wooden piers: yes
Dockside power connections: 30 & 50 amps
Dockside water connections: yes
Showers: yes
Laundromat: yes
Waste pump-out: can be arranged
Mechanical repairs: independent contractors
Ship's & variety store: yes
Restaurants: several nearby

Salty Dawg Marina is located at the foot of the Shallowbag Bay entrance channel just before it turns northwest into Doughs Creek, southwest of unlighted daybeacon #6. This fine facility offers extensive dockage at two sets of piers. The outer docks overlook Shallowbag Bay and are composed of typical fixed wooden piers. The inner, more sheltered slips feature wooden pilings and tiny finger piers set against a concrete sea wall. Salty Dawg's entrance channel has minimum 6½-foot depths, with 6 to 12 feet of water at the slips. All berths have full power and water hookups. The older piers of the inner harbor provide excellent shelter, while the outer docks might get a little bumpy in strong northeasterly or southeasterly blows. Gasoline and diesel fuel are readily available, as are mechanical repairs for gasoline engines. The marina can contract for diesel repairs through an independent mechanic. Waste pump-out can be arranged through a local sewage contractor. A proud, new shower building now graces the Salty Dawg, where you will also find a well-stocked ship's store that offers NOAA charts. Salty Dawg features a large, metal dry-stack storage building for small power craft.

The Food-A-Rama supermarket is located just across U.S. 64 from the marina's shoreside entrance. Retail shops, restaurants, and a laundromat are only a short step away. It's a brisk walk of less than a mile to the historic downtown district. If you opt for automobile transportation, the marina has a courtesy car for visitors, or car rentals can be arranged. All in all, Salty Dawg is a nice alternative to the Manteo waterfront docks.

### Salty Dawg Marina
### (919) 473-3405

Approach depth: 7–12 feet
Dockside depth: 6–12 feet
Accepts transients: yes
Fixed wooden piers: yes
Dockside power connections: 30 & 50 amps
Dockside water connections: yes
Showers: yes
Laundromat: nearby
Waste pump-out: can be arranged
Gasoline: yes
Diesel fuel: yes
Mechanical repairs: available for gasoline engines; diesel repair through independent contractors
Ship's store: yes
Restaurants: several nearby

Boaters should also know that Salty Dawg's owner, Harry Schiffman, was instrumental in short-circuiting a state program to charge a leasehold fee for the bottom land over which North Carolina's marina docks are located. A useful compromise was worked out that has saved Tar Heel boaters a wad of money in the increased dockage fees that would have resulted from the ill-starred program. Please join me in congratulating Harry on a job well done.

## Roanoke Island Attractions, Restaurants, and Lodgings

Boaters entering Doughs Creek will immediately be struck by the huge, three-story condo/retail/dining complex known as "The Waterfront." This unusual structure has resident parking on the ground floor, a host of retail shops and two restaurants of note on the middle level, and private condos on the top floor. It is a genuine pleasure to frequent this attractive complex. Famished cruisers will want to make the acquaintance of Clara's Seafood Grill (919-473-1727) on The Waterfront's second level. This striking restaurant has large glass windows as well as outside dining overlooking Doughs Creek and Shallowbag Bay. The seafood is excellent (give the curried scallops a try), and the desserts are not bad either. Clara's is a great spot to unwind after a long day on the water.

You might try the Full Moon Café (919-473-6666), also located in The Waterfront. This informal dining spot offers good sandwiches.

Separated from The Waterfront by another complex of retail shops, the three-story Tranquil House Inn (919-473-1404) proudly overlooks the northerly stretch of Doughs Creek. This inn has been constructed to resemble the down-east architecture of an earlier day. The architects have succeeded admirably. Inside, visitors will be struck by the gracious manner of the inn's personnel and the high-gloss wooden floors. The inn's third-story suites boast a view that must be experienced to be understood. While the accommodations are not the most inexpensive, cruisers who want to take a break from the live-aboard life are encouraged to call ahead for reservations at this most distinctive inn.

Recently, the Tranquil House Inn expanded its appeal by opening its own, in-house dining establishment, known as the 1587 Restaurant (919-473-1587). The food can only be described as "high gourmet" and the atmosphere as most attractive. While one could never call the prices budget-minded, you get what you pay for. You might want to dig out your last clean shirt—you know, the one buried under the forward V-berth—for a dinner at 1587.

*Salty Dawg Marina*

The White Doe Inn (319 Sir Walter Raleigh Street, 800-473-6091 or 919-473-9851) is accessible via a quick walk from Manteo Waterfront Marina. It's a bit farther from Salty Dawg, but the friendly innkeepers will be glad to provide complimentary transportation. The White Doe is housed in a historic 1896 structure which was expanded to its present dimensions during the early part of this century. To this writer's eyes, it is one of the most striking Victorian homes in Manteo. A full breakfast is served (to guests only) every morning.

Just across Doughs Creek from the Manteo waterfront, the Elizabeth II State Historic Site on Ice Plant Island is well worth your attention. This fascinating exhibit's star attraction is, of course, the *Elizabeth II*, a faithful replica of one of the ships that brought the Lost Colonists to the shores of Roanoke Island. The *Elizabeth II* was painstakingly built by hand on the Manteo waterfront as part of the celebration of the 400th anniversary of Sir Walter Raleigh's colonies. Only traditional methods and materials were used in its construction. The opportunity to visit this remarkable replica is a chance you will not want to miss. Costumed attendants interpret the ship and its functions for visitors and add greatly to the feeling of being transported to the 17th century. Most of the time, you need only walk across the short bridge spanning Doughs Creek to visit the *Elizabeth II*. Occasionally, the ship is away on cruises to other North Carolina ports of call.

Another attraction at the *Elizabeth II* park is the Outer Banks History Center. Thanks to the efforts of noted area historian David Stick and other local volunteers, visitors interested in the rich heritage of the Outer Banks will find a wealth of information at this unusual facility. According to the center's first director, Wynne Dough, as reported in *Outer Banks Current*, "The purpose of the Outer Banks History Center is to preserve the cultural and human heritage of the North Carolina coast and to encourage the public to become more interested in it."

As this guide went to press, ground had already been broken on Ice Plant Island for the $10 million Outer Banks Cultural Heritage Center. When complete, this new attraction will add immensely to Manteo's offerings.

I am sorry to report that one longtime downtown Manteo tradition, The Duchess of Dare Restaurant, is no more. The restaurant has changed hands several times recently. It is currently known as The Two Sisters.

Downtown Manteo teems with all types of retail enterprises including ice-cream shops, gift shops, and a movie theater. Take plenty of time to stroll the downtown streets and sample all the attractions. If you are interested in things literary, be *sure* to check out Manteo Booksellers (105 Sir Walter Raleigh Street, 919-473-1221), located just behind The Waterfront shopping complex. This is simply one of the nicest and best-stocked independent bookstores this writer has ever come across.

Manteo is an ideal base for exploration of those parts of the Outer Banks not readily accessible from the water. Rental cars are available from several local firms which offer dockside pickup and delivery. Call Barry's Automotive at 919-473-6111 or Arty Sawyer at 919-473-2141. Ask the dockmaster at Manteo

Waterfront Marina or Salty Dawg for assistance. These rental vehicles can be used to visit *The Lost Colony* outdoor drama, Nags Head, Kitty Hawk, or even the Cape Hatteras Lighthouse. On the other hand, I do not recommend taxi service in Manteo, as all the local services are based on the Outer Banks. Patrons must usually pay a minimum $15 charge for a taxi to cross over to Manteo.

The most popular attractions of Roanoke Island—Fort Raleigh, the Elizabethan Gardens, and *The Lost Colony*—are located together 4 miles north of Manteo's waterfront.

At Fort Raleigh and the nearby visitor center and museum, you can see the unearthed remains of the colonists' original fort. The museum paints a fascinating portrait of those early colonial days. A movie and an occasional performance of period music add to the attraction.

The Elizabethan Gardens are an extravaganza of native and imported English plants. A walk through the green paths is definitely recommended for cruising boaters who have seen one too many waves. The grounds are open daily from 9 A.M. to 5 P.M. year-round. In the summer, when *The Lost Colony* is in production, the gardens remain open until 8 P.M.

Undoubtedly, Roanoke Island's greatest tourist attraction is *The Lost Colony* outdoor drama, written by Pulitzer Prize–winning playwright Paul Green. The waterside theater has been playing to packed houses since 1937. *The Lost Colony* was the state's first outdoor drama, and it remains one of the best. The play is a moving narrative of the fortunes of Sir Walter Raleigh's ill-fated settlement. It is presented from June 15 to August 15 at 8:30 P.M. Advance reservations (which are recommended) can be obtained by writing to The Lost Colony, Box 40, Manteo, N.C. 27954.

There is one other attraction on Roanoke Island worthy of every visitor's attention. While motorized transportation and directions from a friendly local are required to reach its doors, Queen Anne's Revenge (919-473-5466) may just be the best restaurant on the northern North Carolina coast. Because of the restaurant's rather out-of-the-way location in Wanchese, the management feels it must serve the best food to attract patrons. All steaks are the finest grain-fed Iowa beef, and the seafood is hand-selected daily for freshness. Do yourself a big favor and try the combination platter, either fried or broiled. Desserts, soups, and appetizers all bear the same mark of total quality. While most assuredly hazardous to the waistline, a visit to Queen Anne's Revenge is a prerequisite for any visit to Roanoke Island.

## Pirate's Cove Yacht Club

Pirate's Cove Yacht Club & Marina sits perched on the southwesterly tip of a dredged canal which cuts the shores of Roanoke Sound southeast of unlighted daybeacon #24B, just northwest of the sound's fixed high-rise bridge. Most of the canal carries 8-foot depths, and similar soundings are found at the piers. There is one spot at the canal's northeasterly entrance with 6½ to 7 feet of water, but this is a concern only for deep-draft vessels.

Pirate's Cove Marina is associated with a burgeoning condo and townhouse complex which seems to gobble up more of the sound's shoreline every year. During my visit, the well-sheltered dockage basin was crowded with power craft, but there was not a single mast in sight. Transients are now accepted. Berths are provided at ultramodern fixed wooden piers with every conceivable utility connection. Gasoline and diesel fuel are at hand, as are good showers and a laundromat. The marina staff will be glad to call an independent mechanic if you are in need of repairs. A full-line ship's and variety store overlooks the fuel dock. The on-site Pirate's Cove Restaurant and Raw Bar is quite good, even if a trifle pricey.

### Pirate's Cove Yacht Club & Marina (919) 473-3906

Approach depth: 6½–8 feet
Dockside depth: 8 feet
Accepts transients: yes
Fixed wooden piers: yes
Dockside power connections: 30 & 50 amps
Dockside water connections: yes
Showers: yes
Laundromat: yes
Gasoline: yes
Diesel fuel: yes
Mechanical repairs: independent contractors
Ship's & variety store: yes
Restaurant: on-site

*Pirate's Cove Yacht Club & Marina*

## Wanchese

The town of Wanchese is one of the most active commercial fishing centers on the entire North Carolina coast. Its very existence, however, is threatened by shoaling problems in nearby Oregon Inlet. When local fishermen and the state made their investments in the Wanchese area some years ago, it was with the understanding that the Corps of Engineers was to build stone jetties to stabilize the inlet as a ready access to the open sea. As a result of objections by environmentalists and the National Park Service, construction of the jetties has never even begun. Several dredges labor periodically, and not always successfully, to keep the cut open.

The Wanchese Harbor entrance channel strikes southwest from Roanoke Sound abeam of flashing daybeacon #16. As all the commercial fishing traffic around Wanchese might lead you to expect, the channel is deep, with at least 10 feet of water. You can expect minimum 8-foot soundings inside the harbor.

There are only minimal overnight facilities for pleasure boaters at Wanchese. A shoreside restaurant, Fisherman's Wharf, guards the harbor's southwestern shores just inside the entrance. Vessels with an adroit crew may find room to tie to the adjacent fixed wooden pier. This dock is often crowded with small commercial fishing craft and is not in the best of repair. Depths alongside range from 8 to 10 feet.

Mill Landing Marine (919-473-3908) occupies the harbor's northerly corner. This repair firm specializes in service work for pleasure craft. Complete mechanical repairs for both gasoline and diesel engines are available, and haul-outs are accomplished by a modern, extrawide travel-lift with a 50-ton capacity. Cruisers in need of repairs could scarcely do better than this fine facility. A few overnight slips with freshwater and 30- and 50-amp power connections are available at Mill Landing.

## Oregon Inlet Fishing Center

The long, plentifully marked channel leading to Oregon Inlet Fishing Center strikes generally east from flashing daybeacon #52. This marina has a definite flavor of sportfishing—in fact, a large charter fishing fleet that plies the waters off Oregon Inlet is based here. The marina does accept transient sailcraft and power craft on a space-available basis. It is wise to call ahead and check on slip availability before committing to a plan that calls for an overnight stop here.

Minimum depths on the long entrance channel run 6 feet, and visiting cruisers should find 8 to 10 feet of water in the slips. Berths at the center are comprised of wooden pilings and

**Oregon Inlet Fishing Center
(919) 441-6301**

Approach depth: 6 feet (minimum)
Dockside depth: 8–10 feet
Accepts transients: yes
Fixed wooden piers: yes
Dockside power connections: 30 & 50 amps
Dockside water connections: yes
Gasoline: yes
Diesel fuel: yes
Mechanical repairs: independent contractors
Ship's & variety store: yes
Restaurant: on-site (breakfast only)

small finger piers set out from a concrete sea wall. The harbor is well sheltered from inclement weather except in strong southwesterly blows. Water and 30- and 50-amp power connections are found at each berth. Gasoline and diesel fuel are currently dispensed through shoreside tanker trucks. There is a large ship's, tackle, and variety store on-site, as well as a breakfast-only restaurant.

### Old House Channel

The marked cut known as the Old House Channel provides access from Roanoke Sound's southern foot to the northern headwaters of vast Pamlico Sound. This passage is one of the most changeable that cruisers will encounter on the North Carolina coastline. Markers are frequently shifted, deleted, added to, and re-numbered to follow the ever-changing shoals.

In mid-1997, boaters could count on minimum 7-foot depths in the Old House if and only if they stayed to the marked channel. Outside the cut, soundings often rise to mere inches. Despite its changeable nature, the Old House Channel can be used with reasonable confidence by cautious mariners who are careful to identify each marker as they cruise. Obviously, this is not the sort of place to go charging ahead at full speed. Take your time, keep an eagle eye on the sounder, and have your entire crew help pick out the various aids to navigation along the way. With these precautions, you'll probably come through with nothing worse than a few beads of sweat on your brow.

## ROANOKE SOUND NAVIGATION

It is critically important to correctly identify markers on the Roanoke Sound channel. This seemingly simple task is a bit daunting because several of the markers tend to blend with the Roanoke Island shoreline. Northbound craft have the most difficulty with this problem. Be sure to have your binoculars close at hand to help pick out the daybeacons.

From flashing daybeacon #3, which marks the northern headwaters of Croatan Sound, set course directly for flashing daybeacon #42, to the west of Northwest Point. From #42, point to pass unlighted daybeacon #41 to its fairly immediate northwestern side and come abeam of flashing daybeacon #40 by 30 yards to its southern side. Do not cruise to the north of #40, where there is a fish haven. Set course from #40 for flashing daybeacon #39, which marks the northern entrance to the Roanoke Sound channel. Come abeam of #39 to its northern side. From this point, as you move south and southeast on the Roanoke Sound channel (but *not* the Shallowbag Bay entrance channel), you should take all green markers to your starboard side and all red beacons to port. This color scheme holds as far as the intersection with the Oregon Inlet channel. Since you are now headed *toward* the open sea, the color configuration makes sense.

From #39, continue on an easterly heading, passing unlighted daybeacon #37 to its northerly side, and point to eventually come abeam of flashing daybeacon #36 to its southerly quarter. At

*Bodie Island Lighthouse*

#36, the Roanoke Sound channel swings sharply south. Pick up unlighted daybeacon #34 and flashing daybeacon #33 with your binoculars. Pass to the west of #34 and to the east of #33.

From #33, the channel remains fairly straightforward as far as unlighted daybeacon #30. South of #30, the Manteo–Shallowbag Bay entrance channel will come abeam to the southwest.

**Manteo**    From unlighted daybeacon #30 on the Roanoke Sound channel, set course to pass flashing daybeacon #M to its easterly side. Do not approach #M closely. Shoal water seems to be building around this aid to navigation. Continue southeast on the main channel for a short distance past #M, then turn 90 degrees to the southwest, setting a new course to come abeam of and pass unlighted daybeacon #1 to your port side. From #1 to flash-

ing daybeacon #4, the channel is a straight shot through Shallowbag Bay. You're entering port now, so keep red markers to your starboard side and green aids to port.

While cruising from flashing daybeacon #2 to flashing daybeacon #4, you may catch sight of another aid northwest of your course. With your binoculars, you may be able to spot this flashing daybeacon's designation as #2. *Visiting cruisers should ignore this beacon.* It has been placed next to the shores of Ice Plant Island to mark a canal that was dredged to give commercial fishermen on upper Doughs Creek (cut off by the low-level fixed bridge leading to the *Elizabeth II* park) access to Shallowbag Bay.

Abeam of flashing daybeacon #4, the main channel cuts west on its way to Doughs Creek. Point to come abeam of unlighted daybeacon #6 to your starboard side. From #6, cut northwest and enter the centerline of Doughs Creek. You will quickly spot the *Elizabeth II* to starboard, and the extensive piers of Manteo Waterfront Marina will come abeam to your port side.

Southwest of #6, several small, privately maintained, uncharted nun and can buoys outline the Salty Dawg Marina entrance channel.

**South on Roanoke Sound**    The Roanoke Sound channel from Shallowbag Bay to Wanchese has been improved by periodic dredging and remarking, but it still winds this way and that. Some additional markers outlining the channel's edge would be ever so helpful. Even so, cautious skippers piloting craft that draw 5 feet or less should be able to reach the Old House Channel with minimal problems.

North of the Roanoke Sound Bridge, the channel jogs first one way and then another. It is important to correct course immediately after coming abeam of one marker to bring the next aid abeam to its proper side. Again, southbound cruisers should take all red, even-numbered aids to their (the boaters') port side and green beacons to starboard.

Southeast of unlighted daybeacon #24B, the channel quickly flows under the U.S. 64-264 Roanoke Sound Bridge. This high-rise fixed span has a vertical clearance of 65 feet.

Just northwest of the fixed span, the entrance canal leading to Pirate's Cove Yacht Club & Marina will come abeam to the southwest.

**Pirate's Cove**   To visit Pirate's Cove Marina, be sure to select the wider and southeasternmost of the two canals which cut the shoreline to the southwest. Enter the canal on its mid-width and track your way upstream to the dockage basin.

**On the Sound**   To continue south past the Roanoke Sound Bridge, pass fairly close to the southwestern sides of unlighted daybeacons #24A and #24. From #24 to flashing daybeacon #16, the channel is deep and relatively easy to follow. Watch carefully for leeway. Don't let a stiff breeze ease you out of the channel between markers. At flashing daybeacon #16, the Wanchese channel lies to the southwest.

**Wanchese**   To make your entrance into Wanchese Harbor, leave the Roanoke Sound channel abeam of flashing daybeacon #16 and cut sharply to the west-southwest. Point to pass between nun buoy #2 and can buoy #1. Remember the "red-right-returning" rule. Cruising into Wanchese Harbor, you should pass all red beacons to your starboard side and green markers to port.

The Wanchese entrance channel is well outlined with unlighted nun and can buoys. Soon, the harbor entrance will open out dead ahead. After passing a motley collection of semisunken vessels to port, you will see the harbor swinging sharply to the northwest. Watch to port again and you should spy the Fisherman's Wharf restaurant and its adjacent dock. Mill Landing Marine is on the harbor's northerly corner.

**On the Sound**   South and southeast of flashing daybeacon #16, the channel remains fairly straightforward as far as the gap between flashing daybeacon #1 and unlighted daybeacon #2. In fact, the channel is far better outlined by aids to navigation along this stretch than is the track north of Wanchese.

After leaving #1 and #2 behind, you will next find flashing daybeacon #55. For the moment, the same color scheme continues, and as #55 is a green marker, you should pass it to your starboard side.

As you can guess from the above comments, markers are frequently shifted on this lower portion of the Roanoke Sound channel (much as they are on the Old House Channel). Things may easily change by the time you read this account. Be ready to discover new and different aids to navigation than those described below.

From #55, the channel swings southwest. You will next pass between flashing daybeacon #52 and unlighted daybeacon #53. East of #52, the Oregon Inlet Fishing Center channel swings in toward the Outer Banks.

**Oregon Inlet Fishing Center**   To enter the channel leading to Oregon Inlet Fishing Center, head straight for flashing daybeacon #52. Just before reaching the aid, turn sharply to port and follow the well-marked channel east to the marina docks. Take your time, watch for leeway, and remember your "red-right-returning" rule.

**Toward the Junction**  From flashing daybeacon #53, the Roanoke passage hurries toward a major intersection. You will find many more markers in this area than pictured on chart 12205. Be sure to pass unlighted daybeacon #42 to your port side. This aid marks a shoal building into the channel from the southeast.

Eventually, you will cruise between a series of floating nun and can buoys as you near the intersection with the Oregon Inlet channel. After leaving buoy #37 behind, watch for a short, lighted red buoy. This important aid to navigation marks the intersection of three channels: the just-reviewed Roanoke Sound channel; the Oregon Inlet channel, which stretches back to the east; and the Old House Channel, which continues to the southwest toward Pamlico Sound.

Boaters are often confused by the change in color configuration at this intersection. Stop to consider for a moment. As you traveled down the Roanoke Sound channel, your track was headed out to sea, via Oregon Inlet. But once you begin cruising the Old House Channel, you are headed away from the open sea. There is thus a logical reason for the color shift, even if that reasoning doesn't do much to help you on the water.

Point to leave the flashing junction buoy to port, then look ahead to pick out the first markers on the Old House Channel, unlighted can buoy #1 and unlighted nun buoy #2. You will quickly note that all red markers should now be passed to your *starboard* side and all green aids to *port*.

The remainder of the Old House Channel is well outlined by both fixed and floating aids to navigation. Hopefully, skippers who carefully identify the color of each aid as they cruise will not have further difficulty. They will receive no guarantees from this writer, however, as the channel can change in a proverbial heartbeat.

**Oregon Inlet Channel**  As mentioned above, a second cut leads east from the unnumbered flashing junction buoy toward Oregon Inlet. The initial portion of this channel is wide and well marked. Though many aids are not charted, the adventurous but careful skipper may be able to cruise as far as the bridge without mishap. This is a popular area for bottom-fishing, and many small craft can usually be seen trying their luck.

Seaward passage through Oregon Inlet is strictly not recommended unless you can follow in the wake of a local captain who knows the twisting turns of the channel.

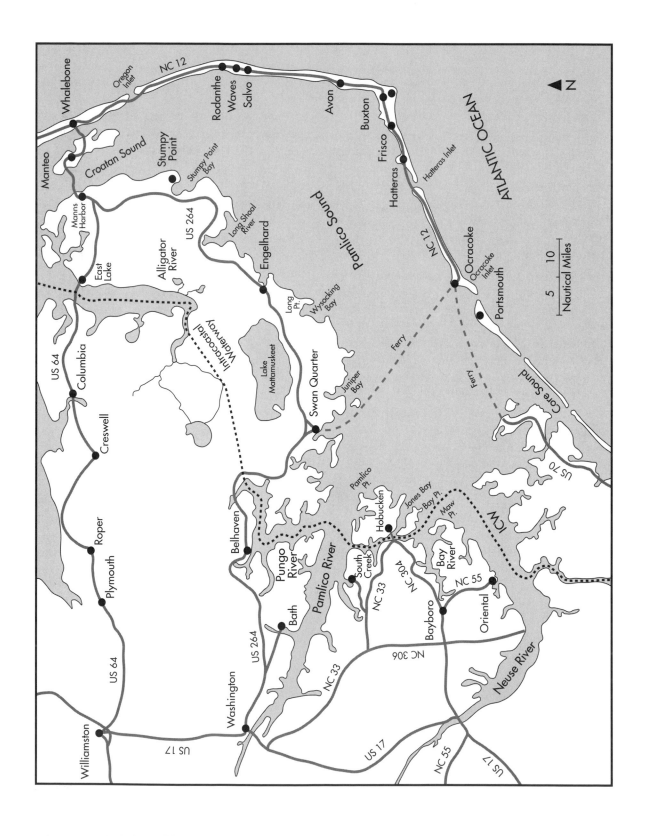

# The Pamlico Sound

Pamlico Sound is one of the largest essentially landlocked bodies of water on the East Coast. In fact, it is second only to Chesapeake Bay. The sound's vastness becomes evident when one cruises its waters. Often, neither the eastern nor western shoreline is visible, and cruisers can easily imagine that they are well out to sea. Charts simply do not convey the sound's immensity to those who have never cruised it.

Pamlico Sound has never been fully appreciated by pleasure boaters. I have traversed the sound's entire length many times and have seldom seen another noncommercial craft north of Hatteras. The Pamlico can, however, serve as ideal cruising ground when weather conditions permit. Sailcraft in particular should find the sound well suited for their purpose. With elementary coastal navigation, sailors can cruise at length without frequent course changes.

Pamlico Sound is 70 nautical miles in length from its headwaters at the foot of Croatan Sound to its southernmost point at the northern entrance of Core Sound. It encompasses more than 1,700 square miles and was once mistaken by an early explorer for the Pacific Ocean.

The Pamlico is bordered to the west by the North Carolina mainland. The western shore is mostly saltwater marsh, and only a few villages are to be found along its banks. On the eastern shore are the fabled Outer Banks. In places, these unstable sand spits are less than a mile wide, but they do protect the Pamlico from the violent storms that often batter the coast.

One particularly noteworthy geographical feature of the Outer Banks is Cape Hatteras. Here, the warm Gulf Stream and the cold Labrador Current meet. The violent clash of these conflicting waters has formed the cape and vast offshore shoals. Diamond Shoals has long been known as "the Graveyard of the Atlantic." Many, many ships have found a watery grave in the furious storms of the Diamond.

Two inlets today serve the Pamlico. Hatteras Inlet is a capricious cut that requires frequent dredging. It is used on a regular basis by the large sportfishing fleet based at Hatteras village. Ocracoke Inlet, once of considerable commercial importance, currently boasts a fairly reliable channel. This cut also requires periodic dredging, and most of its aids to navigation are not charted.

Two major rivers, the Neuse and the Pamlico, empty into the sound's southwestern corner. Don't be confused by the names of Pamlico Sound and the Pamlico River; they are two distinct bodies of water. Both the Neuse and Pamlico Rivers have more than a little to do with the formation of inlets on the Outer Banks. The enormous drainage from these two streams must find outlet to the sea. Cruisers traversing Pamlico Sound can use either river to connect with the ICW or to travel farther inland.

Pamlico Sound has several bays. Wysocking Bay is located on the central Pamlico's western shore, but most of the others lie along the northern bank of the sound's southwestern corner. Surprisingly few of these waters provide enough depth or protection to serve as overnight anchorages.

A reputation for wicked wind and waves has long been the Pamlico's lot. It is quite true that breezes over 10 knots, particularly from the northeast, can stir up a nasty chop. A 15-knot wind can render a cruise downright uncomfortable, and gusts of 25 knots or more are dangerous. The shallow depths aid in the formation of short but steep waves, quite different from rolling offshore swells.

What is often ignored, however, are the many days of light to moderate breezes when cruising the Pamlico is a most pleasant experience, particularly for sailors. Many boaters will find it gratifying to navigate such vast waters successfully. With a craft over 25 feet in length, and with a wary eye and ear on the weather, cruising boaters should not hesitate to explore the sound.

Though lunar tides have only a negligible effect on depths in most parts of Pamlico Sound, strong winds can affect water levels to a surprising degree. Fresh northeasterly blows can actually cause minor flooding in portions of southern Pamlico Sound, while sustained southwesterly winds have the same effect in northern sections.

Aids to navigation on Pamlico Sound are tall and well placed but widely separated. Runs between daybeacons can be as long as 20 nautical miles, which means that skippers must run careful compass courses while watching for leeway. With careful attention to compass, sounder, log, and chart, plus Loran or GPS if you have it, fair-weather passage of the sound should not be too great a problem.

Fish traps and stakes of all kinds pose a special hazard throughout Pamlico Sound. Skippers and their crews must be alert at all times to spot these numerous pests. You may even find your intended course blocked. A good procedure to follow in such circumstances is to pick out a stake that intersects your course. After detouring around the hazard, realign your stern with the stake and resume course.

Generally, the sound exhibits depths ranging from 8 to 20 feet between its mid-width and the mainland shore. A large shelf of shoal water extends westward into the sound from the Outer Banks. Bluff, Bryant, and Royal Shoals are three shallow-water patches in the southern Pamlico that warrant particular respect, as the incautious boater can run aground without any shoreline in sight. Bottom configurations can and do shift in the Pamlico, particularly near Ocracoke and Hatteras Inlets. Proceed cautiously at all times.

Facilities on Pamlico Sound are few and far between. A friendly marina welcomes transient boaters on Far Creek at the mainland village of Engelhard. Two facilities offering full services are to be found at the foot of the Rollinson Channel at Hatteras village. National Park Service docks and one private marina are available at Ocracoke. The community of Swan Quarter in the southwestern Pamlico boasts a marina that welcomes transient boaters. These are the only facilities accessible to cruising pleasure craft on the vast Pamlico. It is often a long trek between marinas. For this reason, cruisers should make sure that their craft are in top condition and their tanks topped off before tackling the sound.

The Pamlico offers the opportunity to cruise in open water without ever putting to sea. And few bodies of water anywhere can lay claim to such a rich historical heritage. Only by cruising this impressive inland sea can boaters come to understand the sound's true nature.

## THE OUTER BANKS

The history of Pamlico Sound is closely interwoven with the story of the Outer Banks. Because of the marshy quality of the mainland shore, few have settled there. By contrast, the Outer Banks have seen some of the Tar Heel State's most colorful incidents. Skippers cruising Pamlico Sound will find their trip enhanced by a knowledge of the special qualities of the Banks. A brief historical and cultural summary will be given here, but the most complete account of the history of the region is to be found in David Stick's *The Outer Banks of North Carolina*.

The Outer Banks long lay in a state of isolation. The Banks were not bridged from the mainland until 1931, and a paved road did not span the full length of the islands until 1952. This isolation has actually been a boon; not only have the Banks been largely spared the eyesores of rampant commercial development, but close-knit communities have survived with their own accent, customs, and folk heritage. Even with the recent influx of seasonal and permanent non-native residents, the "Outer Banker" is still readily identifiable. You may well meet some true Outer Bankers when cruising Pamlico Sound, and you will be richer for the experience.

Many and entertaining are the tall tales of Hatteras, Ocracoke, Nags Head, and other communities of the Banks. The courage and self-reliance of the Outer Banker as portrayed in these legends will stir the hearts of all who love the water. Charles Harry Whedbee chronicled many of these intriguing stories in his five books of coastal folklore. Those fine works are highly recommended to cruising boaters. Also, Ben Dixon MacNeill gives a penetrating look into the cultural character of the Banks in his two books, *The Hatterasman* and *Sand Roots* (now out of print).

The Outer Banks have undergone a radical transformation in natural character since they were first sighted by early European explorers. In those days, the Banks were covered by dense forests. As early settlers cut trees to build their homes and ships, and as stock roamed at will grazing the land, the sand was no longer held in place by vegetation. The ever-present wind began to move the sand, piling it upon the remaining trees and killing them, which in turn caused more and more sand to be blown up and down the Banks. This sad process continued unabated until the 1930s. Except for Nags Head Woods and a small wooded area near the present-day village of Frisco, grass and scrub brush became the only cover on the Banks.

As part of President Franklin Roosevelt's New Deal programs, the Civilian Conservation Corps erected sand fences and planted new trees and grasses on the Outer Banks. The CCC's efforts and later work by the state of North Carolina were at first considered partially successful. In recent years, however, it has become apparent that these practices have actually served to weaken the structure of the Banks. The so-called overwash theory claims that before stabilization occurred, large storms washed sand from the ocean side of the Banks to the sound side. Thus, while the easterly side decayed, the shores facing the mainland were nourished. The Banks were slowly migrating to the west, but at least they were surviving. Now, with many dunes stabilized by grass and sand fences, storms do not usually overwash the Banks. Thus, the ocean shores seem to be eroding without any compensating buildup on the sound-side banks. While the overwash theory is still controversial, it does explain what seems to be happening on the Banks today. The Outer Banks are indeed a land in constant flux.

Over the years, the inlets on the Banks have also displayed a distressing tendency toward not staying put. As many as 24 inlets have opened and closed at one time or another in the recorded history of the Banks. Today, only three remain. With an exasperating unpredictability, cuts open, deepen, shoal, and sometimes close altogether. Historically, whenever a new inlet has opened and become deep, commerce has arisen in the area. And whenever a cut has shoaled and perhaps eventually closed, the prosperity of the region has become a thing of the past. One example of an inlet's influence on a coastal village can be seen in the abandoned town of Portsmouth on the southern shore of Ocracoke Inlet. Once the largest and most commercially important trading center on the Outer Banks, it is now a ghost town.

Today, there are 14 communities on the banks, but once there were many more. Some, such as Little Kinnakeet and Wash Woods, have faded into memory. Even the towns that remain are

*Cape Hatteras Lighthouse*

not named as they once were. When post offices were established along the Banks in the early part of the 20th century, the federal government showed an exasperating tendency to change the names of the villages without any apparent logic. Big Kinnakeet became Avon, for instance, and Chicamacomico became Rodanthe. The Cape became Buxton.

The founding fathers of many Outer Banks families came to the islands in a rather ignoble fashion. They were sailors who washed up on the beaches from their stricken craft and later showed an understandable aversion to returning to the open sea. Many settled on the Banks and came to love these lonely sand spits. Whether because of the region's long isolation or the English descent of many shipwrecked mariners, an Elizabethan accent continues to survive on the Banks. Fried seafood is "froid" seafood, and high tide is "hoi toide."

As early as 1794, the new American government realized the necessity of lighting the ship-killing shoals of the Outer Banks. The idea was to place a series of readily identifiable lights from Cape Henry, Virginia, to Cape Lookout so that the offshore sailor could easily track his progress. In the early days, many sailcraft traveling northward came perilously close to the great Diamond Shoals by following the Gulf Stream to increase their speed. This rendered the need for lighting the North Carolina coast acute. Unfortunately, the early lights were neither tall enough nor bright enough, and new ones had to be built. Many lighthouses have come and gone since the first light at Cape Hatteras went into service in 1802. Today, five lights remain in operation on the Outer Banks—at Corolla, Bodie Island, Cape Hatteras, Ocracoke, and Cape Lookout.

The Cape Hatteras Lighthouse proudly stands 208 feet above the ocean and is the tallest masonry lighthouse in America. Tragically, the sea is cutting ever closer to the base of this magnificent sentinel. A campaign is currently under way in North Carolina to save the light, but unless action comes quickly, the Cape Hatteras Lighthouse may become only a memory. For many years, visitors were allowed to climb the lighthouse for a magnificent view. Then, for almost a decade, the light was closed due to structural problems. Recent repairs have allowed visitors to once again make the long, long climb up the spiral stairs to the dizzying catwalk circling the lighthouse's crown. Even though the closest port of call for cruising boaters is 13 miles from the Cape Hatteras Lighthouse, I urge all visitors to make every effort to view the light before it is too late!

According to David Stick, piracy seriously affected North Carolina for only a 12-month span around 1718, but this short period left an indelible print on the Banks. Stories involving Edward Teach, better known as Blackbeard, are numerous and absorbing. Near-superhuman feats have been credited to this rascal. He is said to have lived at various times in Bath, Hatteras, and Ocracoke. Tales of Blackbeard's buried treasure are still told over more than a few campfires along the islands. Many people have searched for Teach's treasure, but no one has ever admitted to finding it.

The Outer Banks can lay claim to many other accomplishments and distinctive qualities. The Wright brothers first flew near Kitty Hawk in 1903, ushering in the era of aviation. For many years, wild ponies, possibly the descendants of shipwrecked Spanish steeds, wandered the Banks at will. Today, they can still be seen in the "pony pens" of Ocracoke. In 1848, the United States Lifesaving Service began its service on the Outer Banks, which continued until 1950. Tradition claims that no member of any lifesaving crew—or any rescued sailor—was ever lost from a surf boat.

By now, you have probably begun to realize that I could write volumes about the Outer Banks. Read all you can about the history and culture of the Banks before visiting the region. Your trip will be much the better for the effort.

## Rodanthe

Rodanthe, once known by the Indian name Chicamacomico, is today a community rapidly losing its old Outer Banks look. New multilevel construction is very much in evidence. The fairly well-marked entrance channel south of charted Round Hammock Bay now holds 3½- to 4½-foot depths, and the cut is subject to constant shoaling. There is little to interest cruisers here. The passage eventually leads to a small harbor where you will most likely find all available dockage taken up by local craft. Because of the channel's uncertain nature and the general absence of berths, Rodanthe can only be recommended as a shelter from unexpected foul weather, and only for craft drawing less than 3½ feet.

## Rodanthe Custom

The village of Rodanthe maintains the colorful custom of celebrating "Old Christmas." Although the tradition has been forgotten by most modern cultures, the whole Christian world once celebrated Christmas on January 6. In 1752, the Gregorian calendar came into worldwide use, and Christmas Day was moved to December 25. Only a few isolated places have clung to the old date and continue to observe Christmas on January 6, and Rodanthe is one of those. The village continues this quaint custom on the Saturday that falls closest to January 6.

The traditional celebration begins early in the morning with a parade, which eventually includes all the villagers and their guests. All roads lead to the community church, where a huge banquet awaits. Festivities and visiting continue until night falls and it is time to call out "Old Buck."

The most unique part of Rodanthe's Old

Christmas is the beating of a traditional drum to call out the spirit of a bull once shipwrecked on the island and supposedly endowed with the spirit of a dragon. Old Buck, as he is known, never fails to appear, although today he looks a bit like papier-mâché. No one minds, though. Island children are just as delighted as their mainland counter-parts are with the more familiar figure of Santa Claus.

## Avon

Avon, once known as Big Kinnakeet, is today a community composed mostly of resort homes and a few small stores. The channel leading from Pamlico Sound to the small harbor holds 3½- to 4-foot depths but is subject to shoaling and the considerable side-setting effect of beam winds. Shallow-draft vessels might be able to find berths at the small public dock, but neither power, wa-ter, nor fuel is to be found. Because of the en-trance channel's uncertain nature, Avon can only be recommended for small power craft.

## Hatteras

Hatteras village is one of the older settlements on the Outer Banks and one of the few to retain its original name. This community should not be confused with Cape Hatteras, located 13 miles to the northeast, or with Hatteras Inlet, about 4 miles down the island.

The Rollinson Channel affords reliable access from Pamlico Sound to Hatteras village and Hatteras Inlet. Named for John Rollinson, who managed a porpoise-processing factory in the area about 1885, the cut is well marked and holds minimum depths of 7 feet. Though the channel is subject to shoaling, the Corps of Engineers can

*Sunset over the Hatteras Harbor Marina Charter Fleet*

usually be relied upon to quickly clear away major obstructions. An excellent series of daymarks fa-cilitates navigation. These aids are so numerous that first-timers may become confused. Be sure to read the navigational account of the Rollinson Channel later in this chapter before making your first visit.

Hatteras boasts some of the most extensive facilities available to cruising craft on Pamlico Sound. Southeast of flashing daybeacon #HR, you can cruise into a sheltered harbor whose entrance is marked by flashing daybeacon #2. Almost immediately, you will spy Oden's Fuel

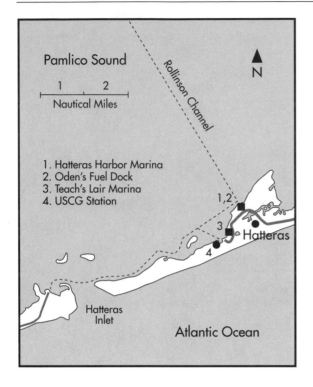

Dock (919-986-2555) straight ahead. This is a great spot to fuel up with either gasoline or diesel fuel. The friendly staff can often call ahead for you and arrange dockage at either Hatteras Harbor Marina or Teach's Lair Marina. Oden's also features a large variety and tackle store just behind the fuel dock.

If a visit to Hatteras Harbor Marina is your goal, continue cruising southwest from Oden's Fuel Dock and the marina slips will eventually come abeam to port. Most of the facility's dockage is on the harbor's well-protected southwesterly tip in a basinlike area that cuts back to the southeast. Hatteras Harbor Marina is a modern facility oriented toward power craft. It offers berths set inside wooden pilings standing out from the concrete sea wall. Entrance and dockside depths run 6 to 9 feet. Transients are readily accepted, and

there is no longer a requirement that guest craft be equipped with diesel power plants. Diesel fuel is available, but gasoline is not. Mechanical repairs can be arranged by way of independent technicians. Showers and a laundromat are on the grounds, and there is a large, well-stocked ship's, variety, and tackle store (plus a dockmaster's office) just behind the northeasterly slips. The on-site Harbor Seafood Deli is open from lunch until 7 P.M. The seafood is undeniably fresh and quite tasty. A grocery store is accessible via an 0.25-mile walk.

After docking, visiting cruisers will most likely find themselves surrounded by a large portion of the Hatteras charter-fishing fleet. The presence of the resident charter craft can contribute to an interesting stay.

---

**Hatteras Harbor Marina**
**(919) 986-2166**

Approach depth: 7–9 feet
Dockside depth: 6–9 feet
Accepts transients: yes
Fixed concrete piers: yes
Dockside power connections: 30 & 50 amps
Dockside water connections: yes
Showers: yes
Laundromat: yes
Diesel fuel: yes
Mechanical repairs: independent contractors
Ship's & variety store: yes
Restaurants: on-site, with several nearby

---

Access to Hatteras village's other full-service facility is gained by way of a short cruise southwest on the Hatteras Inlet channel. Southeast of flashing daybeacon #24, follow the Hatteras Inlet ferry channel for a stretch, then cut east into the marina's sheltered basin.

Teach's Lair Marina, formerly Hatteras Fishing Center, welcomes all transient boaters. Overnight berths at fixed wooden piers with water and 30- and 50-amp power connections are usually available. Call ahead to ensure that all available dockage has not been taken up during one of Hatteras's many fishing tournaments.

Some low-tide entrance and dockside depths of as little as 4½ feet can be a bit of a problem for long-legged vessels. Gasoline and diesel fuel are on hand, and mechanical repairs can be arranged. Visiting cruisers may make use of the shower facilities to wash away the day's salt and grime. Teach's Lair features a large ship's and variety store. Several restaurants and the grocery store mentioned above can be reached by way of a walk ranging from several blocks to 0.5 mile. A new Holiday Inn is located next door to this marina, a convenient choice for those who want to leave the water for a bit. Teach's Lair is an unusually friendly marina even in this land of friendly marinas, and I recommend it.

*Teach's Lair Marina–Hatteras Village*

Several restaurants, motels, and grocery stores are within walking distance of Hatteras village's marina facilities. Many veteran Hatteras visitors beat a path year after year to the Channel Bass Restaurant (919-986-2250). This wonderful dining spot is located to the north on the main road, N.C. 12. The few extra steps are well worth the effort. The Channel Bass has the reputation of being one of the best seafood eateries on the Outer Banks. Don't miss the Hatteras chowder, a unique soup with a deep and hearty flavor all its own.

Hatteras village retains some of its early charm. While new construction is very much in evidence, a few old homes remain. These veterans of many a storm speak of a simple elegance so characteristic of the Outer Banks. Take the time to stroll through the village at your leisure.

### Hatteras Village History

No one seems exactly sure when Hatteras village was founded, but a post office was established here in 1858. During the Civil War, the Hatteras region became the first portion of

**Teach's Lair Marina**
**(919) 986-2460**

Approach depth: 4½–7 feet
Dockside depth: 4½–5 feet
Accepts transients: yes
Fixed wooden piers: yes
Dockside power connections: 30 and 50 amps
Dockside water connections: yes
Showers: yes
Gasoline: yes
Diesel fuel: yes
Mechanical repairs:: independent technicians
Ship's & variety store: yes
Restaurants: several nearby

the Confederacy to fall to Union forces. A life-saving station was built near the village in 1878. This station was originally called Hatteras, but its name was later changed to Durants to avoid confusion with the Cape Hatteras Lifesaving Station, just to the north.

In 1923, Brigadier General Billy Mitchell used a nearby landing strip as the takeoff point for his now-famous exhibition of air power against naval ships. History suggests that the formation of the modern United States Air Force was a direct, if delayed, outgrowth of this demonstration.

Paved roads did not reach Hatteras village until the 1950s. In 1936, the Corps of Engineers dredged the Rollinson Channel, allowing ready access from the sound to Hatteras Inlet. Soon, a sizable fishing fleet began to develop. Relatively easy access to the waters off Cape Hatteras, one of the world's great natural fisheries, and to Pamlico Sound made the village a natural location for the angling trade.

Today, the future of Hatteras appears bright, and its rich past is far from forgotten.

## Hatteras Inlet

If Teach's Lair Marina was your choice for an overnight berth or a fuel stop, you have already traversed the initial approach to Hatteras Inlet. This seaward cut is used on a daily basis by the local fishing fleet, and the Corps of Engineers labors diligently to maintain the channel. Some markers are not charted, and local knowledge is advisable, even if not absolutely necessary, before running the cut.

In 1997, I found the approach channel reasonably deep, with 6½- to 7-foot minimum soundings. The passage out to sea was marked but ringed with breakers. It's obviously not for the faint of heart. Consider stopping at one of the local marinas or fuel docks to check current conditions before making the attempt. Better yet, watch for a resident sportfisherman traveling seaward and follow in his wake.

## Hatteras Inlet History

The modern Hatteras Inlet is actually the second cut to bear that name. An earlier inlet located some miles south of the present stream closed about 1764. It was not until September 7, 1846, that the present inlet was opened by a violent gale. This was the same storm that opened present-day Oregon Inlet to the north.

The initial invasion of the North Carolina coast by Union forces began at Hatteras Inlet in 1861. Two Confederate forts guarding the cut quickly fell, opening the entire coastal region to eventual occupation.

Following World War II, a private ferry began operating across the inlet to connect Hatteras and Ocracoke Islands. The state took over the ferry in 1957, and it has continued in operation until the present.

## Hatteras Legend

The Hatteras region is the setting for many moving legends. One of the best is the story of Hatteras Jack, a tale sure to bring a smile to anyone who has ever watched the fluid play of a bottle-nosed dolphin. By 1790, the story goes, most shipping had moved north from Ocracoke to the new Hatteras Inlet. Just as it is today, the channel was a twisting snake liable to convulse into new turns with every tide. Those were the days before buoys, daymarks, and any other aids to navigation. Passage of the tortuous cut was fraught with peril.

Help for distressed mariners came in a most unusual form. Pilots began to notice the lithe figure of a snow-white albino dolphin preceding each boat through the cut. Amazingly, the creature seemed always to follow the ever-changing channel. Soon, captains came to trust Hatteras Jack, as he was called. They would blow their foghorns just outside the inlet to summon this master of sea and sand. Legend says that Hatteras Jack would appraise the draft of an incoming vessel and carry it through only when the tide was high enough for safe passage. Once the boat was through the passage, the porpoise would invariably put on a fascinating show of tail walks, jumps, and barrel rolls, seemingly in delight at a job well done.

As the federal government began to place aids to navigation in the inlet, Hatteras Jack must have felt his work was no longer needed. He was seen less and less until finally his visits ceased altogether.

Hatteras Jack has not been forgotten. As Charles Harry Whedbee writes, "Many remember him and speak of him with love and with gratitude. He is part and parcel of their tradition. He, too, was a real Outer Banker."

## Ocracoke

Ocracoke is the only settled portion of the Outer Banks that can be reached by water alone. Though tourists have been discovering the charms of Ocracoke in increasing numbers during the last decade, the community has kept its distinct character perhaps better than any other village on the Banks. Many original homes

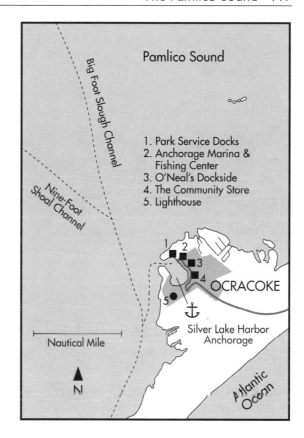

remain, some streets are still sandy lanes, and the native Ocracoker can still be heard discussing the next "hoi toide." Ocracoke may well be the friendliest spot on the Banks. Visitors, particularly those who arrive by boat, are always welcome. In my opinion, cruising boaters who have not seen Ocracoke have not seen the Outer Banks.

Ocracoke is served by a reliable, well-marked channel with minimum depths of 8 feet. The state provides regular ferry service through this cut to the mainland ports of Cedar Island and Swan Quarter. For this reason, the channel is maintained with particular care.

*National Park Service Docks—Ocracoke*

The entrance cut leads to Silver Lake harbor, a pond-shaped, sheltered body of water dredged from Old Cockle Creek by the Corps of Engineers in 1931. The harbor has depths of 8 feet or better and makes an excellent spot to drop the hook if you do not choose to use the village facilities. Anchoring on Silver Lake, with the venerable Ocracoke Lighthouse and many old homes overlooking the harbor, is usually an idyllic experience.

Ocracoke now has its own commercial marina in addition to the National Park Service docks, which have been around for time out of mind. The National Park Service docks have always been popular, probably because they were essentially free in the past. That policy has changed, and visiting skippers now have reason to consider both the public piers and private dockage on Silver Lake harbor.

Upon entering Silver Lake harbor, you will first spy the Coast Guard headquarters and the North Carolina ferry docks to port. The fixed concrete National Park Service docks are next to the ferry piers. All visiting cruisers may tie to these piers on a first-come, first-served basis. There is a 14-day time limit for dockage, and fees are charged commensurate with those of local private facilities. Thirty-amp power and low-pressure water connections are available at all berths. There are no showers on the premises, but bathrooms are available from Memorial Day to Labor Day at the National Park Service headquarters, located across the street from the dockage complex.

> **National Park Service Docks on Ocracoke (919) 928-4531**
>
> Approach depth: 10–15 feet
> Dockside depth: 8–13 feet
> Accepts transients: yes
> Fixed concrete piers: yes
> Dockside power connections: 30 amps
> Dockside water connections: yes
> Restaurants: many nearby

The three fixed wooden piers of Anchorage Marina flank Silver Lake's northeastern shores a short jog southeast of the National Park Service piers. Just look for the multistory, brick-faced Anchorage Inn behind the docks. You would just about have to be blind to miss this incongruous structure.

Anchorage Marina accepts transients and provides berths with water and power connections. Most slips feature 7 to 10 feet of water, but some low-water soundings of 6 feet are found here and there. Gasoline and diesel fuel are available dockside, and mechanical repairs can be arranged. Bicycles are provided dockside for visiting cruisers—a real plus for making the acquaintance of the more distant portions of Ocracoke Island. Transients are also afforded guest privileges at the harborside swimming pool. The marina features an on-site grill which serves hamburgers, hot dogs, sandwiches, steamed shrimp, and other items from 10:30 A.M. until sunset.

The adjacent Anchorage Inn is very convenient if you want to sleep ashore for a few evenings. The view from the upper-story rooms is absolutely spectacular.

---

**Anchorage Marina & Fishing Center (919) 928-6661**

Approach depth: 10–15 feet
Dockside depth: 6–10 feet
Accepts transients: yes
Fixed wooden piers: yes
Dockside power connections: 30 & 50 amps
Dockside water connections: yes
Gasoline: yes
Diesel fuel: yes
Mechanical repairs: independent contractors
Restaurants: grill on-site, with many
    other choices nearby

---

O'Neal's Dockside (919-928-1111) is located southeast of Anchorage Marina. Low-water depths alongside run about 8 feet. Currently, all of O'Neal's slips are filled by local craft.

The small dock of the Community Store (919-928-3321) gazes out over the northeastern shore of Silver Lake Harbor a short jog southeast of O'Neal's. Gasoline and diesel fuel are available for all craft, but there is nothing else in the way of transient services available here. However, this is *the* place to buy food and supplies on Ocracoke Island. Though there are larger stores north of the village on N.C. 12, a visit to the Community Store goes hand in hand with a visit to Ocracoke. It's like stepping back in time 30 years to the local corner grocery store. The shelves

are surprisingly well stocked with a full array of food items, including some fresh produce and frozen meats.

One of Ocracoke's great attractions is its many fine restaurants. All are within a short walk of the waterfront. Captain Ben's (919-928-4741), Pony Island Restaurant (919-928-5701), and the Island Inn Dining Room (919-928-7821) are all justly famous for their seafood. Captain Ben's is a particularly attractive establishment, its walls covered with watercolor and oil seascapes.

My personal favorite on the island is the Back Porch Restaurant (919-928-6401). As its name implies, some tables are set on a delightful screened porch, but inside dining is also available for inclement weather. All seafood items on the menu are served broiled; fried seafood is available by request. Many recipes are old Ocracoke favorites, and the quality of each dish is superb. Picking out one single item for praise is difficult, but the fillet of flounder dredged in nuts is certainly worthy of note. Visiting cruisers should do themselves a big favor and take advantage of this unusual dining opportunity.

Another dining spot of note is the Cafe Atlantic (919-928-4861). It takes a walk of almost 2 miles north of Ocracoke harbor to reach this restaurant, located on the west side of N.C. 12, but the exercise should only serve to whet your appetite. The preparation of local seafood at Cafe Atlantic is a bit more sophisticated than what you might find at the other island eateries. Believe you me, the results are more than satisfying.

There are a number of motels, grocery stores, and gift shops within a hefty walk of the harbor. The local post office is located on the harbor's northeastern shore. Just behind this modern building, visitors will discover the Old Post Office, which now houses Sally Newell Interiors and Homeport Realty and Construction.

The National Park Service maintains an office just north of the docks. There, you can see displays detailing the natural history of the Outer Banks and check on the various talks and field trips given on a daily basis by the rangers. Ocracoke's Coast Guard station is just west of the National Park Service office.

Just south of Silver Lake harbor, the snow-white Ocracoke Lighthouse stands over the village. Consider renting a bicycle at one of the many roadside rental facilities and visiting this splendid old sentinel. Built in 1823, Ocracoke Lighthouse is the oldest lighthouse in operation on the Outer Banks. Park rangers periodically open the base of the lighthouse and allow visitors to admire the old masonry, which has withstood so many tempests; check at the National Park Service office for tour times. If you are fortunate enough to take this tour, the park ranger will show you a strange phenomenon of the light's construction. While the inner wall is straight, the outer wall slopes inward from the base to the crown. This was accomplished by laying fewer and fewer courses of brick as the lighthouse rose. Finally, the exterior was finished with smooth, white-washed plaster.

For many years, wild ponies, probably the descendants of abandoned or shipwrecked Spanish stock, wandered at will on Ocracoke Island. Ocracoke's Boy Scout troop once patrolled the island's beaches atop these sturdy beasts. In those days, the annual "pony penning" was an event of great local interest. Today, for their own protection and preservation, the ponies are kept penned

*Anchorage Marina & Inn*

year-round in spacious fields well north of the village. You will probably need a ride from a friendly native to see the herd.

If you are interested in visiting Portsmouth Island (see the section on Ocracoke Inlet History below) and its deserted village via commercial charter, inquire at the National Park Service headquarters or ask the dockmaster at Anchorage Marina or O'Neal's Dockside. Several local captains pilot flat-bottomed boats across southern Ocracoke Inlet's shallow waters and discharge visitors at Portsmouth. Most of these excursions are day trips, though overnight camping stays can occasionally be arranged through the National Park Service. Be sure to take along plenty of insect repellent.

## Ocracoke History

In 1715, the North Carolina General Assembly authorized "an act for settling and maintaining Pilots at . . . Ocracoke Inlet." Thus began Ocracoke village, originally a settlement of pilots whose job was to bring inbound vessels safely over the Ocracoke bar. Ocracoke is probably one of the older communities on the Outer Banks.

*Silver Lake Harbor–Ocracoke*

First as pilots, then as commercial fishermen, the islanders have always followed the tradition of the sea. After 1931, when Silver Lake harbor was dredged, commercial fishing operations grew. With the new harbor, local fishermen were able to use larger and deeper-draft vessels. Fishing remained the primary industry until the 1960s, when tourism began to thrive.

In 1953, Cape Hatteras National Seashore was established. It eventually came to include much of Ocracoke Island. When the Ocracoke Highway was built in 1957, tourists began to visit the island in increasing numbers. Stanley S. Wahab and Bill Gaskill built inns on the island and did much to encourage the tourist trade. Today, Ocracoke draws many outsiders each year, but the island native still remembers the old days of isolation.

## Ocracoke Legend

Like Hatteras, Ocracoke has spawned many colorful legends. One of the most intriguing is the story of the pirate Blackbeard's last battle. The bloody fight was supposedly waged in Teach's Hole channel near Ocracoke village. Some historians have cast doubt on this traditional tale, but it

*Ocracoke Lighthouse*

certainly makes an interesting yarn.

The story goes that, near the end of his infamous career, Blackbeard hatched the idea of fortifying Ocracoke as a pirate haven. Hearing of this devilish plan and despairing of any help from Charles Eden, the colony's do-nothing Royal governor, the responsible citizens of coastal North Carolina appealed to Governor Alexander Spotswood of Virginia for aid.

The call was answered with the dispatch of two small sloops under the command of Lieutenant Robert Maynard of the Royal Navy. The two craft sailed to Ocracoke, where they found Blackbeard's ship, the *Adventure*, at anchor in the channel. Maynard sent out two small boats to seek a clear passage to his quarry. These were fired upon. Maynard displayed his colors, and the battle began in earnest.

One sloop soon ran aground, but Blackbeard bore down on the larger vessel, the *Ranger*, which was under Maynard's personal command. The *Ranger* was swept with cannon fire, for the British had only small arms with which to press the attack. Cleverly, Maynard ordered all his men below to escape the murderous fire. Seeing an apparently helpless vessel, Blackbeard brought the *Adventure* alongside and personally led the charge onto the deck of the British sloop. He soon met Maynard face to face, but as Blackbeard charged, the commander grazed his skull with a pistol shot. Charging up from his hiding place below, a Royal marine dealt the pirate a terrible neck wound with his saber. On and on Blackbeard fought with Maynard, until he finally fell dead at his enemy's feet. A later examination revealed that the pirate had suffered over 30 major wounds. In a grisly gesture, Maynard severed Blackbeard's head from his body and hung it upon the bowsprit. The body was flung overboard and is said to have swum three times around the *Ranger* before it sank.

### Ocracoke Inlet

South of Ocracoke village, Ocracoke Inlet provides questionable access to the open sea. Teach's Hole channel leads from Ocracoke harbor to the inlet. When I first researched Teach's Hole in the early 1980s, it was a deep, fairly straightforward cut. That has changed. The present-day channel winds this way and that on its approach to the inlet. The cut is marked by a horde of floating buoys which are frequently shifted in position, added to, removed, and renumbered in response to changes in the bottom strata. Local cruisers have informed me that there are still not enough markers for strangers to reliably keep to the deep water without local advice.

I strongly suggest that visiting cruisers looking to make use of Ocracoke Inlet inquire about current conditions at the Silver Lake facilities before making the attempt. This local knowledge could make the difference between a successful passage and the unhappy sound of a keel meeting up with the sandy bottom.

## Ocracoke Inlet History

Ocracoke Inlet has had a long and eventful history. The expedition carrying the first party of colonists to Roanoke Island put ashore here in 1585. As the colonization of eastern North Carolina went forward, the inlet became the state's primary artery of commercial waterborne traffic. Ocracoke Inlet served both Bath and New Bern, cities of primary importance during the early colonial period. During the Revolution, many of the supplies shipped from France to George Washington's armies entered here.

After the war with Britain, John Gray Blount and John Wallace began a unique enterprise on Shell Castle Island. This small tract of sand in Ocracoke Inlet eventually saw the erection of wharves, warehouses, and even a small lighthouse. Here, long-legged oceangoing vessels could unload their cargo without having to navigate fickle Ocracoke Swash. Small, shallow-draft vessels carried the cargo inland. Wallace took the unofficial title of governor of Shell Castle Island. For

many years, his enterprise prospered. He died in 1809, and the buildings were allowed to deteriorate. Today, nothing remains of this imaginative business venture.

In response to the same need to unload deep-draft vessels, the town of Portsmouth was established in 1753 by act of the state assembly. Located on the southern shore of Ocracoke Inlet, it was for a time the largest settlement on the Outer Banks. In those days, the Ocracoke channel was deep and reliable. At Portsmouth, large ships unloaded their goods, which were temporarily stored in warehouses before being ferried inland by smaller craft.

With the opening of New Hatteras and Oregon Inlets in 1846, the drainage of inland waters flowing through Ocracoke Inlet lessened, and the old cut began to shoal. Though Portsmouth held on in a declining state until the 1950s, the area's commercial activity was gone. Today, the town is deserted and can only be reached by small skiffs.

If you are interested in visiting Portsmouth, there are several commercial captains in Ocracoke village who will carry passengers across the inlet's shoals for a look at the former community. The National Park Service offers a map of Portsmouth Island and provides the names and telephone numbers of those who can provide transportation. If you go, take a liberal supply of insect repellent; the bloodthirstiness of the Portsmouth Island mosquitoes is legendary.

Today, Ocracoke Inlet is used mostly by fishermen and pleasure boaters. If you cruise the inlet, take a moment to reflect on all the history this storied body of water has known.

# OUTER BANKS NAVIGATION

Your cruise of Pamlico Sound will begin at either 42-foot flashing daybeacon #RM, which marks the southern foot of Croatan Sound, or flashing daybeacon #24OH, at the southwestern tip of the Old House Channel from Roanoke Sound. As a quick study of chart 12204 will reveal, there are many possible destinations from either marker, including Rodanthe, the first possible side trip on the Outer Banks. To reach Rodanthe, set course from either aid for flashing daybeacon #1CC at the western entrance of the Chicamacomico channel.

**Rodanthe**   Entrance into Rodanthe's small harbor is not recommended during bad weather or for craft drawing more than 3½ feet. If you choose to enter, pass flashing daybeacon #1CC to its fairly immediate southern side. Pass all other red markers to your starboard side and take green beacons to port. Come abeam of flashing daybeacon #3 by 15 yards to its southern side. Alter your heading immediately to pass between flashing daybeacon #5 and unlighted day-beacon #4. From #4 and #5, you will have to look carefully southeast toward the shoreline to spot flashing daybeacon #6. Set a new course to come abeam of #6 by 5 yards to its northern side. Once you are abeam of #6, the harbor entrance will be obvious.

**On the Pamlico**   From flashing daybeacon #1CC, it is necessary to follow a divided course to flashing daybeacon #1 at the head of the Avon channel. This is a run of 14 nautical miles. A straight course between these aids would land you on the shoals northwest of Gull Island. To avoid this hazard, give way to the west during the first part of your run.

**Avon**   To enter the 4-foot waters of the Avon Harbor channel, come abeam of flashing daybeacon #1 to its fairly immediate southern side. Again, take all subsequent red, even-numbered markers to your starboard side and green aids to port. During the last year or two, this channel has been remarked. The various aids to navigation have been set much farther apart on a northeast-to-southwest axis than was true in times past. Frankly, the new configuration of markers makes this channel harder than ever to navigate. Visiting cruisers are strongly advised that they are entering this channel at their own considerable risk.

If you do choose to make the attempt, set a southeasterly course from flashing daybeacon #1, pointing to pass unlighted nun buoy #2 by 25 yards to its northeasterly side. Continue on the same heading, passing flashing buoy #4 by about the same distance to its northeasterly quarter. Between #2 and #4, you will pass unlighted can buoy #3 well to the northeast of your course line. The same course will lead you past unlighted can buoy #5 well to its southwesterly side. From #5, continue on the same course for approximately 0.5 nautical mile. You will pass flashing buoy #6 well southwest of your course line during this run. Then swing sharply east and set a new course to pass flashing daybeacon #8 by 5 to 10 yards to its northerly side. From #8, the small harbor is easily entered. Remember, this channel may be very different from the way it was when I performed my research. Use extreme caution!

**On the Pamlico**   Probably the best route to Hatteras village is a straight run from Rodanthe's flashing daybeacon #1CC to flashing daybeacon

#42RC at the northwestern tip of the Rollinson Channel. Twenty-two nautical miles of often-rough water separate these two aids. Watch for leeway! Fortunately, this course does not stray near any shallows. If you are careful, you should encounter no difficulties other than fish stakes.

Between the Avon channel and the Rollinson (Hatteras) Channel is a series of daybeacons that is more of a menace than anything else. The seemingly haphazard aids mark shallow channels leading to local boat docks and one repair yard in the Buxton/Frisco area. They can be used only by shallow-draft boats and require specific local knowledge.

**Hatteras**   To enter the Rollinson Channel, come between flashing daybeacon #42RC and unlighted daybeacon #41. This cut is now considered part of the Hatteras Inlet channel, so as you cruise down its length from Pamlico Sound, you are headed toward the open sea  or so the Coast Guard says, despite 100 years of history to the contrary. You should pass all red aids to navigation to your port side and all green markers to starboard. Old editions of chart 11555 may not show this color configuration, but this is the current state of affairs on the water.

Set course down the long channel, pointing to come abeam of and pass each aid on its appropriate side. Minimum depths of 8 feet can be expected. Eventually, you will come abeam of flashing daybeacon #30 hard by the entrance to Hatteras village's harbor. Slow down! This is a difficult portion of the channel that calls for caution.

From #30, look southeast and you will spy flashing junction daybeacon #HR. Come abeam of and pass #HR to its *northeasterly* side. That's not the way chart 11555 depicts the channel, but believe you me, this is the way to hold best depths.

Once past #HR, those cruisers bound for Hatteras village's harbor can continue dead ahead through the opening in an artificial breakwater marked by flashing daybeacon #2. This aid is actually perched atop the southwesterly tier of the breakwater, so if you find yourself entering the harbor at night, don't cruise directly for it.

Oden's Fuel Dock is dead ahead immediately after the breakwater. If Hatteras Harbor Marina is your choice, turn to starboard from Oden's and follow the harbor southwest. The marina office will soon come abeam to port.

If Hatteras Inlet or Teach's Lair Marina is your goal, swing sharply to the southwest just northwest of #HR and point to come abeam of and pass unlighted daybeacon #27 to its southeasterly side. The same color configuration of the various aids to navigation continues along this portion of the channel.

West and southwest of #27, the initial markers on the channel approaching Hatteras Inlet are well charted. After passing flashing daybeacon #25 to its southeasterly side, point for the gap between flashing daybeacon #24 and unlighted daybeacon #23.

To gain access to Teach's Lair Marina, you must follow a portion of the Hatteras Inlet ferry channel. Depart the main inlet channel just short of flashing daybeacon #24. Look to port just before making the turn and you may spot a sign warning of a new shoal. Obviously, you should not cruise too close to the sign. Cut to the southeast and point to come abeam of flashing daybeacon #1 to its southwesterly side. Just short of #1, swing sharply to the east and immediately use your binoculars to pick out unlighted (and poorly charted) daybeacons #2, #4, and #3. As you are now entering the

*Looking out to sea through Hatteras Inlet*

harbor, take the red, even-numbered aids to your starboard side and green markers to port. Don't approach #2 too closely. It marks a shoal which seems to be building into the channel.

Cruisers continuing to Hatteras Inlet will have to rely on the various aids to navigation along the way. Most of the markers past the North Carolina ferry—Teach's Lair channel are not charted, as they are frequently changed.

**On the Pamlico**  It is possible to reach the Ocracoke channel directly from flashing daybeacon #1CC of the Rodanthe channel by following a course to flashing daybeacon #14BF at the northern entrance of Ocracoke's Big Foot Slough Channel. While this route does not pass near any shoals, it is a lengthy run of 36 nautical miles. Leeway is almost sure to be a problem on such a long stretch between markers on the Pamlico. Unless you have a reliable Loran C or GPS aboard, it would be a better idea to use the northwesternmost aid of the Rollinson Channel, flashing daybeacon #42RC, as a midpoint in your trek to Ocracoke. This will lengthen your journey 2 to 3 nautical miles, but it will provide a good midcourse correction.

**Ocracoke**  Always use chart 11550 for the waters surrounding Ocracoke. Its detailed scale makes for significantly easier navigation than the small scale of 11548.

Two channels lead from Pamlico Sound to Ocracoke harbor. The primary cut, known (and charted) as Big Foot Slough Channel, is by far the better of the two. This is the channel used by the Cedar Island and Swan Quarter ferries. The second cut, designated the Nine Foot Shoal Channel, currently has fair depths, but it is quite subject to shoaling. As the two channels are almost side by side, it makes sense to use the more reliable route.

To enter Big Foot Slough Channel, come abeam of flashing daybeacon #14BF by 15 yards to its western side. Set course to pass flashing daybeacon #13 to its eastern side. That's right, you are heading back *toward* the open sea again, so you should take green markers to your starboard side and red beacons to port.

As you pass #13, you will spot two large, rusty smokestacks protruding above the water to the west. These are the only visible evidence of a large dredge that sank on the channel's edge many years ago. Be sure to stay east of #13.

South of #13, set course to pass unlighted daybeacon #12 to its westerly side, then point to pass between flashing daybeacon #10 and unlighted daybeacon #11. From #11, the channel continues wide, deep, and well marked all the way to the gap between unlighted daybeacons #3 and #4. Observe all markers carefully, and be on the lookout for temporary nun and can buoys warning of new encroachments by the surrounding shoals.

South of flashing daybeacon #8, take care not to mistake the southeasternmost markers on the Nine Foot Shoal Channel, unlighted daybeacons #1 and #2, as aids to navigation on Big Foot Slough Channel. This case of easily mistaken identity can be a real problem for northbound boaters on Big Foot Slough. Use your binoculars and be sure of your marks before committing to a particular course.

Between #3 and #4, set course to come abeam of unlighted daybeacon #1 on Big Foot Slough Channel by 30 to 40 yards to its eastern side. From a position abeam of #1, cut sharply to the east and head directly for unlighted daybeacon #2. Twenty yards before encountering #2, swing 90 degrees to the north and set course as if to come abeam of flashing daybeacon #7 to its western side. Between #2 and #7, you will pass unlighted daybeacon #4 and flashing daybeacon #6 to their western sides. Twenty-five yards (but no closer) before reaching a position abeam of #7, swing 90 degrees to starboard and point for the mid-width of the harbor's mouth. As you cruise into Silver Lake, you will pass flashing daybeacons #7 and #9 to port.

As you cruise into the harbor, Ocracoke's Coast Guard station will immediately come abeam to port, followed closely by the ferry terminal and the National Park Service docks, also to port. Anchorage Marina, O'Neal's Dockside, and the Community Store

*Old dock on Silver Lake Harbor–Ocracoke*

overlook the northeastern shore a bit farther to the southeast.

***Ocracoke Inlet*** South of Silver Lake Harbor, Ocracoke Inlet is approached by way of Teach's Hole channel. This cut follows Ocracoke Island's western shoreline until swinging south and heading into the ocean. As noted earlier, this channel is not nearly as straightforward as it once was. Check on current conditions at one of the Silver Lake harbor facilities before attempting the cut. Of course, if you can manage to follow in the wake of a local craft putting out to sea, so much the better.

*Anchored on Silver Lake Harbor–Ocracoke*

# PAMLICO SOUND'S WESTERN SHORE

The western shore of Pamlico Sound is for the most part a marshy tract where few have settled over the years. A long, well-marked channel leads to a commercial dock at the small community of Stumpy Point, but no other facilities are available there. An active marina welcomes cruising boaters at the village of Engelhard south of Stumpy Point. Wysocking Bay has a wide, well-marked entrance but offers little shelter before depths decline. These are currently the only viable cruising possibilities on the Pamlico's western shoreline for craft drawing 3½ feet or more.

Don't be in too great a hurry to pass this shoreline by, however. If you enjoy cruising where few have been before, and if you enjoy viewing (from a distance, at least) bodies of water with such interesting names as Parched Corn Bay, give the western banks a try.

## Stumpy Point

Stumpy Point, once the shad capital of America, is still an active commercial fishing center. This tiny community is served by a well-marked channel which holds minimum depths of 8 feet. Unfortunately, the village does not have any facilities specifically catering to cruising vessels. You might tie up to one of the commercial docks, but no power or water is available. You might purchase gasoline or diesel fuel from a commercial source, but don't count on it. Stumpy Point's emphasis is on commercial fishing, and the village, while friendly, is not geared to pleasure craft.

## Long Shoal River

The Long Shoal River, 10.6 nautical miles below Stumpy Point, is a disappointing body of water. Its mouth is too open to provide protection even in moderate winds, and its upper reaches are too shallow. The shoreline is completely undeveloped, and there are no facilities in the area. It is advisable to bypass the Long Shoal River.

## Engelhard

The village of Engelhard sits hard by the shores of charted Far Creek 5.3 nautical miles southwest of the Long Shoal River's mouth. Engelhard boasts the best facilities available to cruisers on the upper Pamlico's western shoreline. The village is served by a well-marked channel with 7-foot minimum depths. This cut has been dredged twice during the last several years. For the moment, at least, depths are quite reliable.

Big Trout Marina guards the harbor's northerly banks a short distance west of flashing daybeacon #10. This facility enthusiastically welcomes transients and offers overnight berths at fixed wooden slips with water and 30-amp power connections. Depths on the outer docks, where large vessels are accommodated, are 8 feet or better, while 6-foot soundings can be expected at the smaller inner slips. Gasoline is available at the marina, and the management can arrange for you to fill up with diesel fuel at a nearby commercial dock. A few shoreside showers are to be had for the asking. Breakfast and lunch are served in a small cafe on the grounds which is very popular with the local crowd. A second restaurant, the Engelhard Cafe, is only a short walk away in the small downtown district, as are a grocery and hardware store and several other businesses. The food at both restaurants is of the down-home Southern variety and quite tasty. Of the two, I was a bit more impressed with the marina cafe.

**Big Trout Marina**
**(919) 925-6651**

Approach depth: 7–12 feet
Dockside depth: 8 feet at the outer dock
　　　　　　　　6 feet  at the Inner slips
Accepts transients: yes
Fixed wooden piers: yes
Dockside power connections: 20 & 30 amps
Dockside water connections: yes
Showers: yes
Gasoline: yes
Diesel fuel: nearby
Restaurant: on-site (breakfast and lunch only)

Engelhard is quite small and very sleepy. Its existence seems to depend equally on commercial fishing and agriculture. While docked at Engelhard, I stood for 15 minutes in the cockpit and heard only the sighing of the wind. After joining me, my mate remarked, "Have we slipped into the twilight zone?" If you enjoy getting away from it all in as friendly a town as you are likely to find, then by all means put a red circle around Far Creek and Engelhard.

## Wysocking Bay

Wysocking Bay is another open sidewater of Pamlico Sound that offers almost no protection for overnight anchorage. The bay has a well-marked entrance holding 6-foot minimum

*Stumpy Point*

depths, but shoals extend outward from the western shore. There are no facilities or development along the banks. Because of the lack of shelter, consider entering the bay only for sightseeing.

# WESTERN SHORE NAVIGATION

To visit Stumpy Point from Croatan Sound or Roanoke Sound, head for flashing daybeacon #2SP at the southeastern tip of the Lake Worth channel. If you are cruising from Croatan Sound to Stumpy Point, it is necessary to deviate your course to the east in order to avoid the shallow water near Drain Point.

*Stumpy Point*   Navigation of the excellent Stumpy Point entrance channel is facilitated by pairs of green and red daybeacons stretching almost to the harbor's entrance. Simply pass between each pair and come abeam of flashing daybeacon #10 fairly close to its southwestern side. From #10, you have only to pass

*Engelhard–Far Creek entrance channel*

between a last pair of aids, unlighted daybeacon #13 and flashing daybeacon #11. The harbor entrance then opens out to the northeast.

*On the Pamlico*   Flashing daybeacon #LS2, just east of Long Shoal, is a convenient starting point for the remaining destinations on the mid-Pamlico's western shore. Long Shoal has built out farther to the east and southeast than is shown on the latest edition of chart 11555 and has encroached upon #LS2. For best depths, do not approach this aid any closer than 50 yards to its eastern side.

Be sure to avoid wandering into the charted "Danger Zone" southeast of #LS2, marked by flashing daybeacon #W. The charted "Targets" within this zone are actively used by United States Marines aircraft flying out of Cherry Point.

From #LS2, boaters can access the Long Shoal River by setting course for flashing daybeacon #1PS near Pingleton Shoal, at the river's southern entrance. This is a run of 6 nautical miles through open water.

To reach Engelhard, site of the best boating facilities on the western shore of the mid-Pamlico, set a direct course from flashing daybeacon #LS2 to flashing daybeacon #1 at the eastern entrance of the Engelhard cut. This passage also passes through open water and does not present any difficulty.

*Engelhard*   Come abeam of flashing daybeacon #1, at the channel's eastern entrance, to its fairly immediate northern side. Set course to come abeam of and pass unlighted daybeacon #3 and flashing daybeacon #5 to their northern sides. Pass all subsequent red beacons to your starboard side and green aids to port.

At flashing daybeacon #9, the channel takes a small jog to the southwest. Point to pass flashing daybeacon

*Engelhard fishing craft*

#10 to its southeasterly side. Soon after you leave #10 behind, Big Trout Marina will come abeam to starboard.

**Wysocking Bay**   Wysocking Bay is easily accessible from the Long Shoal beacon. If you decide to enter, set a course to come abeam of unlighted daybeacon #2, at the bay's eastern entrance, by 100 yards to its southern side.

Set a new course to pass between flashing daybeacon #3 to its northerly side and unlighted daybeacon #4 to its southerly quarter. Come abeam of unlighted daybeacon #5 by 100 yards to its northerly side. From #5, point to come abeam of flashing daybeacon #6 by 100 yards to its westerly side. Be careful in cruising past #6, as depths soon decline.

## SOUTHERN PAMLICO SOUND

The southern portion of Pamlico Sound is pierced by many bays and small sidewaters. Some of these provide poor protection, and a few are even too shallow to enter safely. But at least two offer excellent overnight anchorage, and another leads to the southern Pamlico's only marina facilities, at the village of Swan Quarter. Both the Pamlico and Neuse Rivers make into the western banks of the southern Pamlico, and Core Sound opens out from the extreme southeastern corner. These three major bodies of water offer a wealth of cruising opportunities, which will be discussed in the next three chapters.

Until now, few pleasure boaters have availed themselves of the southern Pamlico's cruising opportunities. If you dream of visiting bays and

secluded coves where yours may be the only pleasure craft in sight, yet still want access to marina facilities, the southern Pamlico may be for you.

Accounts of the various shoreside destinations in southern Pamlico Sound follow. This review begins at the eastern tip of the northern shore near Gull Shoal and moves westward to the Pamlico River's entrance. Moving south, it then outlines the banks between the Pamlico and Neuse Rivers. Finally, it examines the sound's southernmost shore between the Neuse River and the northern entrance of Core Sound.

### Outfall Canal

Marked by one unnumbered flashing daybeacon, the entrance to Outfall Canal lies east of East Bluff Bay. The canal acts as a feeder ditch to Lake Mattamuskeet some miles inland. The stream's 3-foot depths are not practical for cruising-size vessels.

### East Bluff Bay

Located east of Bluff Point, East Bluff Bay is an open body of water that offers little protection from stiff winds. No development or facilities are to be found. A wide shelf of shoal water extends out from the shoreline for 0.3 nautical mile, but the bay's midsection does hold 6 to 7 feet of water. In very light airs, or in light to moderate northerly and northwesterly breezes, the bay offers some protection. However, unless you are in immediate need of shelter, consider some of the more reliable anchorages to the west.

### West Bluff Bay

West Bluff Bay is another of the open, undeveloped sidewaters so common in Pamlico Sound. Southwesterly winds can stir up a wicked chop in the bay. Good depths of 6 feet are held to within 0.1 nautical mile of shore. In light winds or moderate northeasterly breezes, you might consider anchoring here, but again, better places to drop the hook are not far to the west.

### Juniper Bay

The deep, reasonably well-marked channel in Juniper Bay provides access to one of the most reliable overnight anchorages on Pamlico Sound. Entrance depths run 6 to 9 feet. The waters north of flashing daybeacon #4 hold minimum 5-foot depths and are quite sheltered from all but gusty southerly blows. Swinging room should be sufficient for craft as large as 45 feet. The surrounding

shores are composed mostly of undeveloped marsh. Juniper Bay is a rather isolated body of water where visiting cruisers will likely spy few fellow pleasure craft. This is backwater anchoring at its best.

### Swan Quarter Narrows

The body of water known as Swan Quarter Narrows affords reliable passage from Juniper Bay to Swan Quarter Bay. The broad path of the narrows is sandwiched between Great Island to the south and the mainland shoreline to the north. Minimum depths are 7 feet in the marked channel, and typical soundings run 8 to 12 feet. In spite of its name, Swan Quarter Narrows is a rather open body of water that affords no protected spots to set the hook.

### Swan Quarter

The tiny village of Swan Quarter sits perched on the northeastern extreme of Swan Quarter Bay. Among the many quaint, sleepy communities along the North Carolina coast, Swan Quarter is one of the quietest and friendliest. Take a moment to stroll the village's lovely lanes. You will discover that time has passed pleasantly here.

Swan Quarter boasts the only facility catering to cruising boaters on southern Pamlico Sound. Clark's Marina overlooks the northern banks of the canal running east-northeast from flashing daybeacon #10. Approach depths are 8 feet or so, but caution is required to avoid the surrounding shallows. Boaters can expect 6½ to 8 feet of water at the marina docks. You will spy Clark's dockage basin to port as you cruise upstream on the canal. Most of the fixed wooden slips are covered, but there are enough open spaces for a very few sailcraft. Water and 30-amp power connections are available at all berths. The marina's fuel dock, office, and variety store flank the canal's northern banks several hundred yards upstream of the dockage basin. Both gasoline and diesel fuel are available here. The variety store is surprisingly well stocked; fresh seafood can often be purchased.

There is currently no restaurant operating within easy walking distance of the Swan Quarter waterfront. Michael's Munchies, a convenience store/grill that offers breakfast items, sandwiches, and a daily lunch special, is located on N.C. 45 approximately 1 mile from the downtown business district. I suggest you purchase some of the ultrafresh seafood often available at Swan Quarter Harbor or the Clark's Marina store and have a fish fry in your own galley.

### Clark's Marina
### (919) 926-3801

Approach depth: 8–12 feet
Dockside depth: 6½–8 feet
Accepts transients: yes
Fixed wooden piers: yes (many are covered)
Dockside power connections: 30 amps
Dockside water connections: yes
Gasoline: yes
Diesel fuel: yes
Variety store: yes
Restaurant: requires a long walk

## Swan Quarter History

Though located on the mainland, Swan Quarter has the flavor of the Outer Banks. Established in 1812, the village was named for the many swans that once frequented the bay. The town became the seat of Hyde County in 1836. Before eastern North Carolina enjoyed a good

*Engelhard Harbor*

road system, there was much travel across Pamlico Sound from Swan Quarter to Ocracoke. It is likely that in those days, the village felt closer to the Banks than to Washington or Bath, even though those North Carolina towns are geographically closer.

Fishing, oystering, and crabbing have long been the principal occupations of Swan Quarter citizens. This salty duty is supplemented by farming the rich land about the town. Today, the village sees many more visitors than in times past. Tourists pass through on their way to and from the Ocracoke–Swan Quarter ferry, located nearby. The increased traffic doesn't seem to have changed the town much, however.

## Swan Quarter Tale

Sometime in the 1870s, the good citizens of Swan Quarter decided that it was high time to build a church. Various local craftsmen offered to donate their services. All that was needed was a lot on which to build. After a diligent search, a prime parcel was decided upon, and representatives of the future congregation went to call upon the owner. Much to their dismay, he courteously

*Near Swan Quarter*

but firmly refused to sell. A second lot was chosen. Soon, the proud new structure began to take shape.

Just as the church neared completion, a terrific storm struck the North Carolina coast. The screaming winds backed more and more water into Swan Quarter Bay, flooding the town. The new church actually floated off its foundation and proceeded "before the wind" down what was the main street. After colliding with the general store, it eventually came to rest on the lot the congregation had first chosen.

Apparently seeing the hand of providence, the owner ceded the property to the church. Not long afterward, Providence Church sat atop a new foundation on its chosen land.

Today, a new brick structure has replaced the original building, but the old church that floated down the street is still used for Sunday school. If you are interested in visiting the church, walk north along the main road and you will see the new brick structure on the left. The old church is just behind it.

## Swan Quarter Canal

West of flashing daybeacon #5, a deep canal connects Swan Quarter and Deep Bays. Strong tides flow through this cut, scouring the stream's bottom. Depths of 8 to 14 feet can be expected on the canal's centerline. However, the approach to this useful channel from Swan Quarter Bay carries only 5 feet (maybe slightly less) at low tide.

Swan Quarter Canal serves as a convenient and mostly reliable route between the two bays. By using this cut, boaters can avoid the long cruise south into the sound's unprotected waters. Such a cruise is otherwise necessary to bypass the shoal water near Swan Quarter Island.

## Deep Cove

Deep Cove is a small body of water straddling the gap between Judith and Swan Quarter Islands. The cove's entrance is marked by flashing daybeacon #1. At first glance, these waters might be looked upon as a potential overnight stop. However, extensive shoaling north of #1 has not been noted on the current edition of chart 11548. Depths of 3 and 4 feet are all too common. Both Swan Quarter and Judith Islands are composed entirely of marsh grass, and they do not give much protection in foul weather. Most cruisers will probably want to bypass Deep Cove.

## Three Bay Area

West of Judith Island and north of flashing daybeacon #2, three large bays open out to the north. Spencer, Rose, and Deep Bays form a distinctive three-fingered body of water which is far larger than a casual inspection of chart 11548 might lead one to believe. All three bodies of water offer cruising possibilities, but only Deep Bay boasts good anchorage.

Spencer Bay, the westernmost of the three, has a marked channel which eventually leads to the coastal village of Germantown. This tiny community is composed mostly of a few homes owned by the local fishing folk. A low-key campground does flank the northern shores of the first westward-running cove, located north of unlighted daybeacon #9. Bayside Campground and Marina allows boats to tie off to its wooden bulkhead, but no real docks or slips are available. The Spencer Bay channel holds at least 5½ feet of water, but you must plow through some 4-foot depths to reach the campground's waterfront. A few 15-amp connections might be available for those with long power cables, and there are a few wa-

*Oyster Shells at Swan Quarter*

ter hookups. One low-key shower is located in the campground. A small variety store sits just behind the waterfront.

If you do make it to the campground, be sure to say hello to the real boss, B. J., a black Labrador who can usually be found in deep slumber on a couch with his legs stuck up in the air. Give him a pat for me.

---

### Bayside Campground and Marina (919) 926-6621

Approach depth: 4 feet
Dockside depth: 3½–4 feet
Accepts transients: limited basis
Fixed wooden bulkhead: yes
Dockside power connections: 15 amps (limited basis)
Dockside water connections: limited basis
Shower: one
Variety store: yes

---

Most of the remaining shoreline waters on Spencer Bay are shoal, and the mid-waters are much too open for anchorage in anything but very light airs. All in all, large cruising craft should probably look elsewhere for both anchorage and marina facilities.

Lower Rose Bay is surprisingly large. Don't look for shelter on these wide-open spaces. Captains with wanderlust in their hearts might choose to cruise carefully into the bay's upper reaches and drop anchor in 6 feet of water northeast of flashing daybeacon #6. It's all too easy to wander into 4½ to 5 feet of water while making this passage, even when you are trying to be cautious. The surrounding shores are composed of undeveloped scrub marsh and are not the most attractive you will ever find. There is enough elbow room only for boats as large as 36 feet.

Much of Rose Bay's eastern shoreline is part of the Swan Quarter National Wildlife Refuge. As you cruise between flashing daybeacons #5 and #6, you will see the refuge's only public facility, a large observation pier, on the northeastern banks. Don't attempt to tie to this dock, as the surrounding waters are quite shallow.

A small power-craft marina is located on the northerly arm of Rose Bay north of flashing daybeacon #6. Unfortunately, approach depths of less than 4 feet relegate this facility to our outboard and I/O brethren.

Deep Bay strikes east off lower Rose Bay and eventually leads to deep Swan Quarter Canal (see the account above). This bay boasts two aids to navigation and minimum depths of 7 feet or better. There is one unmarked shoal which requires extra caution.

Flashing daybeacon #2 marks the western entrance to Swan Quarter Canal. The large cove south-southwest of #2 makes an excellent overnight stop when winds are blowing from the south, southwest, or southeast. Breezes of even moderate strength from the west, north, or northwest make this anchorage most uncomfortable. Minimum 6-foot depths run to within 250 yards of the southern Judith Island banks. There is enough room for craft as large as 48 feet to swing comfortably. The adjacent shores are the usual undeveloped marsh and do not provide enough shelter in strong storms. In fair weather, this is a wonderful spot to watch the day's light fade from the waters.

## Between Pamlico and Neuse Rivers

Four bays flank Pamlico Sound's western shores between the mouths of the Neuse and Pamlico Rivers. None offers much in the way of good cruising for large pleasure craft. Mouse Harbor, Big Porpoise Bay, and Middle Bay all have winding, treacherous, and unmarked entrances. They should definitely not be attempted.

Jones Bay, the southernmost of the four waters, might at first glance appear to be a good sidewater possibility. The entrance, though partially surrounded by shoal water, is well marked. However, extensive shoaling not shown on the latest edition of chart 11548 has occurred 2 nautical miles northwest of flashing daybeacon #3. Depths fall off to 4 feet on these waters. The deep section of the bay to the east is too open for practical anchorage. For all its promise, Jones Bay should probably be avoided without specific local knowledge.

## West Bay

Located on the Pamlico's southernmost shore between the mouth of the Neuse River and the headwaters of Core Sound, West Bay is a large, delightful body of water which has heretofore remained undiscovered by pleasure boaters. The bay has good depths and ample markings. Even more promising, there are at least two good anchorages on its upper reaches. Except for a few deserted buildings in the restricted area north of Corn Sage Point, the bay's shoreline is completely undeveloped. This body of water has a feeling of deep isolation. Many will find exploration of these seemingly forgotten waters an exciting and rewarding experience.

South of flashing daybeacon #7WB, West Bay divides into two arms. The southeastern branch is known as West Thorofare Bay and the southwestern as Long Bay. Both are excellent evening stopovers.

West Thorofare Bay eventually leads to Thorofare Canal, which connects in turn with Thorofare Bay and Core Sound. This useful passage will be reviewed in chapter 7.

The waters of West Thorofare Bay west of flashing daybeacon #11WB offer good overnight anchorage. Depths run 6 to 10 feet, and there is ample room for a 38-footer. Shelter is quite good for all but strong northerly blows. Be sure to drop the hook west of the main channel to avoid any local fishing craft which might happen along.

Long Bay runs southwest from flashing daybeacon #7WB. West of flashing daybeacon #4, the large cove south of Corn Sage Point makes a good spot to pitch the hook in moderate winds. Blows of 20 knots or more from the east or southeast make for a bumpy night. Consider anchoring about halfway between flashing daybeacons #4 and #6, where there is good shelter. Although

these waters are not quite as protected as the anchorage on West Thorofare Bay, the setting is just as lovely and isolated.

West of flashing daybeacon #6, an old canal connects Long Bay with Turnagain Bay, a sidewater of the Neuse River. Several local historians have suggested that this small stream was dug by Native Americans before the first European ships touched the North Carolina coastline. Today, this venerable waterway has shoaled to depths of 3 feet or less. Don't attempt to enter unless your craft draws less than 3 feet.

## Cedar Island

Between the mouth of West Bay and the northern entrance of Core Sound, two flashing daybeacons, #1 and #2, mark the entrance to the Cedar Island–Ocracoke ferry terminal. No dockage or facilities are available for cruising boaters at the ferry piers. Don't attempt to enter.

## SOUTHERN PAMLICO NAVIGATION

In planning a cruise of southern Pamlico Sound, it soon becomes evident that there are many possible course combinations that can lead captains where they wish to go. There is no single "best" route. Some of the more practical passages will be reviewed in this section, but the list is by no means exhaustive. With the current edition of chart 11548 in hand, wandering navigators can plot many a course to a wide variety of destinations.

If you followed the Outer Banks route southward down the Pamlico, your cruise of the sound's southern quadrant will probably begin from flashing daybeacon #14BF at the northern entrance of Ocracoke's Big Foot Slough Channel. If the mainland route via Far Creek and Engelhard was your choice, 45-foot flashing daybeacon #GS at the eastern tip of Gull Shoal makes a good starting point. Passages from #14BF will first be reviewed, followed by those from Gull Shoal light. After these discussions, specific accounts of each possible destination will be presented.

***Routes from Ocracoke***   To reach most any southerly point on Pamlico Sound from #14BF, consider setting a course for flashing daybeacon #1 at the southerly foot of Bluff Shoal. From #1, it is a quick hop to flashing daybeacon #3 on the northeasterly flank of Royal Shoal. A vast array of possible courses and destinations is available from #3.

**To the Northern Shore**   You can reach Juniper Bay by following a direct course from #3 to flashing daybeacon #2 near the bay's mouth. This is a run of 11.4 nautical miles through open water. As you begin your approach to Juniper Bay, be on the watch for flashing daybeacon #1, which marks a long, long shoal stretching southeast from Great Island. Be *sure* to pass well east of #1. Point to come abeam of flashing daybeacon #2 at Juniper Bay's entrance by 50 yards to its western side.

To reach Swan Quarter Bay and the village of Swan Quarter, site of the southern Pamlico's only facilities for cruising boaters, set course from #3 to come abeam of 40-foot flashing daybeacon #LM by 0.5 nautical mile to its northeastern side. From #LM, point to come abeam of flashing daybeacon #1SQ by 100 yards to its eastern side. Set a new course to come abeam of flashing daybeacon #3, at the southern entrance to Swan Quarter Bay, by 25 yards to its eastern side. Be on guard against the shallow water surrounding Great Island as you cruise between #1SQ and #3. You may spot flashing daybeacon #2, which marks the northwestern tip of the Great Island shoals, well east of your course about 1 nautical mile before reaching #3.

**To Pamlico River**   The Pamlico River, described in the next chapter, can be reached from #3 by first setting course for flashing daybeacon #M at the southern tier of Middle Ground Shoal. Some 9.9 nautical miles separate these two aids. Alter course to the southwest 0.3 nautical mile before reaching #M and come abeam of the aid well to its southwestern side. This maneuver will help you avoid the sunken wreck to the south of #M, clearly shown on chart 11548. Set a new course to come abeam of and pass flashing daybeacon #UM, located well south of Swan Quarter Island, by at least 100 yards to its southwestern side. From #UM, it is a straightforward run of 5.7 nautical miles to the 40-foot flashing daybeacon #PP, which marks the river's entrance just to the east of Pamlico Point.

**To Neuse River**   A visit to the Neuse River, detailed in chapter 6, carries cruisers across a wide section of southern Pamlico Sound. Set course from #3 to come abeam of flashing daybeacon #5RS, located to the west of Royal Shoal, well to its northern side. This will help you avoid the charted sunken wreck north of #5RS. From a position abeam of #5RS, set a new course for the 40-foot flashing daybeacon #BI at the eastern tip of Brant Island Shoal. After sighting #BI, be sure to identify flashing daybeacon #WR2, a smaller marker east of #BI that marks the sunken remains of a screw-pile lighthouse. Pass well south and east of both aids to navigation. From #BI, it is a long run of 9.1 nautical miles to the 24-foot flashing daybeacon #NR near the Neuse's entrance.

**To the Southern Shore**   To reach West Bay, a large body of water on the Pamlico's southern shore, follow the courses recommended for passage to the Neuse River as far as flashing daybeacon #BI. From #BI, set course to come abeam of flashing daybeacon #2WB by 10 to 15 yards to its southern side. Set a new course to come abeam of and pass flashing daybeacon #5 by 100 yards or more to its northwestern side. Don't slip to the southeast between #2WB and #5. The charted shoal water off North

Bay is waiting to trap incautious navigators. From #5, the main body of West Bay lies due south.

**To Core Sound**   Before deciding to enter Core Sound, read the general description of the sound's water at the beginning of chapter 7. If you decide to cruise this delightful but treacherous sound, you must first skirt Royal Shoal. Use flashing daybeacon #5RS to work around the shoal's western boundary. Point to eventually come abeam of flashing daybeacon #SW, at the southern tip of Royal Shoal, by 300 yards to its southern side. Do not approach #SW too closely, as it guards the charted sunken wreck of a screw-pile lighthouse. From #SW, set course to come abeam of flashing daybeacon #HL, near the western boundary of Hodges Reef, by 50 yards to its western side. Along the way, you will pass between flashing daybeacon #HR to the southeast and unlighted daybeacon #OS to the northwest. Don't approach either of these aids, as they are surrounded by shoal water. Once abeam of #HL, carefully set a new course for flashing daybeacon #2CS at Core Sound's northern entrance. Watch for leeway! To the east, Hodges Reef threatens with 1- and 2-foot depths. South of #2CS, refer to chapter 7 for further navigational information.

**Routes from Western Pamlico**   From 45-foot flashing daybeacon #GS at the eastern tip of Gull Shoal, you can easily reach most destinations by cruising to unlighted daybeacon #2A, south of Hog Island. Stay well south of #2A to avoid the shoal water on the aid's northern quarter.

**To the Northern Shore**   To reach Juniper Bay, set course for the unnumbered flashing daybeacon to the east of Bluff Point. From this marker, follow a bisected course to round Bluff Point and come abeam of unlighted daybeacon #2 by 25 yards to its northerly side. Be careful to avoid the shallow-water patch southeast of #2. From #2, set a new course to come abeam of flashing daybeacon #2 at the entrance to Juniper Bay by 0.4 nautical mile to its southerly side. You will pass unlighted daybeacon #1 north of your course line along the way. Once abeam of #2, point to pass this aid well to its westerly side as you enter Juniper Bay.

To visit the village of Swan Quarter, use the same course described above for Juniper Bay as far west as flashing daybeacon #2. From #2, follow the mid-width of Swan Quarter Narrows north of Great Island. You should then come abeam of another flashing daybeacon #2, to the west of Great Island, by 30 to 50 yards to its northerly side. Do not drift south or southeast of the second #2. This aid marks a long tongue of shoal water building west from Great Island. Once abeam of #2, set a new course for flashing daybeacon #3, which marks the entrance to Swan Quarter Bay.

**To Pamlico River**   For passage to the Pamlico River, follow the same course used to reach Swan Quarter Bay to flashing daybeacon #2, located northwest of Great Island. From #2, set course for the unnumbered flashing daybeacon south-southwest of Shell Point. Come abeam of the unnumbered daybeacon to its northerly side. From this aid, it is a run of 2.9 nautical miles through open water to the 40-foot flashing daybeacon #PP east of Pamlico Point, which marks the river's entrance.

**To Neuse River**   Access to the Neuse River from #2A calls for a long cruise. Carefully set course for flashing daybeacon #BI to the east of Brant Island Shoal. A gap of 17.4 nautical miles separates #2A and #BI. On the first portion of this run, you will pass unlighted daybeacon #1 and a charted but unnumbered warning beacon northwest of your track. Stay to the southeast of these markers.

Do not closely approach #BI or the adjacent flashing daybeacon #WR2, which marks a sunken wreck. From #BI, set course for the 24-foot flashing daybeacon #NR at the Neuse's eastern entrance.

***To the Southern Shore***   You can reach West Bay, on the Pamlico's southern shore, by cruising to flashing daybeacon #BI, as in the passage to the Neuse River detailed above. From #BI, set course to come abeam of flashing daybeacon #2WB, at the northern entrance of West Bay, by 25 yards to its southern side. From #2WB, point to come abeam of and pass flashing daybeacon #5 by 100 yards or more to its northwestern side. Don't slip to the southeast between #2WB and #5. The charted shoal water off North Bay is waiting to trap errant skippers. From #5, the main body of West Bay lies due south.

***To Core Sound***   Core Sound, marking the southernmost point of Pamlico Sound, is a charming but difficult body of water. Before deciding to enter, read the detailed description presented in chapter 7. If you decide to cruise the sound, set course from #2A to come abeam of flashing daybeacon #5RS, at the western edge of Royal Shoal, by 300 to 400 yards to its western side. From a position abeam of #5RS, follow the body of Royal Shoal to the south, staying well away from the edge of the shallow water. Point to eventually come abeam of flashing daybeacon #SW, which marks a charted sunken wreck at the southern tip of Royal Shoal, by 300 yards to its southern side. Don't approach #SW closely. Set course from #SW to come abeam of flashing daybeacon #HL, just west of Hodges Reef, by 50 yards to its western side. Between #SW and #HL, you will pass flashing daybeacon #HR to the southeast of your track and unlighted

daybeacon #OS to the northwest. Both of these aids mark shallow water and should not be approached. Carefully set a new course from #HL to flashing daybeacon #2CS at the northern entrance of Core Sound. Don't allow leeway to ease you onto the shoal waters of Hodges Reef to the east.

***Juniper Bay***   Pass flashing daybeacon #2 well to its westerly side and set course to come abeam of unlighted daybeacon #3 by 50 to 100 yards to its easterly side. Past #3, bend your course to the northwest to avoid the shallows that extend out from the northeasterly shore, clearly shown on chart 11548. Come abeam of flashing daybeacon #4 to its westerly side. After passing #4, continue cruising upstream by following the bay's mid-width. Soon, depths decline to low-water soundings of 5½ to 6 feet. Anchor along the bay's centerline between #4 and the channel's charted 90-degree turn to the east.

***Swan Quarter***   Enter Swan Quarter Bay by passing flashing daybeacon #3 to its fairly immediate eastern side. Set course to pass flashing daybeacon #3A to its eastern side. Come abeam of flashing daybeacon #5 by 100 yards to its eastern side. Bend your course to the northeast and point to come abeam of flashing daybeacon #5A to its immediate southeastern side.

As you approach #5A, you will spot two uncharted and unlighted daybeacons, #1 and #2, to the east. These errant aids mark the Ocracoke ferry channel leading toward Long Point. Ignore these markers! Instead, set course to come abeam of unlighted daybeacon #6 to its westerly side. Avoid the ferry channel entirely. There are no facilities whatsoever for pleasure craft at the ferry docks.

From #6, set a new course to come abeam of flashing daybeacon #7 to its eastern quarter. Once abeam of #7, immediately set a new course to come abeam of flashing daybeacon #8 to its immediate western side.

From #8, look to the northeast and identify flashing daybeacon #10. This aid marks the entrance to a deep, sheltered canal leading to Clark's Marina. To enter, proceed directly from #8, pointing to pass #10 to your fairly immediate starboard side. Cruise into the canal's mouth, favoring the starboard shore slightly. As you cruise northeast on the canal, you will pass several private docks to port. About halfway between the entrance and the stream's headwaters, watch carefully to port for a group of covered slips. The fuel dock and marina office are upstream of the covered slips, also on the port shore.

### Swan Quarter Canal    To approach Swan Quarter Canal, which serves to connect Swan Quarter and Deep Bays, depart the main Swan Quarter channel 30 yards south of flashing daybeacon #5. Use your binoculars to carefully identify flashing daybeacon #2, which marks the canal's easterly entrance. This aid can be hard to spot, and the approach is not nearly as simple as it appears on chart 11548.

Cruise west from #5, pointing to come abeam of and pass #2 to its southerly side. Expect some 5-foot depths (or slightly less at low water) between #5 and #2. Once you are abeam of #2, the canal's entrance will be obvious.

For good depths, simply hold to the canal's midline as you cruise to Deep Bay.

Another flashing daybeacon #2 marks the canal's southwestern exodus into Deep Bay. Southwest of this second #2, boaters have access to the Deep Bay cove and anchorage described earlier. If you stay at least 200 yards off all the shorelines, you should not have any difficulty with shallow water.

### Three Bay Area    To enter Spencer, Rose, and Deep Bays directly from Pamlico Sound, come abeam of flashing daybeacon #2, west of Judith Island, by 100 yards to its westerly side. Soon after you pass #2, the entrance to Spencer Bay splits off to the northwest.

To follow Spencer Bay to Germantown, cruise 0.5 nautical mile north from #2 before turning sharply northwest, pointing to come abeam of unlighted daybeacon #2 by 10 yards to its southwesterly side. Be careful to avoid the long finger of shallow water extending northeast from Willow Point, clearly shown on chart 11548. Minimum depths of 7 feet can be expected between the two aids. To continue upstream, cruise past #2 on the same course for 200 yards. Then turn sharply north and set a new track to come abeam of and pass flashing daybeacon #3 by 50 yards to its easterly side.

You may continue cruising north to Germantown by passing all red markers to your starboard side and green daybeacons to port. North of unlighted daybeacon #9, you will sight the village's commercial fishing docks dead ahead. The shallow wooden bulkhead of Bayside Marina lies west of the commercial piers.

Those cruisers bent on exploring Rose Bay should follow a northeasterly course from a position abeam of flashing daybeacon #2 to a point 50 yards east of unlighted daybeacon #3.

North of #3, the next upstream aid to navigation, unlighted daybeacon #4, is hard to spot. The marker appears to be much farther from the eastern banks than chart 11548 leads you to believe. Come abeam of #4 to its *western* side. Very shoal water lies east of #4. Point to eventually come abeam of flashing daybeacon #5 to its eastern quarter.

Past #5, the main body of Rose Bay veers to the northwest. Hold scrupulously to the mid-width as you cruise upstream, pointing to eventually come

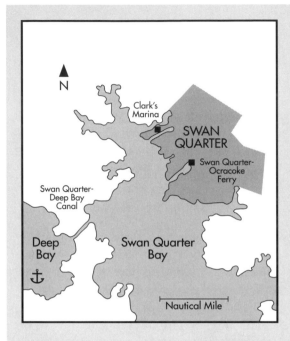

abeam of flashing daybeacon #6 to its easterly side. At #6, the waters turn again, this time to the east. There are no additional aids to navigation upstream of #6. Hold to the mid-width as you follow the narrowing waters to the east. This is the trickiest portion of the passage; depths of 4½ to 5 feet are possible. Drop anchor before the stream swings back to the northeast.

Deep Bay, the easternmost of the three bays, boasts two lighted aids to navigation. One trouble spot is not marked, however. When entering Deep Bay from the southerly waters of Rose Bay, take extra care to avoid the lengthy patch of shallow water extending northward from Judith Island. Pass flashing daybeacon #1, located south of Judith Marsh, by 50 yards to its southerly side. Set course to come abeam of flashing daybeacon #2 to its im-

mediate northerly side. From #2, the entrance to the Deep Bay–Swan Quarter canal is deep and easily identified.

To anchor on the cove southwest of #2, simply stay at least 200 yards off all the surrounding shores.

*West Bay*    As you approach West Bay from Pamlico Sound, set course to come abeam of flashing daybeacon #2WB by 25 yards to its southeasterly side. Continue on a southwesterly track, pointing to come abeam of flashing daybeacon #5 by 300 yards to its northwesterly side. Take extra care to avoid the shoal waters extending outward from the westernmost point of North Bay. Do not drift east of #5!

Once abeam of #5, swing to the south and follow a new course designed to bring unlighted daybeacon #6 abeam by at least 200 yards to its easterly side. Shallow water lies west of #6. Be sure to stay east of this aid. Between #5 and #6, you will pass flashing daybeacon #3 well west of your course line.

At unlighted daybeacon #6, the bay's easternmost arm will come abeam. Bypass this section. While the mouth between Western and Tump Points holds 8-foot depths, 4-foot readings are encountered southeast on the arm before the waters narrow enough for effective shelter.

From #6, cruising boaters have access to the two southern tiers of West Bay. The southeastern branch is known as West Thorofare Bay and the southwestern as Long Bay.

To enter West Thorofare Bay, set course from your position abeam of unlighted daybeacon #6 for flashing daybeacon #7WB. Pass #7WB to its westerly side and set a new course to come abeam of and pass flashing daybeacon #8WB well to its easterly quarter. Point to come abeam of flashing daybeacon #10WB by 25 yards to its easterly side.

Continue past #10WB on the same course for 300 yards before setting a new course to come abeam of flashing daybeacon #11WB to its westerly side.

To make use of the anchorage west of #11WB, depart the main channel 50 yards north of #11WB. Feel your way slowly west with your sounder. Drop the hook as soon as you've left the channel far enough behind to facilitate the passage of any commercial fishing vessels which happen by.

Cruisers following West Thorofare Bay to Thorofare Canal should pass unlighted daybeacon #13WB and flashing daybeacon #15WB to port. From #15WB, Thorofare Canal opens to the east and southeast. This useful link to Thorofare Bay, an auxiliary water of Core Sound, is described in chapter 7.

Long Bay boasts additional anchorage possibilities. To enter it from flashing daybeacon #7WB,

set course down the mid-width of Long Bay, passing flashing daybeacon #2 well to its southeasterly side. Watch out for the charted but unmarked patch of 3-foot shoals southwest of #7WB. Continue past the next upstream aid, flashing daybeacon #4, passing it well to its easterly side.

Some 10 yards past #4, bend your course sharply to the west and point toward flashing daybeacon #6, which marks the old Indian canal leading to Turnagain Bay. Past #4, depths of 8 to 10 feet can be expected. Approaching #6, depths fall off to 5 and 6 feet. Consider anchoring about halfway between #4 and #6.

Don't attempt to enter the Long Bay–Turnagain Bay canal unless your craft draws 2½ feet or less.

Continued passage southwest on the main body of Long Bay past #4 is not recommended. Unmarked shoals are pronounced, and chart 11548 correctly predicts a patch of 3-foot shallows on the stream's midline.

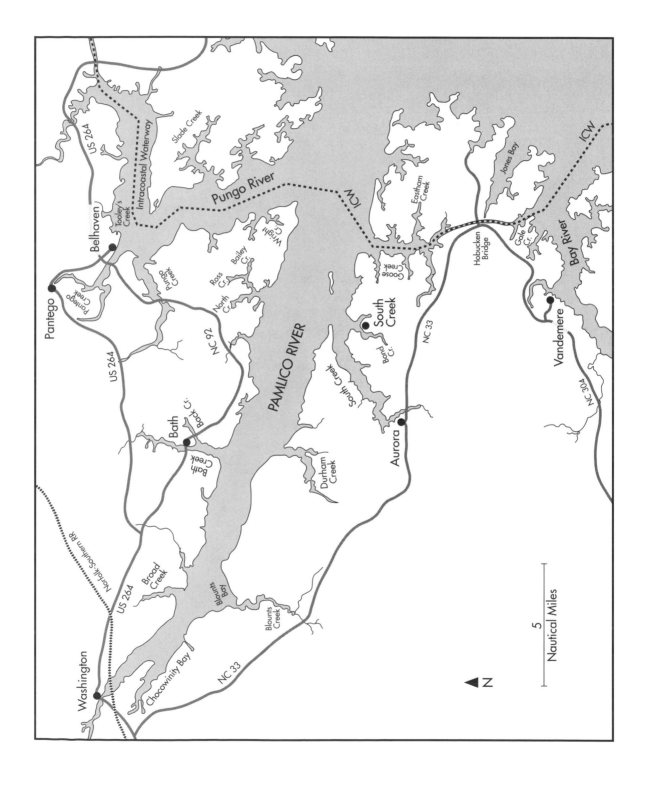

Nautical Miles

5

N

# The Pamlico River

The Pamlico and its sister river, the Neuse, empty into the southwestern corner of Pamlico Sound. The Pamlico is about 30 nautical miles in length from its mouth to its headwaters at the town of Washington, and it is 3.5 nautical miles across at its widest point. Because of its position with reference to northeast and southwest winds—the two predominant wind directions—the Pamlico is less subject to rough water than is the Neuse. This generally benevolent disposition renders the Pamlico one of North Carolina's finest cruising waters. Though wide swaths of the river's banks remain untouched, there are sufficient facilities for the cruising boater's needs. The Pamlico also boasts many interesting sidewaters useful for gunkholing and overnight anchorage.

During the colonial era, the Pamlico River was the "great highway in the wilderness," upon which the resources of the region's settlements were carried to the markets of the world. The ships returned laden with provisions and merchandise needed by the colonists. The Pamlico was truly the lifeline of North Carolina's earliest settlers.

---

### Charts

You will need three NOAA charts for navigation of the Pamlico:

**11548** covers the river's entrance from Pamlico Sound

**11553** covers the ICW route from its entrance into the headwaters of the Pungo River to its exit from the Hobucken Cut into the Bay River

**11554** details the Pamlico River from Indian Island to Washington and includes the South Creek channel to Aurora

# ICW AND PUNGO RIVER

The ICW enters the headwaters of the Pungo River, a major sidewater of the Pamlico, at the foot of the Alligator River–Pungo River Canal, where we left it in chapter 2. The Waterway flows down the Pungo, crosses the Pamlico River, and enters the Hobucken Cut, thereby connecting ICW cruisers to the Neuse River. The Pungo River offers several interesting sidewaters worthy of exploration, as well as a number of secluded overnight anchorages. The charming, sleepy coastal community of Belhaven, located on the Pungo, is one of the most popular overnight stops on the North Carolina ICW. Belhaven offers every facility for the cruising boater, including good dining and complete marine repairs.

## The Upper Pungo (Standard Mile 127.5)

The uppermost waters of the Pungo River, abandoned by the ICW, strike north and west from flashing daybeacon #23 a short jog west of the Alligator River–Pungo River Canal's southerly entrance. This body of water supports minimum 8-foot depths along its centerline and boasts at least two well-protected overnight havens. The shores are mostly in their natural state, with a wide buffer of marsh grass flanking much of the shoreline. Here and there, a few private homes peep out over the tranquil waters.

With fresh winds blowing from the east, north, or northeast, consider dropping anchor in the large, charted cove indenting the eastern banks north-northeast of flashing daybeacon #23. Chart 11553 correctly predicts depths of 8 feet running to within 150 yards of the eastern shores.

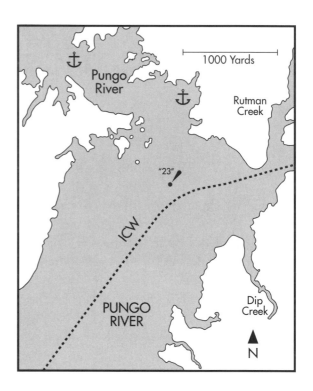

The banks are guarded by a deep pine wood. There is enough swinging room for all but the largest pleasure vessels.

In western or strong southern blows, follow the upper Pungo River as it rounds its first point and strikes to the northwest. One good spot to anchor under these conditions is off the stream's third east-side point, located east of charted Styron Creek. Depths run to 10 feet, and there is almost enough room for the *Trump Princess.*

## Scranton Creek (Standard Mile 130)

Scranton Creek, located on the Pungo's south-eastern shore (southeast of flashing daybeacon

#21), has a deep, unmarked channel that is flanked by shallower depths. Craft 34 feet and under that draw less than 5 feet should be able to explore and anchor on the creek, provided their skippers exercise proper caution. The shoreline is essentially undeveloped, but if you go upstream far enough, you will see many old pilings along the water's edge. These are evidence of a once-thriving lumber business, now long gone.

While the explorers among us may find many places to drop the hook, one of the best spots is abeam of the first small creek making into the southern banks. Though you must be careful to avoid the surrounding shallows, these waters promise depths of 6 feet or better. Swinging room is definitely a bit tight for vessels larger than 34 feet.

## Upper Dowry Creek
## (Standard Mile 131.5)

Upper Dowry Creek cuts into the Pungo's northern shore north of unlighted daybeacon #15. For many years, this stream has provided protected anchorage in a completely untouched atmosphere. Development is now going forward on the creek's western banks just inside the entrance. Part of this complex is an excellent marina with transient services. As part of the new construction, the stream's entrance channel has been marked with numerous unlighted daybeacons. With these fortunate aids now in place, any craft drawing 6 feet or less may choose to visit Upper Dowry Creek during daylight with little difficulty. Though the facilities are certainly welcome, you can still settle down for the night on the stream above the marina in about as beautiful a

spot as you are likely to find on the North Carolina coastline.

Upper Dowry Creek is being developed by Harbour Point Associates as a sumptuous residential and marine community. An integral part of this complex, Dowry Creek Marina operates a bevy of fixed wooden slips featuring all power and water connections. This facility suffered fairly extensive dock damage during Hurricane Fran, but most of the piers had been reconstructed by the time of this writing. You may not even notice any evidence of the great storm during your visit.

Depths at Dowry Creek Marina are 6 feet or better. Transients are eagerly accepted for overnight or temporary dockage. Gasoline and diesel fuel are readily available. A combination ship's and variety store overlooks the piers. Shoreside, visiting mariners will find new showers, a laundromat, and a swimming pool. Mechanical repairs can be arranged through private contractors operating out of nearby Belhaven. Future plans call for the construction of tennis courts and a restaurant, but the completion date for

**Dowry Creek Marina
(919) 943-2728**

Approach depth: 7–8 feet
Dockside depth: 6–8 feet
Accepts transients: yes
Fixed wooden piers: yes
Dockside power connections: 30 & 50 amps
Dockside water connections: yes
Showers: yes
Laundromat: yes
Gasoline: yes
Diesel fuel: yes
Mechanical repairs: independent contractors
Ship's & variety store: yes

these amenities was uncertain at the time of this writing. Dowry Creek provides a courtesy car for visitors who need to reprovision or visit one of the restaurants in Belhaven. Nestled in the beautiful confines of Upper Dowry Creek, this marina can lay claim to an incredible setting.

Good depths of 5 to 6 feet run several hundred yards upstream past the new marina docks. I am happy to report that the upstream portion of the creek remains untouched at this time. Swinging room is sufficient for boats as large as 45 feet, and there is super protection from all save southerly winds over 30 knots.

### Battalina and Tooleys Creeks (Standard Mile 135)

Two creeks break the Pungo's shoreline just north of Belhaven, west of flashing daybeacon #1.

The southernmost of the two, Tooleys Creek, offers protected overnight anchorage for craft that can stand some 5-foot depths. Exercise caution when entering Tooleys Creek or you could find yourself in 3 feet of water. The shoreline exhibits moderate residential development that is quite pleasing to the eye. Swinging room is more than adequate for a 40-footer.

Battalina Creek lies just north of Tooleys Creek. An indifferently marked channel tracks its way upstream to a full-service boatyard. The Smith family, proprietors of Belhaven's River Forest Manor (see below), own this repair facility, which was renamed Belhaven Shipyard (800-346-2151) several years ago. Full mechanical repairs for both gasoline and diesel engines are offered, and boats can be hauled via the yard's 40-ton travel-lift. For cruisers plying the Waterway, Belhaven Shipyard specializes in

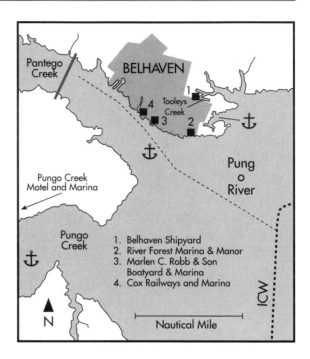

quick in-and-out repairs to get you on your way. The management suggests that patrons first call at River Forest Manor. One of the friendly staff will then pilot your boat to the yard, or you can follow one of the marina's boats into the creek. The channel on Battalina Creek is quite tricky and not adequately outlined. This passage certainly calls for local knowledge.

### Belhaven (Standard Mile 135.5)

Belhaven is a charming, sleepy riverside village that boasts the greatest collection of marina facilities directly on the North Carolina portion of the ICW north of Oriental. The Belhaven waterfront guards the northeastern shore of Pantego Creek west-northwest of flashing daybeacon #10. The entrance channel is well marked and holds at least 10 feet of water. The harbor is partially protected by an artificial wooden breakwater. The entrance between the two arms of the breakwater is marked by flashing daybeacons #5 and #6.

Hurricane Fran passed well west of Belhaven, but due to wind and storm surge, the town experienced quite a flood. The resilient citizens already have repairs well under way and, with luck, little evidence of the great storm should be visible by the second quarter of 1997. Both local marinas are near to restoring full services.

Belhaven, whose name means "beautiful harbor," was founded upon the resources of its waters and woods. Originally called Jacks Neck, the town began to grow about 1900, when railroad magnate John A. Wilkinson founded a lumber business. Crabbing also became a large local enterprise. The railroad and the Pamlico River have provided the means of transportation necessary to keep the wheels of commerce turning for this community. The river and the woods still offer excellent opportunities for hunting and fishing.

Belhaven has some charming homes, most in the traditional North Carolina down-east style. A stroll down the quiet, wooded lanes—particularly Water Street, adjacent to both marinas—is definitely recommended. This quiet river town has changed little in the past 50 years.

One local attraction of note is the Belhaven Memorial Museum, housed on the second floor of the town hall. Though it is necessary to walk several blocks from either of the town's marinas to visit the museum, it is well worth the trouble. This remarkable exhibit houses the antique and curiosity collection of Eva Blount Way, donated to the town in 1965. Mrs. Blount began collecting oddities as a way of raising money for the

American Red Cross. Originally, she opened her house to visitors. Now, the collection is better housed in the town hall. According to the museum pamphlet, visitors can view "30,000 buttons, preserved snakes, an eight legged pig, whale bones, kitchen and farm artifacts, petrified walrus tusks millions of years old, ten-cent paper money, a watch fob made from the first Atlantic cable, a 200-year-old pitcher, dressed fleas, and many, many more items too numerous to mention."

## Belhaven Marinas

Visiting cruisers will spy Belhaven's first facility to the northeast soon after passing through the Pantego Creek breakwater (which is also undergoing repairs following Hurricane Fran). River Forest Marina and Manor has been welcoming wandering boaters for better than 60 years. The marina has a marked entrance channel with 8 to 10 feet of water. The fixed wooden slips, newly decked after the hurricane, feature water connections. At the time of this writing, the docks were without power due to the storm, but a new system—including some 100-amp hookups—should be in place by the time this account finds its way into your hands. A stone breakwater flanking the slips to the south and southeast provides some protection when winds are blowing from this quarter. Depths alongside range from 10 feet on the outer berths to 5½ feet on the innermost slips. A ship's and variety store just behind the docks can usually handle basic supply needs. Mechanical repairs can be arranged on-site or at nearby Belhaven Shipyard. Gasoline, diesel fuel, and waste pump-out services are readily available. Cruising visitors can

*River Forest Manor*

**River Forest Marina and Manor**
**(919) 943-2151 or (800) 346-2151**

Approach depth: 8–10 feet
Dockside depth: 5½–8 feet
Accepts transients: yes
Fixed wooden piers: yes
Dockside power connections: 30, 50, & 100 amps
Dockside water connections: yes
Showers: yes
Laundromat: yes
Waste pump-out: yes
Gasoline: yes
Diesel fuel: yes
Mechanical repairs: yes
Below-waterline repairs: Belhaven Shipyard
Ship's & variety store: yes
Restaurant: on-site

take advantage of River Forest's tennis courts, hot tub, and swimming pool. They are also given free use of electric golf carts and bicycles to visit town. A supermarket, a drugstore, an ABC store, and several other businesses are easily within golf-cart range.

River Forest is, as you would expect, quite popular. Advance dockage and/or lodging reservations are highly recommended during the spring, summer, and fall months.

River Forest Marina is the "backyard" of River Forest Manor, one of the most famous restaurants and inns on the ICW. A beautiful combination of the plantation and Victorian eras, the house was built in 1899 by John Wilkinson for his bride. Axson Smith, Sr., bought the mansion in 1933 and converted it to an inn. His spectacular nightly buffets soon became known far and wide. The Smith family still runs this showplace with warm hospitality. A large cocktail lounge with an eye-pleasing view of the water has been added. In addition to the sportsmen and boaters who have long enjoyed the manor, the Smiths have been host to such notables as Theodore and Franklin Roosevelt, Tallulah Bankhead, Harvey Firestone, James Cagney, and Roy Clark.

As you move northwest, Belhaven's second facility is located northeast of unlighted daybeacon #9. Marlen C. Robb & Son Boatyard & Marina offers extensive transient dockage at fixed wooden piers with water and 30- and 50-amp power connections. Depths at the piers run from 6½ to 9 feet. The mostly enclosed dockage basin is well protected from all but strong southwesterly blows. The harbor is beautifully landscaped, and the marina features spotless bathrooms and showers and an on-site laundromat. An extensive ship's store is on the premises, and full mechanical repairs for both gasoline and diesel engines are available. There is also a prop repair shop on-site. Haul-outs and below-waterline repairs are quickly accommodated via the marina's 75-ton travel-lift. Gasoline and diesel fuel can be purchased dockside, and waste pump-out service is available. Like River Forest, Robb Marina provides electric golf carts for trips to nearby supermarkets and other retail firms and tours of downtown Belhaven. A one-block walk leads famished cruisers to The Helmsman Restaurant (919-943-3810), which serves first-rate seafood.

---

**Marlen C. Robb & Son**
**Boatyard & Marina**
**(919) 943-2110**

Approach depth: 8–10 feet
Dockside depth: 6½–9 feet
Accepts transients: yes
Fixed wooden piers: yes
Dockside power connections: 30 & 50 amps
Dockside water connections: yes
Showers: yes
Laundromat: yes
Waste pump-out: yes
Gasoline: yes
Diesel fuel: yes
Mechanical repairs: yes
Below waterline repairs: yes
Ship's store: yes
Restaurants: several nearby

---

Cox Railways & Marina (919-943-6489) lies immediately northwest of Robb Marina. This yard can handle all mechanical and below-the-waterline haul-out repairs. Haul-outs are by way of two marine railways rated at 50 and 100 tons.

A fourth facility, Pantego Creek Marina, will appear to starboard just short of the Pantego Creek Bridge. Currently, this marina caters exclusively to the local boat trade.

Some boaters choose to anchor in Pantego Creek rather than make use of the marina facilities. The waters southwest of unlighted daybeacon #8 make a good spot. Depths run 8 to 10 feet, but protection is not adequate for nasty weather. Even in fair weather, the "rock-'n'-roll" on these waters can be annoying. It's a long dinghy trip ashore from this anchorage.

## Pungo Creek and Hub's Rec Marina (Standard Mile 136)

A large sidewater known as Pungo Creek pierces the Pungo River's western banks well west-northwest of the ICW's flashing daybeacon #8. The creek's mouth is a short distance south of Pantego Creek and Belhaven Harbor. This stream is wide, well marked, and uniformly deep, with minimum soundings of 7 feet in the channel.

Pungo Creek's shoreline is sparsely developed and quite attractive. Because of its wide, well-marked entrance and uniform depth, Pungo Creek is an excellent side trip or overnight anchorage for any craft drawing less than 6 feet. Good depths run to within 200 yards of shore on the stream's most protected section, located west of flashing daybeacon #3 off Windmill Point. Pick a spot adjoining the lee shore and settle down for the evening. The creek's large size does not render particularly good protection in a heavy blow.

For several years now, the docks and motel building of Hub's Rec Marina have flanked Pungo Creek's shoreline west of Windmill Point. Early in 1997, it appeared as if this dated complex was going to pass to new owners and a comprehensive refurbishment was to be undertaken. Unfortunately, that deal fell through, and cruisers can now expect fewer services than might have been in the offing.

The motel at this location is closed and will probably remain so for the foreseeable future.

The marina is open, but the dockmaster is only a part-time employee. You can usually find Wes on the grounds most weekday evenings and on weekends. Otherwise, the docks are unattended. Transients are accepted for overnight stays, and quite a number of slips are set aside for this purpose. It would be wise to call well ahead of time and make advance arrangements rather than arriving during a period when the dockmaster is absent.

Those who do find overnight berths at Hub's Rec Marina will coil their lines at fixed wooden piers with some water and 15-amp power hookups. Expanded water service and 30-amp power hookups are planned for the future. Soundings alongside run 5 to 6 feet, and there is at least 6 feet of approach depth. Showers are available shoreside, as is a nice screened-in picnic porch with a fine view of the creek. Visiting mariners are welcome to use the on-site swimming pool during the summer months.

Be sure to bring your own galley supplies. There is no restaurant within walking distance, and taxi service is not available to ferry visitors to nearby Belhaven. Only those up for a

true long-distance hike should attempt this trip by foot.

Hub's Rec Marina is a well-placed facility with good shelter and eye-pleasing surroundings. It is to be hoped that some upgrading and modernization will take place during the next several years. As it now stands, this facility can be recommended only to skippers who are willing to secure a berth through advance preparations.

## Slade Creek (Standard Mile 140)

The broad mouth of Slade Creek yawns its way into the Pungo River southeast of unlighted daybeacon #5. This stream is a controversial sidewater. Another cruising guide used to recommend it as a good overnight anchorage. However, during on-site research, I tried to enter the creek from three separate angles, only to encounter 3- and 4-foot depths each time. Clearly, the charted channel has suffered extensive shoaling along its flanks. Based on this experience, Slade Creek is not recommended for cruising-size vessels.

## Jordan Creek (Standard Mile 140)

Lying well to the west-northwest of flashing daybeacon #4 along the Pungo's westerly banks, Jordan Creek is home to the friendly River Rat Yacht Club. This club's facilities line the southerly banks a short distance west of the stream's easterly mouth. Transients who are members of accredited yacht clubs and who are piloting craft up to 40 feet in length can sometimes secure overnight berths at the club's fixed wooden piers. Water and 20- and 30-amp power connections are available, as are shoreside showers and a club-

---

**Hub's Rec Marina
(919) 964-6151**

Approach depth: 6 feet
Dockside depth: 5-6 feet
Accepts transients: yes (dockmaster not
   always in attendance)
Fixed wooden piers: yes
Dockside power connections: 15
   amp ( 30 amp planned in future)
Dockside water connections: limited
   (slated for future expansion)
Showers: yes

house. Minimum dockside depths run 6 to 7 feet. Advance arrangements are recommended. Give the club a call at 919-964-6100.

Jordan Creek features a well-marked channel maintained by the North Carolina Wildlife Service. Surprisingly enough, the various aids to navigation are not charted. This state of affairs stretches back more than 10 years. Minimum 6-foot depths can be carried in the cut as far as the club's docks.

Boaters intent on spending a night at anchor might also consider pitching the hook west of the club's docks short of the charted split in Jordan Creek. Protection is excellent for all but gale-force easterlies.

### Wright Creek (Standard Mile 142)

The marked entrance to Wright Creek makes into the Pungo's western shoreline southwest of flashing daybeacon #3. Minimum depths of 7 feet can be carried on the entrance cut and well into the stream's interior sections. Extensive but not unattractive residential development overlooks the shoreline.

As a side trip, Wright Creek is recommended for almost any cruising craft drawing less than 6 feet. As an overnight anchorage, however, the creek is rather narrow, and there is extensive local boating activity. Boats larger than 30 feet will probably not find enough room for a comfortable stay. If you do manage to find a spot to drop the hook, the surrounding shores provide superior protection from all winds.

## ICW AND PUNGO RIVER NAVIGATION

This chapter rejoins the ICW at the fixed, high-rise Wilkerson Bridge, which spans the southern foot of the Alligator River–Pungo River Canal. The span has a vertical clearance of 64 feet (at best).

West of the bridge, a marked, improved channel leads through adjoining shallows into the headwaters of the Pungo River. You will observe that daybeacon colors are suddenly reversed. The river channel takes precedence, and as you are now going downriver, take all red markers to your port side and green markers to starboard. This color scheme holds down the length of the Pungo River and across the Pamlico, until markers resume their normal ICW configuration at the northerly entrance of the Goose Creek–Hobucken Cut.

West of flashing daybeacon #25, the ICW passes into the deeper waters of the Pungo. Point to come abeam of unlighted daybeacon #24 to its northerly side. North of #24, cruisers might choose to explore or anchor on the upper portion of the Pungo River, bypassed by the ICW.

*The Upper Pungo*  Continue cruising west on the Waterway until you are about halfway between unlighted daybeacon #24 and flashing daybeacon #23. Then leave the ICW by swinging sharply north-northwest, pointing for the stream's broad entrance channel. Soon, the first east-side cove will come abeam to starboard. Drop anchor at least 150 yards offshore for best depths.

To continue upstream on the main track, simply keep within shouting distance of the midline and you should find minimum 8-foot depths to the charted limits of the stream. Eventually, the upper Pungo leaves chart 11553. Cruising past this point is not recommended without specific local knowledge.

**On the Pungo**   Southbound cruisers on the ICW should proceed from flashing daybeacon #23 down a well-marked channel to flashing daybeacon #21. Be sure to come abeam of and pass #21 to its southeasterly side, as shoal water is found north, west, and northwest of this marker. Scranton Creek, another sidewater possibility, beckons south-southeast of #21.

**Scranton Creek**   Unmarked shoals extend out from Scranton Creek's shores for quite some distance. Take your time and watch the sounder when cruising this body of water.

Should you decide to enter, be sure to avoid the lengthy patch of shallows extending out from Broad Creek Point. Soon after entering the creek, watch out for a sharp point of land on the northern shore, where water less than 5 feet deep extends well out into the stream. After passing this trouble spot, hold to the mid-width and you can proceed upstream amidst minimum depths of 6 feet. Eventually, you will observe a small bridge which should be approached only if you draw 3 feet or less. Soundings decline significantly near the span.

**On the Pungo**   Back on the Pungo, the ICW extends generally southwest down a well-marked and consistently deep channel. Don't be tempted by Smith Creek, located south of flashing daybeacon #18. In spite of what chart 11553 would lead you to believe, you will quickly encounter 3- to 4-foot depths if you attempt to enter.

Downriver, no navigational problems or sidewater possibilities present themselves until unlighted daybeacon #15. At #15, boaters may choose to enter the attractive Upper Dowry Creek.

**Upper Dowry Creek**   As mentioned earlier in this chapter, successful entry into Upper Dowry Creek is now facilitated by a series of privately maintained, unlighted, and mostly uncharted daybeacons outlining the entrance channel. To make your entry into the creek, depart the ICW at unlighted daybeacon #15. Set a careful compass course to avoid the broad shelf of shallows extending southeast from the stream's western entrance point.

Use your binoculars to pick out the privately maintained markers, then follow them into the creek. Immediately after swinging north and passing into the main body of Upper Dowry Creek, you will see the docks of Dowry Creek Marina to port.

Good depths continue along the stream's mid-width as far upstream as the first charted offshoot on the western banks. Past this point, soundings deteriorate to 5 feet and eventually less.

**On the Pungo**   From #15, the ICW channel remains broad and easy to follow down the Pungo River to unlighted daybeacon #11. At #11, boaters may choose to enter the protected but shallow Tooleys Creek.

**Tooleys Creek**   The entrance to Tooleys Creek lies almost due west of flashing daybeacon #1, itself well northwest of the ICW's unlighted daybeacon #11. Don't try to enter Battalina Creek, a bit farther to the north. Battalina Creek is home to Belhaven Shipyard. It is highly advisable to have one of the personnel at River Forest Manor pilot your craft or at least lead you through the yard's entrance channel.

To enter Tooleys Creek, come abeam of #1 by 30 to 50 yards to its northerly side. Shallow water lies southwest of #1. Curl around to the west and point for the middle of the stream's entrance. The initial depths of 6 feet drop off to 5 feet as you cruise upstream. Don't try to follow the creek as it swings to the south. Soundings decline to 3 feet or even less past this errant turn.

**On the Pungo**   It is a short run from unlighted daybeacon #11 to flashing daybeacon #10. Come abeam of #10 well to its northerly side to avoid the charted obstruction east of #10. From #10, boaters have access to the village of Belhaven, one of the most popular overnight stops on the ICW.

**Belhaven Harbor**   To enter Pantego Creek and Belhaven Harbor, leave the ICW at flashing daybeacon #10. Pass between flashing daybeacon #1 and unlighted daybeacon #2, between unlighted daybeacons #3 and #4, and finally between flashing daybeacons #5 and #6, which mark the entrance in the wooden breakwater that protects the harbor. Once inside the breakwater, you will be cruising on the waters of Pantego Creek. Almost immediately after passing the breakwater, you will observe the piers and marked entrance channel of River Forest Manor to the northeast.

Don't be too casual about navigating Pantego Creek. There is shoal water abutting the northeastern shore and a few other shallow spots. Pass all red markers to your starboard side and green beacons to port. Watch out for the 3-foot shallows southwest and northwest of unlighted daybeacons #9 and #11. You will spot Robb Marina's dockage basin northeast of #9, followed closely by Cox Railways & Marina.

**Pungo Creek**   The eastern mouth of Pungo Creek is only a short jog downriver from Pantego Creek. Use chart 11553 when entering the creek, but switch to chart 11554 for navigating the waters west of Windmill Point. Pass to the south of unlighted daybeacon #2 and to the north of flashing daybeacon #3 to avoid the shallow waters shelving out from Persimmon Tree and Windmill Points. Past #3, hold to the creek's central waters for minimum depths of 7 feet until you reach the low-level, fixed Pungo Creek Bridge. This small span blocks passage farther upstream for all but small craft.

**On the Pungo**   South of Pungo and Pantego Creeks, the ICW remains its easily followed self to a point halfway between unlighted daybeacon #5 and flashing daybeacon #4. Along the way, be sure to pass well east of flashing daybeacon #7. A shoal is building toward this marker from the west. North of #4, it is theoretically possible to enter Slade Creek on the river's eastern shore or Jordan Creek on the western shore. Slade Creek, however, has a shoaly entrance and should only be attempted by very small craft

Fortescue Creek, east of the Pungo's flashing daybeacon #3, is too shallow for cruising-size vessels. Wright Creek, on the western shore, makes for an interesting side trip.

**Jordan Creek**   Jordan Creek is best approached from a position well south of flashing daybeacon #4. Set a careful course for the southerly flank of the creek's mouth. As you approach the entrance, keep a sharp watch for three pairs of green and red markers which will lead you on a northwesterly course into the stream's interior reaches.

Once past the last set of aids, swing to the west and follow the creek's mid-width upstream. Soon, the docks of River Rat Yacht Club will come abeam to the south. Cruisers looking to anchor on Jordan Creek can continue a short distance farther to the west and drop the hook short of the stream's charted split.

***Wright Creek***   Enter Wright Creek by cruising southwest from flashing daybeacon #3 to the first marker on the improved Wright Creek entrance channel, flashing daybeacon #2. Just as you would expect, pass all subsequent red aids to your starboard side and all green markers to port. At flashing daybeacon #5, Wright Creek splits. Don't take the southern fork; it is too shallow for all but the smallest craft.

Good depths continue on the principal northerly arm of Wright Creek to unlighted daybeacon #10. A commercial seafood dock flanks the creek's southeasterly banks just past #10. The diplomats among us may be able to purchase fresh seafood here from time to time.

***On the Pungo***   South of flashing daybeacon #3, southbound ICW cruisers should set course for the 29-foot flashing daybeacon #PR, which marks the intersection of the Waterway and the Pamlico River. It is a run of 3.1 nautical miles between #3 and #PR. Come abeam of #PR to its easterly side. A long shoal is building southeast from Wades Point toward this marker.

A continuing account of the ICW can be found in the "ICW to the Neuse River" section later in this chapter.

## UP THE PAMLICO

The upper portion of the Pamlico River east of the Pungo River intersection offers excellent facilities and several overnight anchorages. The towns of Bath and Washington are interesting ports of call. If you have not visited these communities, they are well worth a deviation from your trek down the Waterway.

### Four Creek Area

As you enter the Pamlico River from Pamlico Sound east of the Pamlico River–Pungo River intersection, the first sidewater of any consequence is located on the southern shore between Pamlico and Fulford Points. This complex body of water appears on charts 11553 and 11548 as a four-fingered hand. It is comprised of Oyster Creek, James Creek, Middle Prong, and Clark Creek. The entrance is marked, but the channel is still not particularly reliable. There seems to have been quite a bit of shoaling not noted on the latest edition of chart 11553. The trouble spots on Middle Prong, probably the most reliable of the four creeks with respect to depth, are not marked. While it is theoretically possible to hold depths of 6 feet or better into Middle Prong, there are vast tracts of unmarked 3- and 4-foot shoals to avoid. The shoreline is essentially in its natural state, though there appears to be some sort of commercial fishing facility on shallow Oyster Creek.

Boaters cruising in all but shallow-draft outboard-powered vessels would do well to bypass this four-creek body of water. However, for those with wanderlust in their hearts, a navigational sketch of these waters is presented later in this chapter. Just remember, when you hear that sad sound of your keel scraping in the mud, I warned you.

## South Creek

Magnificently undeveloped Indian Island sits south of the Pamlico River's flashing daybeacon #3. A broad and deep channel runs westward to the south of this isle into one of the most interesting sidewaters on the Pamlico River, South Creek. This long and complex stream offers many overnight anchorages, as well as the opportunity to visit one of coastal North Carolina's most isolated communities. There is some residential development along the shore, but most of the creek's banks are still in their natural state.

Bond Creek strikes south from South Creek's easterly entrance and boasts a marked channel leading to the village of South Creek. This tiny community lines the southeasterly banks of Bond Creek southwest of unlighted daybeacon #3. Minimum depths on the cut run about 6 feet, though care must be exercised to avoid the shoals flanking either side of the channel.

The village of South Creek was originally named Oregon in honor of the first steamship to enter the mouth of the creek. Not long after its voyage on South Creek, the *Oregon* became a floating store, taking produce of the Pamlico region to Norfolk, Virginia, and returning with merchandise for this riverside community. Today, South Creek is a residential village consisting of a few private homes. There are no facilities catering to cruising craft.

It is quite possible to anchor in 6 to 7 feet of water just off the village waterfront southwest of unlighted daybeacon #3. Protection is good from all but strong northern and northeastern winds. There is enough room for vessels as large as 38 feet.

As you move up South Creek toward Aurora, there are dozens of places to drop the hook in safety. Typical depths are 7 feet or better. Usually, shallows extend out 200 yards from the shoreline, so you should not approach the banks too closely. Don't anchor right on the channel either, as South Creek supports some commercial barge traffic. Otherwise, simply select a spot that is to your liking and settle down for an on-the-water evening you will not soon forget.

South and west of unlighted daybeacon #12, depths on South Creek deteriorate, but the marked channel continues to the village of Aurora. Even in the channel, soundings rise to 5 feet or slightly less.

South of unlighted daybeacon #25, you will observe the sparse Aurora waterfront along the western banks. The downtown section of Aurora, adjacent to the water, has cleaned up its act a bit during the past year or two, but it still has a rather depressed look. There is one interesting attraction within walking distance of the city "marina." The Aurora Fossil Museum (919-322-4238) guards the northern side of Main Street a few blocks west of the waterfront. Here, visitors can gaze at an astounding collection of fossilized remains gathered from the surrounding region. Seldom will cruising boaters find a more out-of-the-way attraction.

Aurora also offers a Piggly Wiggly supermarket. It's a hike of about 0.25 to 0.5 mile from the waterfront. Ask any local for directions.

The Aurora city marina, located along South Creek's westerly banks south of unlighted daybeacon #25, was opened with high hopes 15 years ago. Unfortunately, this facility has not met with success. The few low-level fixed wooden piers were largely destroyed by Hurricanes

Bertha and Fran. Reconstruction dates are uncertain. In the meantime, it would probably be best to anchor off along the centerline of South Creek abeam of the marina (identifiable by the public launching ramp) and dinghy ashore. All in all, as it now stands, Aurora is a stop only for the most adventurous boaters who enjoy truly off-the-beaten-path ports of call.

### Aurora History

This village was originally called Betty's Town but was renamed by its founder, the Reverend W. H. Cunningham. Aurora, whose name means "new light in the East," was for a time the potato capital of the state, if not the nation. A popular tale is told about the planter who asked to be excused from jury duty because he had planted 1,000 acres in potatoes and it was digging time. "Excused," said the judge. "Anybody who'll plant 1,000 acres in potatoes is too crazy to serve on a jury anyway." They still plant a lot of potatoes around Aurora, but corn, soybeans, and tobacco have also become important crops.

Dr. John Bonner tells of another citizen of Aurora, Michael Megear Gray, a New Jersey emigrant who came to South Creek on the steamboat *Oregon* and remained. Gray invented the steel-jacketed bullet. An ardent Confederate, his job was to sink the navigation buoys set out by the Yankees. Lead bullets wouldn't penetrate the metal of the buoys, so he encased his projectiles in steel and sank the buoys easily by rifle fire from shore.

Just prior to and during the Civil War, Aurora was populated by free Negroes, fugitive slaves, and a few Indians. This community was later broken up.

### East Fork

North-northwest of flashing daybeacon #3, a series of creeks makes into the Pamlico's northern banks. Chief among these streams is East Fork, which offers overnight anchorage for vessels under 40 feet in length that draw no more than 4 feet. Depths in the largely unmarked channel run 6 feet or better, but substantial shallows abut both shorelines and extend for quite some distance into the main body of the creek. Extra care and a careful watch on the sounder are required.

Northeast of unlighted daybeacon #4, visiting cruisers can throw out the hook on East Fork's mid-width in 6 to 6½ feet of water with good protection from all but strong northeastern and southwestern blows. There are a few houses along the shore, but most of the banks are delightfully untouched.

Cruising craft that can stand some 4½- to 5-foot depths might consider entering North Creek north of unlighted daybeacon #4. This is a lovely body of water with excellent protection from all but strong southerly breezes. There is enough swinging room for a 40-footer, but be sure your craft draws 4 feet or preferably less before beginning an exploration of North Creek.

### Durham Creek

Durham Creek cuts a broad swath in the Pamlico's southern shoreline southeast of flashing daybeacon #5. This well-favored stream is enchanting, isolated, and protected from foul weather. There is a house on Garrison Point; otherwise, the shoreline is untouched. Though entrance depths run 7 feet or better, there is plenty of shallow water to avoid. The creek has one aid to navigation, but some additional markers would greatly facilitate safe entry.

Nevertheless, captains whose craft draw 4½ feet or less may well consider entering Durham Creek for one of the Pamlico's loveliest and best-sheltered overnight anchorages. The creek is buffered from all but strong northerly winds. I suggest anchoring between the two points of land south of charted Garrison Point; one is to the east and the other to the west. Once the hook is down, break out the dinghy and go exploring.

Garrison Point, which lines the easterly flank of Durham Creek's entrance, is believed by some authorities to have been the site of Fort Reading, built before 1711. It is quite possible that the point's name was derived from its association with the fort.

## Bath

Bath, the state's oldest incorporated community, is an enchanting, lovely village that sits quiet and serene on the eastern shores of Bath Creek. This fortunate stream makes into the Pamlico River north-northeast of flashing daybeacon #5.

Bath is steeped in history, lovingly cared for, and well preserved. The village lies almost entirely within the boundaries laid out by John Lawson in the late 17th century. It is a memorial to the courage and diligence of our ancestors.

Visiting cruisers are welcome to use the state dock lining Bath Creek's eastern banks just short of Bath Creek Bridge, located north of flashing daybeacon #4. These piers, rebuilt in 1994, are much sturdier than their predecessors. In fact, Hurricanes Fran and Bertha, which caused widespread dock destruction elsewhere on the Pamlico

River, did not disturb these piers whatsoever. Depths alongside run about 6 feet near the outer portion of the state dock, 5 to 5½ feet on the middle section, and 4 feet nearer to shore. With this new state-sponsored facility, Bath can now lay claim to some of the best public dockage on the Pamlico River.

Closer to Bath Creek Bridge, also on the eastern shore, Bath Harbor Marina gazes out over the waters of Bath Creek. This facility has recently been purchased. The new owners plan to refurbish the facility and set aside two slips for transients. Dockage is provided at fixed wooden piers with water, 30-amp, and some 50-amp connections. Depths alongside range from 6 feet at the outermost slips to 4½ and 5 feet nearer to shore. Shoreside showers are available. The new management will probably be able to help with transportation to the nearby restaurant and grocery store (see below).

> **Bath Harbor Marina**
> **(919) 923-5711**
>
> Approach depth: 6-7 feet
> Dockside depth: 6 feet at outer slips,
>     4½-5 feet at inner slips
> Accepts transients: 2 slips available for visitors
> Fixed wooden piers: yes
> Dockside power connections: 30 amps & some
>     50 amps
> Dockside water connections: yes
> Showers: yes
> Restaurant: transportation usually available

If your craft can clear the charted 13-foot fixed bridge, you may cruise 0.1 nautical mile upstream from Bath Creek Bridge in depths of 6 feet as long as you hold to the creek's mid-width. If you are seeking a secluded anchorage, this

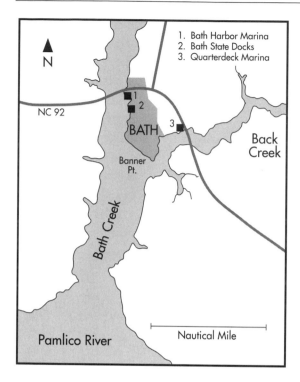

1. Bath Harbor Marina
2. Bath State Docks
3. Quarterdeck Marina

upstream portion of the creek is an excellent bet.

## Bath Attractions

The Historic Bath Commission (919-923-3971) has restored three of the town's many old houses, including the Palmer-Marsh House, one of the oldest surviving homes in North Carolina. Within the Bonner House, visitors can view an interesting display dedicated to Bath's historic renovation efforts. The North Carolina Department of Cultural Resources offers guided tours of these splendidly renovated structures.

It is a short and pleasant walk from the state docks to the Historic Bath Visitor's Center. Simply walk up the grassy plot behind the docks to Water Street and turn left. Two blocks will bring you to Carteret Street (N.C. 92), the main road through Bath. Turn right. Two more blocks will bring you to the visitor's center, housed in a brick building to the right of the main road. A modest fee will enable you to view a movie portraying Bath's colorful history and take a guided tour of all three restored homes.

After you have completed your tour, make sure to visit St. Thomas Church, the oldest church building in continuous use in the state. The church itself was organized in 1701, but the present building was constructed between 1734 and 1759. It is generally open on weekdays and is a short walk from the last stop on the guided tour. Be sure to study the silver candelabra on the altar, which dates back to the time of King George III. The church bell was a gift from Queen Anne around 1732.

Bath boasts a restaurant and a small grocery store. Both Old Towne Country Kitchen (919-923-1840) and Brooks Grocery Store (919-923-4361) overlook the northern flank of Carteret Street approximately 0.25 mile east of the Historic Bath Visitor's Center. This location is very convenient to anchorage on Back Creek (see below) but is a bit of a walk from the state dock and Bath Harbor Marina on Bath Creek. Old Towne is open for breakfast and lunch seven days a week and for the evening meal every night except Sunday.

## Bath History

Most books say that Bath was named for the English town of the same name. However, some historians suggest it was more likely named for Lord Proprietor John Granville, the earl of Bath. The town's primary founder, John Lawson, was commissioned by the Lords Proprietors to make a survey of the Carolina interior and to map the province. Lawson, in addition to being an explorer, surveyor, and mapmaker, was a natural scientist and the region's first historian. There is today in the British Museum an exhibit of carefully pressed leaves of 30 species of trees labeled "Lawson's Virginia Trees."

Lawson had ambitions for Bath as a major port and center of culture and politics. Deeply concerned about relations between settlers and Indians, he said the Indians "met with enemies when we came among them." It is ironic that he lost his life to a band of Native Americans while exploring the Neuse River in 1711.

At dawn on September 22, 1711, Tuscarora warriors and members of other tribes attacked the settlers along the Pamlico River, murdering men, women, and children and putting houses and fields to the torch. Peace did not fully return to the region until a treaty was signed with the Tuscaroras four years later. Bath survived the onslaught, but its population was greatly reduced.

Edward Teach, better known as Blackbeard,

*Bath State Docks (before reconstruction)*

is said to have married a local girl and briefly settled in the little harbor town about 1716. There have always been legends that Blackbeard struck bargains in Bath with Royal Governor Charles Eden. The pirate did obtain a Royal pardon, and it was the violation of that pardon that led to his death at the hands of Lieutenant Robert Maynard at Ocracoke in 1718.

Thanks to its natural harbor and rich surrounding bottom lands, Bath prospered in the early 18th century. Its inhabitants included men of culture, education, and wealth. The North Carolina Colonial Assembly met in Bath in 1743, and the town was almost made the capital of the state.

The Reverend George Whitfield, the Methodist revivalist who personified the Great Awakening in the colonies, visited Bath four times between 1747 and 1762. Bath enjoyed the usual merrymaking and festivities expected in a seat of government and a prospering seaport; Whitfield preached vehemently against the sins of the town, to no avail. On his fourth visit, the church refused to allow him to preach. In retaliation for this final insult, the reverend cursed the town. Bath, said Whitfield, would not prosper and would never be more than a village.

Whether because of the curse or other circumstances, Bath has remained very much a village. Internal rebellion, a religious uprising, the Tuscarora massacre followed by four years of intermittent warfare, a hurricane that struck the town with devastating ferocity in 1769, and an epidemic of yellow fever all served to halt Bath's progress.

## Bath Legend

An interesting tale concerns a set of mysterious hoofprints located near the outskirts of Bath not far from the road to Washington. The story goes that during the riotous frontier days, there was a gentleman farmer by the name of Elliot who, with his compatriots, was given to wagering and horse racing on the Sabbath. One Sunday morning, Elliot was heard to order his horse to take him to victory or take him to hell. The horse suddenly veered from the path, dug in his hooves, and hurled his master against a tree, causing his immediate death from a broken neck.

For almost 200 years, hoofprint-like impressions have remained at that spot in spite of every effort to erase or change them. It is said that birds and chickens will not eat any seed that falls within the hoofprints. The prints returned, distinct and uniform, even after pigs occupied the area. No satisfactory scientific explanation has yet been offered.

## Back Creek

Back Creek splits off from Bath Creek at Bonners Point, east of unlighted daybeacon #3. You may expect to hold 6-foot depths on Back Creek if you stay to the mid-width. The waters of Back Creek make a good overnight anchorage. When the hook is safely down, you can dinghy ashore to Quarterdeck Marina (see below) and, after obtaining permission from the ship's store, tie to the small pier here. It's then only a short step to both Old Towne Country Kitchen and Brooks Grocery Store.

Quarterdeck Marina and Ship's Store (919-923-2361) maintains a pier along Back Creek's northern banks just west of the charted, low-level fixed bridge. A gas dock is available, though no diesel fuel is sold. Though low-tide depths of only

3 feet limit access, shallow-draft cruising boats up to 30 feet should be able to gas up comfortably at high water.

## Blounts Bay

Blounts Bay, named for a famous Washington mercantile family, is a large body of water flanking the southern shore of the Pamlico River south of flashing daybeacon #9. The bay is uniformly deep to within 0.1 nautical mile of its banks. Because of its size, Blounts Bay does not offer particularly good protection for overnight anchorage. The shoreline is sparsely developed, and no facilities are available.

## Blounts Creek

Blounts Creek makes off from the southerly tip of Blounts Bay. This stream boasts sheltered anchorage but has a difficult approach channel. The shoreline exhibits sparse residential development. A country store overlooks the banks.

The creek's entrance is marked by a welcome aid to navigation, but the approach channel is still tricky and requires extreme caution. Cruisers who carefully sound their way into the creek will discover that this body of water is well worth their time.

North of the 15-foot fixed bridge, you can drop anchor in depths of 8 to 17 feet in about as protected a spot as you are ever likely to find. The surrounding scene is absolutely idyllic. The heavily wooded shores and attractive country homes are often reflected perfectly in the creek's mirror-smooth waters. But because of the approach's navigational difficulty, this haven is not recommended for craft over 36 feet or those drawing more than 4 feet.

## Broad Creek

North of flashing daybeacon #9, Broad Creek (one of many North Carolina streams with this name) throws out the red carpet along the Pamlico's northern banks. Broad Creek offers the best facilities for cruising craft on the Pamlico River. All marine services, including overnight dockage and full repairs, may be obtained here.

The entrance channel into Broad Creek is well marked but subject to continual shoaling. I found good depths of 6½ to 8 feet along the cut at the time of this writing, but the situation could be different in a few years.

Pamlico Plantation, a large, sprawling condo project, overlooks Broad Creek's eastern banks. The complex's extensive collection of fixed wooden piers can be readily spied from the main channel. Visitors are sometimes accepted at Pamlico Plantation under special conditions, but the marina does not employ a regular dockmaster. Unless you are lucky enough to know one of the property owners here, it is probably best not to count on finding a transient berth.

Broad Creek's conventional facilities include two marinas, a host of small repair firms, and the Washington Yacht Club, all located on the stream's western shoreline. As you move upstream from south to north, the first facility you will come upon is Broad Creek Marina. The vast majority of this marina's slips are rented to local boaters, and the docks are unattended. Call ahead of time to see if any berths happen to be available for transients.

Broad Creek Marina features fixed wooden piers with water and 30-amp power connections. Bathrooms are located just behind the piers.

Depths alongside run 5 to 5½ feet at the outer slips and around 4 feet at the inner docks.

### Broad Creek Marina
### (919) 975-2046

Approach depth: 6–8 feet
Dockside depth: 4–5½ feet
Accepts transients: limited basis
Fixed wooden piers: yes
Dockside power connections: 30 amps
Dockside water connections: yes

Located just across the street, Eastern Carolina Yacht Service (919-975-2046) performs haul-outs from Broad Creek Marina via a 20-ton travel-lift. This outfit also helps to oversee the day-to-day operation of Broad Creek Marina.

Next up is McCotter's Marina, the largest facility on Broad Creek. In fact, it's one of the largest marinas in North Carolina. The extensive piers, many of them covered, line the western banks south of unlighted daybeacon #6. There are also plenty of open spaces for sailcraft. McCotter's suffered dock damage courtesy of Hurricane Fran, but at the time of this writing, repairs were well under way, and I expect all traces of the storm will be erased by the time of your visit.

The excellent management at McCotter's Marina seems to be very much in touch with the needs of visiting cruisers. Transients are eagerly accepted for dockage at extensive fixed piers with all power and water connections. Soundings on the inner slips run to 5½ feet, while 6 to 6½ feet of water can be expected at the outer berths. Gasoline, diesel fuel, waste pump-out service, and shoreside showers are all readily available. Full mechanical repairs for both diesel and gasoline power plants are offered, and haul-outs are readily accomplished by the marina's two 30-ton travel-lifts. Marine canvas repair can also be obtained, and McCotter's offers dry storage for power craft. The large ship's store on the premises maintains an impressive inventory of spare parts. Visiting cruisers who need to restock their larders or who just want to visit one of the restaurants in nearby Washington can usually rely on the dockmaster to arrange complimentary trans-portation. Transport to and from nearby rail- and air-service facilities is also available with advance warning. Seldom will cruising boaters find a better-appointed marina than McCotter's.

The Washington Yacht Club (919-946-1514), the northernmost facility on Broad Creek, is a large and active organization. The club tries to leave several slips open for the use of transients who are members of accredited yacht clubs. The facilities include a large clubhouse with a

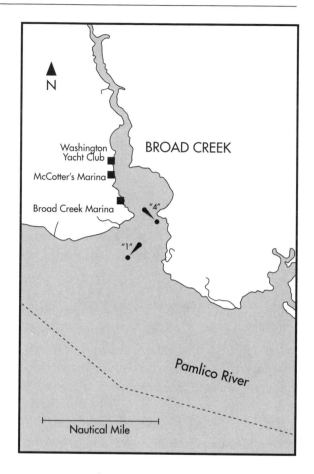

## McCotter's Marina
## (919) 975-2174

Approach depth: 7–8 feet
Dockside depth: 5½–6½ feet
Accepts transients: yes
Fixed wooden piers: yes
Dockside power connections: 30 & 50 amps
Dockside water connections: yes
Showers: yes
Waste pump-out: yes
Gasoline: yes
Diesel fuel: yes
Mechanical repairs: yes
Below-waterline repairs: yes
Ship's store: yes
Restaurants: transportation can usually be
   arranged

restaurant and a swimming pool, in addition to slips with all power and water connections.

## Chocowinity Bay

Northwest of Broad Creek, the large body of water known as Chocowinity Bay splits off from the Pamlico River at Fork Point. For those who successfully avoid the surrounding shallows, minimum depths of 6 feet continue upstream 1 nautical mile past Fork Point. There is some residential development on the bay's shores, and it must be said that this is not the most attractive of the Pamlico's sidewaters. A low-key small-craft marina is located at charted Whichard Beach, but approach depths of 3 and 4 feet relegate this facility to small, shallow-draft powerboats.

Chocowinity Bay is an interesting side trip and a nice spot to drop the lunch hook. It may also be used as an overnight anchorage, but not as a place to ride out a heavy blow. The bay's size gives the wind too much fetch for comfort, particularly in a fresh southeasterly breeze.

## Washington

West of the charted railroad bridge, the thriving riverside city of Washington guards the Pamlico's northern banks. The town's waterfront is beautifully landscaped with picnic tables and shade trees. The unattended municipal docks are comprised of a long concrete sea wall fronting the waterfront park. Wooden pilings set against the sea wall help boaters keep the rub rail away from the concrete. There are some low-key 15-amp power connections and standard water hook-ups. Depths alongside are only 5 feet, and the bottom is *rocky!*

The adjacent downtown district features a convenience store and several other retail businesses. It's a long walk of better than a mile from the waterfront to a supermarket. You may want to consider a taxi when it comes time to seriously restock the galley. Call Joe Duck Cabs (919-946-6054) or L-Cheapo's (919-975-1384). For rental cars, check with Day by Day (919-946-1142).

During summer weekends, an informal farmers' market is often held just across from the waterfront park. Ah, the smell of fresh veggies cooking in the galley is ever so sweet!

Also in the downtown district is the new headquarters of the Washington/Beaufort County Chamber of Commerce (919-946-9168). The impressive George H. and Laura E. Brown Public Library (122 Van Norden Street, 919-946-4300) is only a two- to three-block walk away.

Downtown Washington boasts several interesting dining spots. The Curiosity Shoppe and Coffee Company (201 West Main Street, 919-975-1397) offers wonderful cuisine, served in the evenings only. For lunch, check out The Meeting Place (225 West Main Street, 919-975-6370). Both these establishments are within easy walking distance of the municipal docks.

You might also consider PJ's Creekside Lounge and Restaurant (919-946-9483). This restaurant is located well east of the downtown district and is a bit too far for walking. Consider taking a taxi.

While you are strolling around downtown Washington, be sure to check out Sunflower Books (109 West Main Street, 919-975-1001). This is a superb book shop with something for readers of most any taste.

Several years ago, Carolina Wind Yachting Center (919-946-4653) took up residence at historic Havens Wharf, a stone's throw west of the municipal docks. This facility was heavily damaged by Hurricane Fran, but repairs were well under way at the time of this writing. Carolina Wind offers sailcraft charters from its offices in Washington, from the Sheraton Marina in New Bern, and from Northwest Creek Marina in Fairfield Harbor. All the facility's fixed wooden piers at Havens Wharf are currently rented to local boaters, and there is no room for transients. A ship's store now occupies the lower level of Havens Wharf, the oldest commercial structure

*Washington City Docks and Riverfront Park*

in Washington. Marine electrical, refrigeration, and air-conditioning repairs are offered.

For boaters ready to take a break from the live-aboard routine, Washington has two bed-and-breakfast inns that are happy to pick up and deliver patrons dockside from either the Broad Creek facilities or the city docks.

Pamlico House Inn (400 East Main Street, 919-946-7184 or 800-948-8507) is housed in a lovely Colonial-style house. The friendly, gracious innkeepers serve a wonderful breakfast, and the rooms look like they are ready for the pages of *Colonial Homes* magazine. I have had the good for-

tune to lodge here on several occasions, and my stays have been memorable.

Acadian House Inn (129 Van Norden Street, 919-975-3967) is run by a former cruising couple that has been very generous in helping me with my research. This hostelry serves a fine breakfast and is highly recommended.

## Washington History

In 1771, the North Carolina legislature authorized Colonel James Bonner to found a town at the "Forks of the Tar." The community was laid out in 1776 and named for George Washington. Washington was incorporated in 1782 and became the county seat in 1785. During the Revolutionary War, the town was the principal mainland port for boats plying Ocracoke Inlet. In 1790, Congress authorized a custom house at Washington. At that time, the town's waterborne traffic was exceeded in North Carolina only by Wilmington.

In 1862, the town was occupied by Union forces and was briefly declared the capital of North Carolina. The period following the Civil War was a harsh time for Washington. But when the railroad came in 1878, the lumber business began to boom. Today, Washington boasts many modern industries, and the agriculture and tobacco trades continue to prosper.

## PAMLICO RIVER NAVIGATION

The Pamlico River does not pose any special navigational problems. The channel is quite broad and very well marked. The longest run between daybeacons is 6.3 nautical miles. The river is generally deep to within 0.2 nautical mile of its banks. In some instances, good depths run even closer to shore. Many sidewaters have well-marked entrances.

**Entrance from Pamlico Sound** The Pamlico River's entrance from Pamlico Sound is bordered by Willow Point to the north and Pamlico Point to the south. Cruisers entering from the sound should consider setting their course for the 40-foot flashing daybeacon #PP, located 1.3 nautical miles east of Pamlico Point. Come abeam of #PP by 0.6 nautical mile to its northerly side. From this aid, you have access to all points west on the river.

**Four Creek Area** Incautious cruisers who choose to enter the four creeks should set course from a position abeam of #PP (to its northerly side) for flashing daybeacon #2, located at the creek's mouth.

Between #2 and #PP, you will pass north of unlighted daybeacon #1. Pass flashing daybeacon #2 by 50 yards to its southerly side and set a new course to come abeam of flashing daybeacon #4 to its southerly quarter. You can expect 7- to 8-foot depths between these daybeacons. As noted on chart 11553, there is shallow water on both sides of the channel.

At flashing daybeacon #4, the channel to Middle Prong cuts 90 degrees to the south, while the marked track continues west past unlighted daybeacons #6 and #8 into Oyster Creek. If you decide to explore Oyster Creek, a risky proposition at best, pass to the south of #6 and #8. Don't continue upstream on Oyster Creek to flashing daybeacon #10 unless your craft draws less than 3 feet.

Your best bet for an overnight anchorage is Middle Prong. Be careful to avoid the shallow water around Beard Island Point, Dicks Point, and Clark Point. After passing Clark Point, you may anchor in relatively protected water.

Don't attempt to enter James Creek or Clark Creek unless your craft draws less than 3 feet. James Creek has 3-foot depths in spite of what is noted on chart 11553, and Clark Creek's unmarked entrance and winding channel are treacherous for large craft.

**On the Pamlico**   To proceed up the Pamlico and bypass the four creeks, consider setting a course from a position north of flashing daybeacon #PP to the 29-foot flashing daybeacon #PR at the southern mouth of the Pungo River. During this run, you will pass Abel Bay on the northern shore. Abel Bay has flashing daybeacon #1 marking its entrance, but the bay is much too shallow for cruising craft.

Flashing daybeacon #PR marks an intersection of the Pamlico and Pungo Rivers and the ICW. If you entered the Pamlico River by way of the ICW and wish to explore the river's western (upper) reaches, your trip will begin at #PR.

To continue upriver, set course from #PR to flashing daybeacon #3 on the northern side of Indian Island. Do not approach Indian Island! As noted on chart 11554, it is surrounded by extremely shoal water. To play it safe, come abeam of #3 by at least

*Carolina Wind Yachting Center–Haven's Wharf*

50 yards to the aid's northern side.

Between flashing daybeacons #PR and #3, you will pass Goose Creek on the southern shore. Goose Creek is part of the ICW and will be discussed later in this chapter. East of #3 and Indian Island, you may choose to enter South Creek, an interesting sidewater on the southern shore.

**South Creek**   To enter South Creek, work your way carefully around the extensive shoals off the eastern and southern shores of Indian Island. Pass well east of the charted, unlighted, and unnumbered daybeacon lying off the eastern tip of the island. Watch to the west for unlighted daybeacon #2. As this aid comes abeam well west of your track, swing to the west and point to pass #2 by at least 50 yards to its southern quarter.

As you continue tracking your way west into South Creek, pass flashing daybeacon #4 to its southern side and unlighted daybeacon #5 to its northern quarter. Shortly thereafter, the mouth of Bond Creek will come abeam to the southwest.

**Bond Creek**   Two unlighted daybeacons, #2 and #3, guide boaters around the shoals near Fork and Gum Points. Pass #2 to your starboard side and take #3 to port. From #3, follow the mid-width of Bond Creek as it flows to the southwest. Minimum depths of 7 feet can be expected as far upstream as the waters adjacent to the village of South Creek. There is good anchorage abeam of the small waterfront. Don't cruise upstream on Bond Creek farther than the waters abeam of the village or up Muddy Creek. Depths are much too shallow for all but small craft drawing less than 3 feet.

**On South Creek**   West of unlighted daybeacon #7, good depths open out in a broad path on South

Creek. Shallows abut both shorelines, so stay at least 200 yards off the banks. As you are now going upstream, pass all red aids to navigation on your starboard side and green markers to port. You should not encounter any navigational difficulties short of unlighted daybeacon #10.

West-southwest of #10, you will spot unlighted daybeacons #1 and #2. These aids mark a side channel leading to a cove which serves as a barge-loading area. Ignore #1 and #2. To continue upstream from #10, you should instead set course to come abeam of and pass unlighted daybeacon #12 to its easterly side.

Do not attempt to cruise between #1 and #2 and then set course for #12. The hapless boater who attempts this procedure will land himself in 3 feet of water.

**South Creek to Aurora**   Surprisingly enough, on-site research revealed that depths from unlighted daybeacon #12 to the Aurora waterfront now run at least 5 feet, with most soundings in the 6- to 9-foot range. But considering the minimal facilities available at Aurora, only boaters who really enjoy cruising off the beaten path should undertake this stretch of South Creek. Depths outside the marked channel rise quickly.

It is a long run between unlighted daybeacons #20 and #21. Watch the track over your stern as well as the course ahead to make sure leeway isn't easing you out of the channel.

At #21, the creek takes a sharp turn to the south. Several more aids lead upstream to unlighted daybeacon #25. As you come abeam of #25 to its westerly side, you will spy a long dock on the westerly shore. This pier belongs to Aurora Marina, but there are no facilities for visitors. Continue upstream past #25, holding to the mid-width. The town ma-

rina will soon come abeam to the west just short of the low-level fixed bridge that spans the creek.

**On the Pamlico**   Back on the Pamlico River at flashing daybeacon #3, located north of Indian Island, another sidewater on the river's northern shore beckons. This series of creeks is known collectively as East Fork.

**East Fork**   If you choose to enter, set a course from flashing daybeacon #3 for flashing daybeacon #1, which marks East Fork's southerly mouth. Come abeam of #1 to its fairly immediate easterly side. Point to come abeam of the next upstream aid to navigation, unlighted daybeacon #2, to its fairly immediate westerly quarter.

Once abeam of #2, set a careful course for unlighted daybeacon #4. Study chart 11554 for a moment and notice that a straight course between #2 and #4 could land you in the 3-foot shoals extending southeast from Little Ease Creek. Give way to the east a bit to avoid these shallows.

Unlighted daybeacon #4 marks the entrance to the northeasterly arm of East Fork, your best bet for overnight anchorage. You may proceed as far as 0.5 nautical mile past #4 and still hold minimum depths of 5½ to 6 feet by sticking scrupulously to the mid-width.

Little Ease, Frying Pan, Bailey, and Ross Creeks, all sidewaters of East Fork, should be entered only by craft drawing 3 feet or less.

Boats drawing 4 feet or less can enter North Creek, located north-northwest of unlighted daybeacon #4, on its mid-width. Discontinue your explorations before passing through the stream's first turn to the northwest.

**On the Pamlico**   To cruise west on the main body

of the Pamlico River, consider setting a course from flashing daybeacon #3 for flashing daybeacon #4, located southwest of Gum Point. This run of 6.3 nautical miles is the longest stretch between aids to navigation on the Pamlico River.

Along the way, you will pass Gaylord Bay to the north and Long Point to the south. These points are connected by the Pamlico ferry, which traverses the river regularly. Both terminals have marked channels, but no facilities or anchorage possibilities for cruising boaters are present.

South of flashing daybeacon #4, you will observe the huge Texas Gulf Chemical Company, a phosphate-manufacturing facility on the river's southern shore. Chart 11554 indicates that the plant has its own marked and dredged entrance. This channel is for the exclusive use of commercial traffic to and from the plant. However, curious boaters may approach to within 0.4 nautical mile of the southern shore for a closer view of this behemoth.

From flashing daybeacon #4, two more sidewaters, Durham and Bath Creeks, present themselves for exploration and anchorage.

**Durham Creek**   Approach Durham Creek from the northeast in order to bypass the shallows running off Durham Creek Point. Point to pass unlighted daybeacon #2 to its fairly immediate easterly side. Then cruise due south into the creek's interior reaches. A study of chart 11554 shows that this procedure will help you avoid the shoal waters reaching west from Garrison Point. Once past this potential trouble spot, swing back to the creek's mid-width. You can then proceed 0.2 nautical mile upstream in minimum depths of 6 feet. Only craft drawing less than 3 feet should proceed farther.

**Bath Creek**   To enter Bath Creek, come abeam of flashing daybeacon #1, the first aid on the entrance channel, by at least 0.6 nautical mile to its southerly side, a position well out into the main body of the Pamlico River. Only then should you turn north and point to pass flashing daybeacon #1 to its fairly immediate easterly side. Do not cut either of the creek's entrance corners too sharply. Continue cruising into Bath Creek by coming abeam of and passing unlighted daybeacon #2 by 20 yards to its westerly quarter.

North of #2, good water spreads out almost from shore to shore on Bath Creek as far as unlighted daybeacon #3. Minimum depths of 7 feet may be expected to Bath Creek Bridge provided you keep to the mid-width. Avoid Banner Point, the area between Bath and Back Creeks that is unnamed on the chart; this point seems to be building outward.

If you choose to enter Back Creek, leave the main stream abeam of unlighted daybeacon #3. Cruise carefully into Back Creek's westerly mouth on its midsection, keeping a weather eye on the sounder. The stream's mouth is constricted by shoals to both the north and south.

Cruisers continuing up Bath Creek to the state docks should pass west of flashing daybeacon #4. The state docks will eventually come abeam along the easterly shoreline.

**On the Pamlico**   Cruisers plying their way upstream on the Pamlico from flashing daybeacon #4 should set a course for flashing daybeacon #5 off Core Point. Pass #5 by several hundred yards to its northern side.

From #5, set a course for flashing daybeacon #7, deviating from a straight run between these two in order to avoid the spoil area clearly shown on chart 11554. Come abeam of #7 to its northerly

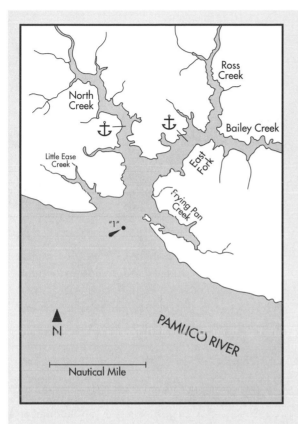

side. Shallow water lies south of #7.

Northwest of #7, Broad Creek, home of the best facilities on the Pamlico River, beckons.

**Broad Creek**    Though it is well marked, the entrance to Broad Creek requires careful study of chart 11554. To enter from flashing daybeacon #7, set a northwesterly compass course to avoid the shallows and the charted spoil banks north and northwest of unlighted daybeacon #8 and flashing daybeacon #9. As you approach the entrance to Broad Creek, curl slowly around to the north and bring flashing daybeacon #1 abeam to its immediate easterly side. Watch out for the extensive shoals stretching from the easterly shores and for the

patch of 4- and 5-foot shallows southwest of #1.

From #1, point to pass unlighted daybeacon #3 to your port side and flashing daybeacon #4 to starboard. The channel is narrow between #1 and #3. I almost wandered into grounding depths the last time I cruised into Broad Creek. Watch where you are going and keep an eye on the sounder.

North of #4, hold to the mid-width. Soon, the docks of Broad Creek Marina will come abeam to port, followed by the extensive piers of McCotter's Marina. If your destination is the Washington Yacht Club, be sure to pass west of unlighted daybeacon #6.

**On the Pamlico**    West of #7, the Pamlico River channel remains fairly straightforward to flashing daybeacon #9.

At #9, Blounts Bay and Blounts Creek lie to the south. The latter stream offers wonderful anchorage, but only by way of a tortuous channel.

**Blounts Creek**    Should you decide to enter, be careful to avoid the shallow water along the bay's shoreline. Point to come abeam of unlighted nun buoy #2 by 25 yards to its eastern side. Take your best guess as you try to follow the otherwise unmarked channel as it curls back around to the west and then plunges sharply south around the creek's east-side entrance point. Favor the eastern and southeastern shores heavily. Depths of 12 feet run almost to shore on the eastern quarter of the entrance, but the western shore is shoal. After entering the creek, keep to the mid-width and you can expect depths of as much as 12 feet, unusual for a stream in this region.

After you safely negotiate its entrance, Blounts Creek provides an attractive and safe haven to ride out a storm or just rest for the night. Travel farther upstream on the creek should be attempted by only very small craft. A fixed bridge with a vertical clearance of 15 feet soon blocks passage upstream, and an overhead power line with less than 10 feet of vertical clearance spans the creek immediately beyond the bridge.

**On the Pamlico**　Boaters continuing past Broad Creek to Washington can follow the well-outlined track to flashing daybeacon #14 near Fork Point. West of #14, it is possible to enter Chocowinity Bay.

**Chocowinity Bay**　To enter Chocowinity Bay, give the shoal waters around Fork Point a wide berth. It is a good idea to run a compass course from flashing daybeacon #14 to a point abeam of the bay's mid-width (well to the northwest) and then turn into the bay itself. As Fork Point comes abeam to starboard, begin slightly favoring the northeasterly shoreline. With judicious use of your compass and chart 11554, you can hold minimum depths of 6 feet for 1 nautical mile upstream past Fork Point. Do not proceed farther unless your craft draws less than 3 feet.

**On the Pamlico**　From flashing daybeacon #14, the channel to Washington follows a dredged cut. Northwest of flashing daybeacon #19, a low-level railroad bridge with only 7 feet of closed vertical

*Palmer-Marsh House–Bath*

clearance spans the Pamlico River. Fortunately, this span is usually open unless a train is due. Beyond the bridge, the thriving city of Washington lies sprawled along the northern shore.

**Washington**　West of the railway span, cruisers will soon spot the long city docks along the northern shore, followed by Carolina Wind Yachting Center. The river is then blocked by an automobile swing bridge with 6 feet of closed vertical clearance. This span requires 24 hours of advance notice to open; even then, I wouldn't hold my breath. Beyond the bridge, the Pamlico becomes known as the Tar River. Depths become inconsistent, and the waters are not well charted.

## ICW TO NEUSE RIVER

From the mouth of the Pungo, the ICW darts across the width of the Pamlico River and enters the Hobucken Cut. This section of the Waterway is formed by Goose and Gale Creeks, which are connected by a man-made canal. Several fine anchorages are found along this route,

and some very minimal facilities are located near the Hobucken Bridge. Construction is currently well under way to replace the old Hobucken swing bridge with a fixed high-rise structure. In the meantime, the Hobucken swing span has restrictive opening hours from April 1 to November 30. The entire route is well sheltered, and cruisers need not be concerned about rough water.

## Lower Spring Creek (Standard Mile 151)

Lower Spring Creek, located west-southwest of flashing daybeacon #6, is an emergency anchorage only. Depths run as little as 3 feet near the stream's mouth and on its interior reaches, but the waters just to the east are much deeper. It is quite possible to get off the main ICW route and drop the hook, should you be desperate to do so. But failing an emergency, boaters should probably continue down Goose Creek to a more reliable anchorage.

If you decide to drop anchor here anyway, the best spot lies southwest of #6. Depths run between 7 and 9 feet, and there is plenty of swinging room for pleasure craft of most any size. Fair protection is afforded from eastern and western breezes, but strong winds from the north or south make for an uncomfortable evening. The surrounding shoreline is flanked by sparse residential development.

## Eastham Creek (Standard Mile 154)

Eastham Creek spreads its broad mouth along the Waterway's eastern banks east-northeast of unlighted daybeacon #13. The stream features a marked channel with minimum 7-foot depths, as well as some good water off the main cut. The shoreline is undeveloped to Mill Seat Landing. Cruising captains with craft less than 40 feet in length that draw 5 feet or less should have no problems entering.

While there are a number of possible overnight havens, two spots merit particular attention.

The charted bay northwest of unlighted daybeacon #4 holds surprising depths of 5½ to 6 feet to within 150 yards of its rear banks. Protection is superb from all but unusually strong southerly winds. Depths a bit closer to #4 are even better.

Another anchorage worthy of consideration is just off the marked channel south of unlighted daybeacon #7. Good depths of 5 to 6 feet hold to within 50 yards of the southerly banks, though there is one unmarked shoal to avoid. There is good shelter from all winds and enough room for a 40-footer.

## Campbell Creek (Standard Mile 154)

Campbell Creek indents Goose Creek's shoreline west of the gap between unlighted daybeacons #13 and #14. Attractive, heavily wooded, all-natural shores lead off a list of the fortunate qualities of this notable sidewater. Once safely past an unmarked shoal at the creek's entrance, you may expect minimum depths of 6 feet on the mid-width as far upstream as the waters abeam of charted Smith Creek, a small sidewater on the southern shore of Campbell Creek. You may proceed even farther up the creek, but 5-foot depths soon become the norm. Campbell Creek is an excellent overnight anchorage that offers superior shelter from all but strong eastern blows for craft drawing 5½ feet or less.

## Hobucken (Standard Mile 157)

At the time of this writing, construction was about two-thirds complete on a 65-foot fixed high-rise span crossing the ICW at Hobucken. The new bridge is located a few hundred yards north of the old swing span. When the new span is completed, the old bridge will be removed.

Immediately south of the Hobucken Bridge, the long face dock of the R. E. Mayo Seafood Company will come abeam to the west. Fresh seafood can often be bought here, and gasoline and diesel fuel are usually available. A small variety store just behind the fuel dock carries snacks and basic food items. Diplomatic captains may even be able to arrange for an overnight berth among the numerous shrimp trawlers. However, R. E. Mayo is primarily concerned with the commercial seafood trade, and pleasure craft are very much a sideline.

### Jones Bay (Standard Mile 157.5)

South of the Hobucken Bridge, the upper reaches of Jones Bay meet the ICW hard by flashing daybeacon #21. Jones Bay eventually flows southeast to Pamlico Sound. Chart 11553 would lead you to believe that it is possible to use this cut-through as a short route from the ICW to the sound; however, on-site research revealed that 3-foot depths are encountered 0.3 nautical mile down the bay.

Boaters in need of shelter can ease off the ICW into the headwaters of Jones Bay just south of #21 and drop the hook with good protection from all but easterly winds. There is plenty of swinging room, and depths run 5 to 7½ feet. Passing shrimpers may disturb your nighttime or early-morning rest. Be sure to show an anchor light!

## ICW TO NEUSE RIVER NAVIGATION

To continue southward on the ICW from the Pungo River, set your course across the Pamlico River from a position abeam of flashing daybeacon #PR to flashing daybeacon #1 at the mouth of Goose Creek. It is a run of 2.9 nautical miles between #PR and #1. Come abeam of #1 to its northwesterly side.

The northern entrance to Goose Creek and the Hobucken Cut is well marked and presents no unusual navigational difficulty. Be sure to pass southeast of unlighted daybeacon #4. Shoal water is building southeast from Reed Hammock around this marker.

Note that the configuration of aids to navigation reverts to the usual ICW pattern at the mouth of Goose Creek. Southbound boaters should once again pass green, odd-numbered aids to their (the boaters') port side and take red markers to starboard.

From #4, point to pass north of flashing daybeacon #5. Shallows lie east and southeast of this aid to navigation. Don't allow leeway to ease you to the south when cruising between #4 and #5. Such a navigational error could land you in the broad tongue of shallow water striking northwest from Fulford Point.

After #5, the Waterway cuts sharply south. Take a slow turn around #5, pointing to pass flashing daybeacon #6 by 25 yards to its easterly side. Southwest of #6, the first of Goose Creek's many anchorages presents itself.

*Lower Spring Creek* If you need to stop here, leave the main ICW channel about halfway between flashing daybeacon #6 and the next southerly aid to navigation, unlighted daybeacon #7. You can cruise as much as 0.2 nautical mile west of the ICW's course and hold minimum depths of 6 feet. A closer approach to Lower Spring Creek will land you in 3- and 4-foot depths.

**On the ICW**   Between #7 and unlighted daybeacon #13, several small streams lead east and west from Goose Creek. None of these sidewaters is useful to the cruising boater. Peterson and Dixon Creeks are too shallow for craft drawing more than 3 feet, and Snode Creek is rendered dangerous by several submerged pilings.

At #13, captains may choose to make use of the Hobucken Cut's first sheltered sidewater, Eastham Creek.

**Eastham Creek**   Cruise into the creek's entrance from unlighted daybeacon #13, pointing to pass unlighted daybeacons #1 and #3 to your port side and unlighted daybeacon #4 to starboard.

To utilize the excellent anchorage northwest of #4, depart the main channel abeam of this marker and cruise into the bay's midline. Good depths continue to within 150 yards of the rear banks.

Upstream from #4, a well-marked channel continues all the way to Mill Seat Landing. Take all green markers to your port side and red aids to starboard.

The anchorage south of unlighted daybeacon #7 is accessible simply by cruising carefully south from that aid to navigation. Avoid the sharp, charted point of land southwest of #7. An uncharted shoal is building from this small promontory. Be sure to drop the hook before approaching to within less than 50 yards of the southerly shoreline.

**Campbell Creek**   The entrance to Campbell Creek cuts into the Waterway's western shore between unlighted daybeacons #13 and #14. Enter the creek by favoring the northern banks slightly. Take extra care to avoid the extensive shallows pushing north from Huskie Point, located on the southern flank of the creek's entrance. Once you are through the entrance, keep to the centerline for best depths. Captains should be warned that the mouth of the creek is often dotted liberally with crab pots; consequently, nighttime entrance can be dangerous.

Deep-draft vessels should stop before coming abeam of charted Smith Creek to the south. Upstream of this point, soundings decline to 5 feet or so.

**On the ICW**   The Waterway continues tracking its way generally south down a well-marked channel to flashing daybeacon #19. There, Upper Spring Creek splits off from the eastern shore. Do not attempt to enter. Depths run to 3 feet. Apparently, extensive shoaling not noted on chart 11553 has taken place at the mouth of the creek.

South of #19, the ICW enters a man-made canal. This canal runs southward for 1.6 nautical miles to the Hobucken Bridge.

**Hobucken**   As mentioned above, a new, fixed 65-foot bridge will soon replace the older Hobucken swing span. If you happen to arrive before the swing bridge is removed, you will likely find that it opens only on the hour and the half-hour from 7 A.M. to 7 P.M. between April 1 and November 30. Given the bridge's closed vertical clearance of only 6 feet, most boaters will have to contend with these pesky restrictions until the new high-rise is in place.

**Jones Bay**   Flashing daybeacon #21 marks the intersection of the ICW and the upper reaches of Jones Bay. Should you decide to try this cut-through to Pamlico Sound, sound your way carefully. Remember, depths fall off to 4 feet along the way.

The headwaters of Jones Bay, immediately off the ICW near #21, offer depths of 7 and 8 feet. Enter on the mid-width of the bay's mouth 30 to 50 yards south of #21. For best depths, drop anchor before cruising more than 100 yards east of the ICW. Be sure to show an anchor light, and be prepared for nighttime passage by local shrimp trawlers.

**On the ICW**   South of flashing daybeacon #21, the ICW passes through another man-made canal for 1.5 nautical miles before emptying into Gale Creek at flashing daybeacon #22 (Standard Mile 159.5). Gale Creek is a sidewater of the Bay River, which is itself a side body of the Neuse River. This chapter's account of the ICW's southward trek is discontinued at #22. To pick up the route again, see chapter 6.

*R.E. Mayo Seafood Company Docks–Hobucken Cut*

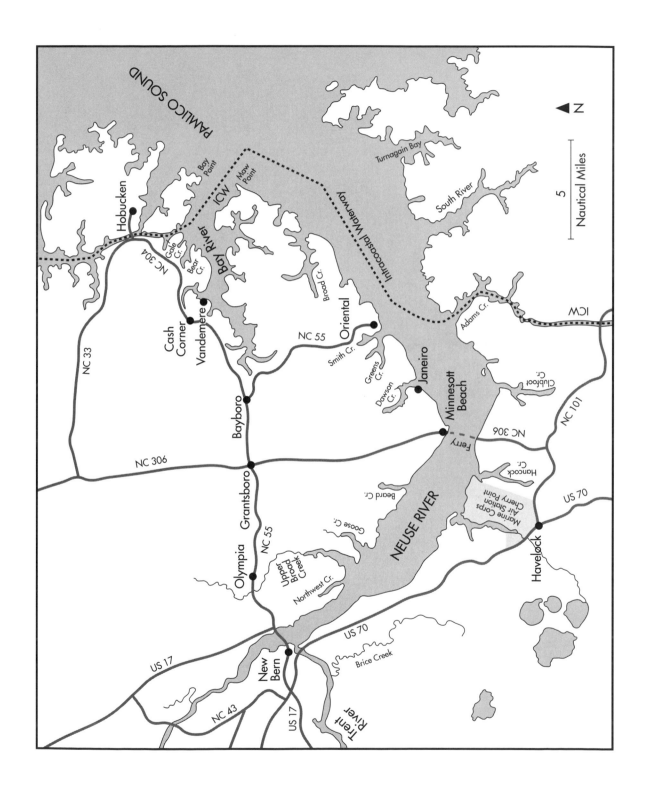

# The Neuse River

The Neuse River, named for an Indian tribe that once lived along its banks, is the southernmost of the two major rivers that empty into southwestern Pamlico Sound. The Neuse is 34 nautical miles in length from its mouth to New Bern and 6 nautical miles in width at its widest point, making it one of the widest rivers in the United States. The Neuse River is rich in sidewaters and overnight anchorages. Facilities catering to cruising boaters are reasonably numerous and of good reputation.

On the negative side, the river has a deservedly nasty reputation for rough weather. Northeasterly and southwesterly winds, the two winds that predominate, tend to blow up or down the river's entire length, allowing enough fetch for a teeth-rattling experience.

The Neuse has little in the way of lunar tides, but sustained winds from the south and southwest can lower water levels significantly, while long-lived blows from the north and northeast tend to have the opposite effect.

The Neuse flows past several picturesque coastal towns. The largest, New Bern, is a thriving city that retains much of its earlier charm. It is well worth a visit. Oriental, located almost halfway between the river's mouth and New Bern, is one of the most unspoiled river villages on the entire coast. This small, quaint town offers excellent facilities for cruisers and is a favorite stop on the North Carolina ICW.

## Charts

You will need four charts for successful navigation of the Neuse and its various sidewaters:

**11548** details the river's entrance from Pamlico Sound and certain portions of Bay River

**11553** details the Bay River section of the ICW and Bay River's intersection with the Neuse

**11552** covers general navigation of Neuse River and all sidewaters from Oriental to New Bern, including Trent River

**11541** details the ICW and the Neuse to Adams Creek, as well as certain creeks between Bay River and Oriental

The Bay and Trent Rivers are two major auxiliary waters of the Neuse. The Trent River joins the Neuse at New Bern and provides several miles of excellent cruising. The Bay River, located near the Neuse's exit into Pamlico Sound, offers an isolated cruising opportunity and plentiful anchorages well off the beaten path.

The ICW enters the Bay River from Gale Creek, passes into and up the Neuse for 16 nautical miles, and then enters Adams Creek. From Adams Creek, the Waterway follows a man-made canal until it flows into Core Creek and the Newport River. Because of the Neuse's geographical position, the ICW section on the river is considered the second-roughest of the entire Waterway. Boaters must keep a wary eye on wind conditions or their cruise could be an unpleasant, wet experience.

## Neuse River History

"The Neuse is one of America's great streams," comments Bill Sharpe in *A New Geography of North Carolina*. Indeed, the Neuse was the route by which almost all settlement and commerce reached the surrounding region during colonial times. Much of southwestern Pamlico Sound's shoreline is marshy, but the Neuse allowed colonists to build ports and made the sound accessible. Ocracoke, of prime importance as a port of entry before the Revolutionary War, was and still is easily reached from the Neuse.

The river gave rise to one of North Carolina's most successful coastal cities, New Bern. Settled in 1710 by Swiss and German colonists, New Bern is located at the intersection of the Neuse and Trent Rivers. This prime location led to the establishment of New Bern as North Carolina's capital prior to the Revolutionary War.

Much later, the Neuse served as a means of transportation for several small riverside communities of Pamlico County, including Bayboro, Stonewall, Oriental, and Minnesott Beach. These villages have always depended on the abundant seafood of the Neuse's waters for their commerce.

Around 1850, an attempt was made to connect the Neuse with the port of Beaufort. The Harlowe Canal was dug between Clubfoot Creek and the Newport River. The canal was only in use a short time before cave-ins forced its abandonment. Later, the dream was realized when Adams and Core Creeks were connected by a stable man-made waterway.

## Neuse River Legend

During the Revolutionary War, a privateer, the *Cornelia*, operated on the Neuse. The *Cornelia* had a rather inexperienced crew. In order to encourage practice in climbing the ship's rigging, the captain lashed the handle of the water pump high above the deck; any crew member wanting a drink was obliged to go aloft and retrieve the handle before he could quench his thirst.

The story goes that one day, the *Cornelia* met a ship flying the British flag. In an attempt to lull the other craft into a false sense of security, the *Cornelia* also ran up the Union Jack. The two ships approached each other. The *Cornelia* hauled down its false colors and prepared to fire, only to learn that its opponent was an American privateer out of Charleston. It, too, was trying to lure unsuspecting British ships into an easy trap. Both crews must have had a good laugh.

# BAY RIVER

The Bay River offers many miles of isolated but lovely cruising. The varied charms of its waters are consistently overlooked by most cruising boaters. This is unfortunate, as you will seldom find a stream with a more picturesque shoreline or as many lonely but enchanting overnight anchorages. Chapel and Trent Creeks are especially appealing.

The Bay River serves two small coastal towns, Vandemere and Bayboro. Neither offers substantial facilities catering to pleasure vessels, but fresh seafood can often be purchased at the commercial fisheries located in the harbors of both villages.

Most of the Bay River's shoreline is in its natural state, though there are residential developments along sections of the banks. At times, it seems as if you are cruising in that far-removed time when only Native Americans plied the waters. A trip on the Bay River is almost always an appealing experience.

The ICW enters the Bay River at Gale Creek not far from the river's mouth, then passes through its lower reaches before entering the Neuse. This discussion follows the Bay from its intersection with the Neuse to its headwaters at Bayboro. The ICW passage from Gale Creek to Oriental and Adams Creek will be reviewed in the next section.

## Bear Creek

Bear Creek, west of the ICW's flashing daybeacon #27, was once the home of a marina which catered to cruising captains. Unfortunately, this establishment is long out of business, and the creek's winding, unmarked entrance is probably too tricky for strangers. Cruisers would be well advised to bypass Bear Creek.

## Bonner Bay

Bonner Bay is a good-sized body of water that lies south-southeast of the Bay River's flashing

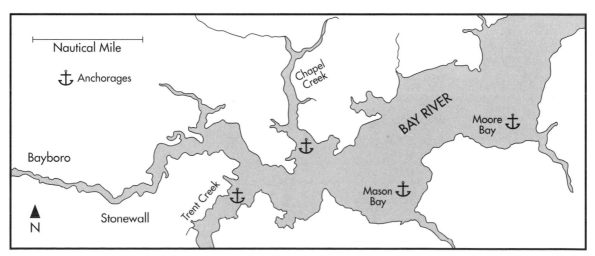

daybeacon #4. The bay might at first glance seem a possibility for anchorage. However, the winding, unmarked channel is more difficult than might be expected from a quick inspection of chart 11553. Shoals abound outside the channel, and it's easy to wander into 3 feet of water even when you are trying to explore with care. With the exception of one incredibly isolated cabin, the shoreline is untouched by the hand of man.

Truly adventurous boaters may find a safe path through Bonner Bay's channel to its best anchorage. This spot is on Long Creek (the bay's eastern arm) short of the intersection with Dipping Vat Creek. Minimum 6-foot depths are held in the channel, and there is enough room for a 34-foot craft to swing comfortably. There is good protection from northern and eastern winds, but not from western and southern blows. Please keep in mind, however, that the anchorage and the path to this haven are surrounded by unmarked shallows. Unless you are in great need of shelter, I recommend traveling farther upriver to a more reliable spot.

### Vandemere

Vandemere, once the seat of Pamlico County, is today a small fishing village whose harbor is lined by picturesque seafood docks. The village harbor guards the Bay River's northwestern banks northwest of flashing daybeacon #5. Minimum approach depths run around 6 feet.

Fresh seafood can often be purchased at the town wharves, but there are no facilities catering specifically to cruisers. You might try anchoring abeam of the waterfront and dinghying ashore to make your purchases. Be sure to leave enough

*Dusk on Bayboro Harbor*

room between your craft and the wharves for the ready passage of local shrimpers.

Vandemere Creek, located north of the town docks, is shown on chart 11548 as having 8- and 9-foot depths. But due to the creek's tricky entrance, it is all too easy for strangers to go aground in 3 feet of water.

### Moore Bay

Moore Bay lines the southeasterly banks well south of unlighted daybeacon #6. Minimum depths of 8 feet run to within 0.2 nautical mile of the rear banks. The bay affords good protection from southerly, southeasterly, and southwesterly winds, but there is virtually no shelter from northerly blows. The shoreline is surrounded by fairly extensive residential development. All in all, Moore Bay is only a fair anchorage among the Bay River's memorable overnight stops.

## Mason Bay

Mason Bay is not as deep as Moore Bay, but its shoreline is delightfully undeveloped. You will spy the bay's broad waters south of unlighted daybeacon #8. Minimum depths of 6 feet can be held to within 0.2 nautical mile (but no closer) of the southerly shore. The bay's waters offer pleasant overnight accommodations when light to moderate southern, southeastern, or southwestern winds are in the offing. During heavy weather or northern breezes, wise captains would do well to consider one of the more sheltered anchorages farther upriver.

## Chapel Creek

Idyllic Chapel Creek wanders lazily into the Bay River's northerly banks almost due north of flashing daybeacon #9. Quite simply, there is no better spot to spend an evening on the Bay River. Minimum depths of 5 feet are held into the outer reaches of the creek's mouth; typical soundings run 6 to 7 feet. Shelter is quite good from all but unusually strong southerly and southwesterly winds. The shoreline is heavily wooded and completely untouched. If nature chooses to cooperate, the nighttime sky as seen from this pristine haven is nothing short of spectacular. It's not stating the case too strongly to note that a night spent on the placid waters of Chapel Creek can lead you to believe you have traveled to a simpler, long-forgotten time. If you anchor only once on the Bay River, this is the place to be.

## Trent Creek

Trent Creek makes into the southern shoreline of the Bay River southwest of unlighted daybeacon #11. This creek is easy to enter, uniformly deep, and well protected. While most any craft up to 45 feet can gunkhole on Trent Creek, swinging room is sufficient only for craft as large as 36 or possibly 38 feet. The shoreline is in its natural state and is quite attractive.

Trent Creek is rich in fish, as evidenced by the large number of traps and net lines that can often be observed along the shoreline.

Large craft will find the most swinging room just inside the creek's mouth. Vessels under 34 feet can track their way upstream for quite some distance to any spot that strikes their fancy.

## Bayboro

The river village of Bayboro, perched at the headwaters of the Bay River, remains much the same as it was in the 19th century. Unfortunately, no berths for pleasure boaters are available. A visit to the town, now the seat of Pamlico County, is worthwhile, but your only opportunity to dock temporarily lies in negotiating a space at one of the commercial seafood piers. Success in such an enterprise will require real diplomacy. Speaking of which, fresh seafood can often be purchased at the Bayboro docks. Minimum approach and pier-side depths run about 5 feet, though typical soundings range from 6 to 10 feet.

Bayboro boasts some lovely old homes, and its courthouse is an imposing structure. Several shoreside businesses, including a laundromat and a convenience store, are located within a four- to five-block walk of the waterfront. If you are lucky enough to find a temporary berth, don't pass Bayboro by too quickly.

# BAY RIVER NAVIGATION

The Bay River's entrance from the Neuse is bordered to the north by Bay Point and to the south by Maw Point. The river's mouth is wide, generally deep, and well marked. Use chart 11553 for navigation from the entrance to flashing daybeacon #4. This chart's large scale provides the best detail of the Bay River's lower section.

No significant navigational difficulties are posed by the river's entrance. A careful study of chart 11553 should be sufficient. Once abeam of flashing daybeacon #3, you can begin a gentle curve to the southwest and enter the main body of the river. As you are following this bend, you will pass Gale Creek and the ICW route to the north.

Point to come abeam of and pass flashing daybeacon #4 by 100 yards to its southerly side. Don't drift north of this aid. Shoal water is building out from the northerly banks toward #4.

***Bonner Bay***   If you are the devil-may-care variety of captain and choose to explore Bonner Bay, strike a course from flashing daybeacon #4 to avoid the considerable patch of shallow water flanking the westerly side of the bay's entrance. As can be seen from chart 11553, it will eventually be necessary to swing to a more southerly course to avoid the 2- and 3-foot shoals near the southwesterly point of Davis Island. Even if you follow these directions and stay in the channel, soundings on this portion of the bay are not as deep as shown on chart 11553. Depths of 7 to 8 feet can be expected.

South of Davis Island, swing to the east and enter the mouth of Long Creek along its centerline. Stick to the mid-width and you will soon find yourself in protected waters with depths of 7 feet. Don't at-

tempt to follow the creek as it swings to the south. Depths become even more uncertain on this upstream portion of the stream. For maximum swinging room, drop anchor abeam of the first charted point of marsh on the north side.

Do not attempt to explore Spring Creek or Riggs Creek. Both are too treacherous for cruising craft.

***On Bay River***   From flashing daybeacon #4 to unlighted daybeacon #6, use chart 11548 for navigational purposes. It is a simple process to continue upstream from #4. Hold to the river's midsection and point to come abeam of flashing daybeacon #5 by 100 to 200 yards to its northern side.

***Vandemere***   Once abeam of #5, skippers might consider cruising north to the village of Vandemere. Depart the main Bay River channel at flashing daybeacon #5 and set a careful compass course for the town docks, being careful to avoid the charted tongue of 2-foot shallows just south of the wharves. This shoal is the result of sailing ships' off-loading of ballast stones during their calls at Vandemere long before the first power craft ever plied the river's waters.

Remember, continuing north into Vandemere Creek past the village waterfront is not recommended, as you will likely meet up with 3-foot depths.

***On Bay River***   From flashing daybeacon #5, it is another easy upriver run to unlighted daybeacon #6. Again, simply stick to the mid-width and come abeam of #6 well to its southeasterly quarter.

At #6, begin using the Bay River section of chart 11552 for continued upriver navigation. Chart 11552 gives a more detailed picture of the river's upper section than does 11548.

**Moore Bay**  Moore Bay, located south of #6, holds good depths of 8 feet or so to within 0.2 nautical mile of its shoreline. Simply drop the hook before approaching the banks too closely.

**On Bay River**  It's yet another simple run from #6 to unlighted daybeacon #8. Come abeam of #8 to its southeasterly side. Again, stick to the river's mid-width.

**Mason Bay**  Mason Bay, to the south of #8, has minimum depths of 6 feet running to within 0.2 nautical mile of its rear banks. Drop anchor at any likely spot short of these shallows.

**On Bay River**  Upstream of unlighted daybeacon #8, the Bay River curves to the west. Come abeam of flashing daybeacon #9 by 25 yards to its northerly side. Don't cut Chapel Creek Point, located north of your course, too closely. As chart 11552 clearly shows, shoal water surrounds this point. At #9, Chapel Creek beckons to the north.

**Chapel Creek**  Cruisers who decide to anchor on Chapel Creek should strike a north-northwesterly course from #9 into the mid-width of the stream's entrance. You can cruise 0.25 nautical mile past #9 into the creek's entrance and hold minimum depths of 5 to 6 feet. Don't attempt to cruise into Chapel Creek's first small jog to the northwest. Depths rise to 4 feet in the body of this turn.

**On Bay River**  From flashing daybeacon #9, cruisers continuing upriver should pass unlighted daybeacon #10 on its southerly side, then come abeam of unlighted daybeacon #11 by 25 yards to its northerly quarter.

**Trent Creek**  At #11, Trent Creek, another excellent anchorage, presents itself. Enter the stream by slightly favoring its northwesterly banks. This maneuver will help you avoid the band of charted 4-foot shallows abutting the southeasterly shoreline. Good depths of 6 feet are held upstream until Trent Creek turns to the south. Past this point, the shoals encroaching from both shorelines become a worry. I suggest anchoring short of the southerly turn.

**Bay River to Bayboro**  Past unlighted daybeacon #11, the Bay River channel continues to follow a deep and well-marked track all the way to Bayboro. There are no overnight anchorages along the way, so this trip is strictly a gunkholing prospect. However, for those who have the time, the voyage is highly recommended for its scenery.

The only tricky section is between #11 and unlighted daybeacon #12. The problem is that #12 blends into the background, and it is all too easy to proceed mistakenly toward unlighted daybeacon #14, the next daybeacon upriver. Boaters who make this mistake will find themselves in 4-foot waters along the river's southwestern shore. Use your binoculars and make sure you identify #12. Except for this one trouble spot, you can expect 8-foot minimum depths until you begin your approach to Bayboro.

**Bayboro**  Just short of the Bayboro docks, west of unlighted daybeacon #22, you will encounter one patch of 5-foot depths. A bit farther upstream, water levels again deepen to 6 feet or more.

Bayboro marks the headwaters of the Bay River.

# ICW AND NEUSE RIVER

The ICW enters the Bay River from Gale Creek at Standard Mile 160.5, then passes down the lower confines of this stream until swinging southwest into the Neuse River at Maw Point. The Waterway follows the Neuse for 16 nautical miles before again ducking south on Adams Creek. There are many good overnight anchorages along this section of the ICW, and marina facilities are fairly abundant. The riverside village of Oriental, a charming overnight stop, is quickly becoming one of the most popular ports of call on the North Carolina portion of the ICW.

As noted earlier, the geographical position of the Neuse tends to allow the predominant northeasterly and southwesterly winds to blow up or down a good portion of the river's length. This condition of high wind fetch has earned the Neuse River portion of the ICW the reputation of being the second-roughest section of the entire Waterway. Wise captains will take a careful look at the weather before tackling this stretch of water.

## Gale Creek Anchorage (Standard Mile 159.5)

West of flashing daybeacon #22, the upper reaches of Gale Creek, abandoned by the ICW, can serve as a good overnight anchorage for vessels drawing 4 feet or preferably less. Depths of 4½ to 5 feet hold along the stream's centerline as far as the waters abeam of the first charted offshoot on the southerly banks. Obviously, you should anchor east of this point unless your craft

requires 3 feet or less of water to stay off the bottom. There is good cover from all but strong westerly and, to a lesser extent, easterly blows. The surrounding shores are mostly undeveloped marsh backed by higher, wooded banks. One attractive home overlooks the creek's south-side entrance point. Swinging room is ample for a 45-footer. If your craft fits the draft requirements, this is a convenient haven for waiting out bad weather on the Neuse.

## Waterway Anchorage (Standard Mile 160)

Study chart 11553 and notice the 6-foot cove indenting the Waterway's eastern banks between unlighted daybeacons #23 and #24. This used to be the best anchorage along this portion of the ICW, but shoaling during the last several years has lessened its desirability. Entrance depths are now only about 5 feet. And while it used to be possible to hold good depths into the stream's southern fork, depths now rise to 4 feet as you approach the charted split in the stream.

Instead, anchor well west of the split. You can then count on your anchor rode finding 5 to 6 feet of water; you can also count on enough swinging room for boats as large as 40 feet. The surrounding shores are natural marsh, though a few private homes can be spied in the distance to the north.

Boaters should be aware that the entrance to this creek is no longer portrayed accurately on chart 11553. Consult the navigational data in the next section of this chapter for more information.

## Turnagain Bay (Standard Mile 173)

Turnagain Bay's yawning mouth makes into the Neuse's southern banks 5 nautical miles south of flashing daybeacon #4, which is itself southeast of Piney Point. Shoaling has made this body of water inaccessible to large cruising craft. Depths near flashing daybeacon #1, which marks the bay's entrance, have shoaled to 4 feet or slightly less.

These shallow depths are unfortunate, as Turnagain Bay is connected to West Thorofare Bay, an auxiliary water of southern Pamlico Sound, by an old canal. West Thorofare Bay is in turn connected by Thorofare Canal to Thorofare Bay, a sidewater of Core Sound. If navigation of Turnagain Bay were feasible, it might be possible to travel from the Neuse to Core Sound without ever venturing into the often-choppy waters of Pamlico Sound. With depths as they are, however, this interesting passage must be consigned to our outboard and I/O brethren.

## Turnagain Bay Legend

There is an interesting story of how Turnagain Bay acquired its name. According to *The North Carolina Gazetteer*, a local farmer named Joseph Pittman "ran an Indian out of his sweet potato patch" one day in 1774. The Indian swam across a narrow section of the bay and emerged on the opposite shore. He turned and made an "insulting remark" to Pittman, then prepared to go on his way. "Pittman told him to turn again and repeat what he had said. This the Indian did, and Pittman shot him."

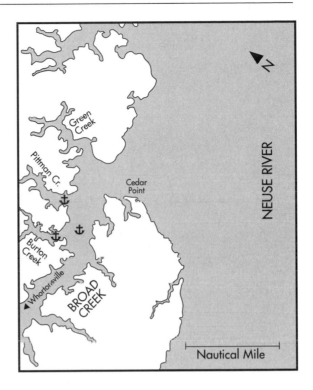

## Broad Creek (Standard Mile 173.5)

Broad Creek opens out along the Neuse River's northwesterly banks between flashing daybeacons #4 and #6. It is well marked and fairly deep and offers excellent overnight anchorage and two marina facilities. This impressive stream provides the most reliable sanctuary along the Neuse River portion of the ICW east of Oriental.

Minimum depths on the Broad Creek entrance channel from the Neuse River were about 6½ feet at the time of this writing. Typical soundings range from 7 to as much as 11 feet. Depths outside the marked cut rise rapidly, and the channel wanders a bit among the various markers. Navigational caution is required for a successful entry.

Pittman Creek makes into the northwestern shores of Broad Creek southwest of unlighted daybeacon #3. Minimum 5-foot depths hold upstream until the creek begins a gentle curve to the north. Craft drawing 4 feet or less can find good anchorage short of the northern bend. Protection is adequate for all but gale-force winds, and there is plenty of swinging room for craft of most any size. The starboard shore is delightfully undeveloped, while the opposite banks display moderate residential development.

Burton Creek cuts into the northwestern shore of its larger sister, Broad Creek, and offers yet another excellent overnight anchorage. Minimum depths are 5 feet, and typical soundings run 6 to 8 feet. This body of water offers better shelter than its neighbor to the northeast and enough swinging room for boats up to 50 feet. A large forest of virgin pines lines the southwestern shores, but there is fairly heavy residential development along the opposite banks.

Back on the main body of Broad Creek, a wide, privately marked channel continues upstream west and southwest of unlighted daybeacon #4 to a large fork near the tiny village of Whortonsville. Typical depths continue to top the 7-foot level. Along the way, the stream's shores continue beautiful and mostly undeveloped. Without a doubt, no cruising boater will ever fault this body of water for its natural scenery.

Even before reaching the split, pleasure craft under 45 feet can drop the hook most anywhere near the edge of the broad channel. While not quite as sheltered as some other spots, these waters provide adequate protection from winds under 15 knots.

Just short of Broad Creek's split, Point Marina overlooks the northerly banks at Whortonsville. This small but friendly facility sports a nice lounge with first-class showers. Point Marina lacks a dockmaster, but visitors are sometimes accepted with advance arrangements on a space-available basis. The piers are of the fixed wooden variety with water and 30-amp power connections. Approach depths run 6 to 6½ feet, and you can expect the same soundings dockside. A small country store just behind the marina is convenient for restocking your larder, but there is no restaurant within walking distance.

**Point Marina**
**(919) 249-2670**

Approach depth: 6–6½ feet
Dockside depth: 6–6½ feet
Accepts transients: limited basis
Fixed wooden piers: yes
Dockside power connections: 30 amps
Dockside water connections: yes
Showers: yes
Variety store: nearby

If your cruising travels bring you to Whortonsville on the Fourth of July, be sure to stop for one of the most special parades you will ever see. This tiny village does an amazing job of putting on a celebration.

Broad Creek's northwesterly fork west of Whortonsville is known as Brown Creek. A few privately maintained buoys line the channel into this body of water. Minimum 5-foot depths continue well upstream. Thanks to its ample swinging room, Brown Creek makes a superior anchorage in all but gale-force winds. The light residential development along both shores is interspersed with undeveloped, heavily wooded areas.

Broad Creek's principal southerly branch continues to hold 6-foot depths for a short distance, but soundings soon deteriorate to 5 feet or less. Short of the shallows, Boone Docks lines the creek's northerly banks west of shallow Ship Creek. Approach and dockside depths run 6 to 6½ feet. Most of this facility's fixed wooden slips are usually filled by long-term residents, but if space is available, transients are accepted for overnight or temporary dockage. Water and 30-amp power connections are at each slip, and shoreside showers and bathrooms are available.

### Boone Docks
### (919) 249-1400

Approach depth: 6–6½ feet
Dockside depth: 6–6½ feet
Accepts transients: if space is available
Fixed wooden piers: yes
Dockside power connections: 30 amps
Dockside water connections: yes
Showers: yes

Ship Creek Boat Works (919-249-1902) is located on the creek of the same name just east of Boone Docks. An entrance bar crossing the mouth of Ship Creek carries only 3 to 4 feet of water. Most of this firm's work is performed on boats berthed at Boone Docks or other nearby marinas. The yard specializes in mechanical repairs and complete reconditioning of both fiberglass and wood vessels.

The waters of Broad Creek immediately west of Boone Docks offer good anchorage for vessels drawing 4 feet or less. Depths run around 5 feet, and there is ample elbow room for a 40-footer.

The surrounding shores are eye-pleasing, with just one or two attractive homes peeping from the wooded banks. Protection from all winds is quite good.

### South River (Standard Mile 178.5)

The South River is a large, uniformly deep, and well-marked sidewater on the southeastern shore of the Neuse 4.5 nautical miles south of flashing daybeacon #6, itself located off Gum Thicket Shoal. The river has a narrow entrance, but it is marked in a more-than-adequate fashion. Most of the shoreline is completely untouched and is overlooked by a fascinating collection of pines and hardwoods. As you enter the South River, you will spy one wooden structure along the northeastern banks. This is a private hunting lodge, and visitors are not permitted.

This entire body of water is well sheltered, and good possibilities for anchorage abound. The South River is one of those delightful sidewaters that combines good depths, attractive and isolated scenery, and an excellent series of daymarks.

Study chart 11541 and notice the location of "Lukens" on the river's northeastern shore. Several interesting cemeteries are left from this long-deserted community. Old families in Carteret County that have roots in Lukens still make regular trips to these graveyards to visit the resting places of their ancestors.

One of the South River's best anchorages lies along the northeastern banks southeast of Big Creek. Notice the correctly charted 10-foot depths that run to within 100 yards of the banks.

### Pierce Creek (Standard Mile 179)

Pierce Creek, located on the Neuse River's

northern shore north of flashing daybeacon #7, is the home of Sea Harbor Yacht Club (919-249-0808). This facility does not currently offer any dockage for transients, but gasoline and diesel fuel can usually be purchased during daylight hours. The entrance channel has been dredged to a depth of 7 feet; dockside depths run in the 6- to 7-foot range. Unless you are in immediate need of fuel, you should probably bypass Pierce Creek and Sea Harbor in favor of Whittaker Creek or Oriental Marina.

## Whittaker Creek (Standard Mile 181)

The well-marked channel to Whittaker Creek strikes northeast from flashing daybeacon #1 at the southeastern tip of the Oriental Harbor channel, located west of the ICW's flashing daybeacon #7. One large marina and two repair yards on this stream's shores eagerly await the cruising boater.

Whittaker Creek's entrance channel was dredged during the spring of 1997. For now, the cut is some 100 feet in width with 9 feet of depth at low water. This passage is subject to future shoaling, however, if history is any judge. Captains piloting vessels that draw more than 6 feet should probably call Whittaker Creek Yacht Harbor's ultra-friendly management (919-249-1020) ahead of time to check on the latest depth conditions.

Whittaker Creek Yacht Harbor occupies the point separating the two major branches of the creek. This large, friendly facility is eager to greet visiting cruisers. It offers extensive overnight dockage for transients at fixed wooden piers with all power and water connections. Depths alongside run 6 to 8 feet. Clean showers and a laundromat are offered. Gasoline, diesel fuel, new waste pump-out service, full mechanical repairs, and a refreshing swimming pool are available, and the marina maintains an unusually well-stocked ship's store. Ask for Lila, and tell her I sent you. A courtesy car is available for ferrying visitors to nearby restaurants and grocery stores. Sometimes, transportation can be arranged through the local restaurants as well. The latest addition at Whittaker Creek is an on-site restaurant that was closed and undergoing a change of ownership at the time of this writing. Several potential proprietors were bidding for this site, so the restaurant may be back in operation by the time of your visit. While it seems that far more sailors than power-craft skippers call Whittaker Creek home, this facility can be unreservedly recommended to cruising boaters of either persuasion.

It should also be noted that Whittaker Creek offers a sailcraft charter fleet of 12 vessels. For information, call 800-525-7245. I highly recommend this charter service to my fellow cruisers.

### Whittaker Creek Yacht Harbor (919) 249-1020

Approach depth: 6 feet (minimum)
Dockside depth: 6–8 feet
Accepts transients: yes
Fixed wooden piers: yes
Dockside power connections: 30 & 50 amps
Dockside water connections: yes
Showers: yes
Laundromat: yes
Waste pump-out: yes
Gasoline: yes
Diesel fuel: yes
Mechanical repairs: yes
Ship's store: yes
Restaurants: several nearby

*Whittaker Creek Yacht Harbor*

Two large, full-service boatyards face each other across the mouth of the big offshoot making off to the southwest from Whittaker Creek's southwesterly fork.

Deaton Yacht Service (919-249-1180) occupies the creek's southeastern banks. It offers full mechanical, below-the-waterline (haul-out), and topside repair services for even the largest pleasure craft. The yard's travel-lift is rated at 25 tons. Marine painting, repairs to hull blisters, gel-coat, and marine carpentry services are also available. Deaton's struck me as an ultramodern yard that can handle just about any repair problem you might encounter.

Opposite Deaton's, the docks and travel-lifts of Sailcraft Service (919-249-0522) also wait to greet those who need marine service. In addition to all mechanical and below-the-waterline (haul-out) repairs, the yard specializes in fiberglass refurbishment and refinishing. The on-site travel-lift is rated at 16 tons.

Thanks to Whittaker Creek Yacht Harbor and the two boatyards, Whittaker Creek can lay claim to some of the most extensive facilities on the North Carolina portion of the ICW. Considering all these advantages, cruising boaters, particularly those who need repairs, should think long and hard before bypassing this well-appointed body of water.

### Oriental (Standard Mile 181)

Oriental, which lies northwest of the ICW's flashing daybeacon #7, is one of the most unspoiled river villages on the entire North Carolina coast. Commercial fishing is still the principal occupation of the local residents. In fact, a commercial fishery occupies one side of the harbor. Happily, there does not seem to be an odor problem from this facility.

One of the most lovely walks you will ever take is along the banks of the Neuse in Oriental. Beautiful old houses, many exhibiting down-east architecture, line South Avenue, which parallels the river. It is easy to see why Oriental has attracted such a horde of resident pleasure craft.

Oriental preserves the delightful atmosphere of earlier days. Its residents are usually far more interested in how the fish are biting than what's happening in the larger world. If you want to unwind, don't pass Oriental by.

Oriental's entrance channel from the Neuse River is deep and quite reliable, maintaining at least 8 feet of water. At flashing daybeacon #8, the cut skirts around a rock breakwater and turns hard to the east-northeast on its way to the sheltered inner Oriental Harbor. As you enter this quaint basin, a wonderful facility will come abeam to starboard.

*Oriental Marina*

Oriental Marina, Motel, and Restaurant occupies the southeastern banks of Oriental Harbor. It welcomes transients, offering well-sheltered dockage at fixed wooden piers with water and 30- and 50-amp power connections. Depths alongside run 6 to 7 feet. Slip space is sometimes at a premium, so call ahead to check on availability.

Clean showers and a laundromat are available at the motel office. Diesel fuel, gasoline, and some mechanical repairs via independent contractors may also be purchased. The adjacent, full-line Harborside Grocery (see below) is very convenient. A marine-equipment supplier is also within an easy walk of the docks. For those who need a break after a hot day on the water, the adjacent swimming pool is open to transient dockers. The on-site restaurant and upstairs lounge are highly recommended for excellent seafood.

Oriental Marina, Motel, and Restaurant has undergone a change of ownership during the last three years. Though the new management seems quite friendly and anxious to please, Waterway veterans will look in vain for the smiling face of former owner Brenda Harris. Nevertheless, Oriental Marina is still a real standout. You simply cannot do better than to coil your lines here, whether for an overnight stay or a week's stop.

**Oriental Marina
(919) 249-1818**

Approach depth: 8–11 feet
Dockside depth: 6–7 feet
Accepts transients: yes
Fixed wooden piers: yes
Dockside power connections: 30 & 50 amps
Dockside water connections: yes
Showers: yes
Laundromat: yes
Gasoline: yes
Diesel fuel: yes
Mechanical repairs: independent contractors
Restaurant: on-site

Oriental also offers a small city-owned pier occupying the inner harbor's northeasterly tip. There is just room enough for two 35-foot craft to tie off to this fixed wooden structure. Depths along the outer portion run 5 feet, with 4½-foot soundings immediately adjacent to the shoreline. No power or water connections or other marine services are available.

The nearby Trawl Door Restaurant (919-249-1232) serves some memorable repasts. A new addition to the Oriental dining scene is the M & M Café (919-249-2000). This three-meals-a-day dining attraction is housed on South Water Street (which parallels the harbor's northwesterly shores) in what looks to be a private home just beside Truitt's General Store (see below). The locals swear by the food here. Breakfast is of the continental variety. During the summer

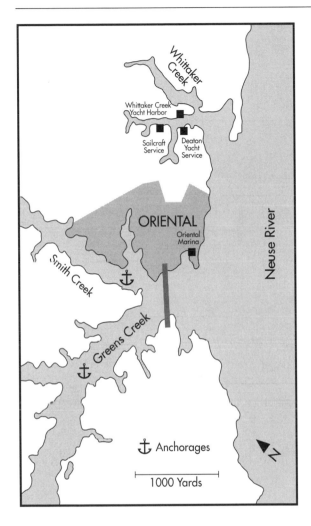

in Oriental Harbor and are in need of any marine paraphernalia, then by all means spend a few minutes browsing the store's shelves. Interestingly enough, Inland Waterway Treasure Company maintains a courtesy car for the exclusive use of visiting cruisers. Ask any of the staff for help.

Cruising chefs will be interested to learn that the proprietors of Inland Waterway Treasure Company, Jay and Paula Winston, are now the owners of nearby Harborside Grocery (300 Hodges Street, 919-249-1707) as well. Paula has done a magnificent job of turning this once rather ordinary grocery operation, located at the northwestern corner of the harbor, into a real gourmet food store. The selection of baked goods (especially the home-made chocolate chip cookies), meats, and seafood is outstanding. Even if your galley isn't in dire need of restocking, don't miss Harborside.

Cruisers can step back in time with a visit to Billy and Lucille Truitt's general store, located just off the harbor's northwestern shore on South Water Street. The combination of odd antiques and just plain junk makes for one of the most unique collections I have ever seen. If things are a bit slow, ask Billy and Lucille about their lives along the Neuse River. If fancy takes them, this salty couple can relate many fascinating tales. You may learn more about the surrounding region on the shop's steps than in all the books you might ever read.

## Oriental History

In 1870, Lou Midgett was fishing on the Neuse when a violent storm suddenly approached. He took shelter in a harbor formed by the intersection of five creeks. After the storm,

months, some screen-porch dining is available. Truly, there is little fear of gastronomic boredom in Oriental.

The cool, white walls of the Inland Waterway Treasure Company (919-249-1797) gaze out over the northeastern shore of Oriental Harbor. This firm features one of the most extensive collections of marine equipment, publications, and coastal clothing on the North Carolina coast. Be sure to check out the book section! If you dock

*House on Cedar Creek off Adams Creek*

Midgett decided the area was a natural place to settle down. Soon, he returned with his family. Thus, the village of Oriental was founded. Others quickly saw the community's natural advantages for commercial fishermen, and Oriental began to grow into the quaint riverside community that still looks to the Neuse for its principal livelihood.

Oriental was named in unique fashion. It seems that Becky Midgett, the wife of the village's founder, was visiting at Hatteras when she found the cabin nameplate of a vessel named the *Oriental*, which had sunk off the cape. She took the plate home. When the time came to name the new village, she suggested calling it Oriental.

Apparently, Oriental was once a walled city. The wall was designed not for protection against a hostile enemy but to keep livestock from roaming the village streets. Anyone coming in or leaving had to open and close the gate.

### Oriental Anchorages (Standard Mile 181)

Cruisers making the approach to Oriental

Harbor will notice a large bridge to the northwest. If you wish to anchor-off rather than enjoy the village's many attractions, the two creeks on the far side of the bridge, Smith and Greens Creeks, offer 5- to 6-foot depths. Of course, you must be able to clear a 45-foot fixed span to reach these waters.

Past the bridge, Greens Creek strikes off to the west, while Smith Creek opens out to the north. Greens Creek is deeper than Smith and offers better anchorage. Navigation of Greens Creek can be a bit confusing for strangers. Be sure to read the navigational information about this stream in the next section of this chapter.

Once you figure out the channel, it is possible to hold minimum 5-foot depths as far upstream as the waters 150 yards east-southeast of the point of land where the creek splits into two major branches (where chart 11541 notes a 6-foot sounding). Drop the hook 150 yards short of the point and settle down for a quiet evening. The delightful shoreline features a deep pinewood set just behind the northwesterly point of land. There is ample swinging room for a 45-footer and good protection from all but strong easterly breezes.

Smith Creek offers an excellent anchorage amidst heavier residential development. Several banks of private docks flank this stream's easterly shoreline, but there is still plenty of room to drop the hook. Depths of 5 feet or better hold for several hundred yards upstream. Consider anchoring just north of unlighted daybeacon #10. Farther upstream, soundings rise to 4-foot levels.

### Adams Creek and Core Creek

From the Neuse River's flashing daybeacon

#7, southbound Waterway cruisers will set their course southwest to flashing daybeacon #1AC (Standard Mile 185), which marks the northerly mouth of Adams Creek. Adams Creek and Core Creek, along with a connecting man-made canal, provide ICW access from the Neuse to the Newport River, which serves the Morehead City–Beaufort region. Thankfully, the old, pesky low-level bridge spanning the canal has been replaced with a new, fixed high-rise span. This structure greatly facilitates passage by sailcraft on this portion of the Waterway. A single overnight anchorage and two marinas welcoming transients are found between the Neuse and Newport Rivers. Most of the shoreline is in its natural state, but several attractive and isolated homes inhabit the banks here and there. Depths are reliable, and the route is well marked.

Many a boater has breathed a sigh of relief when entering the calm waters of Adams Creek after the choppy conditions of the Neuse. You can depend on this cut to provide safe and reliable access to Beaufort and Morehead City.

## Cedar Creek (Standard Mile 188)

The only reliable anchorage on the Adams Creek–Core Creek section of the ICW lies east of flashing daybeacon #9. Cedar Creek features minimum depths of 6 feet, good protection, and excellent holding ground. Boats as large as 50 feet should find enough swinging room. The shores are overlooked here and there by a few private homes, but most of the banks are well wooded and undeveloped. With its good depths and more-than-adequate protection, Cedar Creek can be unreservedly recommended.

Deep-draft vessels would do well to anchor on the broad band of correctly charted 7-foot waters east of flashing daybeacon #9. Depths farther upstream are less certain.

## Sea Gate Marina (Standard Mile 194)

You will sight the entrance to Sea Gate Marina along the Waterway's western shore 2.4 nautical miles south of flashing daybeacon #18. The location is designated "4A" on chart 11541. This small but friendly marina is tucked into its own dredged basin, which offers 5- to 6-foot entrance and dockside depths. Overnight berths are available at fixed wooden piers featuring all power and water connections. Showers and a laundromat are found shoreside. Gasoline and diesel fuel are readily available, and there is a ship's and variety store on the grounds. Mechanical repairs can be arranged through independent technicians. This is a particularly well-located facility for southbound cruisers who can't quite make it to Beaufort or Morehead City at the end of the day but would like to continue past Oriental and Whittaker Creek a few extra miles.

**Sea Gate Marina**
**(919) 728-4126**

Approach depth: 5–6 feet
Dockside depth: 5–6 feet
Accepts transients: yes
Fixed wooden piers: yes
Dockside power connections: 30 & 50 amps
Dockside water connections: yes
Showers: yes
Laundromat: yes
Gasoline: yes
Diesel fuel: yes
Mechanical repairs: independent technicians
Ship's & variety store: yes

## Bock Marine (Standard Mile 196)

A short jog south of the new high-rise Core Creek Bridge, the single fixed wooden pier of Bock Marine guards the eastern banks. This firm specializes in haul-out, below-the-waterline repairs. Mechanical services for both gasoline and diesel power plants are also offered through an independent contractor. The yard's travel-lift is rated at 60 tons, and crane service is available for larger craft.

Overnight transients are accepted at the yard's one dock, though the management warns that it is best to put out your largest fenders, as the occasional wake from a passing vessel can produce a bit of "rock-'n'-roll." Depths alongside run 6 to 8 feet. Water and 30- and 50-amp power connections are at each berth. Surprisingly enough for a repair yard, Bock Marine offers a very nice

**Bock Marine**
**(919) 728-6855**

Approach depth: 8–12 feet
Dockside depth: 6–8 feet
Accepts transients: yes
Fixed wooden pier: yes
Dockside power connections: 30 & 50 amps
Dockside water connections: yes
Showers: yes
Laundromat: yes
Mechanical repairs: independent contractor
Below-waterline repairs: extensive

boaters' lounge with bathrooms, showers, and a laundromat. Visitors may even make use of a courtesy pickup truck to drive into town for supplies. All in all, Bock Marine is a friendly establishment with much to offer visiting cruisers. Just be sure to have those fenders out.

# ICW AND NEUSE RIVER NAVIGATION

Use chart 11553 for all ICW navigation between Gale Creek and Maw Point Shoal. Study the chart carefully before cruising this portion of the Waterway. There are several shoals along the way which, though well marked, can ground unwary navigators.

**On the ICW**　Southeast of flashing daybeacon #22, the ICW leaves the sheltered canal which runs south from the Hobucken Bridge and follows a dredged channel into the lower reaches of Gale Creek. This stream in turn carries Waterway cruisers into the Bay River.

West of #22, skippers have access to the upstream waters of Gale Creek, abandoned by the Waterway, and the first of many anchorages lying between Gale and Adams Creeks.

**Gale Creek Anchorage**　Abandon the Waterway about halfway between flashing daybeacon #22 and the southerly entrance point of upper Gale Creek. Cruise into the stream on its midline. Drop anchor before coming abeam of the first unnamed offshoot on the southerly banks.

During on-site research, I did not sight the charted unlighted daybeacons lying farther upstream. As depths west of the previously described offshoot seem to rise to 4 feet or less, I suggest you not go looking for these aids to navigation unless your vessel draws 3 feet or less.

**Waterway Anchorage**　Remember that the anchorage flanking the ICW's easterly shoreline between unlighted daybeacons #23 and #24 has now shoaled, and that some 5-foot depths can be expected. Also, note that the entrance to this unnamed stream is now very different from what is pictured on chart 11553. Apparently, a portion of the marshy south-side entrance point has washed away, leaving what appears to be a marsh island flanking the southerly quarter of the stream's entrance.

Stay away from the marsh island and enter the stream along its mid-width. Drop anchor well short of the split in the creek. Depths rise to 4-foot levels as this division is approached.

**On the ICW**   To cruise south on the ICW, pass unlighted daybeacon #24 to its easterly side and unlighted can buoy #25 to its westerly quarter. Continue on the same course, pointing to come abeam of flashing daybeacon #27 to its fairly immediate westerly side. Don't slip to the west between #25 and #27. Gale Creek Point continues to build out into the Bay River, and 1- and 2-foot waters wait to trap the foolhardy. Flashing daybeacon #27 marks the Waterway's intersection with the main body of the Bay River.

Marker colors are reversed between #27 and Maw Point. As you are going downriver, pass all green markers to your starboard side and red beacons to port. The usual ICW configuration begins again after you round Maw Point and head up the Neuse.

From #27, the ICW cuts southeast and follows the Bay River past two patches of shallow water. Flashing daybeacon #3 warns of a large shoal near Pine Tree Point, and flashing daybeacon #1 marks a similar section near Deep Point. Pass both these aids by at least 100 yards to their northeasterly sides. Do not approach either daybeacon closely. Both points are building outward.

**Intersection with the Neuse**   Southeast of flashing daybeacon #1, cruisers have two choices.

The shorter but more dangerous route is to proceed directly from #1 to a position northeast of flashing daybeacon #2 near Maw Point Shoal. This course is reasonably safe if you are careful not to drift west or southwest along the way. Such a miscalculation can carry sloppy navigators onto Maw Point Shoal and cause a dangerous grounding.

The longer but safer route involves cruising from #1 to the unnumbered "Neuse River Junction" flashing daybeacon, located northeast of #2. This course will lead you well away from Maw Point Shoal and shallow water.

**On the Neuse**   After rounding Maw Point Shoal, switch to chart 11541 for continued southerly navigation on the ICW. From either #2 or the unnumbered flashing junction daybeacon, the Waterway flows generally southwest to flashing daybeacon #4, located off Piney Point. Though this run is uncomplicated and does not stray near shoal waters, care must be exercised in approaching #4. An obsolete skeletal-steel warning beacon, now located inside Piney Shoal and obscurely marked on chart 11541, can be mistaken for #4. Watch carefully for #4 (which will appear as the smaller of the two structures) well southeast of the old warning beacon.

Come abeam of and pass #4 by at least 100 yards to its southeasterly side. Recently, flashing daybeacon #WR2 has been placed southwest of the old beacon to warn of a semisubmerged wreck. Don't confuse #WR2 with #4; ignore #WR2.

**Entrance from Pamlico Sound**   Cruisers entering the Neuse River from Pamlico Sound rather than by way of the ICW should set course from the 24-foot flashing daybeacon #NR, at the river's mouth, to flashing daybeacon #4, near Piney Point. Again, be sure not to mistake the old skeletal warning beacon or flashing daybeacon #WR2 for flashing daybeacon #4. Stay at least 100 yards southeast of #4. This is a fairly lengthy run of 3.4 nautical miles. Fortunately, there are no shallows along the way.

**On the Neuse**   From flashing daybeacon #4, it is a simple run of 2 nautical miles southwest to flashing daybeacon #6 off Gum Thicket Shoal. Come abeam of #6 by 100 yards to its southeasterly side. Northwest of #6, the shallows of Gum Thicket Shoal are building out toward the marker. Halfway between #4 and #6, Broad Creek, the Neuse's first reliable side trip and anchorage, lies to the northwest.

**Broad Creek**   To enter Broad Creek, use chart 11541. Come abeam of flashing daybeacon #1 by 25 yards to its northeastern side. Curl around #1 to the west-southwest and point to pass unlighted daybeacon #2A by 20 yards to its southern side. Chart 11541 indicates 9- to 10-foot soundings between these two daybeacons, but on-site research revealed that 7-foot minimum depths can now be expected.

From #2A, the channel cuts to the northwest. Take a lazy turn around #2A and then set course to pass unlighted daybeacon #3 by 25 yards to its northeasterly side. Maintain course past #3 until the mid-width of the creek's main body comes abeam to the southwest. Turn 90 degrees to port and enter the centerline of the creek.

As you cruise past #3, you may spy the entrance to Green Creek north of your course. Do not attempt to enter this sidewater. Its narrow, unmarked entrance is too unreliable for large cruising craft.

After making your turn into the main body of Broad Creek, point to eventually come abeam of unlighted daybeacon #4 to your starboard side. Residents living along Broad Creek have placed a host of white PVC pipes in the waters between #3 and #4 to mark the shallows flanking the channel to the northwest and southeast. Though they are not charted and cannot be considered wholly reliable, these unofficial aids to navigation are nonetheless welcome.

Before reaching #4, you will pass two of Broad Creek's best anchorages to the northwest.

As you cruise southwest between #3 and #4, the mouth of Pittman Creek will soon come abeam. If you choose to enter, strike a course for the stream's mid-width. Minimum depths of 5 feet continue upstream until the creek bends to the north. Past this point, soundings rise to 4 feet.

The entrance to Burton Creek is just southwest of Pittman Creek. Again, enter on the middle and hold to the centerline. Craft drawing less than 4½ feet should have no difficulty cruising as far as the second large, charted offshoot on the starboard shore. Depths fall off to the 4-foot range farther upstream.

To continue cruising upstream on the main body of Broad Creek, set course to come abeam of unlighted daybeacon #4 to its southeasterly side. Be careful to avoid the charted shallows lining both banks between #3 and #4.

Past #4, a broad, privately marked channel leads to Whortonsville. You will need chart 11552 for navigating this portion of Broad Creek. Remembering the "red-right-returning" rule, pass all red markers to your starboard side and take green markers to port.

As you approach the major split in Broad Creek where Brown Creek strikes off to the northwest, you will spy the Whortonsville waterfront and Point

Marina to the north. Cruise into the marina docks without cutting any corners.

To anchor on or explore Brown Creek, enter this stream via its marked channel. The few floating buoys soon give out, but reasonably good depths can be carried for several hundred additional yards by simply keeping to the midline.

A few markers outline the channel into the main, southerly fork of Broad Creek. Observe these aids and generally keep to the middle as far as Boone Docks. Good depths continue for only 100 yards or so west of Boone Docks. Discontinue your Broad Creek explorations at this point unless your boat draws less than 3½ feet.

**On the Neuse**    From flashing daybeacon #6, it is a long but straightforward run of 5.5 nautical miles to flashing daybeacon #7. Daybeacon #7 is a centrally located aid to navigation. Cruising boaters have access to no fewer than four viable sidewater possibilities: the South River, Pierce Creek, Whittaker Creek, and Oriental.

**South River**    Use chart 11541 for entry into the South River. Set course from a position about halfway between flashing daybeacons #6 and #7 to come abeam of flashing daybeacon #1, which marks the South River's entrance, by 25 yards to its southwestern side. Then set course to pass flashing daybeacon #2 fairly close on its northeastern side. Immediately after passing #2, bend your course to a more southern track and pass unlighted daybeacons #WR3 and #5 fairly close to their western sides. Once past #5, simply stay within shouting distance of the river's midsection. Minimum depths of 8 feet can be carried for several miles upstream.

Some 1.2 nautical miles past #5, you will en-counter flashing daybeacon #6 near the river's southwestern shore. This daybeacon marks the entrance to Big Creek, home of a fish-processing house.

One of the best spots to anchor lies southeast of #6 where chart 11548 correctly notes 10-foot depths running to within 100 yards of the northeasterly banks. Ease into this cove, feeling your way with the sounder. Be on guard against the charted pool of 4-foot waters to the southeast.

**Pierce Creek**    Another sidewater accessible from flashing daybeacon #7 is Pierce Creek, located on the Neuse's northwestern shore. Pierce Creek is well marked. Simply pass all red aids to your starboard side and green markers to port. Eventually, you will spot the docks of Sea Harbor Marina along the creek's southwestern banks.

**Whittaker Creek**    The recently dredged channel into Whittaker Creek is subject to shoaling, and depths outside the marked cut quickly rise to grounding levels. Come abeam of flashing daybeacon #2, the first of the channel's aids to navigation, to its fairly immediate northwesterly side. Set a course to the northeast, pointing to pass all red aids to your starboard side and green markers to port. After passing unlighted daybeacon #4, use your binoculars to pick out a set of range markers to the northeast. *Stay on this range* until you pass flashing daybeacon #5. This is the trickiest portion of the Whittaker Creek channel. A number of sailcraft skippers have come to grief over the years by not paying adequate attention to these important range markers.

Northeast of #5, the channel swings sharply northwest and enters the main body of Whittaker Creek. Pass unlighted daybeacon #7 well to its

*Inland Waterway Treasure Company–Oriental*

northeasterly side. Soon, you will spy Whittaker Creek's fuel dock dead ahead; it occupies the point at a major split in the creek. If you are continuing upstream to either of the repair yards, cruise up the creek's southwesterly branch, favoring the northeasterly banks as you pass the yacht harbor's slips. Soon, both yards will be obvious to port.

**Oriental**   The entrance to Oriental Harbor is well marked and easy to navigate. Come abeam of flashing daybeacon #1 to its northeasterly side and continue cruising northwest down the marked track. After passing between flashing daybeacon #6 and unlighted daybeacon #5, the channel cuts farther to the north. Point to pass flashing daybeacon #8 to its westerly quarter. This aid marks a stone breakwater; be sure to pass it on the proper side.

After rounding #8, swing sharply to starboard and set an east-northeasterly course parallel to the stone breakwater into Oriental Harbor. As you cruise into the sheltered basin, you will spy Oriental Marina to starboard.

**Oriental Anchorage**   Cruisers choosing to an-

chor on the waters of Greens or Smith Creeks, located northwest of Oriental Harbor, should set course from flashing daybeacon #8 for the central pass-through of the fixed span lying to the northwest. This bridge has a vertical clearance of 45 feet. Skippers whose craft need more clearance are out of luck.

Once through the span, look to starboard and you will spy a small orange-and-white warning buoy set out from a mass of semisubmerged pilings. Stay well away from these hazards.

To enter Greens Creek, cut west and pass between the first pair of unlighted red and green daybeacons. Ignore the second pair. These latter aids lead to a private dockage complex in the charted offshoot striking northwest from the main body of Greens Creek.

Instead, continue tracking upstream on Greens Creek along its midsection. Soon, you will approach a major parting of the waters. Anchor 150 yards short of (east of) this major split. Depths on both the northwesterly branch and the principal southwesterly arm of Greens Creek deteriorate past this point of land.

Enter Smith Creek by passing unlighted daybeacon #9 to your port side and unlighted daybeacon #10 to starboard. Cruise upstream from #10 on the midwidth for another 100 yards or so and drop anchor. Depths rise to 4 feet or so farther upstream.

**On the ICW**   From flashing daybeacon #7, it is a run of 2.6 nautical miles southwest to flashing daybeacon #1AC, which marks the mouth of Adams Creek. If you are interested in cruising the upper Neuse River, see the "Up the Neuse" section below. To continue south on the ICW, pass #1AC on its southwestern side and cut sharply southeast. Point to pass between red nun buoy

#2 and flashing daybeacon #3. Don't drift southwest of #2. Shoal water seems to be building out from the adjacent point.

The Waterway now swings almost due south, directly into the mouth of Adams Creek. Set course to come abeam of flashing daybeacon #4 to its northeasterly side. The channel shifts once again, this time back to the southeast. Observe the usual ICW color scheme by passing unlighted daybeacons #4A and #6 to their northeasterly sides. The charted range southeast of #7 is not particularly important to pleasure craft along this track.

After passing flashing daybeacon #7, point to come abeam of flashing daybeacon #9 to its southwesterly side. This aid doubles as a forward range marker, and its appearance is not typical of the fixed aids to navigation along the ICW. Be sure not to mistake the 35-foot rear range marker for #9. At #9, boaters may choose to enter Cedar Creek, an excellent overnight anchorage.

**Cedar Creek**   To enter Cedar Creek, leave the ICW at flashing daybeacon #9 and cut east into the mid-width of the stream. You may cruise as far as 0.3 nautical mile from #9 and hold minimum depths of 6 feet. Farther to the east, some 5-foot depths will be encountered.

Cedar Creek joins two smaller creeks to the north and south; the one to the north is named Jonaquin Creek. Both branches are excellent gunkholing prospects, but do your exploring by dinghy. Depths on both streams run 4 feet.

**On the ICW**   Northbound boaters on the ICW are advised to make use of the charted range that employs flashing daybeacon #9 as the forward marker in the pair. These aids to navigation help passing cruisers avoid the charted shallows flanking the

Waterway's northwestern flank between unlighted daybeacon #12 and flashing daybeacon #9.

Don't attempt to anchor on the bubble of deep water abutting the southeastern side of the ICW between #9 and unlighted daybeacon #10. The dump symbol on chart 11541 denotes a foul bottom in this area.

Back Creek makes into the ICW southeast of unlighted daybeacon #12. Don't be tempted to enter. Depths between the Waterway and Back Creek have shoaled to 3½ feet or less.

Pay particular attention to the various markers south and southwest of unlighted daybeacon #12. Depths outside the ICW are quite shallow.

South of flashing daybeacon #17, the ICW flows into a man-made canal connecting Adams and Core Creeks. These waters are sometimes fouled with floating debris. Keep a sharp watch for floating logs and other large obstructions.

The entrance to Sea Gate Marina will come abeam on the western banks 2.4 nautical miles south of flashing daybeacon #18. Enter the canal leading to the dockage basin on its midline. Don't cut either corner at the entrance. Soon, the fuel dock and ship's store will be obvious to starboard, followed a bit farther upstream by the dockage basin.

The fixed, high-rise Core Creek Bridge crosses the ICW approximately 1.4 nautical miles south of Sea Gate Marina. The span has a delightful vertical clearance of 65 feet.

You will spot Bock Marine along the Waterway's eastern banks a short distance south of the high-rise. Be sure to cruise past the piers at idle speed.

South of the Core Creek Bridge, the Waterway follows a clear, straight, and well-marked route down the length of Core Creek. Between flashing daybeacons #19 and #20, no-wake regulations are in effect to protect a set of commercial fishing wharves along the eastern banks.

South of flashing daybeacon #20, the waters begin to widen. Don't be fooled. The ICW channel parallels the western banks between #20 and unlighted daybeacon #21. The waters farther to the east are quite shoal.

Once abeam of unlighted daybeacon #21, point for the gap between flashing daybeacon #24 and

unlighted daybeacon #23. The charted range is useful in helping you keep to the channel's mid-width.

From #24, the ICW cuts southeast into the wide and mostly shallow waters of the Newport River. This body of water is associated with the Morehead City–Beaufort region and will be discussed in chapter 8.

This chapter now returns to a discussion of the upper Neuse River from the ICW to New Bern.

## UP THE NEUSE

From Adams Creek to New Bern, the Neuse continues to be easily navigable, offering many cruising opportunities and overnight anchorages. Good marina facilities are at Clubfoot Creek, Minnesott Beach, Fairfield Harbor, and New Bern. The Trent River, which intersects the Neuse at New Bern, offers even more cruising potential. Most Waterway boaters turn south at Adams Creek. It is their loss not to experience the charms of the upper Neuse.

Cruising mariners should know that the twin 1996 hurricanes, Fran and Bertha, visited some of their worst damage on the New Bern waterfront. Happily, one large marina is up and running again with full facilities for cruising visitors. One of the other principal New Bern marinas wasn't so lucky.

### Clubfoot Creek and Matthews Point Marina

Clubfoot Creek has undergone a radical change since I first visited in 1980 and almost ran aground. This body of water lies along the Neuse's southern shoreline southwest of charted Great Island. The entrance channel is well marked, and pleasure craft of most any size can enter with confidence. Entrance depths range from 8 to 15 feet, and much of the creek carries a similar water level. Several good anchorages and a first-rate marina should attract more than a few passing skippers. As a bonus, the creek's beautifully natural banks present as attractive an appearance as you will find in this land of lovely shorelines.

Matthews Point Marina sits proudly on the creek's sheltered westerly shores south of the charted village of Temple, at the intersection of Clubfoot and Mitchell Creeks. Of all the North Carolina marinas I have reviewed, Matthews Point fits the "charming" description as well as any. Set in a little-frequented body of water, surrounded by virgin shores, and peopled by some of the most knowledgeable and friendly staff a boater could ask for, Matthews Point Marina deserves a red circle on any cruiser's chart.

The marina management is eager to greet transient cruisers. Dockage is available for a night, a week, or even longer at fixed wooden piers and slips with the latest power and water connections. Dockside depths range from 6 to 8 feet. The clubhouse boasts a bar, a magnificent view of the surrounding waters, and several nice showers. Because of this facility's rapidly increasing popularity, it might be best to call ahead for slip reservations.

Gasoline, diesel fuel, and waste pump-out are available, and mechanical repairs can be arranged through independent contractors. A very small ship's store is located in the dockmaster's office. About the only thing missing is an on-site restaurant, but the food cooked in your own galley will be ever so much tastier when enjoyed with a view of the tranquil creek.

Matthews Point's commitment to happy patrons can be seen in the frequent barbecues and other special events held by the owner at the new clubhouse. In short, I recommend Matthews Point Marina without reservation.

## Matthews Point Marina
### (919) 444-1805

Approach depth: 8–15 feet
Dockside depth: 6–8 feet
Accepts transients: yes
Fixed wooden piers: yes
Dockside power connections: 30 & 50 amps
Dockside water connections: yes
Showers: yes
Waste pump-out: yes
Gasoline: yes
Diesel fuel: yes
Mechanical repairs: independent contractors
Ship's store: limited

I should also note that the owner, Jet Matthews, was a key player in the effort to prevent the state of North Carolina from implementing a disastrous easement-fee program for bottom lands over which marina docks are lo-

cated. If it had not been for Jet, Harry Schiffman of Salty Dawg Marina in Manteo, and many other dedicated individuals in the North Carolina marine community, this program would almost certainly have resulted in vastly increased dockage fees statewide.

For those who fancy a night swinging at the hook, Clubfoot Creek offers some excellent anchorages. The main body of the creek north of the marina is broad, but in light airs, craft of most any size can drop the hook along the creek's central axis. Other captains sometimes choose to anchor abeam of Matthews Point's entrance channel when winds are less than 15 knots. For a really snug overnight stay, Gulden Creek, located on the eastern shore, maintains 4½- to 5-foot depths on its northwestern reaches and offers good protection. Even better is the main body of Mitchell Creek, located past the marina docks. Minimum 5-foot depths carry well upstream; most soundings are in the 5- to 8-foot range. The wooded shores are lovely and provide superior protection from all airs. Finally, the southern branch of Clubfoot Creek itself, located north of the charted position of Blades, holds 5- to 9-foot depths and provides good protection from eastern and western winds. Strong northern blows call for a different plan.

## Minnesott Beach Yacht Harbor

West of unlighted daybeacon #8, a ferry regularly crosses the Neuse River from the tiny village of Minnesott Beach to Cherry Point. Study chart 11552 and notice the marked channel a short jog west of the village's position. This cut leads to Minnesott Beach Yacht Harbor, yet another in the Neuse's long chain of first-rate

*Minnesott Beach Yacht Harbor*

facilities. The marina's dockage basin has been carved out of the surrounding swamps and is shown on chart 11552 as an unnamed creek. Entrance depths at the time of this writing ran about 6 to 7 feet. This facility owns its own dredge, and it is to be hoped that these soundings can be maintained indefinitely. Dockside depths range from 6 to 8 feet. Transients are readily accepted for overnight berths at fixed wooden docks with water and 30- and 50-amp power connections. Slip space has been vastly expanded over the past several years; those who have not visited for some time will be in for quite a surprise.

Gasoline and diesel fuel can be purchased at a new fuel dock you will spy to port as you enter the basin. An on-site ship's and variety store is perched beside an air-conditioned lounge graced by a color TV and a paperback exchange library. The adjacent showers and laundromat are excellent. The marina even maintains a swimming pool to give visitors a refreshing end to those long, hot summer cruises. Waste pump-out service is available. The nearby Minnesott Restau-rant provides complimentary transportation to and from the marina docks.

All these impressive facilities notwith-standing, Minnesott Beach's marine repair services are the star attraction for many boaters. The friendly yard crew can handle just about any mechanical or below-the-waterline repair problem you are ever likely to encounter. The space and facilities devoted to service work are quite impressive indeed. A travel-lift rated at 60 tons is available. The yard also specializes in topside and hull repairs and refinishing, including Imron and Awl-grip. If you are in need of service work or just a new coat of antifouling for your bottom, you could scarcely do better than this notable facility.

### Minnesott Beach Yacht Harbor (919) 249-1424

Approach depth: 6-7 feet
Dockside depth: 6–8 feet
Accepts transients: yes
Fixed wooden piers: yes
Dockside power connections: 30 & 50 amps
Dockside water connections: yes
Showers: yes
Laundromat: yes
Waste pump-out: yes
Gasoline: yes
Diesel fuel: yes
Mechanical repairs: extensive
Below-waterline repairs: extensive
Ship's store: yes
Restaurant: nearby

### Hancock and Slocum Creeks

Two streams on the Neuse's southern shore-line well west of flashing daybeacon #9 are best avoided. Both Hancock and Slocum Creeks cut into the Cherry Point Marine Base and are pretty much off-limits for private pleasure craft.

## Goose Creek

The wide mouth of Goose Creek cuts into the Neuse River's northeastern banks well northeast of flashing daybeacon #17. This inviting body of water has an unmarked channel, but depths will allow cautious mariners to enter without too much difficulty. You can expect minimum soundings of 7 feet anywhere in the wide channel. The creek's shoreline is composed alternately of undeveloped marsh and heavily wooded banks.

Goose Creek makes a fine overnight anchorage. But before deciding to spend an evening here, you should read the section on Upper Broad Creek, the next sidewater discussed. The two creeks are similar in character, but Upper Broad Creek, unlike Goose Creek, is marked.

If you decide on Goose Creek for an overnight stop, consider anchoring on the correctly charted 6-foot waters short of the stream's first turn to the north. This spot is open to southwesterly winds but well sheltered from all other breezes. There is enough elbow room for vessels up to 50 feet in length.

## Upper Broad Creek

Upper Broad Creek, one of the finest overnight anchorages on the Neuse River, cuts the northeastern banks well east-northeast of flashing daybeacon #19. It is well marked and consistently deep and boasts good protection and solid holding ground. Blackbeard Sailing Club overlooks the creek's western shore north of unlighted daybeacon #3, but this organization does not offer any services for visitors. Otherwise, the shoreline is dotted with minimal residential development. Elementary coastal navigation should allow you to cruise upstream to the charted 35-foot power line in minimum depths of 6 feet. Most of the channel is considerably deeper.

In light to moderate winds, you can anchor anywhere on Broad Creek. In heavy weather, cruise up the creek to the waters just south of the overhead power lines. There, you can anchor in 6- to 7-foot depths with good sanctuary from all but southerly winds.

## Northwest Creek Marina and Fairfield Harbor

Just northwest of Upper Broad Creek on the Neuse River, Northwest Creek provides access to Fairfield Harbor, a large, luxurious condominium development, and full-service Northwest Creek Marina. The marked entry channel carries 6½- to 7-foot depths, and 8- to 14-foot soundings can now be expected dockside, following the completion of a recent dredging project. This well-appointed marina welcomes transients and offers berths at extensive fixed wooden piers set in a well-sheltered basin surrounded by a tasteful condo/retail complex. Northwest Creek Marina survived Hurricanes Fran and Bertha with very little damage.

All slips have power and water connections. Plans are going forward for a 1997 expansion of dockage. When the project is completed, 270 slips should be available to visiting and resident mariners. Gasoline, diesel fuel, and waste pump-out service are in the offing, and mechanical repairs can be arranged. The on-site Harbor Breeze General Store (919-635-1066) can usually supply your grocery, marine, and snack needs; the luncheon sandwiches are nothing to sneeze at either. An air-conditioned boaters' lounge with a paperback exchange library overlooks the docks. The adjacent showers and laundromat are extraclean and climate-controlled. Transients have guest privileges at the nearby swimming pool, tennis courts, golf course, and exercise room.

The adjacent Captain Bordeaux Restaurant (919-637-2244) has a good reputation. It is open evenings only during the fall months but usually for both lunch and dinner during the spring and summer. It is closed entirely in December and January.

I found the staff of the entire Northwest Creek Marina complex ready to go the extra mile to meet visiting cruisers' needs.

*Neuse River as seen from Oriental*

**Northwest Creek Marina
at Fairfield Harbor
(919) 638-4133**

Approach depth: 6½-7 feet
Dockside depth: 8+ feet
Accepts transients: yes
Fixed wooden piers: yes
Dockside power connections: 30 & 50 amps
Dockside water connections: yes
Showers: yes
Laundromat: yes
Waste pump-out: yes
Gasoline: yes
Diesel fuel: yes
Mechanical repairs: independent contractors
Ship's & variety store: yes
Snack bar: yes
Restaurant: on-site

## New Bern

New Bern guards the crucial intersection of the Neuse and Trent Rivers. Ideally situated for waterborne commerce, this city has been important in North Carolina history since its found-ing in the 1700s. In fact, New Bern served as the colonial capital until the Revolutionary War, then as the first capital of North Carolina until the early 1790s.

Today, New Bern is a thriving coastal city that has managed to retain much of its earlier charm. Excellent motels and restaurants are within easy walking distance of the waterfront. Currently, one large marina on the Trent River provides excellent dockage. Keep in mind that you must pass through a swing bridge with 13 feet of closed vertical clearance and a restricted opening schedule to reach this facility.

New Bern boasts a dynamic, revitalized down-town business district and many historical build-ings, including Tryon Palace, one of the most memorable structures in all of North Carolina. It's easy to see why more and more cruisers are setting their sights on this fortunate community on the banks of the Neuse and Trent Rivers. I highly suggest you join this happy throng.

Visitors to New Bern in need of taxi service can call New Taxi Service (919-636-9000). Car rentals are available from Hertz (919-637-3021),

Avis (919-637-2130), and Enterprise (919-514-2575).

## New Bern Marinas

In the fall of 1996, New Bern's waterfront suffered extensively from Hurricanes Bertha and Fran. The popular Ramada Marina, flanking the Trent River's southerly banks directly across from the Sheraton Marina, was all but destroyed. During this writer's visit in January 1997, not a single dock remained standing. Many of the basin's pilings survived, however, and plans are going forward for a full restoration of this facility. A visit in the summer of 1997 confirmed progress on rebuilding that should be complete as this goes to press.

Similarly, the Comfort Inn Marina, which fronted the western banks of the Neuse River near unlighted daybeacon #34, was laid waste by the twin storms. After Bertha, this writer took a photograph, later used in *Soundings* magazine, of a power cruiser originally berthed at the Comfort Inn whose bow was pointed at the sky. Rumor has it that this marina may not be rebuilt. Only time will tell.

Fortunately, New Bern's largest pleasure-craft facility, the Sheraton New Bern Hotel and Marina, suffered only minor damage and is up and running at full capacity. Cruising visitors can still be confident of finding first-class slips at the Sheraton. You will spot the marina's extensive floating, wooden-decked deepwater docks on the Trent's northern banks between the low-level Trent River highway and railroad bridges. Minimum depths alongside are 8 feet, with 12-foot soundings typical. A 700-foot floating dock designed as a breakwater fronts the dockage com-

plex, providing not only additional berth space but good shelter for the remaining slips. All docks have ultramodern power, water, and cable-television connections. Gasoline and diesel fuel can be purchased, and transients are free to make use of the hotel's swimming pool. Free waste pump-out service is offered, sponsored by the local Rotary Club. Clean showers, a laundromat, and a well-outfitted exercise room are available on the first floor of the adjacent convention center. The friendly dockmaster can often arrange for mechanical repairs via independent technicians.

Cruisers in need of galley supplies will be glad to learn that the Pak-A-Sak supermarket (215 East Front Street, 919-633-0020) is located within a three-block walk. Ask the dockmaster or one of his staff for directions. The Sheraton's docks also allow quick access by foot to the downtown business district and the city's many historic attractions.

The marina is overlooked by a large Sheraton

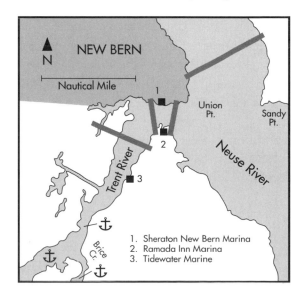

1. Sheraton New Bern Marina
2. Ramada Inn Marina
3. Tidewater Marine

Hotel which features a good restaurant and extensive convention facilities. Passing cruisers will quickly note the complex's huge secondary building (which contains suites) gazing serenely over the Trent River just east of the original hotel building.

---

**Sheraton New Bern Marina**
**(919) 638-3585**

Approach depth: 12+ feet
Dockside depth: 8–12 feet
Accepts transients: yes
Floating wooden piers: yes
Dockside power connections: 30 & 50 amps
Dockside water connections: yes
Showers: yes
Laundromat: yes
Waste pump-out: yes
Gasoline: yes
Diesel fuel: yes
Restaurant: on-site, with several nearby

---

For many years, a set of poorly maintained and rather shallow town docks was located hard by Union Point at the intersection of the Trent and Neuse Rivers. These structures were backed by a public park with a few interesting but neglected historical displays. The Union Point piers were destroyed by the twin hurricanes, but plans call for new docks to be rebuilt in the near future and for the park itself to receive a thorough renovation. Unless dredging is also undertaken, however, depths alongside may well revert to their old 4-foot levels.

## Downtown New Bern

Begin your visit to downtown New Bern at the new headquarters of the Craven County Visitor's Information Center (919-637-9400 or 800-437-5767) and the New Bern Chamber of Commerce (919-637-3111). This combined office is located at 316 Tryon Palace Drive, within a block of the Sheraton's docks. Be sure to ask for the "New Bern Heritage Tour" brochure and map. This useful document will lead you on a walking tour of the city's historic district and its more than 140 historic sites. You can also get all sorts of other useful information and advice from the office's helpful staff.

After leaving the visitor's center, walk west on Tryon Palace Drive and turn right (north) on Middle Street. On the corner, you will discover one of this writer's favorite coastal North Carolina shops. Captain Ratty's Gifts (202 Middle Street, 919-633-2088) is owned and managed by Pete Driscoll, an ultrafriendly, died-in-the-wool boater and lover of things nautical. Among a host of offerings, Captain Ratty's features over 300 nautical-book titles and a full selection of quality boating gear, including charts, clothes, and shoes. Don't miss the new selection of imported wines and beers. Captain Ratty's is a "can't miss" spot for cruisers.

Middle Street and nearby Craven Street are chock-full of interesting shops, many of the antique variety. Be *sure* to drop by Mitchell Hardware (215 Craven Street, 919-638-4261). Walking through the door at Mitchell's is like stepping back in time about 100 years. Seldom will you find a more extensive collection of interesting, hard-to-find equipment and hardware of most every description.

## New Bern Restaurants

When it comes to fine-dining choices, downtown New Bern has an embarrassment of riches. You could spend a week or two tucked snugly in one of the Sheraton's docks and not exhaust the city's culinary possibilities.

Of course, you might want to start your gastronomical review at the restaurant housed in the Sheraton complex. Normally, I am not impressed with hotel (and motel) restaurants, but this operation is an exception. An outstanding breakfast and a notable luncheon buffet are offered here.

The Harvey Mansion Restaurant and Lounge (211 Tryon Palace Drive, 919-638-3205) is housed in an impressive, three-story historic mansion overlooking the Trent River. Once owned by one of New Bern's most successful merchants, this venerable homeplace subsequently served as a boarding school, a military academy, and an apartment house; it was also the quarters for Craven Community College. After lying va-

cant for years, the mansion was restored as one of New Bern's finest restaurants. New owners took over in 1993, and they have vastly improved this dining spot's offerings. The seafood and veal dishes are absolutely spectacular. And recently, the chef has begun to prepare unusual game dishes which are nothing short of extraordinary. The Harvey Mansion is open seven days a week for dinner only. While this restaurant and its white-tablecloth atmosphere will never be described as inexpensive, the Harvey Mansion receives this writer's vote for the most distinguished dining spot in New Bern.

For something a little more informal, try Chelsea's Restaurant (335 Middle Street, 919-637-5469). The owners have recently remodeled and expanded the upstairs dining space to accommodate large parties. The Chelsea serves

*Sheraton New Bern Marina*

lunch and dinner. Both my mate and I were quite taken with the Maryland Crabcake Sandwich for our midday meal, and the Pan Barbecued Voodoo Shrimp were wonderful in the evening.

Those seeking a good lunch spot need look no farther than Fred & Clair's Restaurant (247 Craven Street, 919-638-5426). The sandwiches here are delicious and the lunch specials tasty and unique.

Cruisers with a flair for northern Italian cuisine should check out Scalzo's Restaurant (415 Broad Street, 919-633-9898). I have not yet had the opportunity to dine here, but reports from locals paint a picture of gastronomical pleasure.

Are you looking for some scrumptious baked goods to take back to your galley? Well, search no farther than Sweet Bears Pastry Company (301 Middle Street, 919-635-5325). The cookies here are "to die for," and the Italian Bread—well, words just fail me. Sweet Bears is open for breakfast, and the staff will prepare box lunches.

If you're into coffee houses, New Bern is ready for you. Within the past several years, two such establishments have opened in the downtown district. Trent River Coffee Company (208 Craven Street, 919-514-2030) is housed in an old brick building with hardwood floors and a thoroughly charming atmosphere. The cappuccino and *caffè latte* are memorable. Marina Sweets (208 Middle Street, 919-637-9307) serves not only good coffee, but hand-dipped ice cream as well. On a hot summer day, it's ever so wonderful!

## New Bern Attractions

New Bern is a must stop for those interested in the history of coastal North Carolina. The city is proud of its heritage and has worked diligently to maintain and restore many artifacts of its rich past.

It's only a short step from the waterfront to New Bern's premier historical attraction. Tryon Palace (600 Pollock Street, 919-514-4900 or 800-767-1560) and two other associated houses of later vintage are "must see" points of interest. Though the main building was destroyed by fire during the late 1700s, and though all but one of the original outlying structures fell victim to the slow march of years, the entire complex has been lovingly restored to the specifications of Governor Tryon's day.

Guests of the palace may now choose between two different types of tours. The more traditional excursion runs every half-hour from 9 A.M. to 4 P.M. Monday through Saturday and from 1 P.M. to 4 P.M. Sunday; this tour lasts a little over two hours. Guests are accompanied by a costumed interpreter who provides thorough insight into the life of Tryon Palace in the days when it was the colonial capital of North Carolina. From Memorial Day to mid-August, visitors may select a more novel approach, the so-called Dramatic Tour of the palace. Those lucky enough to take this journey back to the 18th century will find themselves treated as if they were the guests of Governor Tryon and his fair lady at a ball given just before the governor left in 1771 to take up his new post in New York. Actors and actresses portray carefully researched composite characters in an informative, often humorous way most visitors find delightful.

In addition to the tours, the palace complex offers daily demonstrations in colonial cooking, basket and candle making, and blacksmithing. I found the costumed craftspeople to be knowledgeable and responsive to visitors' questions. In my opinion, the palace craft activities compare favorably to similar attractions in Williamsburg, Virginia.

For those who do not wish to visit the palace, a "gardens only" ticket is available at a reduced price. This ticket allows visitors to tour the extensive gardens and the two gift shops on the grounds.

Tryon Palace boasts two additional points of interest.

Just to the left of the palace's main gate, the 1828 Dixon-Stevenson House gladly accepts visitors. This magnificent Federal-style house features a widow's walk and an impressive collection of authentic Federal furnishings. The house was built on land auctioned off from the palace grounds following the destruction of the main building. During the Civil War, it served as a hospital for the Ninth Vermont Regiment.

The nearby 1783 John Wright Stanly House features memorable Georgian architecture. Stanly was one of New Bern's staunchest patriots during the American Revolution. However, he did not live to see that war's greatest hero visit his beloved mansion. Two years after Stanly's death, in 1789, President George Washington spent several days at the late patriot's homeplace during his tour of the Southern states. Visitors will be impressed by this historic home's luxurious trappings.

The New Bern Academy Museum (at the corner of Hancock and New Streets, 919-514-4874) gives a penetrating insight into early North Carolina education. New Bern architecture and builders and the city's Civil War history are also featured.

The New Bern Historical Society, one of the most diligent organizations of its type in the state, maintains the 1790 Attmore-Oliver House (511 Broad Street, 919-638-8558). Tours are given from 1:00 P.M. to 4:30 P.M. Tuesday through Saturday except during January, February, and March; tours are by appointment only during these winter months. The society has worked diligently to acquire and display an impressive collections of 18th- and 19th-century furnishings and memorabilia. Cruising visitors are encouraged to patronize this most worthwhile attraction.

And if all these points of interest are not enough to convince you to visit New Bern, the city has for many years maintained one of the few museums in the country that focuses on firefighting. The New Bern Fireman's Museum (410 Hancock Street, 919-636-4087) is dedicated to the display of early firefighting equipment, including steam pumpers and Civil War relics. This facility, expanded a few years ago through the dedicated efforts of the local fire department and volunteers, is drawing more visitors every month. It is open from 10:00 A.M. until 4:30 P.M. Monday through Saturday and from 1:00 P.M. to 5:00 P.M. Sunday.

One of the community's newest attractions is the New Bern Civil War Museum (301 Metcalf Street, 919-633-2818). This notable museum's sole purpose is to preserve New Bern's rich Civil War history. It houses one of the finest private collections of War Between the States memorabilia and weapons in the United States. The museum is open Tuesday through Sunday from April

1 to September 20 and weekends only between October and March. An admission fee is charged.

Obviously, there is much to see and do in New Bern. The list of attractions has grown quickly since the first edition of this guide was printed in the early 1980s. Now, New Bern can truly lay claim to having one of the most well-appointed historical districts on the North Carolina coast. Thanks to all these attractions and New Bern's impressive docking facilities, this progressive city is becoming a very popular port of call for visiting cruisers.

## New Bern Events

As you might expect from such a vibrant community, New Bern hosts a number of special events and festivals throughout the year which will be of interest to cruising visitors.

Make every effort to attend Ratty's Victorian Regatta, held the last Saturday in September. Pete Driscoll of Captain Ratty's (see above) constructed an exquisite wooden rowing skiff for the inaugural celebration of this festival in 1996. This craft is now on display in the lobby of the Sheraton Hotel.

During the second weekend in April, New Bern hosts the Spring Historic Homes and Garden Tour. Many of the city's private, historic homeplaces are opened to the public. This celebration is held in conjunction with the Tryon Palace Tulip Festival, during which the gardens are open free to the public.

New Bern celebrates the Chrysanthemum Festival from October 10 to October 12, when thousands of mums are in bloom. There is an associated street festival. Again, the Tryon Palace gardens are open to the public without charge.

October 24 and 25 bring on ghostly visitations in downtown New Bern. The "New Bern at Night Ghost Walk" allows visitors to meet "historic ghosts" in many of the town's venerable homeplaces and cemeteries.

During the Christmas season, the evening candlelight tours of Tryon Palace are a must. Call the palace (see above) for times and reservations.

## New Bern History

Almost since its founding in 1710, New Bern has been one of North Carolina's leading coastal cities. Like Edenton and Bath, New Bern was for many years a center of the state's government and culture. New Bern served as the colonial capital, then as the state capital until 1794, when the center of government was moved to the newly created city of Raleigh.

John Lawson, who also had more than a little to do with the founding of Bath, first visited the New Bern area in 1705. He quickly recognized the value of the location between the Neuse and Trent Rivers, both of which are quite navigable. He found an Indian town called Chattawka, meaning "where the fish are taken," and persuaded the Indians to sell him 1,200 acres, on which he built a cabin.

In 1710, Baron Christopher de Graffenried, with the sanction of the British government, led a group of German and Swiss colonists to the region. The settlement grew quickly at first, but the Tuscarora Indian War decimated it in 1711. The colonists had settled on scattered tracts, an arrangement that made it easy for the Indians to quietly and methodically murder the inhabitants.

Around 1720, the town had a second start under the leadership of Cullen Pollock, who had inherited substantial land in New Bern from his father. Pollock tirelessly promoted the community. Soon, the town was well on its way to becoming a major seaport and eventually the capital of the colony.

By 1739, New Bern had apparently recovered from the effects of the Indian wars. In that year, the Reverend George Whitfield visited the town and was "grieved" to see the minister encouraging dancing and even trying to find a dance master.

The colonial assembly first met in New Bern in 1737. By 1746, various state offices were located in the community. When New Bern became the state capital, the city's trade and importance increased. The town surpassed both Bath and Beaufort as a port, and many of its merchants became well-to-do exporters.

In 1749, James Davis brought North Carolina's first printing press to New Bern. He set up shop and began to publish the state's first newspaper, the *North Carolina Gazette*.

Between 1767 and 1770, at the request of Royal Governor William Tryon, a governor's "palace" was built in New Bern; in lovingly restored form, this structure continues to astonish visitors to this very day. Tryon Palace was built at a cost of £16,000, quite a sum of money in those days. The seemingly needless extravagance of this expenditure was apparently one of the leading causes of the War of Regulation, which culminated in 1771 in the Battle of Alamance, fought between the militia of Governor Tryon and a group of backwoodsmen known as the Regulators. The first provincial congress met at Tryon Palace in 1774 in defiance of the Crown. In 1774, Royal Governor Josiah Martin was forced to flee the palace at the less-than-gentle request of New Bern's hostile patriots.

After the Revolutionary War, commerce continued to grow. In 1819, regular steamboat service to New Bern was established. By 1851, it was reported that more than 100,000 barrels of turpentine, 35,000 barrels of resin, 1,900 bales of cotton, and 275,000 shingles had recently passed through the port. The Civil War brought occupation by Union forces, but New Bern continued to progress even after the war.

New Bern can boast several inventors among its one-time citizens. James Gill invented the revolver here in 1829, and Frederick Lente, born in 1823, devised a machine to transfuse blood. Caleb Bradham formulated the first Pepsi-Cola in New Bern during 1898 and served the drink at a downtown drugstore.

The first free public school in North Carolina was established in New Bern in 1766 by Dr. Elias Haroes. For many years, New Bern was known as "the Athens of North Carolina" because of the great local interest in education.

New Bern survives not only as a modern city but as a reminder of a storied past. Today, many buildings more than 200 years old are still standing.

## Trent River

From New Bern, cruising mariners have access to the enchanting Trent River. Well marked and consistently deep, the Trent offers limited pleasure-craft facilities above New Bern. The relatively narrow width of the river makes for small waves and comfortable anchorage most anywhere. A marina and repair yard of good reputation is located not far from New Bern, and the

East Carolina Yacht Club offers limited services for transient cruisers.

Southwest of the Sheraton Marina, cruisers exploring the Trent River must first pass through a (usually open) railway bridge and then under the fixed U.S. 70 Bypass bridge, a high-rise span with 45 feet of vertical clearance. Tall sailcraft that cannot clear this latter bridge must forgo the cruising charms of the Trent.

The docks of Tidewater Marine (919-637-3347) are perched on the Trent's southeastern shores a short jog southwest of the U.S. 70 Bypass bridge. Tidewater's primary emphasis is on repair work. Full mechanical service for both gasoline and diesel engines is offered, and haulouts are accomplished by a 15-ton travel-lift. Fiberglass repairs are also available. The adjacent wet-slip dockage is rented out on a month-to-month basis.

East Carolina Yacht Club (919-637-2389) maintains its docks on the Trent's northern shores near flashing daybeacon #8. Transients may be able to obtain overnight berths by calling the club well ahead of time. The fixed wooden piers feature all power and water connections.

The Trent River shoreline exhibits both undeveloped stretches and areas with light to moderate residential development. Pleasure-craft traffic on the Trent is surprisingly light, lending the waters an off-the-beaten-path quality.

South and southwest of flashing daybeacon #2, shelter is sufficient for skippers with craft as large as 50 feet to pitch the anchor anywhere that strikes their fancy. One of the best spots is between unlighted daybeacons #4 and #4A. The river narrows between these markers, and the

shores are overlooked by moderate residential development, including one condo complex to the north.

### Brices Creek

Brices Creek burrows its way into the Trent's southeastern shoreline between flashing daybeacon #2 and unlighted daybeacon #3. Brices is an unusually deep sidewater that makes an excellent overnight anchorage. Typical depths are 11 to 18 feet; the minimum depth is 8 feet. Visitors should be warned, though, that there are several unmarked shoals which must be avoided.

*Tryon Palace–New Bern*

The unusually deep water calls for a lot of anchor rode to obtain an acceptable scope. Consequently, craft over 36 feet in length might find themselves cramped for sufficient swinging room. A Bahamian mooring would certainly help to offset this problem.

Brices Creek's shoreline features extensive residential development. The creek is quite sheltered and makes an excellent spot to ride out a heavy blow.

Though you can reasonably expect to anchor almost anywhere on Brices Creek short of the charted, low-level fixed bridge, wise cruisers will settle on the 10- to 14-foot waters between the stream's first turn to the west and its next bend to the south. The shoreline here is simply beautiful, and the protection from foul weather doesn't get any better.

# UPPER NEUSE RIVER NAVIGATION

At flashing daybeacon #1AC on the ICW route northwest of Adams Creek, you will need to switch to chart 11552 to cruise west (upstream to New Bern) on the Neuse. A study of chart 11552 might lead you to conclude that two good sidewater possibilities are within easy reach of #1AC. However, one choice, Janeiro, has serious shoaling problems. The other, Clubfoot Creek, is a real cruising find.

**Clubfoot Creek**   Entry into Clubfoot Creek is facilitated by a comprehensive system of daybeacons. Carefully set course from #1AC to come abeam of unlighted daybeacon #1 by at least 0.7 nautical mile to its northerly side. This procedure will help you bypass the shoal waters stretching north from Great Island. Continue cruising upstream on the Neuse River for several hundred yards after coming abeam of #1. Only then should you turn south and point to pass flashing daybeacon #3 by 25 yards to its westerly side.

To enter Clubfoot Creek from #3, point to pass between unlighted daybeacons #5 and #6. Watch your sounder carefully, as shallows lie to the southwest and northeast. After leaving #6 behind, curl around to the south and point to pass unlighted daybeacon #8 by 25 yards to its easterly quarter.

Once past #8, follow the creek's mid-width as it stretches south to the intersection with Mitchell and Gulden Creeks. Here, you can choose to cruise either of these two auxiliary streams.

Enter Gulden Creek on its mid-width. Depths are in the 4½- to 5-foot range near the stream's mouth. Be sure to drop the hook before proceeding more than 100 yards upstream. Past this point, bottom levels begin to rise to 4 feet or less.

Matthews Point Marina has marked a deep channel leading to its docks and the interior portion of Mitchell Creek. You will spy the small, floating markers to the west as you come abeam of Mitchell Creek's mouth. As you enter this channel, you will spot the docks almost dead ahead. The main body of the creek curves away to the southwest. If you choose to berth at the marina, be sure to stay within the stick markers on either side of the docks. These poles outline the main channel.

To visit the upper reaches of Mitchell Creek, depart the marked marina channel just before reaching the docks and cruise back to the creek's mid-width. By sticking to the centerline, you can follow the creek well upstream in minimum 5-foot depths. Eventually, you will spot a small commercial fishery on the port shore, followed by a gray house on the same side. Past the house, depths quickly begin to deteriorate. Be sure to drop the hook well before coming abeam of the house.

Cruisers bent on exploring the southerly reaches of Clubfoot Creek need simply hold to the mid-width for good depths. Watch ahead on the westerly shore and you will eventually catch sight of a large white house. Past this point, there is a deep channel, but there are also several unmarked shoals to avoid. Boaters lacking local knowledge should discontinue their cruise before reaching the white house.

*Janeiro*    Janeiro, a small village on the river's northern shore, is served by a channel marked by unlighted daybeacons #2 and #4. Chart 11552 notes depths of 6 feet in the entrance channel, but extensive shoaling has occurred, and depths of 4 feet or less are now encountered. Additionally, the marked cut leads to a low-level fixed bridge with only 11 feet of vertical clearance. Obviously, this is a "locals only" channel that is of little consequence to cruising skippers.

*On the Neuse*    To cruise upriver on the Neuse from flashing daybeacon #1AC, consider setting a course for flashing daybeacon #9, located north of Cherry Point. A state-operated ferry traverses the Neuse on a regular schedule from Cherry Point to the village of Minnesott Beach. Come abeam of #9 by at least 50 yards to its northerly side. From #9, fortunate cruisers might choose to visit Minnesott Beach Yacht Harbor on the northerly shore.

*Minnesott Beach Yacht Harbor*    To enter Minnesott Beach Yacht Harbor, set course from flashing daybeacon #9 for the creek's entrance west of the marked ferry channel. Watch carefully for several privately maintained daybeacons which will lead you through the channel. As usual in this sort of cut, pass red markers to your starboard side and green markers to port.

The entrance cut leads to a rather narrow but well-dredged stream. This stream winds a bit, but you will soon see the marina nestled between a pine forest and a stand of tall cypress trees. The fuel dock will come abeam to port just short of the first slips.

*On the Neuse*    From flashing daybeacon #9, set course for flashing daybeacon #11 north of Flanner Beach. This is a long run of 7.3 nautical miles. Run a careful compass course and watch for leeway. Fortunately, you need not worry about surrounding shallows, as the river remains deep to within 300 yards of either shoreline.

Between #9 and #11, you will pass Hancock and Slocum Creeks along the river's southern banks. Both streams are best avoided, as they are part of the Cherry Point Marine Base.

You will also pass Beard Creek to the north during the same run. One unlighted daybeacon, #1, marks the entrance, but depths in the creek have shoaled to 2 feet. Do not attempt to enter!

To continue upstream on the Neuse, you can make use of a deep and well-marked channel beginning at flashing daybeacon #11. Pass unlighted daybeacons #13 and #15 to their northeastern sides, then point to come abeam of flashing daybeacon #17 to its northeastern quarter. At #17, Goose Creek, Upper Broad Creek, and Northwest Creek, all good cruising possibilities, are accessible to the northeast.

**Goose Creek**   Enter Goose Creek by striking a compass course from flashing daybeacon #17 for the creek's mouth. Give way to the southeast a bit on the first half of this run to avoid the charted Hampton Shoal shallows.

As you begin to enter Goose Creek, take care to avoid the considerable shallows shelving out from Cooper and Creek Points. As you come abeam of the small, unnamed cove on the creek's northwestern shore northeast of Creek Point, bend your course to the northeast and follow the creek's mid-width upstream. Don't be in a hurry. If you watch your depth, it is quite possible to cruise 0.5 nautical mile upstream from the creek's mouth and hold minimum depths of 6 feet. You can continue even farther in 5-foot depths.

**Upper Broad Creek**   To enter Upper Broad Creek, set a course from flashing daybeacon #17 to come abeam of flashing daybeacon #2 by 100 yards to its western side. From #2, set a new course to come abeam of and pass unlighted daybeacon #3 by no less than 50 yards to its southeastern side. Do not approach #3 too closely. Shoaling has taken place in the vicinity of this daybeacon.

Once past #3, stick to the creek's mid-width. You will soon pass Blackbeard Sailing Club on the northwestern shore. If you choose, you can cruise upstream as far as the overhead power lines in minimum depths of 6 feet. Sailors should note that these shocking obstructions have an overhead clearance of only 35 feet.

**Northwest Creek and Fairfield Harbor**   Boaters bound for Northwest Creek Marina and/or the Fairfield Harbor development should set course from flashing daybeacon #17 for the edge of the deep water southeast of McCotter Point. Keep a sharp watch for a series of green and red daybeacons. These markers will lead you into the mouth of Northwest Creek and to the marina.

**On the Neuse**   North and northwest of flashing daybeacon #17, navigators can follow a well-marked channel to New Bern and an intersection with the Trent River. North-northwest of flashing daybeacon #28, cruisers will quickly note a mammoth on-the-water construction project. A huge, fixed high-rise bridge that will eventually span the Neuse from a point near charted Scotts Creek to the river's eastern banks north of Sandy Point was just getting under way as of this writing. Boaters cruising these waters should proceed at idle speed and keep a sharp lookout for barges and other construction equipment. When the new span is completed, the old Neuse River swing bridge north of unlighted daybeacon #34 will be removed.

From #28 to flashing daybeacon #32 just off charted Union Point, you need only keep to the marked channel. From #32, boaters have access to the New Bern waterfront and the Trent River.

**New Bern**   At flashing daybeacon #32, the Trent River channel cuts sharply west, while a marked track on the Neuse River continues north. Most cruisers will want to turn west from #32 into the Trent River, home of the Sheraton marina.

To access this facility and the waters of the upper Trent River, leave the Neuse at flashing daybeacon #32 and pass through the first automobile swing bridge. As you cruise between #32 and the bridge, the future site of the Union Point town docks will come abeam to the north.

The Trent River highway bridge, which has a closed vertical clearance of 13 feet, currently opens on demand except from 6:30 A.M. to 8:30 A.M. and from 4:00 P.M. to 6:00 P.M. on weekdays. During these two periods, the span opens at 7:30 A.M. and 5:00 P.M. if boats are waiting. From May 24 to September 8, the span is closed on Sundays and federal holidays between 2:00 P.M. and 7:00 P.M. except for openings at 4:00 P.M. and 6:00 P.M. Bridge personnel monitor VHF channels 16 and 13, so don't hesitate to call the tender if you need further information.

After passing through the span, you will soon spy the extensive docks of the Sheraton complex to the north. Be sure to motor along at idle speed until you are well past the marina.

**Neuse River above New Bern**   From flashing daybeacon #32, a well-marked channel continues upstream through two swing bridges that open on demand. The first has a closed vertical clearance of 13 feet. The second (a railroad bridge) has, believe it or not, a closed vertical clearance of 0 feet. Past the second bridge, the river begins to narrow considerably, but a marked track continues for several miles.

This account of the Neuse ends at the second bridge, but adventurous boaters can continue following a 10-foot channel well upriver to the old site of Streets Ferry, today occupied by the Weyerhaeuser mill. Study chart 11552 carefully if you decide to try it, and don't be in a hurry. Should you make the attempt, watch the mainland shore 1 nautical mile above the second bridge for a sight of the Hatteras Yacht plant. Pleasure craft up to 120 feet in length are built and launched from this massive facility.

**Upper Trent River**   After leaving the Sheraton and Ramada marinas in your wake, head directly for the swing span of the railroad bridge, which is usually open unless a train is due. Thankfully, the swing

portion of this bridge has at last been replaced after many years of troublesome operation.

After passing through the railway span, adjust your course to the southwest and begin favoring the southeastern shoreline slightly as you cruise toward the high-rise highway bridge. As chart 11552 correctly indicates, a large patch of shoal water runs quite some distance out from the northwestern and western shorelines.

The U.S. 70 Bypass bridge has a vertical clearance of 45 feet. Sailors that need more height must retrace their steps.

Southwest of the fixed span, continue favoring the southeastern banks slightly as far as the piers of Tidewater Marine, which you will soon sight on the southeastern shoreline.

Continue upstream, holding to the river's midwidth. You will soon pass unlighted daybeacon #1 to its northwesterly side, followed by flashing daybeacon #2. At #2, the river turns a bit farther to the west. The entrance to Brices Creek will come abeam to the southeast.

**Brices Creek**   If you choose to enter Brices Creek, be careful not to cut either the northeastern or southwestern corner of the creek's entrance. Favor the northeastern shore as you pass into the main body of the stream to avoid the patch of shoal water lining the southwestern banks, clearly shown on chart 11552. However, chart 11552 would lead you to believe that deep water runs right up to the northeastern shore. This is incorrect, as there is a narrow shelf of shoal water extending out a short distance from the shoreline.

As you cruise farther upstream, continue to favor the northeastern and eastern shores as the creek turns to the south. Eventually, Brices Creek cuts back to the west. Be sure to favor the southeastern banks as you cruise through this turn.

After the second turn, good depths open out almost from shore to shore until the creek turns again, this time to the south. Depths decline past this point. It would be best to discontinue your explorations short of the southerly bend.

***On the Trent***   From flashing daybeacon #2, it is a relatively straightforward run upriver to flashing daybeacon #10. As you head upstream, pass all red aids to navigation to your starboard side and green markers to port. At flashing daybeacon #8, the piers of East Carolina Yacht Club will come abeam on the river's northern shore.

Soon after passing #10, boaters will encounter flashing daybeacon #13 near the river's southern shore. The channel between #13 and the next upriver daybeacon, #14, has shoaled badly. Visiting cruisers are advised to discontinue their cruise of the Trent at #13. While it is possible to continue upstream past the shallows, local knowledge is almost a necessity.

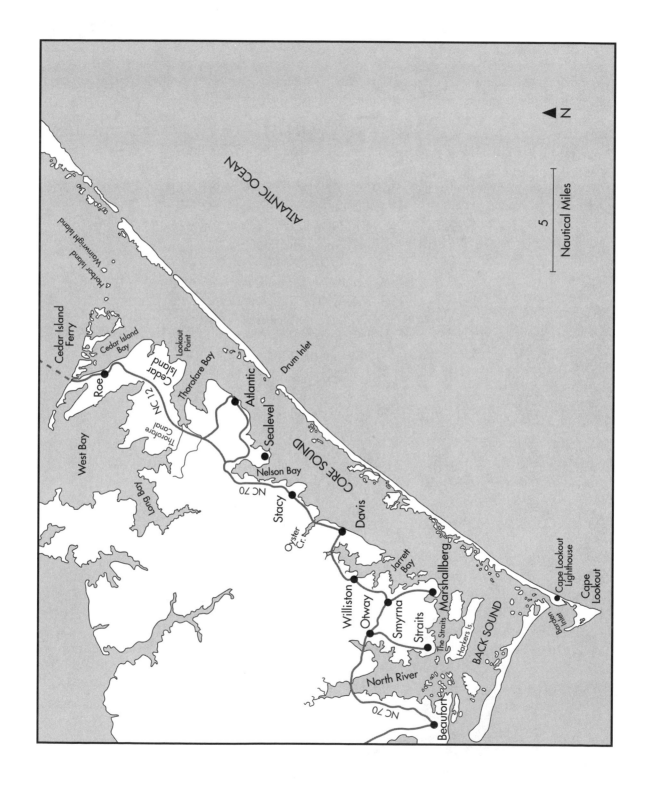

# The Core Sound

**Charts**

You will need two charts for navigation of Core Sound:

**11545** covers the southern quadrant

**11550** covers Core Sound's northern sections

Core Sound is a long but narrow body of water that extends from the extreme southeastern corner of Pamlico Sound southward to Cape Lookout Bight. The sound is approximately 28 nautical miles in length and seldom more than 3 nautical miles wide. Core Sound has an abundance of both desirable and unfortunate characteristics. In fact, seldom will the cruising boater encounter waters whose best and worst qualities are so clearly defined and so at odds with each other.

On the positive side, Core Sound is perhaps the most remote body of water on the entire North Carolina coast. Cruisers can often wander the entire length of the sound without seeing another craft. Should you spot one, it will almost certainly belong to a commercial fisherman rather than a fellow pleasure boater.

Core Sound's abundance of all types of seafood is evidenced in the large number of fisheries along its shores. If you cruise the sound during midsummer, you will probably observe many local residents clamming in the shallows. Core Sound is the only area of the eastern United States other than Chesapeake Bay where the art of "growing" soft-shell crabs is practiced.

Core Sound is a great challenge to the adventurous skipper. If you successfully navigate the Core, you will have a true feeling of accomplishment. You will have done what very few pleasure boaters have even attempted.

The sound affords a wonderful cruising opportunity for vessels under 25 feet in overall length powered by either outboard motors or stern drive. The shallow draft of these craft will make day cruising on the sound an exciting and rewarding experience.

The Core can be successfully navigated by both power craft and sailcraft drawing 4 feet or less. However, sailboats will probably find it best to proceed under power, as the need for changing course can arise suddenly.

As for the sound's negative characteristics, it is extremely shallow throughout. Many channels are badly shoaled. The Core is well marked, but not all the markers are where they should be. Navigation of these twisting channels requires exacting use of compass, chart, log, and the navigational information in this guide. Core Sound offers few reliable anchorages and is almost totally without facilities catering to cruising craft. Many of the region's charming villages can be approached only by dinghy, as their so-called entrance channels are quite shallow. Cruisers should be aware that, with the possible exception of Currituck Sound, Core Sound is the North Carolina body of water on which they are most likely to run aground.

Core Sound is not for the casual boater. However, if you have wanderlust in your heart and are willing to risk touching bottom, if your craft is 35 feet or less in overall length, and, most important, if it draws 4 feet or preferably less, then be assured that passage of the Core is possible. I have safely traversed the sound's entire length on several occasions in a 31-foot craft drawing 40 inches.

Visitors should take careful note of this warning: Core Sound should not be entered during adverse weather. Heavy blows can set you outside the narrow channels before you have a chance to make corrections. Rain showers can lower visibility to the point that you cannot pick out aids to navigation. On Core Sound, it is essential to be able to spot daybeacons without hindrance.

Leeway can be a great problem on the sound. A side-setting wind or current can quickly set you aground on the edge of a narrow channel. It is essential that you keep an eye not only ahead but also over your stern, to quickly note any slippage.

In the final analysis, every cruiser will have to evaluate for him- or herself the disparate qualities of Core Sound. The trade-off between the enchanting backwater character of these waters and their prodigious navigational difficulty is a quandary that can only be resolved by each skipper who contemplates a cruise of Core Sound. Read the information below carefully, study the charts, and have a long thought.

## Core Sound History

Core Sound is named for the Coree Indians, who once lived along the shoreline. This tribe was concentrated in the Cape Lookout and Harkers Island region.

Several old maps show a long, thin island in what is today the central portion of Core Sound. Stories of the island have survived in the sound's oral tradition. If this island did indeed exist, and if for some reason it eroded into the sound's waters, it could very well account for the Core's overall shallow depths.

Commercial fishing has long been the principal occupation of Core Sound natives. In 1806, William Tatham, a noted world traveler of his day, visited the area and saw evidence of the sound's widespread industry. He observed "seven large fishing canoes and several seines" at Cedar Inlet, located across Core Sound from Cedar Island before it closed in 1830.

Many people, some boaters among them, have never heard of menhaden, yet this fish was the source of North Carolina's most important commercial fishing industry until recent times. Though menhaden are considered inedible, their bodies yield valuable oils for cosmetics and are a key ingredient in the manufacture of fertilizer. Before 1900, Core Sound was the principal source of the state's menhaden harvest; however, the sound's annual yield eventually declined. Today, most menhaden are taken offshore.

Before 1935, Core Sound was a duck hunter's paradise. Several gun clubs were built along Core Banks and on Harbor Island. The sound's one-time popularity with waterfowl hunters is evident in the fact that the village of Atlantic was originally named Hunting Quarters. Duck hunting declined in the 1930s, and none of the old clubhouses remains today.

The villages of Core Sound resided in a state of isolation until recent times. Even now, none of the sound's communities has a thriving tourist trade. Most residents seem content to keep it that way. Folklore abounds in the region, a natural development in a community that has lived to itself for many years. The close-knit quality of the "Core Sounders" survives intact. It is refreshing to find a group of men and women who ask little of anyone and just go about their business much as their ancestors did.

In *A New Geography of North Carolina*, Bill Sharpe relates a sea chantey once sung by the fishermen of Core Sound:

> Peace at home
> and pleasure abroad
> Do all ya kin
> and serve the Lord
> Keep all ya got
> and get all ya kin
> Pay your debts
> and owe no man.

## CORE BANKS

Core Sound is bordered on the west by the North Carolina mainland and on the east by Core Banks. The Core Banks are a band of narrow, almost deserted sand spits. Generally, they are marshy on the sound side but have beautiful, lonely beaches on the seaward shore. Unfortunately, they are often rather buggy as well.

The Core Banks have no roads and can be negotiated by four-wheel-drive vehicles only via private, National Park Service–sanctioned ferries leaving from Davis, Atlantic, and Ocracoke. They are difficult to reach even by boat. Depths near shore run as little as 6 inches. If you wish to explore these wild and lonely beaches, approach them by dinghy. And observe one final warning: Take a liberal supply of insect repellent.

## Core Banks History

The earliest European residents of Core Banks were whalers. Whale Creek, Brier Hill, Three Hats Creek, and Jack's Place are long-forgotten names of the whalers' camps. One of the last lifesaving stations established on the North Carolina coast was located near Drum Inlet. First called Core Banks but later renamed Atlantic, the station was decommissioned in 1957.

Core Banks never supported a stable population for any length of time, except for the village of Portsmouth. This now-deserted town, located at the extreme northern tip of Core Banks, was associated with Pamlico Sound, not Core Sound. These forgotten beaches have changed very little in the last 300 years. Fortunately, Core Banks and the village of Portsmouth are now part of Cape Lookout National Seashore and are safe from commercial development.

## Drum Inlet

The seldom-used Drum Inlet lies almost directly southeast across the sound from the village of Atlantic. Unfortunately, Drum Inlet is too shallow for use by cruising boaters. It divides what is sometimes called Portsmouth Island, to the north, from the rest of Core Banks.

## Drum Inlet History

In 1970, the Corps of Engineers used explosives to artificially open the present-day Drum Inlet. This project was undertaken in response to requests from the citizens of Atlantic for a convenient outlet to the sea. Strong ocean tides immediately began to widen the inlet, and it proved impossible to maintain a reliable channel.

In the early 1930s, an earlier Drum Inlet opened to the north of the present-day stream. Not far to the south, the Core Banks Lifesaving Station was established in the late 1930s; it continued in operation until 1957. The earlier Drum Inlet closed naturally around 1960.

At least six different inlets have opened from time to time along this portion of Core Banks. A number have been known as Drum Inlet. It seems that this portion of Core Banks is so low that storm tides, which generally serve to keep inlets open by funneling strong currents through their channels, wash completely over the land. Consequently, all the inlets have been shallow and short-lived.

# UPPER CORE SOUND

If you can reach the towns and fishing villages along the mainland banks of Core Sound, you will experience perhaps the most unspoiled communities in the state. Visitors to these hamlets can acquire an idea of just what life in coastal North Carolina was like when the banks of Core Sound were isolated from the rest of society.

## Wainwright Island

Wainwright Island, near Core Sound's junction with Pamlico Sound west of unlighted nun buoy #4, is named for Colonel James Wainwright, who established a porpoise fishery in 1880 near Hatteras village. Wainwright Island is totally deserted and makes a good lunch spot or even an overnight camp. The island is surrounded by shallows, so your approach must be by dinghy or other shallow-draft vessel.

## Harbor Island

Harbor Island lies a short hop southwest of Wainwright Island. In 1867, this small landmass was the home of a screw-pile lighthouse placed here to aid commercial traffic moving south on Core Sound. A screw-pile lighthouse is a house with a lantern or beacon on its roof; the entire structure is suspended over the water on a series of pilings which are literally screwed into the bottom strata. The Harbor Island light was eventually destroyed in a hurricane, and I have been unable to find any trace of its existence.

In his book *Ocracoke*, Carl Goerch tells of a fishing and hunting club once located on Harbor Island. The building was constructed in the mid-1930s but was already falling into disrepair by the time Goerch's book was published in 1956. Today, the ruins of the old building litter the western tip of the island.

In the same book, Goerch relates the fact that local residents claim Harbor Island has shrunk in size over the years. Old tales speak of the island as being 15 to 20 acres in size; it is less than one acre today. The island makes for an interesting dinghy trip ashore. The ruins are fascinating to explore.

The body of Harbor Island tends to shelter the charted deeper waters south and southwest of the isle from northern and northeastern winds. This channel can serve as an overnight anchorage in light northerlies for boats drawing no more than 4 feet (the less, the better). However, even moderate southern, southeastern, and southwestern winds render this haven uncomfortable or even dangerous.

## Roe

West of the gap between flashing daybeacons #11 and #13, cruising skippers can follow a passable route into Cedar Island Bay and enter the protected harbor at Roe. You can expect minimum depths of 4 to 5 feet at low tide, with most of the route deeper. There are no facilities catering to pleasure vessels at Roe, but it may be possible to temporarily tie to a dock in the small harbor southwest of flashing daybeacon #8.

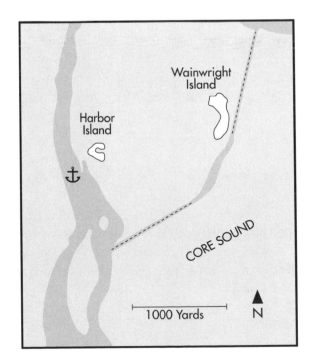

Depths in the sheltered basin run 4½ to 6 feet.

Roe Harbor is leased to various commercial fisheries. Make sure you inquire and obtain the proper permission before tying your lines to someone's leased dock.

### Thorofare Bay and Canal

Thorofare Bay, located along the sound's western shore west of flashing daybeacon #19, leads to a short canal that connects to West Thorofare Bay, an auxiliary water of southern Pamlico Sound. By using an old canal that connects West Thorofare Bay (via West Bay and Long Bay) to Turnagain Bay, a sidewater of the Neuse River, it is theoretically possible for captains piloting craft than can clear a 45-foot fixed bridge to travel directly from Core Sound to the Neuse River without entering often-choppy Pamlico Sound. However, the old canal off Long Bay has shoaled to 3-foot depths and can only be used by shallow-draft vessels.

Adding insult to injury, the approach to Thorofare Canal from Thorofare Bay has shoaled badly in at least one spot. At low tide, cruisers can expect some 3½- to 4-foot depths in the approach channel. Soundings on the canal itself improve to 5 feet or better. If you draw as much as 3½ feet, it would be a good idea to wait until high tide to use the canal.

Traversing Thorofare Canal is a fascinating ecological experience. With the exception of Thorofare Bridge, both shores are part of a huge grass savanna comprising the southern section of Cedar Island.

### Atlantic

A visit to the village of Atlantic, south of Thorofare Bay, is definitely worthwhile if you want to discover an active but unspoiled coastal town. Most of the village's residents are commercial fishermen. Although Atlantic has no facilities catering to cruising craft, there is extensive dockage for commercial fishing vessels. The entrance channel holds minimum 5-foot depths and is quite reliable, if narrow. Depths outside the channel run to grounding levels.

Groceries are available within a healthy walk of the waterfront, and the freshest of seafood can often be purchased at Atlantic's several commercial seafood plants. Currently, there are no fueling facilities for large pleasure craft on the Atlantic waterfront.

The greatest problem in visiting Atlantic is the lack of dockage for cruising boaters. If you are the diplomatic type, you might try negotiating for an empty space at one of the three commercial-craft dockage areas. Your best bet will probably be on the northeasternmost "harbor of refuge" north

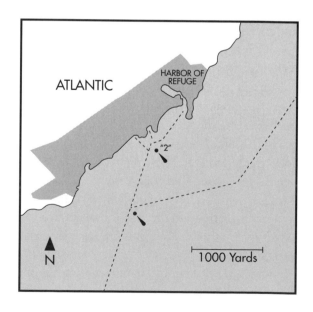

of flashing daybeacon #6. This small but well-sheltered harbor is flanked by an assortment of commercial fishing piers. You should remember that these docks are part of the commercial fishermen's serious business of earning a living, and they may be understandably jealous of their space. Be *sure* to acquire permission before tying overnight (or even longer than a few minutes) to any empty dock.

### Atlantic History

Atlantic is an old town—perhaps even "as old as Beaufort," according to one authority. The village was originally known as Hunting Quarters, a name apparently borrowed from an Indian settlement that once stood near the present town's site.

In 1954, Atlantic was said to produce one of the largest volumes of seafood in North Carolina. Today, commercial fishing and clamming are still the principal occupations of the village's citizens.

For many years, Atlantic was the principal jumping-off point for Ocracoke. A mailboat made daily runs between the two, and passengers were welcome. After regular ferry service was established between Hatteras and Ocracoke, the old mailboat route was discontinued.

### Sealevel

Sealevel is another of the charming, unspoiled coastal villages of Core Sound. The shallow entrance cut well north of flashing daybeacon #28. Sealevel has a protected harbor with depths of 5 to 6 feet, but its approach channel has shoaled to 3-foot depths at low tide. No facilities are available for pleasure craft, though there is a large commercial fishery on the harbor's western banks. There is plenty of room in the harbor to anchor.

*Atlantic harbor*

Visitors can reach a small country store via a long walk from the harbor. Sealevel also boasts a modern hospital and a motel with an excellent restaurant. You will need to obtain a ride from a friendly native to reach these, as neither is within walking distance of the harbor.

### Nelson Bay

The southern mouth of broad Nelson Bay lies northwest of flashing daybeacon #28. This body of water is not as good a prospect for a side trip or overnight anchorage as you might expect from studying chart 11545. The entrance to the bay at flashing daybeacon #1 is rather tricky, and the waters adjacent to flashing daybeacon #3 have shoaled to 3 feet.

Nelson Bay boasts a waterside motel and restaurant with its own fixed wooden pier; this complex overlooks the eastern shore northeast of flashing daybeacon #3. Unfortunately, you must cruise through 3-foot depths to reach the docks of Sealevel Inn (919-225-3651). Obviously, this facility is of little use to large pleasure craft.

Because of the bay's considerable width, even the deep waters between #1 and #3 do not make a particularly good anchorage except in light winds. All things considered, Nelson Bay is really not a good prospect for visiting cruisers.

## Oyster Creek

Oyster Creek cuts the mainland banks of Core Sound west of flashing daybeacon #33. Depths of 4 to 5 feet extend into the creek, and agile, shallow-draft craft might find a spot to anchor. A commercial fishery is located on the creek's northeasterly shore short of the charted, low-level fixed bridge.

Try carefully easing your way a bit to the northeast between flashing daybeacon #2 and unlighted daybeacon #3. Drop the hook as soon as you are clear of the channel. Leave enough room for commercial fishing craft to pass.

## Davis

Davis, named for a once-prominent Core Sound family, is a very old community. The 3-foot entrance channel strikes west between flashing daybeacons #33 and #34. There are no pleasure-craft facilities on the Davis waterfront, but a country store is a short, pleasant walk from the

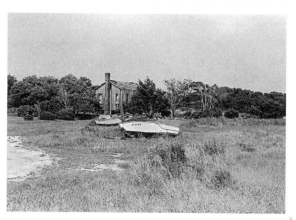

*Near Sealevel*

harbor. A commercial fishery and a machine shop border Davis Harbor.

In fair weather, visiting cruisers can anchor in the 5- to 6-foot waters well southeast of the entrance cut's outermost marker, flashing daybeacon #1, and then dinghy ashore. There is nothing available in the way of dockage for cruising vessels in Davis Harbor, nor is there room to anchor.

Davis is the most unspoiled village accessible to visiting cruisers on Core Sound. A trip to this quaint community, little changed by the passage of years, is definitely worthwhile, if you can stand the shallow depths.

## Davis Legends

Davis is the setting for two legends that illustrate the down-home atmosphere of this village.

The first story is known as "The Incident of Mr. Frisby's Cow." Mary Paul and her husband, the late Grayden Paul, relate this amusing tale in their fine book, *Folk-Lore, Facts and Fiction about Carteret County in North Carolina*. It seems that a certain Captain Frisby came to Davis Harbor from time to time to take on a load of oyster shells or goose feathers. He met a young lady of the village, and they fell in love. Frisby proposed marriage, but his young love said she would never marry a seafaring man. The good captain expressed reservations about whether he could earn a living on land, since the sea was all he had ever known. His lady, however, assured him that she could teach any man to farm, so Captain Frisby gave up the sea and became plain Mr. Frisby of Davis.

Soon after the loving couple was married, Frisby got his first lesson in milking a cow. The peaceful bovine in question had recently borne a calf, and the milk flowed freely indeed. However, the calf was soon weaned. One morning, despite his best efforts, Frisby could not extract any milk. He couldn't decide what the problem was. His wife was not about, so he could not ask her advice. Being a resourceful seaman of many years, he soon hit upon a plan. He passed a rope around the cow's front quarters, threw the other end over a nearby rafter, and hauled the cow up.

Some neighbors passing by asked if Frisby was trying to hang his cow. He replied, "I am just trying to make the milk run aft."

The second legend, the story of the "Davis

*Gathering clams at Davis*

Shore Freeze," is also told by Mary and Grayden Paul. In 1898, the whole North Carolina coast was suffering from the effects of an extremely severe winter. The bad weather seemed to go on forever. The village's food supply, laid up from the summer harvest, was exhausted. To make matters worse, the sound and the creeks were frozen over with a thick layer of ice, making fishing impossible.

Davis was an isolated community, and help could not reach the village overland. The people grew hungry. Finally, a local leader proposed a mass prayer meeting. All the inhabitants of the small community gathered on the shores of Oyster Creek. They humbly asked for the good Lord's help in their hour of need.

As the meeting came to a close, someone spotted smoke rising from Core Banks, across the sound. Immediately, the people of Davis knew that someone was in trouble. There was some reluctance to cross the ice because no one knew if the sheet would support a man's weight, particularly on the sound's midsection. Finally, several brave individuals safely crossed the ice and found a group of shipwrecked sailors huddled around a campfire.

The seamen's ship had grounded on the nearby shoal. It just so happened that the vessel was laden with a cargo of molasses and grain. Most of the goods were salvaged, and the village of Davis was saved from starvation.

## Jarrett Bay

Jarrett Bay, north of Davis Island and flashing daybeacon #36, has an unmarked entrance but does offer some 5-foot depths. Boaters who choose to enter must make judicious use of compass and chart to avoid several shallow patches.

Your best bet for overnight anchorage is on the charted 6-foot waters off Davis Island's western shores. You must cruise through some 5- and possibly 4-foot depths to reach this haven, but boats drawing 3½ feet or less have a fairly good shot of making it without finding the bottom. This anchorage provides fair shelter from eastern and northeastern winds, but there is virtually no protection from southern and northern winds. Clearly, this is not a foul-weather hidey-hole. Make your decision about an overnight stay with the latest weather forecast in mind.

# UPPER CORE SOUND NAVIGATION

Because of the exacting nature of Core Sound navigation, the following information will be presented in greater detail than are any other chapters of this guide. The boater will do well to carefully study his or her charts and the navigational information in this chapter before attempting entry of Core Sound.

Please remember that successful navigation of Core Sound is problematic at best. There is a very real risk of finding the bottom, even with careful navigation.

**Entrance from Pamlico Sound**    Passage of Core Sound begins at flashing daybeacon #2CS, located just off the southern tip of Hodges Reef, in the southeastern corner of Pamlico Sound. You should come abeam of and pass #2CS by 25 yards to its eastern side. As you move south on the main Core Sound channel, pass all red markers to your starboard side and all green beacons to port. This color scheme holds true only as far as the intersection with The Straits.

From #2CS, set course to come abeam of flashing daybeacon #3 by 25 yards to its westerly side. South of #3, you will encounter the sound's first trouble spot. The dredged channel between #3 and the next permanent southerly flashing daybeacon, #5, is subject to shoaling. Low-tide depths in the cut can sometimes run as shallow as 4 feet. If your craft draws more than 3½ feet, plan your passage to coincide with high water.

Between #3 and #5, several unlighted, floating aids have been placed on either side of the narrow channel. These are subject to change according to the latest channel conditions. Southbound boaters should simply continue to pass all red markers to their (the boaters') starboard side and green aids to port. Do not try to put #3 directly to stern and run a straight course to #5. The channel, such as it is, lies west of these two daybeacons. For best depths, bring daybeacons #3 and #5 abeam to their western sides by no closer than 25 yards. Between these two daybeacons, your course will border Wainwright Island to the west. If you choose to visit, anchor in the channel and go ashore by dinghy.

This cut into northern Core Sound is used on a regular basis by the commercial fishermen of Atlantic. Because of their needs, this channel is periodically dredged. Between maintenance periods, shoaling can occur, so proceed with extreme caution and keep an eagle eye on the sounder.

From flashing daybeacon #5 to flashing daybeacon #9, the channel is slightly larger and deeper. It is still narrow, however. Pay close attention to chart 11550. Come abeam of #9 to its fairly immediate northwesterly side. At #9,

Harbor Island, another possible side trip, presents itself.

*Harbor Island*   To visit Harbor Island, follow the main channel southwest from flashing daybeacon #9 for 200 yards. You can then cut to the north-northwest and set course to come abeam of Harbor Island by 100 to 150 yards off its southwesterly tip. Anchor in the channel and dinghy ashore.

*On Core Sound*   South of flashing daybeacon #9, the next aid to navigation outlining the channel is flashing daybeacon #11. Point to come abeam of #11 to its immediate westerly side. Shallow water lies just a stone's throw farther to the west.

Halfway between #11 and the next southerly flashing daybeacon, #13, lies Roe, a possible side trip.

*Roe*   Cruisers voyaging to Roe Harbor should abandon their run between #11 and #13, some 0.8 nautical mile after passing #11. Strike a course for flashing daybeacon #2, which marks the eastern entrance of a short, improved channel leading to the deeper waters of Cedar Island Bay. Come abeam of #2 to its southern side.

From #2, set course to pass unlighted daybeacon #3 to its fairly immediate northern side. You can expect minimum depths of 5½ to 6 feet in this short channel.

Cruise northwest from #3 to unlighted daybeacon #5, which marks the entrance to the improved channel leading to Roe Harbor. Come abeam of #5 to its fairly immediate northeasterly side. From #5, carefully set course to pass flashing daybeacon #6 fairly close to its southwesterly side. Continue past #6 on the same course for 25 yards, then swing a bit farther to the northwest and point

to come abeam of flashing daybeacon #8 by 10 yards to its southerly side. From #8, the entrance to the harbor is obvious.

*On the Sound*   Good coastal navigation should see you safely southward on Core Sound from flashing daybeacon #13 all the way to flashing daybeacon #19. This lengthy, well-marked run is one of the easiest on the sound. A careful study of chart 11550 should be sufficient for navigation. You will probably encounter depths of no less than 7 feet along this section. Between #19 and flashing daybeacon #19A, the next Core Sound sidewaters, Thorofare Bay and Canal, lie to the west.

*Thorofare Bay and Canal*   The canal leading from Thorofare Bay to West Thorofare Bay has shoaled to 4 or 5 feet in places and can only be used by shallow-draft vessels. If you choose this route anyway, depart from the main Core Sound run about halfway between flashing daybeacons #19 and #19A. Set course for flashing daybeacon #1, which marks the eastern entrance of the so-called improved channel leading to the canal. Between the sound's primary north-south route and #1, minimum depths of 6 feet can be expected. From #1, carefully set course to pass flashing daybeacon #1A by 10 yards to its northern side. Come abeam of unlighted daybeacon #2 fairly close on its southern side. You can expect low-water depths of 5 feet along this portion of the approach channel.

The shallowest stretch is between #2 and the canal's entrance. From #2, set course directly for flashing daybeacon #4. Some 25 yards before reaching #4, veer sharply to the southwest and pass #4 by 10 yards to its southerly side. Favor the canal's southeasterly shore as you enter the stream. Pass unlighted daybeacon #6 to your starboard side and unlighted daybeacon #7 to port. This stretch is treacherous. To quote the operator of the old (now replaced) Thorofare Bridge, it "needs dredging badly." Expect 4- or 5-foot depths. According to the bridge's operator, large shrimp trawlers of deep draft use the canal regularly. With a craft that draws 3½ feet or less, you should be able to get through.

Thorofare Canal is spanned by a fixed bridge with 45 feet of vertical clearance. Sailcraft that need more clearance are out of luck.

Once you enter the canal itself, depths improve considerably, typically to 7 to 10 feet; the minimum depth at low tide is 6 feet. As you proceed westward on the canal, hold to the mid-width until you encounter flashing daybeacon #15WB at the canal's western entrance.

From #15WB to flashing daybeacon #11WB, you can expect low-tide depths of 8 to 10 feet. Come abeam of #15WB fairly close to its westerly side. Set course to bring your craft abeam of unlighted daybeacon #13WB and flashing daybeacon #11WB fairly close to their westerly sides. For additional information on West Bay and its anchorages, see chapter 4.

*Roe Harbor*

**On Core Sound**   It is relatively simple to proceed south from flashing daybeacon #20 to flashing daybeacon #22. From #22, cut west-southwest and follow the charted, improved channel to the unnumbered black-and-white flashing junction beacon marking the entrance to the Atlantic channel. Between #22 and the junction beacon, you will pass unlighted daybeacon #22A to your starboard side and unlighted daybeacon #23 to port.

**Atlantic**   Your best bet for visiting Atlantic is probably to anchor near the black-and-white daybeacon marking the entrance to the Atlantic channel. You can then dinghy ashore. The northeasternmost of Atlantic's three channels leads to an enclosed harbor of refuge.

To approach the Atlantic waterfront, cruise to the north-northeast from the junction daybeacon, pointing to come abeam of unlighted daybeacon #1 to your port side. Atlantic's entrance channel splits into three separate branches at #1, each leading to its respective commercial dockage area. Stick to the channels! Outside the dredged cuts, 3-foot depths are immediately encountered. To the south of the southernmost commercial dock is a small-craft marina with gas pumps, but entrance depths of 3 feet or less make this area inaccessible to cruising-size craft.

**Drum Inlet**   At the time of this writing, there was a rather indifferent set of buoys leading from flashing daybeacon #24 to the inlet. Don't use these buoys! Depths are insufficient for all but the smallest craft.

**On Core Sound**   Cruisers continuing south on Core Sound should set course from the unnumbered flashing junction beacon off the Atlantic entrance channel to flashing daybeacon #24. At #24, you will encounter problem waters. The channel from #24 to flashing daybeacon #25, the next southerly daybeacon, is quite narrow. To use the cut successfully, come abeam of #24 by 10 yards to its southeasterly side. Set course to come abeam of #25 by about the same distance to its northwesterly quarter. Continue past #25 on the same course for 0.2 nautical mile before setting a new track for the next southerly aid, flashing daybeacon #27. Watch your stern carefully when cruising between #24 and #25 to make sure leeway is not easing you out of the channel.

No sidewaters or unusual navigational difficulties present themselves until flashing daybeacon #28. From #28, it is theoretically possible to enter the harbor at Sealevel and to enter Nelson Bay. Unfortunately, both waters suffer from shallow depths.

*Sealevel*   Boaters entering Sealevel should set course from flashing daybeacon #28 for flashing daybeacon #1, which marks the southern entrance of the so-called improved channel leading to the harbor. Skippers with boats drawing more than 3 feet should probably anchor south of #1 and dinghy ashore. If you choose to enter the harbor, set course to pass flashing daybeacon #3 to your port side. Remember, you will be traveling through 3-foot depths between #1 and #3.

*Nelson Bay*   Nelson Bay, lying to the northwest, can also be accessed from flashing daybeacon #28. Unfortunately, the bay is not as good a prospect as you would expect from studying chart 11545. The entrance to the bay at flashing daybeacon #1 is rather tricky, and the channel has shoaled to 3-foot depths near flashing daybeacon #3.

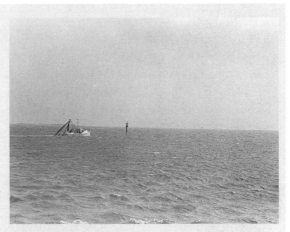

*Shrimping near Atlantic*

Nelson Bay is not particularly recommended, but if you choose to enter, point to come abeam of flashing daybeacon #1 by 15 yards to its easterly side. Be careful to avoid the shallow water east and west of #1. Study chart 11545 and notice the large bubble of 2- and 3-foot shoals surrounding flashing daybeacon #3. You should probably discontinue your explorations south of #3. For those who simply must visit waters where none has gone before, set course to come abeam of #3 by 0.1 nautical mile to its westerly side. Cruisers continuing upstream north of #3 do so at their own peril.

*On Core Sound*   Southwest of flashing daybeacon #28, set your sights on flashing daybeacon #29. At #29, the channel veers to the southwest and narrows on its way to flashing daybeacon #31. This is a harbinger of things to come.

From #31 to the next southwesterly aid to navigation, flashing daybeacon #33, the channel narrows to a 60-foot dredged track. Carefully set course to bring #33 abeam by no more than 30 yards to its northerly side. Take your time, proceed at idle speed, and keep an eagle eye on the sounder.

Navigators cruising north on Core Sound should proceed past #33 for 30 to 50 yards before cutting to the northeast and setting course for #31. As can be seen from a study of chart 11545, these maneuvers will keep you inside the narrow channel. Watch your stern carefully for leeway. The water is quite shallow on both sides of the narrow channel.

From flashing daybeacon #33, Oyster Creek is the next available sidewater.

**Oyster Creek**   Captains who decide to explore Oyster Creek should set course from flashing daybeacon #33 for flashing daybeacon #2, which marks the creek's entrance. Pass #2 on your fairly immediate starboard side and set course to come abeam of unlighted daybeacon #3 to your immediate port side. Be ready for some 4- and 5-foot low-tide depths between these two daybeacons. The same depths persist between #3 and the commercial seafood docks.

**On Core Sound**   Flashing daybeacon #1 and unlighted daybeacon #3 are visible to the south of Oyster Creek's mouth. These beacons apparently once marked a channel to Salter Creek. Don't try it! Extensive shoaling has occurred, and depths of less than 3 feet are encountered before reaching #1. I even observed small trees growing out of the water near #1.

Northbound boaters on Core Sound should take note that flashing daybeacon #33 is quite difficult to spot. The aid seems to blend in with the dark background of Piney Point. Use your binoculars to pick out this marker.

From #33, it is an easy southward run of 2.3 nautical miles to the next flashing daybeacon, #34.

Along the way, the Davis entrance channel will come abeam to the northwest.

**Davis**   Unfortunately, the Davis entrance channel has shoaled badly. In spite of what chart 11545 would lead you to believe, you will encounter 4-foot depths if you approach to within 0.2 nautical mile of flashing daybeacon #1, the outer marker on the Davis channel. Between #1 and Davis Harbor, consistent 3-foot low-water depths can be expected. Because of these shallow soundings, it is almost mandatory for most boaters to anchor in the sound's deeper waters well southeast of #1, then dinghy ashore.

**On Core Sound**   The passage from flashing daybeacon #34 to the next southerly flashing daybeacon, #35, is not as straightforward as some others. A study of chart 11545 shows that best depths can be maintained by not following a straight line from #34 to #35. The channel winds a bit between these two daybeacons, but it is wide enough that judicious use of compass and chart should keep you in the channel.

The run from #35 to flashing daybeacon #36 is a very tricky maneuver. A series of pilings lines the water north-northwest of #36. It is often difficult to discover just which of the structures are pilings and which is the real aid to navigation. Flashing daybeacon #36 is the southernmost of the structures; use your binoculars to pick it out. If you are traveling north on the sound, you will have the same identification problem.

After you pick out #36, set course to come abeam of this aid fairly close to its southerly side. Some 20 yards before reaching #36, alter your course 90 degrees to port and set a new south-southeasterly course to come abeam of flashing daybeacon #37 by 10 yards to its westerly side.

Northbound boaters should set course from #37 to come abeam of #36 by 10 yards to its easterly side. Just before reaching #36, swing sharply northeast and point to come abeam of and pass flashing daybeacon #35 to its northwesterly side.

Watch your stern on these runs. Don't let leeway slippage ease you out of the channel. If your depth falls below 5 feet, you are doing something wrong! The channel holds minimum depths of 5 feet at low tide; in most places, it has 6 to 7 feet of water.

While cruising between #35 and #36, you will notice a beautiful white house on the southern tip of Davis Island, to the north of your course. Do not try to approach this structure, as it is surrounded by extremely shallow water.

At flashing daybeacon #36, devil-may-care cruisers may choose to explore Jarrett Bay.

**Jarrett Bay**   Set a careful course from flashing daybeacon #36 to avoid the 2-foot waters jutting out from the southwestern tip of Davis Island. After coming abeam of the southern tip of Davis Island well to your starboard side, cut back to the north-northeast to take advantage of best depths. Do not proceed up the bay any farther than the waters abeam of Davis Island's northern tip. Contrary to the soundings noted on chart 11545, 3-foot depths will say hello if you cruise farther north.

**The Southern Route Divides**   The southerly run on the Core from #37 to flashing daybeacon #39 presents no difficulty. At #39, cruising skippers must

*Old House on Davis Island–Core Sound*

decide whether to continue south down Core Sound to Cape Lookout and Harkers Island or to turn west into The Straits. Most cruisers should consider discontinuing their southward trek of the Core and entering The Straits. The reason for this recommendation is that south of flashing daybeacon #39, the marked channel continually shoals between unlighted daybeacons #12 and #8. Periodic dredging helps this problem, but between maintenance cycles, a humpbacked sand shoal inevitably builds across the channel from the east near flashing daybeacon #10. If this shoal is present at the time of your arrival and you attempt to bypass it to the west—the only viable possibility—you will encounter 4-foot depths even at high tide. The Straits, on the other hand, presents a fairly wide and deep channel with just one or two tricky spots all the way to westerly Back Sound (or possibly Taylor Creek).

# THE STRAITS

The Straits is a narrow body of water that connects Core and Back Sounds. The channel leading through The Straits provides fair access to the western waters of Back Sound. From this point, vessels drawing 4 feet or preferably less may be able to follow a newly marked but poorly outlined channel into Taylor Creek's eastern entrance. This stream in turn leads to the Beaufort waterfront. Those of us whose craft need 4½ feet or better to stay off the bottom must follow a more lengthy track to the Beaufort docks.

The Straits is bordered to the south by Harkers Island and to the north by the North Carolina mainland. A winding but deep and fairly well-marked channel traverses the length of The Straits. Use of this cut requires extreme caution and careful navigation. The interesting coastal community of Marshallberg, located on the northern shore, offers limited repair facilities. All in all, The Straits affords a pleasant and reliable alternative to the treacherous channel of southern Core Sound.

## Marshallberg

Marshallberg is another charming, sleepy Core Sound community. A great number of wooden ships are built in Marshallberg. If you want to observe nautical craftsmanship practiced in the traditional manner, then by all means consider stopping here.

Cruising boaters can occasionally squeeze into a slip in Marshallberg Harbor at M. W. Willis Boat Works (919-729-3341), but most dockage is usually taken up by resident craft and boats waiting for repair. Call ahead to check on available space before committing to Marshallberg for the evening.

Marshallberg Harbor holds 6 to 7 feet at low tide, as does most of the entrance channel. Unfortunately, there is one spot about a third of the way between unlighted daybeacons #1 and #3 that has shoaled to 4 or 5 feet at extreme low tide. If you need more depth, wait for high water. Many vessels, some of deep draft, use this channel on a daily basis, so you should not have too much difficulty.

## The Core Sounder

The Core Sounder, a famous style of boat with a specialized hull design, originated in Marshallberg. The design evolved from a sailboat known as the "sharpie," which was introduced to Carteret County in the 1880s. The craftsmen of Marshallberg improved the sharpie by adding more flair to the bow and exaggerating the fantail. This configuration resulted in a very dry boat with a shallow draft, both excellent attributes for

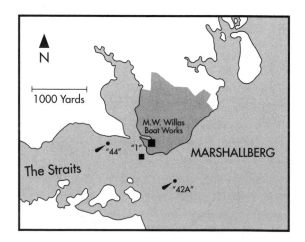

craft plying North Carolina waters.

Today, the design has been transferred to modern power cruisers. Core Sounders are still hand-built, not only in Marshallberg but also at Harkers Island, Hatteras, and elsewhere in eastern North Carolina.

## Passage into Taylor Creek

Since this writer's earliest days exploring the waters around Beaufort, the channel leading from Taylor Creek's easterly exodus into Back Sound has always turned south. During the last several years, this cut has been shoaling at ever more alarming rates. Contrary to what is shown on the May 14, 1994, edition of chart 11545, the southward-running charted passage has been entirely abandoned and unlighted daybeacons #1, #1A, and #2 removed (though a different #2 is still present, as described below).

Instead, an alternate cut—long used by local commercial fishermen and running almost directly east from Taylor Creek into Back Sound—has been newly marked. Unfortunately, the Coast Guard's aids-to-navigation unit did not see fit to outline the route leading from the new channel to the main Back Sound–Harkers Island passage. The result is a state of on-the-water confusion which could be cleared up with just a few additional markers. Are you listening, Coast Guard?

As it currently stands, this passage can be guardedly recommended only for vessels drawing 4 feet or preferably less or those with up-to-date local knowledge. Even so, this is not a run to be taken lightly. Proceed with maximum caution and be ready for the unexpected.

Should you be successful in finding your way into the easterly reaches of Taylor Creek, this fortunate stream provides reliable passage to Beaufort's waterfront, as outlined in the next chapter.

# THE STRAITS NAVIGATION

The rule of thumb in The Straits is that if your depth rises to less than 7 feet, you are doing something wrong. The channel is quite deep if you are anywhere near its mid-width. If soundings do rise to less than 7 feet, assess the situation and decide which side of the channel you are encroaching upon. You can then correct the problem before reaching grounding depths.

To enter The Straits, use your compass and chart 11545 carefully. Depart the Core Sound channel 200 yards north of flashing daybeacon #41. Follow the deep water as it curves slightly on its way to unlighted daybeacon #42. Come abeam of #42 by 25 yards to its southerly side. The channel along this portion of its run is well marked and reasonably easy to follow.

From #42, the channel flows west to flashing daybeacon #42A. Shoals have encroached on #42A. Do not approach to within less than 25 yards of its southerly side. Nearer to the daybeacon, depths rise to 4 feet at low tide.

From #42A, point to eventually come abeam of unlighted daybeacon #1, located at the southern entrance to Marshallberg Harbor, to its southern side. Study chart 11545 and notice that you cannot follow a straight course between these two aids. It

*Marshallberg entrance channel*

is necessary to bend your course to the south in order to stay in the channel's mid-width.

**Marshallberg**   To enter Marshallberg Harbor, pass unlighted daybeacon #1 by 10 yards to your port side and set course to come abeam of unlighted daybeacon #3 by about the same distance to port. Short of #3, the harbor entrance opens out to starboard. Two unlighted daybeacons lead you through the entrance.

**On The Straits**   From unlighted daybeacon #1, the run to the next flashing daybeacon, #44, should not prove too difficult. Come abeam of #44 by 20 yards to its southerly side. As can be seen from chart 11545, a straight run from #44 to the next flashing daybeacon, #46, is not possible. You must follow a significant northerly bend in the channel.

From #46, it is a quick jog to flashing daybeacon #47. Come abeam of #47 by 25 yards to its northerly side. The run from #47 to the Harkers Island Bridge is the most difficult section of The Straits. The channel isn't narrow, but it is a long run of 1.2 nautical miles between #47 and the span. Leeway can easily set you onto the shallow waters

bordering both sides of the channel. Set course carefully and watch your stern and depth finder. If your depth begins to drop below 7 feet, you are nudging the channel's edge. Assess your situation and make appropriate corrections at once.

The Harkers Island Bridge has a closed vertical clearance of 14 feet but opens on demand. West of the span, the marked channel leads into Back Sound and eventually to Taylor Creek.

**Approach to Taylor Creek**   The passage between the Harkers Island Bridge and the easterly genesis of the newly marked Taylor Creek approach channel is fairly reliable, but the waters are subject to shoaling. Boaters should keep to the marked cut and keep a sharp watch for new aids placed to warn of recent channel changes.

Immediately after passing through the bridge, set course to pass unlighted daybeacons #48 and #50 by no more than 10 yards to their southerly sides. Continue on the same course until unlighted can buoy #51 comes abeam south of your course. Once abeam of #51, alter course to the southwest and point to pass flashing daybeacon #55 to its northwesterly side. At #55, it is possible to break off to the south and visit Harkers Island's tiny harbor of refuge. This channel and the other Harkers Island waters are covered below.

From flashing daybeacon #55, it's a quick run southwest to the gap between flashing daybeacons #56 and #1. Flashing daybeacon #1 marks the entrance to a narrow, dredged cut that leads to the main Harkers Island channel. This account now covers the route to Taylor Creek. A discussion of the Harkers Island channel and its approaches will follow.

From a position between #56 and #1, you should continue cruising west to flashing daybeacon

#58. Come abeam of #58 fairly close on its southern side and be on guard against the broad ribbon of correctly charted shallows to the south.

At this point, brave-hearted captains piloting vessels which draw 4 feet or preferably less can leave the main Harkers Island–Back Sound passage and attempt the newly marked channel into Taylor Creek, described above. Captains should be warned that this passage is not shown correctly on the May 14, 1994, edition of chart 11545. They should also be advised that (charted) unlighted daybeacons #1, #1A, and #2 have been completely removed. The southward-running channel that these aids once outlined has now all but ceased to exist.

If you decide to make the attempt, continue cruising 50 yards west of #58. Then cut sharply north and point as if you were going to come abeam of the correctly charted unlighted daybeacon #2 to its fairly immediate westerly side.

Don't let the charted presence of two daybeacons both labeled #2 confuse you. The #2 that has been removed used to lie just off the easterly mouth of Taylor Creek. The existing #2 (the one you will now be pointing for) is farther west; it is located south of the correctly charted unlighted daybeacon #4.

Some 25 yards south of the current unlighted daybeacon #2, turn sharply east and set course for the mouth of Taylor Creek. Along the way, you should pass unlighted can buoys #1, #1A, and #1B to their fairly immediate northerly sides. After leaving #1B in your wake, make directly for the centerline of Taylor Creek's entrance.

One final word on this confusing procedure: Be sure to ignore unlighted daybeacon #4, correctly charted north of the current unlighted daybeacon #2. This aid outlines a channel into the North River which is better left to local fisherman.

Now, wasn't that fun? This freshly outlined entrance into easterly Taylor Creek can be a white-knuckle experience for first-timers. Proceed with the greatest caution and keep one eye locked on the depth sounder. Good luck!

**On to Shackleford Banks**  Cruisers bypassing the entrance to Taylor Creek can continue tracking their way toward Shackleford Banks by setting course from flashing daybeacon #58 to come abeam of the correctly charted flashing daybeacon #59 by 25 or 30 yards to its southerly side.

Remember, the charted channel north of #59 has disappeared and the charted aids to navigation that once outlined this cut (unlighted daybeacons #1, #1A, and #2) have been removed. Stay south of #59.

From flashing daybeacon #59, head toward flashing daybeacon #NR north of Shackleford Banks. Come abeam of #NR on its easterly side. Next, carefully skirt the southerly flank of the charted shallows lying west of this marker. Eventually, you will come abeam of unlighted nun buoy #2 to its fairly immediate northerly side. Do not cruise south of #2, as this aid marks the northerly extreme of an underwater jetty. From #2, you can make your way to the deepwater cut providing access from Beaufort Inlet to the Beaufort waterfront at (Beaufort Inlet's) flashing buoy #21 (currently charted as #17). This route is covered in detail in chapter 8.

# HARKERS ISLAND

The primary channel serving Harkers Island flows from east to west across Back Sound south of the island. A smaller cut referred to above runs south from flashing daybeacon #55 to a tiny harbor of refuge. This latter channel is used almost exclusively by local fishing craft and affords few opportunities for cruising vessels.

Harkers Island's harbor of refuge is located on the island's western shores east of unlighted daybeacon #1. This cramped basin holds 5-foot depths, and its shores are lined with a few fixed wooden piers. These docks are usually occupied by local fishing craft. This harbor should probably be bypassed unless you are in great need of shelter.

The main Harkers Island cut can be entered via the channel running from The Straits to Taylor Creek; via the north-to-south Core Sound channel; or via the Barden Inlet channel, which runs north from Cape Lookout Bight. None of these passages is simple, and the possibility of finding the bottom during your approach to Harkers Island is very real indeed.

Harkers Island's southerly shoreline boasts some facilities catering to pleasure craft. However, all these facilities were affected by the 1996 twin hurricanes, Bertha and Fran. Though reconstruction should be well under way by the spring of 1997, it would be best to call ahead and check on current conditions before counting on spending a night at Harkers.

It should also be noted that the channels south of Harkers Island continue to shoal from year to year. I first researched the various Harkers waterways in the early 1980s, and they weren't a

navigational walk in the park even then. Now, shoaling along the channel's edge has rendered the navigational problems even more acute. It is no small feat to travel from east to west on the main channel without stirring sand.

All the island's marinas have shallow entrances at low water, and great care must be taken to stay off the bottom. Boats drawing more than 3 feet will do well to wait for high tide before attempting to enter any of the small harbors along the southern shore.

The westernmost facility on the island, Harkers Island Fishing Center, is located northeast of flashing daybeacon #3. During my last visit to this facility, in December 1996, only one dock was still standing after the twin hurricanes' wrath. It is to be hoped that more of the piers will be back in operation by the time this guide finds its way into your hands.

Visiting mariners should also know that the marina's entrance channel has some low-tide depths of 3 feet or less. But during high water, several good-sized local power craft regularly make use of the cut. Low-water depths at the docks are 3 feet or less. Transients are accepted for overnight dockage at fixed wooden piers with water and 30-amp power connections. Both gasoline and diesel fuel are available. The marina has an on-site tackle and variety store. Two small-scale grocery stores are within a block of the center's docks. A restaurant, The Captains Choice, is also only a quick step away.

As its name implies, Harkers Island Fishing Center is primarily concerned with sportfishing craft, but cruising boaters can make use of its facilities from time to time. Just watch out for those water depths.

> ### Harkers Island Fishing Center
> ### (919) 728-3907
>
> Approach depth: 3 feet (low water)
> Dockside depth: 2½-3 feet (low water)
> Accepts transients: yes
> Fixed wooden piers: yes
> Dockside power connections: 30 amps
> Dockside water connections: yes
> Gasoline: yes
> Diesel fuel: yes
> Variety store: yes
> Restaurants: several nearby

Harkers Island's other major marina, Calico Jack's, borders the banks northeast of flashing daybeacon #1 not far from Shell Point. This marina also suffered cruelly from the twin hurricanes, but plans called for the docks to be rebuilt by the spring of 1997.

Calico Jack's has a marginally deeper entrance channel than Harkers Island Fishing Center, but you must still carefully follow an unmarked channel to stay off the bottom. Inside the concrete breakwater–enclosed harbor, some slips exhibit low-tide depths of only 3 feet. Large craft should call ahead to check on the availability of deepwater slips before planning to dock here. Transient dockage is available at fixed wooden slips. Each berth has water and 30-amp power connections. Gasoline and diesel fuel are available. Mechanical repairs can be arranged through independent contractors. There is a small ship's, tackle, and variety store on the grounds. Calico Jack's features an adjoining motel with a swimming pool. Wild Will's Restaurant, just across the street, seems to be very popular with the local crowd; there are few better endorsements. All in all, this marina is a rather small-scale operation with a definite emphasis on power craft.

> ### Calico Jack's Marina & Motel
> ### (919) 728-3575
>
> Approach depth: 3-4 feet (low water)
> Dockside depth: 3-4 feet (low water)
> Accepts transients: yes
> Fixed wooden piers: yes
> Dockside power connections: 30 amps
> Dockside water connections: yes
> Gasoline: yes
> Diesel fuel: yes
> Mechanical repairs: independent contractors
> Variety store: yes
> Restaurant: nearby

Harkers Island is another major boat-building center. Everywhere you turn on the island, you can see wooden craft of all sizes in various stages of construction. If you have the time, a stroll along the island's main road is definitely worthwhile.

If your cruising brings you to Harkers Island the first weekend in December, be sure to check out the Core Sound Decoy Festival. In just a few short years, this late-fall celebration has grown into a major event. It features the work of decoy carvers and a variety of other local craftsmen, not to mention more than a little good seafood. Give it a try. I don't think you will be disappointed. For more information, call 919-728-1500 or 919-728-4644.

## Harkers Island History

Harkers Island was originally known as Craney Island. The name was changed when Ebenezer Harker acquired the land in 1730. A long-inhabited piece of real estate, the island was once the home of the Coree Indians, for which Core Sound was named. These Indians were apparently quite fond of oysters. For many years, a huge mound of oyster shells left by the Corees could be seen on the eastern tip of the island. Most have now been removed to serve as road-bed material.

Many citizens from the Shackleford Banks whaling community of Diamond City moved to Harkers Island after their village was hit by a hurricane in 1899. These skilled whalers brought an intimate knowledge of boats and seamanship with them, and their "sea-sense" lives on to this day in the Harkers Island boatbuilders.

## Harkers Island Legends

Ancient Palestine may have had its Samson, but Harkers Island had its Gillikin. Decatur Gillikin, the subject of many legends, lived on Harkers Island around the turn of the century. He reportedly possessed incredible strength.

One day, the story goes, Decatur was hauling logs by oxcart. He discovered that, to get around a fence blocking his path, it was necessary to make a mile-long detour. Not being fond of delays, he picked up each ox in turn and set it neatly on the opposite side of the fence.

Decatur was involved in many fights. Legend has it that he never lost a single one. One story claims that he signed on as a sailor on a British ship. He had not been aboard long before he whipped the ship's champion, which so aroused the nationalistic pride of the crew that he had to fight them all. Before the day was out, Decatur supposedly beat 15 men.

Today, the Gillikin family is still much in evidence on the island. In fact, I spent many of my early years living aboard a Harkers Island craft built by one of Decatur's many descendants.

# HARKERS ISLAND NAVIGATION

To access the small harbor of refuge, leave the channel running from The Straits to Taylor Creek at flashing daybeacon #55 and set course to bring unlighted daybeacon #1 abeam to your port side. Turn sharply east and set a new course to pass unlighted daybeacon #2 to your starboard side. Unlighted daybeacon #3 will lead you farther into the basin.

Don't mistake the unmarked private harbor north of the just-discussed area for the harbor of refuge. This is a very private area where cruising boaters are not welcome even as sightseers.

*Harkers Island Channel*   This account now returns to flashing daybeacon #1 on the passage from The Straits to Back Sound. Visiting cruisers should be warned that almost all the passages around the Harkers Island channel are far more difficult than it would appear from chart 11545. The runs between the various daybeacons are quite long, and leeway can be a serious problem. The channel has shoaled on both sides, and depths shown near the channel's edge on chart 11545 are not reliable.

From flashing daybeacon #1, you must follow an extremely narrow, shoal-prone cut to the un-numbered flashing daybeacon that marks the southeastern tip of the Harkers Island approach channel. Come abeam of #1 by 10 yards to its immediate southwestern side. This looks wrong from the chart, but it is actually the right way to approach the channel. Set a careful course to the southeast, pointing to pass unlighted daybeacon #3 by no closer than 10 yards to its southwestern side. Continue carefully, pointing to pass 10 yards to the eastern side of the unnumbered flashing daybeacon marking the end of the channel. Watch your stern for leeway. This narrow channel is not recommended in high winds or low light.

From the unnumbered daybeacon, another channel bends southwest to Shackleford Banks. See chapter 8 for a description of this passage.

To enter the main Harkers Island channel from the unnumbered daybeacon, set course to come abeam of flashing daybeacon #3 by 25 yards to its northerly side. Watch your stern and don't be in a hurry. On this stretch, there seems to be a tendency to drift onto the shoals north of the channel.

Upon reaching #3, you will be able to see Harkers Island Fishing Center to the north. Remember, the marina entrance carries only 3 feet of depth at low tide. If you need more water, wait until high tide.

*Calico Jack's Marina–Harkers Island*

From #3, it is a long run of 1.45 nautical miles to flashing daybeacon #1. Again, watch carefully for leeway. If your depth drops below 7 feet, you are doing something wrong. Assess the situation at once and make corrections. Bring #1 abeam by 25 yards to its northerly side.

At #1, you will come abeam of Calico Jack's, located to the north. This marina also suffers from a shallow entrance channel. At low tide, you can expect only 4 feet of water in the unmarked entrance cut. Outside the channel, depths are less than 3 feet. To enter, continue cruising east-southeast on the main Harkers Island channel until you are roughly on a line between the marina's entrance, to your port side, and the Cape Lookout Lighthouse, which you will spot in the distance to starboard. Then curl around to port and approach the marina at a 45-degree angle. Follow this line through the breakwater entrance. Ignore the two large pilings directly in front of the marina. They are grounded in very shoal water.

From flashing daybeacon #1, set course to bring flashing daybeacon #35 abeam by 50 yards to its northerly side. At #35, you will intersect the Core Sound channel, to the north, and the Barden Inlet channel, to the south.

***Back on Core Sound*** This account now returns to flashing daybeacon #39 on Core Sound, where we departed from the southward trek down the Core.

From #39, it is a short run to flashing daybeacon #14. Bring #14 abeam fairly close to its westerly side. Notice that the color configuration of the Core Sound aids to navigation suddenly changes. Moving south toward Cape Lookout, you should now point to pass all red, even-numbered markers to your port side and green markers to starboard. Set course to come abeam of unlighted daybeacon

#12 by 10 yards to its westerly side. Minimum depths on both these runs are 6 feet.

***Danger Area***   Between #12 and unlighted daybeacon #8, you will encounter the most treacherous section of the entire Core Sound passage. This portion of the channel is subject to severe shoaling. Time and time again over the past 10 years, a humpbacked sand shoal has built from the east completely across the channel in the vicinity of flashing daybeacon #10. For the moment, dredging seems to have temporarily removed this barrier, but it's a good bet it will be at least partially back in place by the time of your arrival. At times in the past, these shallows have been almost bare of water at low tide and have held only 1 to 2 feet of depth even at high tide.

If you find that the shoal has rebuilt, depart from the southward run at #12. Make a long arc to the west, completely bypassing #10, and rejoin the channel at unlighted daybeacon #8. Make sure you swing far enough west to avoid the "Spoil Area" marked on chart 11545. This patch of shallows is west of #10. Be warned, however, that you will still encounter 3-foot depths at low tide or midtide even if you follow these instructions. Unless you have a boat with a very shallow draft, attempt this section only at extreme high tide. Even then, this passage is not for the faint of heart and definitely not for craft that draw more than 3½ feet.

***South to the Intersection***   From #8 all the way to flashing daybeacon #2, the channel is unusually well outlined by red daybeacons. Pass each marker fairly close to its westerly side. From #2, point to pass unlighted daybeacon #1 to your starboard side, then head straight for flashing daybeacon #35. Some 25 yards before reaching #35, swing either west-northwest into the Harkers Island channel or south to Barden Inlet and Cape Lookout Bight.

# BARDEN INLET

Barden Inlet, also known as "The Drain," is a mostly man-made passage that requires periodic dredging. This channel maintenance keeps depths fairly reliable, but temporary floating markers are often employed to mark new encroachments by the surrounding shoals.

The inlet leads to Cape Lookout Bight and directly past the historic Cape Lookout Lighthouse. This passage is used on a regular basis by local pleasure and fishing craft.

## Barden Inlet History

Barden Inlet was originally a small stream that separated Cape Lookout from Shackleford Banks. In the 1930s, Congressman Hap Barden succeeded in helping Harkers Island residents realize their dream of having a convenient outlet to the sea. Through Barden's influence, the Corps of Engineers was authorized to dredge the inlet. The project was completed in 1938 and has proven invaluable to the island's commerce ever since.

## Cape Lookout Lighthouse

As you cruise south on the inlet, you will see the Cape Lookout Lighthouse to the south, its height painted in a black-and-white diamond pattern. The inlet channel currently runs hard by the inlet's western flank quite some distance from the lighthouse. Formerly, the cut passed much closer. In the absence of specific local knowledge of the now-unmarked channel along the inlet's eastern shore, boaters wishing to visit this venerable sentinel are strictly advised to do so only by dinghy. You can also walk to the lighthouse from the good anchorages in Cape Lookout Bight (see chapter 8), but it's a long hike.

A trip ashore to the lighthouse is highly recommended. Those who undertake this difficult sojourn will not only be able to view the magnificent Cape Lookout Lighthouse from close quarters but will also have the opportunity to inspect the old keeper's quarters and the ruins of the original lighthouse on the site. As a bonus, it is a great walk through a completely undisturbed landscape to the beach opposite the light. See chapter 8 for more details on Cape Lookout Lighthouse.

## BARDEN INLET NAVIGATION

South of #35 to flashing daybeacon #19, boaters cruising the channel from Harkers Island to Cape Lookout should pass all red, even-numbered aids to their (the boaters') port side and take green buoys or daybeacons to starboard. Be alert for low, temporary floating markers as you traverse this channel. Captains are strictly advised to obey all markers, whether permanent or floating.

From #19 to Cape Lookout Bight, the color configuration of the various aids to navigation remains the same, but the buoys that mark the channel are not charted. Most of these southerly markers are green can buoys and red nun buoys.

Again, as you would expect, pass green can buoys to starboard and red nun buoys to port. The channel is well marked with these buoy pairs. If you take your time, you most likely will not encounter any difficulty. Minimum depths of 6 feet can be expected along this cut.

Eventually, the nun and can buoys will bring you abeam of flashing daybeacon #1 to its easterly side. This daybeacon marks the entrance to the navigable waters of the large, popular harbor known as Cape Lookout Bight, which is discussed in detail in chapter 8.

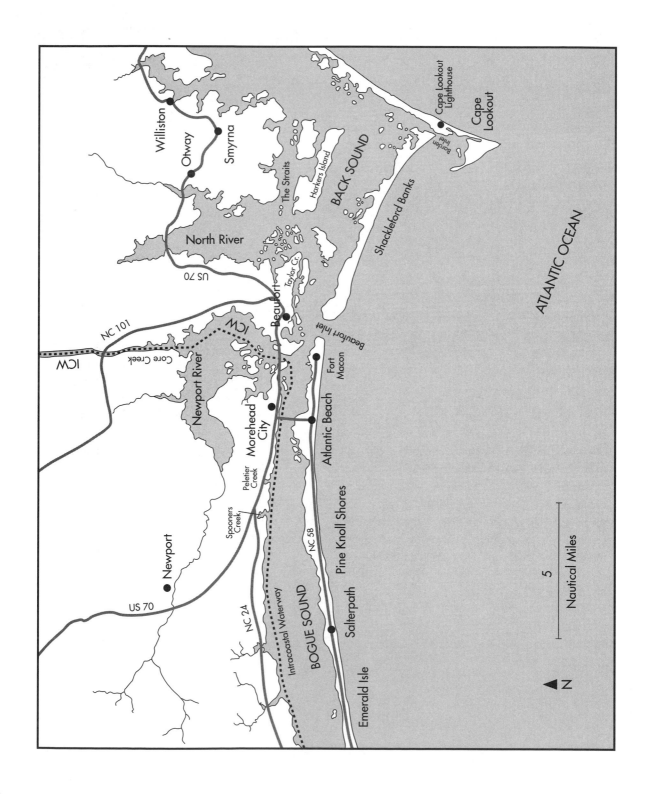

Williston

Otway

Smyrna

North River

US 70

The Straits

Harkers Island

BACK SOUND

Shackleford Banks

Cape Lookout
Lighthouse

Barden Inlet

Cape
Lookout

NC 101

ICW

Core Creek

ICW

Beaufort

Taylor Cr.

Beaufort Inlet

Fort
Macon

Newport River

Morehead
City

Atlantic Beach

Peletier
Creek

Spooners
Creek

Newport

US 70

NC 24

Intracoastal Waterway

BOGUE SOUND

NC 58

Pine Knoll Shores

Salterpath

Emerald Isle

ATLANTIC OCEAN

5

Nautical Miles

N

# The Morehead City–Beaufort Area

The twin cities of Morehead City and Beaufort are considered by many to be the hub of North Carolina pleasure boating. Here, the deep and reliable Beaufort Inlet meets the ICW, as well as the less-traveled Core Sound–Back Sound–Taylor Creek route. Consequently, all inland pleasure and commercial boating is funneled through these waters

Both Morehead City and Beaufort offer a wide variety of facilities and services catering to cruising boaters. You can choose from several marinas that provide transient berths. Practically any necessary service can be obtained. Electrical, mechanical, and hull repairs are all available.

Morehead City and Beaufort are rich in history.

Beaufort's historical district has been restored with excellent taste and careful planning. The Beaufort Historical Association conducts daily tours of several restored homes and public buildings. Additionally, the North Carolina Maritime Museum offers a unique look at how men of the sea practiced their trade in times long past. The Beaufort waterfront on Taylor Creek boasts superb facilities for pleasure craft. A large assortment of restaurants and shops is at hand. Courtesy transportation is usually available to nearby supermarkets.

## Charts

Several NOAA charts are adequate for navigation of the Morehead City, Beaufort, Cape Lookout, and Harkers Island waters and the approaches from Core Sound and the ICW:

**11541** is a specialized ICW chart that follows the Waterway through Morehead City and Beaufort and details the channels leading from the ICW to Beaufort

**11545** is the principal chart covering the waters from Morehead City to Cape Lookout, including Beaufort Inlet, Shackleford Banks, and the Harkers Island channels

**11547** details Morehead City Harbor; many navigators will find they can do without this chart

**11544** covers offshore navigation north, south, and east of Cape Lookout

Morehead City exhibits all the characteristics of a thriving coastal city. This port ranks second only to Wilmington among the state's most important waterborne shipping centers. Morehead City is not as old or as well preserved as Beaufort, but it is a friendly place that welcomes all cruising craft. Three marinas serve the Morehead City area. Additionally, there are several establishments that cater to cruisers' service needs.

Across Bogue Sound from Morehead City, the town of Atlantic Beach offers limited marina facilities. Atlantic Beach is a vacation community composed of a goodly number of cottages and condominiums. Several marinas have sprung up in response to residents' seasonal boating needs.

Cape Lookout, a short cruise from either Beaufort or Morehead City, is perhaps the most popular day-long pleasure voyage on the entire North Carolina coast. The cape forms a large natural harbor known as Cape Lookout Bight, which maintains consistent 20- to 25-foot depths. It can serve as an ideal anchorage either for the day or for overnight.

Shackleford Banks, an oblong island that borders Beaufort Inlet, is another favorite cruising stop. Completely undeveloped, it makes for fascinating exploration by foot.

All in all, the waters and lands lying about Morehead City and Beaufort offer a potpourri of opportunities for cruising skippers. Whether you want to sit idly in a slip and rest from your journey, eat some of the best seafood in the world, or explore the region's fine gunkholing possibilities, Morehead City and Beaufort will not disappoint.

# BEAUFORT

An evening, a week, or a month spent in Beaufort (Standard Mile 201 southbound, Standard Mile 204 northbound), whether tucked into a cozy slip or anchored in Taylor Creek, can be a very rewarding experience. Eighteen years ago, the Beaufort waterfront looked almost like a boarded-up ghost town. Today, the downtown historic district has been tastefully redeveloped as a haven for both landlubber tourists and cruising visitors.

Beaufort's principal waterfront gazes proudly over the northern shore of Taylor Creek. Other facilities are on Town Creek north of the 13-foot bascule bridge (the Grayden Paul Bridge) and on the eastern shore just south of the span.

Courtesy cars are available from the Beaufort Municipal Docks and the North Carolina Mariners Museum, but if you need taxi service in Beaufort, call Yellow Cab (919-728-3483) or Crystal Coast Cab Company (919-728-5365). For rental cars, check with Turners Texaco (919-247-4080), Beaufort Airport (919-728-1777), or Enterprise Rent-A-Car (919-240-0218).

## Beaufort Approaches

Taylor Creek can be approached via four different channels. In former times, most ICW boaters left the Waterway at flashing daybeacon #35 and tracked their way southeast and then south on the so-called Gallants Channel to Taylor

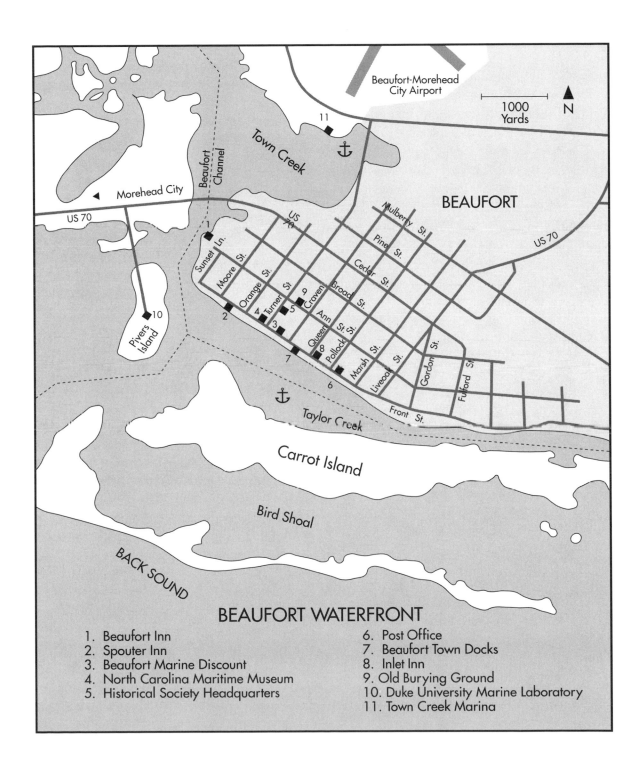

## BEAUFORT WATERFRONT

1. Beaufort Inn
2. Spouter Inn
3. Beaufort Marine Discount
4. North Carolina Maritime Museum
5. Historical Society Headquarters
6. Post Office
7. Beaufort Town Docks
8. Inlet Inn
9. Old Burying Ground
10. Duke University Marine Laboratory
11. Town Creek Marina

Creek. This route is now all but impassable. Serious shoaling southeast of the ICW's flashing daybeacon #35 is waiting to say hello to your keel.

The Russell Slue Channel, which runs south-southeast from the ICW's flashing daybeacon #29, is now far more reliable, particularly for southbound vessels. Though this passage would benefit from a few additional aids to navigation and an update on chart 11541, it is much deeper than the old Gallants cut. You can expect minimum 7-foot soundings on Russell Slue. Typical depths range from 10 to 13 feet, but you may encounter one 7- to 7½-foot spot at low water near flashing daybeacon #5.

Northbound ICW travelers can make use of the deep cut leading from Beaufort Inlet to Taylor Creek north of flashing buoy #21 (charted as flashing buoy #17 on the current editions of charts 11545 and 11541) and immediately southeast of the charted Morehead City Turning Basin. This reliable route is not blocked by any bridges and should probably get the nod if your vessel draws better than 5½ feet.

Another choice for northbound ICW captains is the newly marked southerly portion of the Russell Slue Channel. Though they are not shown on the latest edition of chart 11541, several markers lead cruisers northeast immediately north of the fixed, high-rise U.S. 70 bridge. Be sure to read the navigational information in the next section of this chapter before attempting either the southerly or northerly leg of the Russell Slue cut.

Eventually, both branches of Russell Slue intersect the old Gallants Channel near flashing daybeacon #8. Cruisers can then cut southeast on the deeper portion of Gallants Channel and

*Town Creek Marina*

have easy access to Taylor Creek and the Beaufort marinas.

Visiting cruisers should be warned, however, that they must pass under or through a regulated bascule bridge with 13 feet of closed vertical clearance to reach Taylor Creek via the Russell Slue–Gallants Channel route. Consult the Beaufort navigational section later in this chapter for the bridge's operating hours.

Finally, the adventurers among us who pilot shallow-draft vessels can cruise into Taylor Creek's easterly reaches from The Straits–Harkers Island channel. This route is described in chapter 7.

## Beaufort Facilities and Anchorages

Beaufort boasts some fine dockage facilities for visiting cruisers. The extensive wooden-decked floating docks of Town Creek Marina guard the northerly banks of the like-named creek southeast of Gallant Channel's flashing daybeacon #14. This is the newest of Beaufort's marina facilities. It features full services delivered in a first-class fashion. Transients are readily provided for. All slips feature water and 30- and 50-amp power connections. A new policy concerning live-aboards restricts stays to a maximum 30 days. Low-water entrance and dockside depths range from 8 to 11 feet. Gasoline, diesel fuel, and waste pump-out services are available. Showers, a laundromat, and a full-line ship's store are on the premises as well. Full mechanical repairs for both diesel and gasoline engines, haul-outs via a 50-ton travel-lift, and dry-stack storage are also offered. The Veranda Restaurant (919-728-5352) sits above the ship's store. The Beaufort historic district is within a mile's walk; if that's a bit too far for your feet, call a taxi (see above).

**Town Creek Marina**
**(919) 728-6111**

Approach depth: 8-11 feet (low water)
Dockside depth: 8-11 feet (low water)
Accepts transients: yes
Floating wooden piers: yes
Dockside power connections: 30 & 50 amps
Dockside water connections: yes
Showers: yes
Laundromat: yes
Waste pump-out: yes
Gasoline: yes
Diesel fuel: yes
Mechanical repairs: yes
Below-waterline repairs: yes
Ship's store: yes
Restaurant: on-site

The waters of Town Creek east of the like-named marina are a popular anchorage for sailcraft. While you must carefully avoid the shoals abutting the creek's southerly banks, minimum 6-foot depths can be carried well into the rear portion of Town Creek. There, you will find many other craft, some tied to permanent moorings. Assuming you can find room amidst your neighbors, there is enough swinging room for pleasure craft of almost any size. Town Creek is considered a harbor of refuge, and there is excellent shelter from all winds. The surrounding shores are overlooked by moderate development, the local airport, and the principal highway artery. Passing headlights can be a little annoying at night, though most don't shine directly into the anchorage.

The dockage slips of Beaufort Inn line the eastern banks of Beaufort Channel just south of the Grayden Paul bascule bridge. This notable bed-and-breakfast inn is relatively new, but the architecture and furnishings are very much in keeping with historic Beaufort. The inn is quickly gaining a reputation for friendly service and rooms with magnificent views. Most of the slips are rented to resident boaters, but a couple are sometimes open for transients and inn guests. The berths consist of wooden pilings set out from a fixed wooden pier. Depths alongside run at least 6 to 8 feet. Water and 30-amp power connections are available. If you decide to visit Beaufort Inn by water, it is best to call ahead for reservations.

**Beaufort Inn**
**(919) 728-2600**

Approach depth: 10+ feet
Dockside depth: 6-8 feet
Accepts transients: yes
Fixed wooden piers: yes
Dockside power connections: 30 amps
Dockside water connections: yes
Restaurants: several nearby

A wide array of facilities and docks lines the northern banks of Taylor Creek. The southern Carrot Island–Bird Shoal shores are in their natural state and are protected from development.

*Beaufort Inn*

Visiting cruisers should be aware of the considerable tidal current which regularly moves through Taylor Creek. This rapid water movement necessitates caution when docking.

The single dock of Spouter Inn restaurant lies along the northern shore of the western portion of Taylor Creek. Craft up to 32 feet in length can tie to the dock while patronizing the restaurant. Depths run 10 or more feet.

Farther east, the single floating pier of Harpoon Willie's restaurant will come abeam. A small ferry that offers landlubber access to Bird Shoal (which flanks the south side of Taylor Creek) makes use of this dock, but there is still room for restaurant patrons to tie up while they dine; the pier has sufficient space for one 40-footer. Depths alongside are an impressive 12 feet or more.

A bit farther upstream, passing cruisers will note the Harvey W. Smith Watercraft Center. This facility is associated with the North Carolina Maritime Museum (see below). Traditional wooden sailing and rowing craft are constructed here with time-honored skills.

After passing several private slips, you will spot the long face pier of the Beaufort Gulf Docks (919-728-6000) along the town waterfront. Gasoline and diesel fuel can be purchased at the piers. A small variety store to the rear of the fuel dock sells cold drinks and snack foods. This is also the location of Finz Restaurant (see below).

You will come upon the Beaufort Municipal Docks soon after leaving the Beaufort Gulf Docks behind; the extensive facilities here are mostly fixed wooden slips and piers. Over the past 10 years, Beaufort has vastly expanded its slip space for transients. At the time of this writing, a series of new floating docks designed for small craft was being added to the western end of the complex. Most of this popular port of call's available dockage is occupied night after night. Though you can most likely find a spot without advance preparation, you would be wise to call ahead to check on slip availability.

As you might expect, the Beaufort Municipal Docks feature full water and 30- and 50-amp power connections. A few 100-amp power hookups have just been added as well. Minimum depths at the outer berths run 9 to 12 feet, while some of the inner slips have soundings ranging from 5 to 8 feet. The helpful dockmasters can be relied upon to guide you to a berth appropriate for the size and draft of your vessel. Diesel fuel is available at every slip, and gasoline can be purchased at the central fuel dock. Numerous dockside showers are housed in a large building flanking the complex's westerly tip. There is even a waste pump-out station at the docks. It is quite a walk from the eastside slips to the bathhouse. Beaufort Municipal Docks also offers three courtesy cars that visitors can use for an hour's time to access local supermarkets (located about 2 miles away on U.S. 70) or marine-supply dealers.

A laundromat is located at the General Store on Front Street (see below) just behind the piers. The town dockmaster and his staff are usually quite helpful in arranging for mechanical repairs through local contractors. A vast array of restaurants, gift shops, and other shoreside businesses is only a short step away.

It almost goes without saying that the Beaufort Municipal Docks is one of the most exciting places on the North Carolina coastline to spend an evening, a week, or even longer. Many dyed-in-the-wool sailors stop here year after year on their way to and from the Caribbean. Nearby Beaufort Inlet provides an important connection for this sort of blue-water cruising. Do yourself a big favor and include the Beaufort Municipal Docks in your cruising itinerary.

### Beaufort Municipal Docks
### (919) 728-2503

Approach depth: 12+ feet
Dockside depth: 9-12 feet at the outer berths
  5-8 feet at the inner slips
Accepts transients: yes
Fixed wooden piers: yes
Dockside power connections: 30, 50, & 100 amps
Dockside water connections: yes
Showers: yes
Laundromat: nearby
Gasoline: yes
Diesel fuel: yes
Mechanical repairs: independent contractors
Restaurants: many nearby

Lying amid the Beaufort Municipal Docks is the towering, two-story Beaufort House Restaurant. This dining spot is now closed. Rumors persist that someone will reopen it in the future, but the particulars could not be ascertained at the time of this writing.

The town of Beaufort has thoughtfully provided a nice dinghy dock just east of the Beaufort Municipal Docks. This pier is located in a small public area known as Grayden Paul Park. Cruisers anchored on Taylor Creek will rejoice in the easy access afforded by this addition to the Beaufort waterfront.

Captains preferring to anchor-off will find that Taylor Creek is one of the most popular anchorages on the southeastern coastline. Dozens and dozens of boats, particularly sailcraft, are found year-round swinging tranquilly on the hook in Taylor Creek. Some of these vessels are tied to moorings, while others have anchors down. Depths are typically 8 feet or better. There is good cover for all but gale-force eastern and western winds. Be sure to ease your way toward the southern banks a bit and drop anchor off the main channel. Otherwise, simply select a spot that allows for plenty of clearance from your floating neighbors.

Courtesy of North Carolina's new restrictions on mooring fields, there has recently been some discussion of time limits for boaters anchored on Taylor Creek. No regulations have yet been imposed, and it is to be hoped that none ever will.

## Downtown Beaufort Shops, Restaurants, and Lodgings

If you need any sort of nautical hardware while visiting Beaufort, make your way to Beaufort Marine Discount (421 Front Street, 800-262-8371). Here, you can also purchase NOAA charts and make use of a compressed-natural-gas

*Beaufort boardwalk and Dock House Restaurant*

cylinder exchange. The Rocking Chair Bookstore (400 Front Street, 919-728-2671), housed in the Somerset Square shopping complex, offers a full selection of reading material, including the latest bestsellers. And don't miss The Fudge Shop while you are visiting Somerset Square.

Scuttlebutt Nautical Books & Bounty (919-728-7765) is now in an expanded home at 433 Front Street. This well-appointed shop features a wide variety of marine items, including nautical charts, publications, and gifts. I strongly recommend you stop by and visit with Doreen, Jim, or Jamey.

The General Store (515 Front Street, 919-728-7707) is an interesting stop that offers novelties, personal items, hand-dipped ice cream, and a few basic packaged food items. Perhaps of more interest to cruising types is the new coin laundromat located immediately behind the General Store. This facility has its own outside entrance, or you can access it through the back door of the General Store. The General Store is closed on Sundays.

La Vaughn's Pottery, Coffee, Wines (517 Front Street, 919-728-5353) is one of downtown Beaufort's more unique gift shops. If you are at all interested in pottery or ceramics, by all means stop by this memorable store.

Beaufort boasts a wide variety of excellent restaurants within a short walk of the town docks. Spouter Inn, Beaufort Grocery Company, the Dock House, the New England Net House (133 Turner Street, 919-728-2002), and Clawson's are some of the more notable establishments, but new restaurants seem to spring up daily.

Spouter Inn (218 Front Street, 919-728-5190) is an old favorite of this writer and his first-rate first mate. During the last year or so, Spouter has gone through a change of ownership, managing chefs, and menu. We mourn the loss of the Bird Shoal Sandwich on the lunch menu and the Scallops Parmesan in the evening. Also, the famous Spouter Chowder is now available only intermittently. However, the new bill of fare is quite good. Several luncheon sandwiches have survived, including the Out Island. During the evenings, the menu is more sophisticated. This writer was very much taken with his Mixed Grill. If you have a *big* appetite, be sure to give this entrée a nod. Spouter continues to boast what may be the best atmosphere in Beaufort. Diners look out through large sliding glass doors directly onto the traffic cruising Taylor Creek. We love to watch the sun go down while sipping chilled wine at Spouters. Visiting cruisers are urged to make the acquaintance of this unforgettable dining attraction.

Clawson's Emporium (429 Front Street, 919-728-2133) has just undergone a major expansion. The alley of small shops next door to the restaurant's original location has been turned into a coffee and hand-dipped ice cream bar, a reception room with a fireplace and color television, and a traditional pub. Clawson's coffee bar,

known as Fishtowne Java, offers espresso, cappuccino, *caffè latte*, baked goods, and ice cream. There is an on-site deli that features a wide variety of cold drinks, cold cuts, cheeses, and breads. The restaurant itself, which is joined directly to the addition, continues to boast outstanding seafood entrées. The desserts are also wonderful. Do your palate a favor and give Clawson's a try, particularly if you have not experienced its new menu and expanded facilities.

On spring, summer, and fall evenings, a lively and convivial crowd can be found at the Dock House (500 Front Street directly overlooking the Beaufort Municipal Docks, 919-728-4506). This establishment serves sandwiches and cold drinks (including ice-cold "liquid sunshine") at tables on the waterfront.

The Front Street Grill (419A Front Street, 919-728-3118) serves seafood, chicken, and beef dishes with an unusual mix of herbs and spices. I found the Caribbean-style crab cakes to be absolutely succulent. This restaurant is closed during January.

Harpoon Willie's (1 Orange Street, 919-728-5247), mentioned above as part of the Beaufort

*Beaufort dinghy dock*

*Grave of Otway Burns—*
*Old Burying Ground, Beaufort*

waterfront, is a sophisticated dining establishment with wonderful food a cut above the usual fried seafood.

One of the more popular dining establishments in town is the Beaufort Grocery Company (117 Queen Street, 919-728-3899). It is housed in a building that used to serve as a neighborhood market, hence the name. The food is superb, even if a bit pricey. I love to have lunch here, but the restaurant's atmosphere can be accurately described as "high energy" and a bit noisy during the evenings. If these sorts of surroundings appeal to you, then by all means call for evening reservations. Beaufort Grocery Company features an extensive deli with top-quality cold cuts, a variety of domestic and imported cheeses, and home-baked breads. The take-out sandwiches will travel wonderfully to your on-board galley. This restaurant is closed during January.

For a funky dining experience, try tiny Finz Restaurant (330 Front Street just behind the Beaufort Gulf Docks, 919-728-7459). Lunch and dinner patrons will find themselves seated at a bar or at small tables looking out over the water. I have always found the food and the general air of bonhomie here to be quite pleasing.

As this account was being penned, Blue Moon Café (119 Queen Street) was in the processing of setting up new quarters next to the Beaufort Grocery Company. Word has it that this establishment will be open for breakfast and serve its incomparable muffins. If this rumor proves correct, Blue Moon will be one of the only places open for breakfast in downtown Beaufort.

Several years ago, shoreside lodging in Beaufort was very hard to come by. Now, weary cruisers who would like to rest ashore have a range of options. In addition to the Beaufort Inn, already discussed, several historic bed-and-breakfast hostelries and the Inlet Inn wait eagerly to greet weary travelers.

The Inlet Inn (601 Front Street, 919-728-3600) is an imposing three-story structure which overlooks Taylor Creek within sight of the Beaufort Municipal Docks. The inn's architecture was designed to blend harmoniously with the classic Beaufort down-east look. The result is quite pleasing to the eye. Visitors lucky enough to occupy a room on the top floor have a bird's-eye view of Beaufort Inlet and Shackleford Banks. Unfortunately, the Inlet Inn's rooms could use painting and the furniture refurbishing, but the hotel still has the best view in town.

The Cedars (305 Front Street, 919-728-7036), Captain's Quarters (315 Ann Street, 919-728-7711), and Langdon House Inn (135 Craven Street, 919-728-5499) are all bed-and-breakfasts in historic Beaufort homes. Each has its own unique charm. All are within easy walking distance of the waterfront.

One Beaufort hostelry of special note is the Pecan Tree Inn (116 Queen Street, 919-728-6733). The Pecan Tree is housed in the elegant and historic Franklin Lodge, built around 1866 to serve as a Masonic lodge. It is surely one of the most beautifully decorated and landscaped lodgings you will ever find. For my money, this is *the* spot for shoreside accommodations in Beaufort. Take a moment to stroll the elegant English flower and herb garden and the newly landscaped grounds with fountain and fish pool. The rock-lined pathways are guaranteed to soothe wave-jangled nerves. The breakfasts are spectacular, and the innkeepers are simply wonderful.

## Beaufort Historical District

The vast majority of Beaufort's elegant whitewashed homes have been restored over the last decade. Two houses and several public buildings are owned by the Beaufort Historical Society, which conducts daily tours of these imposing structures. All visitors to this old city by the sea should allow time for this tour. Your cruise will be richer for the effort.

To begin your tour of old Beaufort, take a short walk to the new headquarters of the Beaufort Historical Association, located in the Robert W. and Elva Faison Safrit Historical Center (138 Turner Street, 919-728-5225). Here, you can purchase tour tickets and check out the museum and gift shop as well. The society's new headquarters is a wonderful addition to historic Beaufort. I highly recommend that all who have not yet seen it drop by.

The Beaufort Historical Society sponsors the Old Homes Tour during the last weekend of June. Many of Beaufort's privately owned, beautifully restored homes are open to the public for this event only. Boaters whose visits coincide with the tour should make every effort to attend this worthwhile event.

Another attraction that should not be missed is the North Carolina Maritime Museum (315 Front Street, 919-728-7317). This most informative establishment is located within sight of the Beaufort Municipal Docks. The museum provides an interesting look at the oceanography of the North Carolina coast and a fascinating account of the state's early men of the sea. Seldom will cruising boaters discover a better presentation of North Carolina's coastal history and physical characteristics than that found at the North Carolina Maritime Museum. The museum maintains a courtesy car for the exclusive use of visiting mariners. Check with one of the staff for availability.

The museum's Harvey W. Smith Watercraft Center is located just across Front Street directly overlooking Taylor Creek. Here, students and craftsmen labor to build wooden dinghies and sailcraft of traditional North Carolina design. This exhibit lovingly preserves the art of building boats as it was practiced before the advent of fiberglass and modern technology. The public is welcome at the center. An observation platform is on the western side of the building. If you have the time, drop by and watch the students at their work. For anyone interested in boats and cruising, it is more than fascinating.

During the first full weekend in May, the North Carolina Maritime Museum sponsors the annual Wooden Boat Show along the waterfront. The results of the students' labors are displayed along with many other wooden craft. The event is capped off by a sailing regatta to see whose work of art is best on the water. If you happen to be in the area, don't fail to catch this fascinating event.

Visitors to Beaufort should not even think of leaving before visiting the Old Burying Ground. This historical site is on Ann Street just a two-block walk from the waterfront. No one is exactly sure of the old cemetery's age. The land was deeded by the town as a burial place in 1731, but records indicate that the grounds were already in use as a cemetery.

The Old Burying Ground has many graves with interesting stories. According to legend, one grave contains an English sailor who was buried upright so he could eternally salute his king. Another grave marker bears this inscription:

The form that fills this silent grave,
once tossed on ocean's rolling wave,
but in a port securely fast
he's dropped his anchor here at last.

A free pamphlet available at the headquarters of the historical association will guide you to several of the unique graves and give a short history of each. Don't miss this graveyard! The old oaks swaying in the sea breeze and the seemingly ancient graves exude an atmosphere that must be experienced to be understood.

## Beaufort History

Beaufort was laid out by Robert Turner in 1713. The pattern of streets that he designed remains essentially intact to this day. Several of the streets were named for prominent persons of the time: Ann Street was named for Queen Ann; Turner Street for Robert Turner himself; and Moore Street for Major Maurice Moore, a hero of the Tuscarora Indian wars.

By 1722, Beaufort had become such an active harbor that it was designated an official seaport by the Lords Proprietors of the colony. A customs office was subsequently established in the port. The same year, the so-called Carteret Precinct of Craven County was declared a separate entity, to be called Carteret County. Beaufort became its county seat.

Twice during the summer of 1747, pirates pillaged Beaufort, but they were eventually driven off by local militia. Until a few years ago, this event was remembered by a dramatic reenactment.

During the Revolutionary War, Beaufort was decidedly pro-patriot. Many privateers serving the American cause used the port. Saltworks were built nearby to supply the colony; previously, salt had been imported from England. Near the end of the war, in 1782, the British entered Beaufort Harbor and occupied the town for 10 days. Valiant and determined resistance by the townsfolk eventually discouraged the English forces, and they left for Charleston.

The years following the Revolutionary War were a time of prosperity for Beaufort. The port's commerce enjoyed a notable increase. Many of the fine homes standing today were built in this period. Also during this time, the Harlowe Canal was carved out of the lands separating the Newport and Neuse Rivers. For a brief period, this canal linked Beaufort with the inland ports of New Bern and Bath.

During the War of 1812, Beaufort again played a key role in the American cause. When both Charleston and Baltimore were effectively

*Wild ponies on Carrot Island*

blockaded by the British, the old port town took on added importance as a center of commercial and wartime traffic. One of the heroes of the War of 1812, Captain Otway Burns, used Beaufort as the home port for his privateer, the *Snap Dragon*. Following the war, the valiant captain lived in Beaufort for a while and was eventually buried in the town's cemetery. His unique gravestone is adorned by one of the cannons from the *Snap Dragon*.

Following the War of 1812, Beaufort became a favorite summer retreat for the well-to-do. The cool ocean breezes were welcomed by visitors from the state's interior. During this time, the first Atlantic Hotel was built in Beaufort. This famous establishment was later rebuilt in Morehead City after a hurricane destroyed the original structure in 1880.

The Civil War brought early and prolonged occupation by Union forces. General Ambrose Burnside established his headquarters in an illustrious Beaufort home, and the Atlantic Hotel was converted to Hammond Hospital. Fortunately, the lengthy occupation caused no lasting harm to the community. Following the war, Beaufort again resumed its importance as a summer retreat.

While most of the South suffered the agonies of Reconstruction, Beaufort continued to prosper. The Ocean View and Seaside Hotels were opened. Trade flourished; barrel staves, lumber, rum, and molasses were some of Beaufort's exports. During this period, the menhaden industry became important. Beaufort was home port for a large fishing fleet and the site of the processing plants for a thriving menhaden trade. The fleet plied the waters of Core Sound for this fish, which produces many valuable oils. Today, most menhaden are taken offshore, but Beaufort is still the home of a small fishing fleet and one processing plant.

In 1908, a railroad bridge was built from Morehead City to Beaufort, at last connecting the old port city to the mainland. Although the bridge was welcomed by local residents, as was the first highway bridge in 1926, Beaufort's longtime isolation served it well. Rampant commercial development never gained a foothold. Today, the community leaders' foresight continues to bar unsightly construction. In my opinion, Beaufort is the best-preserved coastal town in North Carolina. Visitors to this historic community owe a debt of gratitude to those who have guarded the town's heritage so successfully.

If you are interested in learning more of Beaufort's history, you should acquire *The Old Port Town: Beaufort, North Carolina* and *Beaufort, North Carolina, in Color*, both by Jean Bruyere Kell. Several entertaining Beaufort legends can also be found in Mary and Grayden Paul's *Folk-Lore, Facts and Fiction about Carteret County in North Carolina*. All three works are available from the Beaufort

Historical Association, the North Carolina Mariners Museum, and Rocking Chair Bookstore on the Beaufort waterfront.

## Morehead-Beaufort Yacht Club and Carolina Marlin Club (Standard Mile 200.5)

Near unlighted daybeacon #27 on the ICW's trek through the Newport River, a prolifically marked channel cuts east to a sheltered dockage basin at Carolina Marlin Club, which is home to my good friends at the Morehead-Beaufort Yacht Club. This dockage facility is composed primarily of private slips, but transients who are members of other yacht clubs with reciprocal

### Morehead-Beaufort Yacht Club (919) 728-1281

Approach depth: 5 feet (minimum)
Dockside depth: 4½-6 feet (low water)
Accepts transients: yes (with reciprocal privileges)
Fixed wooden piers: yes
Dockside power connections: 30 & 50 amps
Dockside water connections: yes
Showers: yes

privileges are sometimes accepted. Dockage is provided at fixed wooden piers with water and 30- and 50-amp power connections. Minimum entrance depths run about 5 feet and low-water dockside soundings 4½ to 6 feet.

# BEAUFORT NAVIGATION

From flashing daybeacon #24, where we left the ICW in chapter 6, the Waterway cuts southeast through a dredged cut in the Newport River's shallow waters. A prolifically marked channel cuts east near unlighted daybeacon #27 to the sheltered dockage basin of Morehead-Beaufort Yacht Club.

At flashing daybeacon #29, the ICW turns south-southwest, while the marked Russell Slue passage strikes south-southeast. Currently, this latter cut is the only reliable means for southbound Waterway cruisers to enter Beaufort Harbor and Taylor Creek directly from this portion of the ICW.

As described earlier in this chapter, the old Gallants Channel entrance from the ICW's flashing daybeacon #35 has experienced serious shoaling. Southbound mariners are now strictly advised to access Town Creek, Taylor Creek, and the Beaufort waterfront via the north or south leg of the Russell Slue Channel or the deepwater connec-

tion with Beaufort Inlet (outlined below).

What remains of Gallants Channel has been completely remarked, and the southerly portion of the Russell Slue Channel has been outlined by aids to navigation for the first time. Unfortunately, the latest edition of chart 11541 available at the time of this writing did not reflect these new aids to navigation. Until NOAA gets around to recognizing the new on-the-water reality, your only choice is to follow the navigational outline below. Proceed with caution and keep a close eye on the sounder.

Though chart 11541 would lead you to believe that all the aids to navigation on the northern link of the Russell Slue Channel are daybeacons, at least one marker is a small, low-lying, unlighted nun buoy which can be hard to spot. Have your binoculars close at hand to help with identification.

To run the northern leg of Russell Slue, depart the ICW 50 yards south of flashing daybeacon #29.

*Entrance to Beaufort Yacht Club*

Pass flashing junction daybeacon #RS to its fairly immediate eastern side and set course to cruise between unlighted daybeacons #2 and #3. To continue south to the old Gallants Channel, continue passing all red, even-numbered aids to navigation to your starboard side and green markers to port. Observe all markers carefully.

From a position between #2 and #3, continue on more or less the same course, pointing to pass unlighted daybeacon #4 to its easterly side and come abeam of flashing daybeacon #5 fairly close to its westerly quarter. At #5, the channel swings a bit to the southwest. Use your binoculars to pick out unlighted can buoy #6A, which is small and uncharted. Unlighted daybeacon #6, a charted aid, was absent during my latest research. Point to come abeam of #6A to its southeasterly side. I found the gap between #5 and #6A to be the shallowest portion of the northern leg of the Russell Slue Channel. For best depths, favor the southeasterly side of the channel between #5 and #6A, but watch out for a semisubmerged snag. It is to be hoped that this obstruction will be removed by the time of your visit.

Eventually, you will catch sight of unlighted daybeacon #7 and (currently uncharted) unlighted daybeacon #8 ahead. Favor #7 slightly. Just before coming abeam of #8, turn to the southeast and set a new course to come abeam of and pass (currently uncharted) unlighted daybeacon #10 by 15 yards to its northeasterly side.

Continue on the same course, passing (uncharted) unlighted daybeacons #12 and #14 to their northeasterly sides. At #14, the channel shifts to a more southerly heading. Point to pass (uncharted) unlighted daybeacon #15 to its westerly quarter. Before you reach #15, unlighted daybeacon #1 will come abeam to the east. This aid marks the entrance to Town Creek and Town Creek Marina.

Before considering Town Creek and the final approach to Taylor Creek, this discussion will turn to the southerly leg of the Russell Slue Channel. This cut is convenient for captains cruising north on the ICW, but those piloting especially large or deep-draft vessels may want to opt for the deepwater approach to Taylor Creek from Beaufort Inlet, as outlined below.

To run this southerly leg of Russell Slue, depart the ICW immediately north of the fixed, high-rise U.S. 70 bridge, which crosses the Waterway south of the ICW's unlighted daybeacon #2. Turn northeast and point for the gap between unlighted #2 and unlighted #3, then swing a bit farther north and set course to pass unlighted daybeacon #4 to its easterly quarter. Keep on the same course line, pointing for the wide gap between unlighted daybeacon #6 and unlighted daybeacon #5.

Once abeam of #6, point to come abeam of (uncharted) flashing daybeacon #8 by 25 yards to its northwesterly side. I found that better depths could be maintained by this procedure than by pointing directly for #8. At #8, you can swing

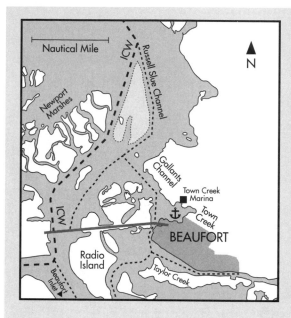

sharply to the southeast and follow the old Gallants Channel to unlighted daybeacon #10, as described above. Come abeam of #10 to its northeasterly quarter. From #10 to Town Creek, the route is the same as that via the northerly leg of the Russell Slue Channel, outlined above.

**Town Creek**    To enter Town Creek, depart Gallants Channel immediately south of unlighted daybeacon #1. Cruise into the creek's interior reaches by heavily favoring the northerly shoreline. Shallows line the mid-width of the creek's entrance and the stream's southerly shoreline. Soon, the docks of Town Creek Marina will be obvious to port.

Cruisers choosing to anchor in Town Creek should cruise past the marina docks at idle speed and pass between unlighted daybeacons #2 and #3. If you stay well north of the two curious black-and-white unlighted daybeacons marking the south-

erly shoals, you can expect 6-foot depths to within 75 yards of the easterly banks.

**Approach to Taylor Creek**    From a position abeam of unlighted daybeacon #15, continue cruising south. Head straight for the central pass-through of the Grayden Paul Bridge. This span opens only on the half-hour between 7:30 A.M. and 7:30 P.M. year-round. It has a closed vertical clearance of 13 feet. There has been some discussion about replacing this structure with a high-rise bridge. As of this writing, funds for a new span had not been obtained and the commencement of construction was uncertain.

The tidal current flowing through the Beaufort–Taylor Creek approach channel in and around the Grayden Paul Bridge can be fierce. Be sure to leave plenty of maneuvering room between yourself, the bridge, and any other vessels that happen to be waiting for an opening.

After passing through the span, hold to the mid-width of the channel until the main body of Taylor Creek comes abeam to the east. Be sure to proceed at idle speed through this portion of the channel, and maintain minimal wake on all of Taylor Creek. The entire stream is now an official no-wake zone. Just before reaching the intersection with Taylor Creek, you will pass the docks of Beaufort Inn to port.

As you approach the main body of Taylor Creek, look west and you will spy the docks and buildings of the Duke Marine Laboratory on the banks of Pivers Island. This impressive facility is one of the most important marine research centers in the United States.

**Approach to Taylor Creek from Beaufort Inlet**
East of the intersection of Taylor Creek and the Gallants approach channel, you have easy access to the principal Beaufort waterfront. You may also find

your way into these waters by making use of the deep, easily navigable, well-charted cut running generally southwest from Taylor Creek's westerly reaches to Beaufort Inlet. This is probably the best route from the ICW to Taylor Creek for northbound ICW captains, and certainly for vessels whose draft exceeds 5½ feet.

Navigators hunting for this convenient cut-through from Beaufort Inlet will now find it opposite flashing buoy #21. The current charts show the channel as being abeam of flashing buoy #17, but as discussed below, the markers on Beaufort Inlet have been renumbered.

The Beaufort Inlet–Taylor Creek channel parallels Radio Island and is clearly shown on charts 11541 and 11545. The cut is well outlined by aids to navigation and does not present any difficulty except at the intersection with Beaufort Inlet.

A sandbar shown on charts 11541 and 11545 is building south from the southwestern tip of Bird Shoal and has begun to impinge on flashing buoy #2. Careless navigators who wander into these shallows may find themselves hard aground. To bypass this hazard, scrupulously avoid the charted shoal waters south, east, and southeast of #2. Come abeam of #2 by 15 yards to its western side. Continue cruising north into the connecting channel by passing unlighted can buoy #3 and flashing daybeacon #1 to your port side. From #1, the channel is well marked and charted to the Taylor Creek intersection.

### Taylor Creek and the Beaufort Waterfront

East of the Gallant approach channel's southern foot lies Taylor Creek. The creek is deep almost to its banks and navigation is straightforward, though docking at the town piers can be complicated by swift tidal currents. You will usually find the western portion of the creek dotted with anchored craft. If you decide to join this happy throng, be sure to select a spot south of the main channel.

The entire length of Taylor Creek all the way to the Back Sound intersection is now an official no-wake zone. Power craft should proceed at slow speed along this entire stretch.

As you move east on Taylor Creek, the Beaufort waterfront will be obvious to port and Carrot Island to starboard. A group of wild ponies makes its home on Carrot Island. You may well see a few of them grazing on the nearby ridge.

Cruising past the waterfront, you will first encounter the docks of Spouter Inn restaurant, followed closely by the single pier of Harpoon Willie's restaurant. After you pass several private and commercial slips, the Beaufort Gulf Docks will come abeam to the north. You will spy the extensive wharves of the Beaufort Municipal Docks shortly thereafter. The dockmaster's office is located on the west side of the Dock House restaurant building. Beaufort Municipal Docks now monitors VHF channel 16.

### East on Taylor Creek

East of Beaufort's main waterfront, Taylor Creek continues deep almost to its banks. You will need to make use of chart 11545, as 11541 ends at Beaufort. Cruising down the creek, you will pass a menhaden-processing plant. You can usually spot several large fishing craft moored here.

As outlined in the last chapter, the newly marked but uncharted channel leading almost due east from Taylor Creek into Back Sound is tricky at best. If you decide to make the attempt, be sure to consult the navigation information in chapter 7. Good luck! You may need it.

## BEAUFORT INLET

Beaufort Inlet (Standard Mile 204.5) is often considered the southern boundary of the Outer Banks. However, Bogue Banks, a vestige of the more prominent northerly sand spits, extends westward for many miles. Beaufort Inlet has long been the most stable cut to and from the sea between Norfolk and the Cape Fear River. This inlet has been known as Topsail Inlet, Core Sound Inlet, Old Topsail Inlet, and Port Beaufort Inlet.

Though the cut has never held a depth of less than 15 feet, its commercial importance was minimal during the state's early history due to Beaufort's isolation from the interior. This situation was remedied in 1858 when Governor John Motley Morehead extended the North Carolina Railroad to Shepherd's Point, thereby founding Morehead City.

In 1880, the Corps of Engineers acquired responsibility for the maintenance of Beaufort Inlet. In 1881, the corps built a series of jetties on both sides of the cut and erected sand fences to stabilize the shoreline. The project was a complete success. Today, the inlet has minimum depths of 35 feet and some soundings as deep as 50 feet.

The point of land that juts out from Bogue Banks into the inlet's western flank has long been recognized for its military importance. Fort Dobbs was constructed on the point in 1756, followed by Fort Hampton in 1808. Finally, a third fort, Fort Macon, was built in 1834. At the outbreak of the Civil War, Fort Macon was seized by the Confederates. Union forces under General Ambrose Burnside assaulted the fort in 1862. Af-

ter a hot battle, the Confederates surrendered. Today, Fort Macon is preserved as a state park. Fort Macon does not have a landing or dock. Your best bet if you wish to visit the park is to put in at one of the marinas at Atlantic Beach and secure a ride from a friendly native.

Today, Beaufort Inlet is a vital artery of waterborne commerce. Many large oceangoing cargo and naval ships enter and exit the channel regularly. The inlet is also popular with blue-water sailors making the offshore jump on their way to the Bahamas or the Caribbean late in the year or returning from those waters in the spring. Every fall and spring, hordes of these hardy seafaring folk descend on Beaufort and spend anywhere from a few days to several weeks resupplying and awaiting favorable weather.

The late-breaking news is the total renumbering of aids to navigation along Beaufort Inlet. During the summer of 1996, the outermost buoy was moved farther out to sea, several buoys were added, and the entire numbering scheme for the extensive collection of aids was changed. Unfortunately, the NOAA charting folks have not yet caught on to this important update. Even the May 11, 1996, edition of chart 11541 still shows the old numbering scheme.

This is not a great a cause for concern. The Beaufort Inlet channel is still extremely well marked and is lit up like a Christmas tree at night. The account below will specify the new numbers where they might be of concern, particularly the turnoff from the main cut to Shackleford Banks and Cape Lookout.

# ICW TO MOREHEAD CITY AND BEAUFORT INLET NAVIGATION

Back on the ICW where this discussion of Beaufort began, you can follow a wide and deep channel to the Morehead City Turning Basin and Beaufort Inlet. As you pass unlighted daybeacon #36 to its southeasterly side, look to port and you will notice an old chimney rising above the small island southeast of the ICW channel. This is all that remains of what was apparently an old saltworks.

Continue on the Waterway, passing can buoy #37 to its northwesterly side, and come abeam of flashing daybeacon #38 to its easterly quarter. From #38, the channel swings south and heads toward the U.S. 70 high-rise bridge, which connects Morehead City and Beaufort. Just north of the bridge, a channel leading to Morehead City Yacht Basin will come abeam to the west. This facility will be discussed in the Morehead City section below.

I no longer recommend anchoring on the charted tongue of deep water northwest of #38. Shoaling has so narrowed this channel as to reduce swinging room to impractical levels.

The U.S. 70 bridge has a vertical clearance of 65 feet. Immediately after leaving the high-rise behind, look east into the charted cove. Three small-craft facilities make their homes in this offshoot. They, too, are reviewed in the Morehead City account below.

As you cruise into the Morehead City Turning Basin, you will spot a series of lighted skeletal-steel buoys leading to the southeast. These mark the Beaufort Inlet channel. Though there is usually plenty of depth on either side of the marked cut, prudent boaters will follow the buoyed route.

Abeam of flashing buoy #21 on the inlet channel, you will encounter the previously discussed cut that leads to Taylor Creek and the Beaufort waterfront. This useful passage is covered in the section on Beaufort above.

The Coast Guard station adjacent to Fort Macon is located southwest of flashing buoy #19. This is a large, active base with one or more large cutters often moored at its docks.

Passing cruisers may well spy the outskirts of Fort Macon State Park on the point of land to the west as they come abeam of flashing buoy #18. A long rock jetty extends seaward from this point. This is a popular spot for surf fishermen.

Once abeam of flashing buoy #17, skippers of boats of all types will discover good access to Shackleford Banks.

Mariners bound for the briny blue should note that flashing daybeacon #16 is now perched directly off the western tip of Shackleford Banks. Obviously, you will want to pass #16 well to its western side.

From #16, the channel continues well marked and reasonably easy to follow all the way into the Atlantic's deep waters. Outbound craft should continue to pass all red, even-numbered markers to their (the boaters') port side and green, odd-numbered buoys to starboard.

# SHACKLEFORD BANKS

Shackleford Banks, an oblong island bordering the eastern side of Beaufort Inlet, is a popular stop for local and transient pleasure boaters. Back Sound, lying north of the island, is a mostly shallow body of water with some deep and reliable channels. Shackleford tends to shelter the waters of Back Sound from the winds that often whip up a nasty chop in the inlet.

A mostly unmarked ribbon of navigable waters with minimum depths of 8 feet lines Shackleford's northerly banks between Beaufort Inlet and unlighted nun buoy #2. Care must be taken to avoid the unmarked shoals to the north.

Once past the island's western tip, boaters can anchor most anywhere and dinghy ashore. One popular spot lies near unlighted nun buoy #2, which marks the northern tip of a rock jetty that protects the waters to the east. You can anchor east of the jetty in minimum 8-foot depths with plenty of swinging room and good sanctuary from southern, southwestern, and southeastern winds. I wouldn't want to be caught here during strong blows from the north, northeast, or northwest. The National Park Service has built a small dock just east of the rock jetty. Though depths alongside run 6 to 8 feet, I would not suggest mooring here. Instead, anchor-off and dinghy ashore.

Local scuba divers frequently explore the rock jetty. Watch for "diver down" flags and don't approach too closely.

Shackleford Banks is almost completely in its natural state. The island is part of Cape Lookout National Seashore and is protected from future commercial development. Camping is allowed without special permits. The island's topography ranges from sand flats at the shoreline to high, rolling dunes with deep intervening valleys. You may observe old cedar stumps on the valley floors. Until a few years ago, wild ponies wandered at will on Shackleford Banks, but they are now being removed by order of the National Park Service. It is believed that the animals have contributed to the deforestation of Shackleford Banks, which promotes erosion.

A variety of seashells can often be found at the western tip of Shackleford Banks, but there are usually not as many as at Cape Lookout. The beaches have been known to yield whole conchs;

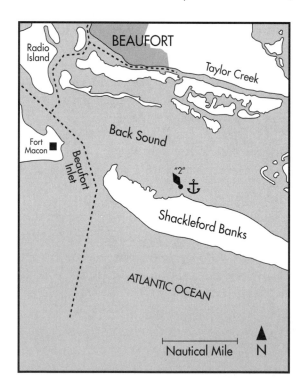

one of these currently sits atop my desk.

If you anchor near nun buoy #2 and come ashore by dinghy, a walk from your landing spot to the ocean will allow an excellent overview of the local topography. You will encounter the rolling dunes, deep valleys, and cedar stumps as you work your way to the beach.

## Shackleford Banks History

Shackleford Banks was purchased by John Shackleford in 1723. There is no evidence that Shackleford ever settled on the island that bears his name to this day.

Shackleford Banks was once green with heavy forests, but many trees were cut to provide lumber for the Beaufort shipbuilders. Several hurricanes, particularly the great storm of 1899, subsequently swept the island clean of all but scrub brush.

In the late 19th century, there were two well-defined communities on Shackleford Banks. Wades Hammock was located near Beaufort Inlet, and Diamond City was directly across Barden Inlet from Cape Lookout. Diamond City was a thriving community of whalers who ardently watched the waters off the cape for migrating schools. Both communities were virtually destroyed by the hurricane of 1899. Within three years, there was not a permanent resident left on Shackleford Banks.

Today, Shackleford Banks stands empty. Diamond City, however, is not forgotten by local residents, who still speak with pride of those early whaling days. Interested readers will find a fascinating account of Diamond City whaling in Mary and Grayden Paul's *Folk-Lore, Facts and Fiction about Carteret County in North Carolina*.

# SHACKLEFORD BANKS NAVIGATION

If you choose to visit Shackleford Banks from Beaufort Inlet, come abeam of flashing buoy #17 as if you were going to sea. Then turn to the east and follow a course parallel to Shackleford's northerly banks, keeping the shoreline 50 yards off your starboard side.

After cruising at least 50 yards past the western tip of Shackleford Banks, you can anchor anywhere in the deep channel. Good depths run to within 25 yards of shore.

To find an even better haven, continue cruising east and pass unlighted nun buoy #2 to its fairly immediate northerly side. The waters east of #2 are Shackleford's most popular anchorage. During summer weekends, this spot is often dotted with craft of all descriptions.

If you choose to make use of this popular anchorage, be careful to avoid the shallow water north of #2, clearly shown on charts 11545 and 11541. East of #2, deep water runs almost to shore.

***On the Shackleford Channel*** Cruising on the Shackleford Channel east of nun buoy #2 is not recommended. As a quick study of chart 11545 will show, unmarked shoals lie south of Middle Marsh. The channels around these hazards are narrow and treacherous.

Should you successfully bypass the shoals, you

will eventually encounter an unnumbered flashing daybeacon. Come abeam of this aid to its southern side. From the unnumbered flashing daybeacon, a wide but unmarked and winding channel leads to Harkers Island. This cut is not recommended. The lack of any navigational aids makes it treacherous. If you do make the attempt, study chart 11545 care-

fully, make use of your compass, watch your depth sounder, and don't be in a hurry.

East of the unnumbered flashing daybeacon, the Shackleford Channel peters out. You will soon encounter shallow water. If you make it to the unnumbered daybeacon, it is highly recommended that you do not proceed any farther.

# CAPE LOOKOUT

Cape Lookout is a hook-shaped landmass that encloses a protected deepwater harbor known as Cape Lookout Bight. Minimum depths of 15 feet run almost to shore. The bight's superior protection and more-than-adequate depths make the harbor an ideal anchorage. On spring and summer weekends, the bight is often crowded with pleasure craft. However, there is always room for one more.

The best spot to anchor is just behind the banks well west of flashing daybeacon #1. Simply avoid the shallows farther to the south and drop the hook at any spot that strikes your fancy.

About the only precaution mariners need take when planning a visit to Cape Lookout is to consult the latest weather forecast. Though the harbor and anchorage are well sheltered from western, southern, and southwestern blows, there is not nearly so much protection from northern winds, particularly strong breezes from the northeast. If these winds are forecast at speeds topping 20 knots, delay your visit until fair weather returns.

Cape Lookout is part of Cape Lookout National Seashore and is protected from commer-

cial development. The National Park Service has established restrooms near the lighthouse and shade shelters at various locations along the banks and is now using the old Coast Guard docks. The Park Service is also considering whether to recondition the decommissioned Coast Guard station for use as a ranger station. No other National Park Service facilities are available ashore or are anticipated for the future. Camping is allowed without special permit.

The Cape Lookout Lighthouse is clearly visible from the bight and is still very much in use. Though you can't climb this structure, you might find a hike to its base interesting. Recently, Barden Inlet has cut closer and closer to this magnificent old lighthouse. Several years ago, an alternate channel was dredged on the inlet's western side to slow the erosion of the beach adjacent to the lighthouse's foundation. For now, the lighthouse is safe, but more permanent measures will eventually have to be taken if this historic landmark is to be preserved.

A dinghy trip ashore to the cape is definitely recommended. It might almost be said that you have not seen the North Carolina coast until you've been ashore at Cape Lookout. Pull your dinghy well up onto the beach, as the tidal range is substantial.

Once ashore, consider hiking the short distance to the ocean side of the cape. The cape itself is generally flat and covered with sand and grass. There were once sand dunes here, but they have long since departed. On the ocean side, you will find an incredible collection of seashells deposited by strong currents. After storms and at low tide, the shell hunting can be spectacular indeed.

On the southern section of the sand spit that forms the northern curve of the cape, a rock jetty extends some distance out to sea. In favorable weather, this jetty makes for excellent scuba diving.

Cape Lookout is an ideal setting for all seashore activities, whether they be picnicking, camping, scuba diving, shell collecting, or just throwing a Frisbee. North Carolina is fortunate to have such an accessible playground that has not succumbed to commercial development, and never will.

*Old cedar stumps–Shackleford Banks*

## Cape Lookout History

Cape Lookout Bight has long been recognized as one of the finest harbors on the North Carolina coast. According to David Stick, a leading authority on the history of the Outer Banks, Spanish privateers used the bight as a hiding place in the 1740s. When Royal Governor Arthur Dobbs visited the cape in 1755, he described it as "the best, altho small, of any harbor from Boston to Georgia." During this period, Cape Lookout was sparsely populated by whalers. Though the largest concentration of these hardy seamen was at Diamond City on Shackleford Banks, many whalers' camps dotted Cape Lookout's shores. Several local names for certain sections of the cape were derived from these old camps.

With some small assistance from the North Carolina government, a group of French volunteers constructed a fort on Cape Lookout during the Revolutionary War and named it in honor of John Hancock. Fort Hancock was garrisoned for two years, but not a trace of the old structure remains today.

The first Cape Lookout Lighthouse was authorized in 1804, but due to considerable time spent in needless surveys, it was not lit until 1812. This first light was a double-walled tower. The inner wall was of brick and the outer was covered with wooden shingles and painted with horizontal red and white stripes. Passing sailors complained that the light was not tall enough to be effective, prompting the construction of a second lighthouse in 1857. During the Civil War, when the immediate coastline was in the hands of Union forces, the Confederates attempted to destroy the lighthouse with dynamite. Nei-

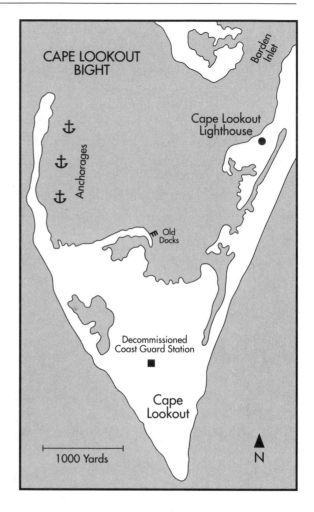

ther of the two daring raids was successful, though the light was put out of commission for a short while.

There is a persistent, controversial story that the distinctive black-and-white diamond pattern of the Cape Lookout Lighthouse was a mistake. The story goes that the Cape Hatteras Lighthouse was the one which was supposed to bear the diamond design, since it guards Diamond Shoals. The Cape Lookout Lighthouse was to receive the black-and-white spiral markings that today adorn the Cape Hatteras Lighthouse. But the painting contractor was confused as to instructions, and the present patterns were the result. Recently, I have received information that casts this tale in a doubtful light, but it makes for a great story over dinner in the cockpit.

In 1880, the Cape Lookout Lifesaving Station was established. It continued in operation under the Coast Guard until 1982. A United States Weather Bureau station saw service at the cape from 1876 to 1904.

In 1912, plans were formulated to make Cape Lookout a major coal port. The North Carolina Railroad was to be extended from Beaufort to the cape, and a rock jetty was planned to lengthen the cape's western point and give additional protection to the bight. Work was begun on the jetty in 1914, and almost 0.5 nautical mile was completed before the outbreak of World War I caused the project to be abandoned. The rock jetty has done its work well; the sand spit at the cape's western tip has been extended nearly 1 nautical mile. This sand bank is often called the Power Squadron Spit.

Cape Lookout has had a long history as a harbor of refuge. As you drop your hook in the bight, take a moment to consider those who have plied these waters: the Spanish, the French, pirates, British warships, American privateers, the Lifesaving Service, the Coast Guard, and now you.

## Cape Lookout Legend

One of the most chilling sea tales you will ever hear had its origin at Cape Lookout. Un-like many coastal legends, this story is quite true. There are still Beaufort natives who will tell you their grandparents saw the events of that terrible night in January 1886.

It seems that a fine three-masted schooner, the *Crissie Wright*, was making its way north along the North Carolina coast when bad weather threatened. The captain decided not to brave Diamond Shoals in the deteriorating conditions, so he set course for Cape Lookout Bight. As the ship approached the harbor, the main mast brace parted. The stricken vessel drifted helplessly onto the shoals, where it lay broadside and was broached by every incoming wave.

The breakers were much too high to allow the launching of lifeboats, so the captain and crew took to the rigging. Meanwhile, most of the residents of nearby Diamond City gathered on the banks to watch the ship's plight. The Diamond City whalers tried repeatedly to launch their small boats, to no avail. The would-be rescuers built a huge bonfire on the beach, hoping some of the crew could swim to shore. It was not to be. As the horrified residents watched, the captain and several crew members were swept overboard.

The night became bitterly cold. To this day, Beaufort natives use the expression "cold as the night the *Crissie Wright* came ashore." The next morning, the waves subsided and the whalers were able to reach the stranded craft. They found four men wrapped in the jib sail. Three were frozen solid, but one, the ship's cook, was alive. He died a scant year later, never having recovered from his ordeal.

This is a tale that should remind all boaters just how fickle the sea can be.

# CAPE LOOKOUT NAVIGATION

To visit Cape Lookout, continue seaward past the gap between flashing buoys #5 and #6. Cruise at least 300 yards past #6 on the inlet channel, then turn sharply east and set a new course for flashing buoy #4, which marks the main entrance to Cape Lookout Bight. Though it is a long run of 6.3 nautical miles between the two buoys, this track does not impinge on any shallows. Soon after departing from #6, you will catch sight of the Cape Lookout Lighthouse. This distinctive landmark will help to keep you pointed in the right direction.

Don't be tempted to turn east toward Cape Lookout short of flashing buoy #6! Though it appears to the uninformed eye that you can cruise through open water without going this far out to sea, a long shoal clearly shown on chart 11545 has built south from the southwestern tip of Shackleford Banks. This hazard blocks the way unless you go far enough out to sea. Any craft that runs aground in the turbulent waters surrounding this bar will be in extreme difficulty.

### Other Approaches to Cape Lookout

While it is possible to reach Cape Lookout via the Harkers Island channel and Barden Inlet, the route is exacting and often tortuous. To use this approach, follow the Harkers Island channel (south of Harkers Island) east until it intersects with Barden Inlet. Barden Inlet, of course, leads to the cape. For a detailed review of these passages, see chapter 7.

***Cape Lookout Bight***   The only aids to navigation within the bight itself are flashing daybeacons #1 and #6. The latter aid marks a safe passage to the old Coast Guard docks, now used by the National Park Service.

If you choose to visit the docks, pass #6 well to its eastern side. Be on guard against the considerable bubble of shallow water striking north and northwest from Catfish Point. Once safely around these shallows and #6, you can cruise right to the piers with good depths all the way. However, most visitors to Cape Lookout wisely choose to anchor in the large section of the bight well northwest of #6. There, deep water runs quite close to shore. It is a quick dinghy trip ashore to the cape.

Flashing daybeacon #1 guards the bight's northeastern corner and marks the southern entrance of Barden Inlet. This route eventually leads to Harkers Island, where there are two low-key marinas. If you choose to make use of the inlet, refer to the appropriate section in chapter 7.

# MOREHEAD CITY

Morehead City's (Standard Mile 205) busy and colorful waterfront offers many attractions for visiting boaters. The Morehead channel strikes north immediately west of the Morehead City Turning Basin near flashing daybeacon #MC. Minimum depths from the channel's eastern entrance to the western tip of the developed waterfront are 10 feet. The cut's western exodus leads back into the ICW at flashing daybeacon #4 and has minimum soundings of 5 to 5½ feet at low water.

Two waterfront restaurants provide temporary dockage for their patrons, and many shops and restaurants are only a short walk away. Twin marinas offer ample dockage on the waterfront for transients. A boatyard near the channel's westerly limits can handle most below-the-waterline repairs.

Since around 1990, Morehead City has spent considerable money rebuilding its waterfront. The result is an eye-pleasing mix of waterside walks surrounded by a colorful array of retail shops, commercial fish houses, and restaurants.

Visiting cruisers and landlubbers alike will want to set their sights on Morehead City for the North Carolina Seafood Festival the first weekend in October. This festival is a potpourri of seafood, arts, and street entertainment. Visitors can really blow their diets by wandering up and down Evans Street sampling the succulent fare at the various booths.

One of the largest charter-fishing fleets on the Atlantic coast is based in Morehead City. Waterfront visitors are sure to notice the long lines of fishing craft advertising for sportsmen to try their luck. Fishing in the Morehead City area can be quite productive.

Cruising visitors in need of shoreside transportation can call Yellow Cab (919-728-3483) or Crystal Coast Cab Company (919-728-5365). For rental cars, check with Turners Texaco (919-247-4080), Beaufort Airport (919-728-1777), or Enterprise Rent-A-Car (919-240-0218).

Cruisers docking along the Morehead City waterfront who are in need of provisions will probably need to take a taxi, as the closest grocery store (the Town and Country on Arendell Street/U.S. 70) is about eight blocks away. On the other hand, captains will find a wonderful array of gift shops and restaurants along both sides of Evans Street within an easy step of either Dockside Marina or the Morehead BP Docks.

## Morehead City Facilities

Cruising along the Morehead channel from east to west, you will first spy a Texaco sign behind an old wooden-face dock. This facility provides fueling service for commercial craft only.

Next door to the commercial fueling dock, the large dry-dock storage building of Portside Marina gazes out over the Morehead waterfront channel. Gasoline can be purchased at the marina's outer dock, but no other services are available for transients. Continuing west, you will soon pass a series of private docks associated with the easternmost of two high-rise condo projects.

West of the private slips, you will encounter the Morehead City waterfront's most modern facility, Dockside Marina and Ship's Store. This facility boasts ample slip space for transients in an area where this sort of dockage was formerly at a premium. Berths are provided at ultramodern floating concrete docks with power, water, and newly installed dockside telephone connections. Showers and a laundromat are available shoreside. Depths alongside range from 11 feet at the outer docks to 6 feet on the innermost slips. Take care when approaching the docks, as swift tidal currents regularly scour the Morehead waterfront channel! Gasoline and diesel fuel are available, and an extensive ship's and variety store is housed on the first floor of the large condo

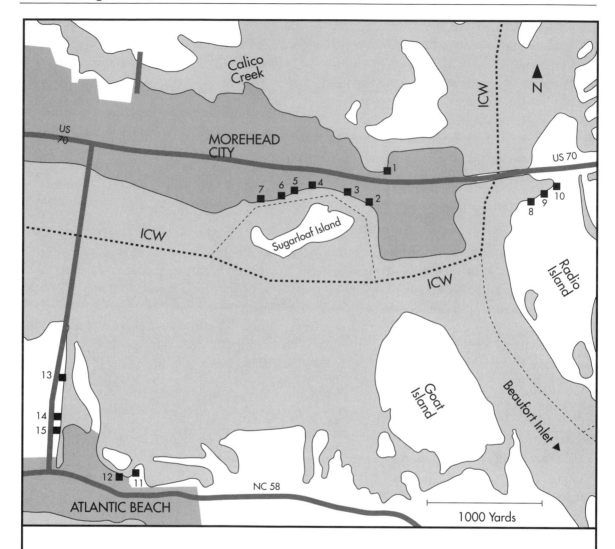

## MOREHEAD CITY AND ATLANTIC BEACH

1. Morehead City Yacht Basin
2. Dockside Marina & Ship's Store
3. Charter Restaurant
4. Sanitary Fish Market
5. Morehead "BP" Docks
6. Captain Bill's Restaurant
7. Russell's Marine Service
8. Morehead Sports Marina
9. Island Marine
10. Radio Island Marina
11. Anchorage Marina
12. Fort Macon Marina
13. Seawater Club Marina
14. Causeway Marina
15. Bailey's Marina

project overlooking the marina. Mechanical repairs can be arranged through several local repair firms. A number of restaurants are within a two-block walk (see below). Over and above these attractions, I found the personnel at Dockside to be friendly and knowledgeable, ready to go the extra mile to help the visiting cruiser with all his needs.

Following Hurricane Fran, an unfortunate rumor arose that Dockside Marina had suffered extensive damage. Nothing could be farther from the truth. In fact, the marina was in full operation within four days. As this account is penned, there is no evidence left of the great storm.

### Dockside Marina and Ship's Store (919) 247-4890

Approach depth: 10+ feet
Dockside depth: 6-11 feet
Accepts transients: yes
Floating concrete piers: yes
Dockside power connections: 30 & 50 amps
Dockside water connections: yes
Showers: yes
Laundromat: yes
Gasoline: yes
Diesel fuel: yes
Mechanical repairs: independent contractors
Ship's & variety store: yes
Restaurants: many nearby

After passing a few private and commercial fishing slips, you will sight the fixed wooden-face dock of Charter Restaurant (405 Evans Street, 919-726-9036) to starboard. Patrons are welcome to tie off while dining, but no overnight stays are allowed. Charter's broiled seafood platters are spectacular, piled high with succulent shrimp, scallops, or flounder. Boats as large as 38 feet should be able to find a place to moor. Mini-

mum low-tide depths alongside run in the 8- to 10-foot range.

Several boats of the local charter-fishing fleet separate Charter Restaurant from Sanitary Fish Market (501 Evans Street, 919-247-3111), one of the most recognized attractions on the Morehead City waterfront. Depths at the pier run an impressive 12 feet or better. This world-renowned seafood restaurant, often referred to as Tony's, provides convenient berths for its patrons. Sanitary has built its reputation on fresh fried seafood. The "Complete Shore Dinner" is spoken of with awe by boaters all along the Waterway. If you have never eaten at Tony's, don't fail to experience the many pleasures of this famous establishment.

Next up is the new Blue Peters Café (509 Evans Street, 919-808-2904), which occupies the old location of Dee Gee's Gift Shop. This dining spot is owned by the same folks as Sanitary Fish Market, but its menu is far more sophisticated. For dinner, consider the Stuffed Flounder Veronique or the Pan-Seared Shrimp and Sea Scallops. By the time this account finds its way

*Dockside Marina and Ship's Store*
*Morehead City Waterfront*

into your hands, Blue Peters should have a floating dock fronting onto the north side of the Morehead waterfront channel. This dock is planned for the use of its dining patrons; it seems probable that no overnight stays will be allowed. Depths alongside should be better than 7 feet.

If the extra weight you acquire at Sanitary Fish Market or Blue Peters Café still allows your craft to float, you can continue cruising west past several more newly refurbished docks. These piers belong to various charter and commercial fishing craft and are used by the annual Big Rock Marlin Tournament.

Next up is Morehead BP Docks, formerly Morehead Gulf Docks. This facility's older slips and one long, fixed wooden-face dock were once the only transient dockage available on the waterfront. That situation has now changed drastically with the advent of Dockside Marina, but the BP slips and piers are still in good repair and well within Morehead City's complex of restaurants and shops. Minimum depths run as much as 12 feet on the outer dock, and the inner slips exhibit 7-foot minimums. Transients are accepted. Each berth has access to water and 30- and 50-amp power connections. Dockage reservations are recommended. As you might expect given this marina's name, gasoline and diesel fuel can be purchased. In fact, the vast majority of Morehead City's charter-fleet captains fuel their craft here. A fairly well-stocked ship's, variety, and tackle store known as the Dock Shop overlooks the BP piers and serves as the dockmaster's office as well.

Past the Morehead BP Docks, you will soon pass Captain Bill's Seafood Restaurant (701 Evans Street, 919-726-2166). There is really

**Morehead BP (Gulf) Docks
(919) 726-5461**

Approach depth: 10+ feet
Dockside depth: 7-12 feet
Accepts transients: yes
Fixed wooden piers: yes
Dockside power connections: 30 & 50 amps
Dockside water connections: yes
Showers: yes
Gasoline: yes
Diesel fuel: yes
Ship's & variety store: yes
Restaurants: many nearby

nothing left in the way of pleasure-craft dockage at this venerable dining spot, but the food is always worthwhile.

A bit farther along, the old piers of Russell's Yachts (919-240-2826) will come abeam to starboard. This facility specializes in all types of below-the-waterline and hull service. Topside repairs and fiberglass refinishing are also offered.

## Morehead City Downtown Business District

Downtown Morehead City, directly adjacent to the waterfront, offers many shops and restaurants well worth exploring. By all means, be *sure* to check out Dee Gee's Gift Shop (508 Evans Street, 919-726-3314). Doug and Jane Wolf have done an outstanding job of assembling an impressive selection of books (including more than a few nautical titles) and gifts. For my money, Dee Gee's is *the* place to shop in Morehead City.

Hungry visitors should spare no pains to find The Plant Restaurant (105 South Seventh Street, 919-726-5502). This unique dining attraction is housed in the thoroughly refurbished former headquarters of the Morehead Gulf Oil Company. Outside dining is offered during fair weather; some tables are elevated on a second-story deck with a good view of the waterfront. While I have not yet had the good fortune to dine here, conversations with several locals suggest that the food is superior.

## Additional Morehead City Marina Facilities

Another large marina is located along the ICW's approach to the Morehead City Turning Basin. The channel to Morehead City Yacht Basin (Standard Mile 204) cuts west from the Waterway between unlighted can buoy #39 and the U.S. 70 high-rise bridge. Morehead City Yacht Basin offers overnight berths at fixed wooden piers with the usual power and water connections. Minimum approach depths run to 8 feet, with most soundings in the 10- to 12-foot range. Cruisers will find 7½ to 9 feet of water dockside. Gasoline, diesel fuel, and waste pump-out services are available, and repairs can be arranged through local mechanics. Showers and a laundromat are adjacent to the docks. A small ship's store is part and parcel of the dockmaster's office. It is a pleasant three- or four-block walk to the many restaurants and shops lining the principal Morehead City waterfront.

In a cove east of unlighted daybeacon #24, three small marinas flank the ICW's approach to the Morehead City Turning Basin. All three are located on the cove's southern shore. The entrance channel carries only 4 feet of water at low tide. Entry by deep-draft vessels is tricky at best.

The westernmost facility is Morehead Sports

**Morehead City Yacht Basin (919) 726-6862**

Approach depth: 8-12 feet
Dockside depth: 7½-9 feet
Accepts transients: yes
Fixed wooden piers: yes
Dockside power connections: 30 & 50 amps
Dockside water connections: yes
Showers: yes
Laundromat: yes
Waste pump-out: yes
Gasoline: yes
Diesel fuel: yes
Mechanical repairs: independent contractors
Ship's store: yes
Restaurants: many nearby

Marina (919-726-5676). This firm caters mostly to small cruising craft. Very limited transient dockage is available for boats as large as 28 feet at a fixed wooden pier with minimal power and water connections. Low-tide depths alongside run as little as 4 feet, the typical low-tide water level for the entire cove. Gasoline is available, but diesel fuel is not. A small travel-lift can haul boats in the 30-foot range. Mechanical repairs for gasoline engines are sometimes available. The marina maintains a ship's store on the premises.

Next up is Island Marine (919-726-5706). As I looked over the old, paint-spattered work shed, I was reminded of boatyards in another, perhaps happier, era. Island Marine has an old 25-ton travel-lift and offers below-the-waterline repairs, mechanical repairs for gas and diesel engines, and topside repairs.

Radio Island Marina (919-726-3773) occupies the rear of the small cove. This facility is primarily concerned with small-craft dry storage, as witnessed by the large, blue storage building visible from the water. The management informed me that overnight berths for transient craft up to 28 feet in length are occasionally provided on weekdays only. There is a large, well-stocked ship's store at the marina, and gasoline can be purchased.

## Morehead City History

Morehead City was the brainchild of John Motley Morehead, governor of North Carolina from 1841 to 1845. Governor Morehead foresaw the commercial potential of Shepherd's Point, the promontory at the intersection of the Newport River and Beaufort Inlet, and envisioned "a great commercial city" there. Morehead and his associates acquired a large portion of the surrounding property and then made plans to extend the North Carolina Railroad from Goldsboro to Shepherd's Point.

A public auction was held in 1857, and 150 lots were sold in the new town. Within three days of the celebration of the railroad's completion in 1858, every property parcel in the city and the surrounding area was sold.

The Civil War interrupted Morehead City's development as a port. Following the war, the shipping terminal deteriorated, but the railroad continued hauling vast quantities of seafood to the state's inland sections.

In the late 1800s, Morehead City received a new group of residents from nearby Shackleford Banks. As discussed in the last chapter, many whaling families were driven from Diamond City and the other Shackleford settlements by the great hurricane of 1899. While most of these salty folk moved to Harkers Island, one group came to Morehead City and settled along present-day Bridges Street in a tract still known as the "Promised Land."

Until recently, Morehead City was known more as a resort community than a major port. A large charter-fishing fleet, the town's central location on the ICW, and the proximity to Atlantic Beach have all served to promote Morehead City as an ideal spot to spend a summer vacation. This popularity continues unabated. It is rare indeed to find a North Carolinian who has not spent at least one vacation in Morehead City.

Governor Morehead's belief in the commercial viability of the city has been vindicated at last. Under Governor Kerr Scott, a large bond program was approved which funded a modern port terminal. Commercial traffic has steadily increased since those early days.

## MOREHEAD CITY NAVIGATION

From a position between flashing daybeacons #34 and #35, where the old (and now all but impassable) entrance to Gallants Channel strikes southeast, set course to eventually come abeam of flashing daybeacon #38 to its easterly side. Anchoring or exploring on the charted tongue of deep water northwest of #38 is no longer recommended. Shoaling has all but erased this cut.

**On the ICW**   From #38, it is a short hop to the

Morehead City Turning Basin. After passing can buoy #39 to its westerly side, set course for the U.S. 70 high-rise bridge's central pass-through. Just before the bridge, a well-marked channel opens out west of the Waterway. This dredged cut leads to Morehead City Yacht Basin. If you enter, pass all red markers to your starboard side and green beacons to port.

**Morehead City Waterfront**   Immediately south of the Morehead City Yacht Basin cutoff, the ICW passes under the U.S. 70 Bypass bridge. Thanks to its 65 feet of vertical clearance, this bridge is high enough that even the tallest craft can pass without difficulty. South of the bridge, the Morehead City Commercial Port Terminal opens out to the west. Large ships are often moored at the facility. Watch your wake and you can cruise quite close to these craft for a firsthand look. To the east, you may spy the small cove containing Morehead City Sports Marina, Island Marine, and Radio Island Marina. If you choose to enter, cruise into the cove's mid-width and watch for several small, floating buoys marking the entrance. Remember, low-tide depths run to 4 feet.

Follow the port's bulkhead and you will soon come abeam of the Morehead City Turning Basin. Here, the ICW takes a 90-degree turn to the west. Though channel markers on Beaufort Inlet have been renumbered and are not yet correctly charted, navigators will be happy to learn that chart 11541 once again begins to reflect aids to navigation accurately west of the Morehead City Turning Basin.

To continue west and south on the ICW, set course to pass between flashing daybeacon #MC

to its southern side and unlighted daybeacon #1B to its northern side. Just east of the gap between these two daybeacons, the entrance to the Morehead City waterfront opens out to the north.

Follow the commercial port's bulkhead as it cuts north. Pass unlighted daybeacon #3 to its eastern side. The channel then cuts back to the west. Favor the northern banks and you can cruise by the waterfront's many facilities in safety. Eventually, you will come abeam of unlighted daybeacon #6 to its southern side.

Past #6, the waterfront channel continues west and eventually intersects the ICW. This section is subject to shoaling. At the time of this writing, however, the cut held minimum depths of 5 to 5½ feet, with most of the route deeper. At the moment, the channel seems safe for all but the deepest-draft vessels. However, prudent boaters piloting craft that draw more than 4 feet will do well to check with one of the Morehead City waterfront marinas about channel conditions before using this cut.

**On the ICW**   Cruisers bypassing the Morehead City waterfront channel should point to pass between flashing daybeacon #MC and unlighted daybeacon #1B, then set course to come abeam of flashing daybeacon #2 to its southerly side. Along the way, you will pass a series of privately maintained daybeacons south of your course. These aids lead to Triple S Yacht Basin. This facility is private and does not offer any transient services.

After passing #2, you should come abeam of unlighted can buoy #3 to its northern side. From #3, it is possible to enter two channels that lead to Atlantic Beach.

## ATLANTIC BEACH

Atlantic Beach (Standard Mile 205.5) has become one of North Carolina's most populous seaside resort communities. Unfortunately, this popularity has led to rampant commercial development that is not always pleasing to the eye.

Two channels striking south and west, respectively, from the ICW at unlighted can buoy #3 serve the Atlantic Beach area. The easternmost cut leads to two marinas, one of which offers very limited transient dockage. This channel is subject to shoaling; at the time of this writing, however, it carried 6-foot depths at low water. Use this approach with caution.

Anchorage Marina lies at the foot of the easternmost channel. Most of this facility's dockage is taken up by seasonal renters, but transients are occasionally accepted for overnight dockage. Space is very limited for this purpose. Visiting cruisers would be well advised to call ahead of time to check on slip availability.

Anchorage has two dockage basins. Large craft are housed at the fixed wooden piers in the easternmost harbor, which has 6-foot minimum depths. The western basin contains the marina fuel dock and compact wooden floating slips appropriate for small power craft. Low-water depths of as little as 4½ feet in this harbor can be a problem for long-legged vessels.

Most berths at Anchorage Marina feature water and 30-amp power connections. One low-key shower is located shoreside. Gasoline and diesel fuel are readily available. The marina also has an extensive tackle shop and supply store. It is a fairly short walk to several nearby restaurants

and motels and to the beach. Ask for directions at the marina office.

### Anchorage Marina
### (919) 726-4423

Approach depth: 5-6 feet (minimum)
Dockside depth: minimum 6 feet in eastern basin and 4½ feet in western harbor
Accepts transients: very limited
Fixed wooden piers: eastern basin
Floating wooden docks: western basin
Dockside power connections: 30 amps
Dockside water connections: yes
Showers: very limited
Gasoline: yes
Diesel fuel: yes
Mechanical repairs: independent contractors
Ship's & variety store: yes
Restaurants: many nearby

Just west of Anchorage Marina is Fort Macon Marina (919-726-2055). This establishment is in the business of dry-storing small powerboats. The large metal building behind the docks houses many craft. Fort Macon Marina has no facilities for transients but does offer gasoline and diesel fuel.

Fort Macon, a restored Civil War fort and state park, is located on the eastern tip of Atlantic Beach. The park is too far away to reach by foot, but if you can secure a ride, it is well worth a visit.

The second Atlantic Beach channel runs west from the unnumbered flashing junction daybeacon south-southwest of unlighted can buoy #3, then turns south, paralleling the easterly banks of the long Atlantic Beach causeway. This cut is rather tricky and is subject to shoaling. At the present time, however, minimum depths of 5 feet can be carried by careful skippers who stick strictly to the marked cut.

The causeway channel is home to several small marinas, none of which offers overnight transient dockage. All of the marine facilities lie along the western shore. Typical low-tide depths on the interior portion of the causeway channel are 8 feet. Almost all of the channel's small marinas feature depths alongside of 5 to 6 feet at low water.

After entering the stream south of unlighted daybeacon #8, you will pass the Showboat Motel and Restaurant, followed by the single pier of the Sailing Place (919-726-5664), owned and operated by Brent Creelman. There are no facilities for visitors here, but if you want to charter a good boat for a day sail, this is the place. Brent provides excellent service and is one of the most knowledgeable people you will ever meet when it comes to cruising the waters lying about Morehead City and Beaufort.

Next up are the docks of the Blue Marlin Motel. These slips are in poor repair and are for the exclusive use of motel guests. They are only large enough for craft up to 26 feet in length.

Next, you will pass the *Captain Stacy IV* docks. This so-called head boat has an alternate dock on the Morehead City waterfront. During the day, the ship takes large parties offshore for bottom-fishing. In the evening, the *Captain Stacy IV* is often used for harbor tours.

Just past the *Captain Stacy IV* docks are the private slips of Sea Water Club Marina. Though there are no dockside services for transients at this facility, the club does maintain a large ship's store which is open to the public.

The fixed slips and piers of Causeway Marina (919-726-6977) are up next. Gasoline and diesel fuel can be purchased dockside, and mechanical repairs for outboards are available. Causeway Marina also offers a "sea-tow" service for those who find the bottom.

Bailey's Marina (919-247-4148) is located next door to Causeway Marina. The friendly management of Bailey's describes its facility as a "family marina." Gasoline and diesel fuel can be purchased here, and the firm maintains a ship's and variety store just behind the fuel dock.

## ATLANTIC BEACH NAVIGATION

Both channels serving the Atlantic Beach waters are narrow, more than slightly tricky, and subject to shoaling. Keep a weather eye on the sounder when traversing either cut and proceed at slow speed. Sailcraft and trawlers should be particularly mindful of the side-setting effect of tidal currents. These slow-moving craft can easily be swept out of the dredged cut unless their captains keep a close watch on their stern for leeway slippage.

The Anchorage Marina channel leads southwest from unlighted can buoy #3. To follow the channel, depart the Waterway at unlighted can buoy #3. Set course to come abeam of the unnumbered flashing junction daybeacon south-southwest of #3 on its immediate eastern side. Between #3 and the unnumbered flashing junction daybeacon, be on guard against the correctly charted tongue of 4-foot water just west of your course line; this water may be even shallower than its charted depth.

From the unnumbered daybeacon, a series of small, floating buoys and more conventional daybeacons leads southwest to the marinas. Hold to the channel's mid-width and don't be in a hurry. This cut is narrow and is subject to shoaling in spots. Keep a sharp watch for temporary markers as you cruise. As usual, pass red buoys to your starboard side and green markers to port.

As you reach unlighted daybeacon #4 near the channel's southwestern end, you will spy a series of daybeacons leading southeast. Don't be fooled! This channel leads to a private condominium dockage complex. To reach Anchorage Marina, continue cruising straight ahead. Fort Macon Marina is just to the west.

Boaters who choose to visit the Atlantic Beach causeway channel, which holds 5-foot minimum depths, should be on the alert for temporary floating aids to navigation. These aids mark new encroachments by the surrounding shoals. Proceed at slow speed and stick strictly to the marked route, as depths outside the channel quickly rise to grounding levels. If your sounder reads less than 5 feet at any time during this passage, you are easing onto the shoals. Stop and make adjustments immediately before you find the bottom.

Set course from unlighted can buoy #3 as if you intend to come abeam of the unnumbered flashing junction daybeacon at the head of the Anchorage Marina channel to its immediate easterly side. Some 20 yards before reaching the marker, cut sharply west and pass the flasher to its fairly immediate northerly side. A study of chart 11541 shows that this plan of action will help you avoid the finger of shoal water building east from unlighted daybeacon #2.

From a position abeam of the junction daybeacon, set a course to come abeam of and pass unlighted daybeacons #3 and #5 by no more than 25 yards to their northerly sides. Don't approach unlighted daybeacon #2, which you will pass north of your course line between the flashing junction daybeacon and #3. This aid lies hard by the north-side shoal and is best avoided.

Point to eventually come abeam of unlighted daybeacon #6 to its immediate southerly side. At this point, the channel begins to bend southwest on its way toward the channel paralleling the causeway. The section between #6 and the inner channel's entrance is the most changeable portion of the cut. Observe all markers carefully and continue to pass red markers to your starboard side and green beacons to port. Be prepared to find a number of small, floating markers. These beacons are frequently moved to follow the latest shifts in the channel.

A few floating markers lead west under the Atlantic Beach Bridge from unlighted daybeacon #8. These aids are easily confused with the causeway channel markers. Ignore the markers running under the bridge. They outline a channel leading to Crows Nest Marina. The clearance along this portion of the bridge limits this cut to small power craft.

Continue cruising almost due south into the mid-width of the causeway channel past unlighted daybeacon #8.

**On the ICW**   To continue west on the Waterway from unlighted can buoy #3, study chart 11541 carefully. It is all too easy to confuse the daymarks of the various Atlantic Beach channels with the

ICW aids. A large shoal lies between the Waterway and the Atlantic Beach causeway channel. It is essential to correctly identify the ICW markers to avoid these treacherous shallows.

Pass flashing daybeacon #4 to its southerly side, then set course for the central pass-through of the Atlantic Beach Bridge. Along the way, you will pass unlighted daybeacon #3A to its northerly side.

Thankfully, the new high-rise Atlantic Beach Bridge is now in place and the old, troublesome bascule span has been completely removed. The new bridge has 65 feet of vertical clearance.

*Anchorage Marina–Atlantic Beach*

## BOGUE SOUND

A fair-weather cruise down Bogue Sound is one of North Carolina's most pleasant boating experiences. Beautiful homes, some with their own private entrance channels, line the northern shore. The sound-side banks are heavily forested with trees that lean toward the northeast, in deference to the prevailing winds.

Bogue Banks, well to the south of the ICW channel, is a series of low barrier islands separating the sound from the ocean. These islands are covered with scrub brush. Bogue Banks is quickly being exploited for commercial development. Housing and condominium projects seem to spring up overnight.

### Crows Nest Marina

Located south of the Waterway channel just west of the Atlantic Beach Bridge, Crows Nest Marina (919-726-4048) is a small-craft dry-dock storage facility with shallow-water problems.

Since the installation of the new bridge, the old channel leading directly from the ICW has disappeared. Several small floating buoys now outline a channel running under the southerly portion of the Atlantic Beach Bridge. This new channel has minimum low-tide depths of 4½ feet, with much of the route deeper. Keeping to the deep water is a tricky process, however. You must pass under a portion of the Atlantic Beach span with minimal vertical clearance to traverse this cut. Only small power craft will be able to make it.

For those who successfully traverse the entrance channel, Crows Nest sometimes accepts transients up to 28 feet in length on weekdays. Gasoline is available, but diesel fuel is not. There is a ship's store on the premises. A large, metal dry-stack storage building overlooks the harbor. A shopping center and several restaurants are only a short walk away.

### Peletier Creek (Standard Mile 209)

Peletier Creek is located on Bogue Sound's northern shore a short hop east of the ICW's unlighted daybeacon #7; the creek's name is spelled and pronounced a variety of ways. This well-sheltered stream is the home of several marinas and boatyards. Though limited transient dockage is available, full repair services and excellent month-to-month slip space are offered by the creek's facilities.

Minimum entrance depths run around 6 feet; many deeper soundings are in evidence. Low-water depths on the stream's interior reaches run 6 to 7 feet, and all the stream's facilities have similar dockside depths.

North of unlighted daybeacon #5, Peletier Creek divides. Some boats anchor just short of the creek's split in 5½ to 6 feet of water. This sheltered haven is a good spot to ride out a heavy blow. Swinging room is sufficient for vessels as large as 45 feet.

With one exception, all of Peletier's facilities are along the creek's northeasterly arm. As you move up this fork, Wilde Boatworks (919-726-9877) will come abeam to starboard. This firm has a marine railway and performs below-the-waterline haul-out repairs.

Next up is Taylor Boat Works (919-726-6374), also to starboard. This venerable yard is known far and wide for having some of the best marine carpenters and technicians in the business. Below-the-waterline and topside repairs for both fiberglass and wooden craft are readily available. Taylor's marine railway can handle the largest pleasure craft. Mechanical repairs are arranged through independent contractors. If you need hull, prop, shaft, or carpentry repairs, you need look no farther than Jack McCallum's talented staff at Taylor Boat Works.

Eventually, the northeastern branch of Peletier Creek cuts back to the east. Just before this final turn, Harbor Master boatyard (919-726-2541) overlooks the southeastern banks. This firm offers quality mechanical repairs for both gasoline and diesel engines. For many years, I have made the trek to Harbor Master to find obscure parts no one else seems to have. The yard also offers haul-out services via a marine railway. If space is available, Harbor Master even accepts transients for temporary dockage. Water and 30-amp power connections are available, as are bathrooms and shower facilities. It is best to call ahead to see if any berths are available.

The largest marine facility on Peletier Creek occupies the farthest upstream portion of the stream's northeasterly arm. As you cruise up the creek, the fuel dock and the 50-ton travel-lift associated with 70 West Marina will come abeam to port. Most of 70 West's dockage stretches east on both sides of the creek. No transient space is available. The month-to-month slips consist of wooden pilings set out from the shore, in some cases backed by a concrete sea wall. It's unfortunate that the marina has not chosen to keep a few spaces open for transients, as the modern slips have all the amenities one could wish for. Water and 30- and 50-amp power connections are at each berth, and new showers are available. Mechanical repairs of both the gasoline and diesel varieties are offered. A large ship's store sits beside the huge dry-stack storage building. All in all, 70 West Marina is a large establishment that offers just about everything except transient dockage.

**70 West Marina**
**(919) 726-5171**

Approach depth: 6-7 feet
Dockside depth: 6-7 feet
Fixed wooden piers: yes
Dockside power connections: 30 & 50 amps
Dockside water connections: yes
Showers: yes
Gasoline: yes
Diesel fuel: yes
Mechanical repairs: yes
Below-waterline repairs: yes
Ship's store: yes

Coral Bay Marine occupies the northern tip of the creek's western branch. This firm features a huge dry-stack storage building. The marina's fixed wooden slips are mostly taken up by resident craft. Gasoline is available, and there is a small ship's store just behind the docks. Otherwise, no services are to be had by visitors.

## Spooners Creek (Standard Mile 210.5)

The well-marked channel leading from the ICW to Spooners Creek cuts north abeam of flashing daybeacon #9. This stream is the home of Spooners Creek Yacht Harbor, one of the finest pleasure-boating facilities in North Carolina. Spooners is my former home port, so I might be a bit prejudiced. For many years, it was one of my fondest cruising memories to hear the dockmaster's hearty salutation, "Welcome back to Spooners Creek!" You, too, will receive the same warm and friendly greeting today.

Spooners Creek features a large number of transient berths at fixed wooden piers with all power and water connections. Recently, many of the marina's slips and pilings have been replaced or refurbished. Entrance depths now run around 5 to 5½ feet at low water, with 6 to 8 feet at the slips. Excellent showers and a laundromat are adjacent to the ship's store and the fuel dock.

Cruisers will discover a good selection of basic foodstuffs and marine items at the on-site ship's and variety store. Captains in need of more extensive provisioning will be glad to learn that a supermarket and a Wal-Mart are located within a pleasant 0.5-mile walk of the dockage basin. After making your purchases, call the friendly marina staff, who will be glad to come and pick you up.

Spooners Creek also offers gasoline and diesel fuel from newly refurbished pumps. Repairs to mechanical equipment, hulls, shafts, and props are readily available. Spooners has a 60-ton travel-lift. The marina also boasts a swimming pool open during the summer months. Tennis courts are available on the premises for an additional fee.

The old, on-site Galley Stack Restaurant is closed and likely to remain so for some time to come. There is no restaurant within easy

*Peletier Creek*

walking distance, though a short cab ride will take you to many restaurants in western Morehead City, including the memorable Mrs. Willis's (919-726-3741).

Like Peletier Creek, Spooners Creek offers excellent protection from heavy weather. When a hurricane threatens, the Coast Guard and Duke Marine Laboratory often use Spooners Creek for shelter.

**Spooners Creek Yacht Harbor
(919) 726-2060 or (888) 808-2060**

> Approach depth: 5-5½ feet (low water)
> Dockside depth: 6-8 feet
> Accepts transients: yes
> Fixed wooden piers: yes
> Dockside power connections: 30 & 50
>     amps
> Dockside water connections: yes
> Showers: yes
> Laundromat: yes
> Gasoline: yes
> Diesel fuel: yes
> Mechanical repairs: yes
> Below-waterline repairs: extensive
> Ship's & variety store: yes

## Island Harbor Marina (Standard Mile 225)

Some 12 nautical miles south and west of Spooners Creek, the channel to Island Harbor Marina cuts south between flashing daybeacon #41 and unlighted daybeacon #42. Most of the channel leading to the marina holds 6 feet or more of water, but a bar has built across the channel's northerly entrance from the ICW. Entrance depths over this obstruction are only 4 feet at low tide. If you need more water, enter and exit at high tide or midtide.

Island Harbor offers transient berths at fixed wooden piers with depths of 4 to 5 feet. Water and 30- and 50-amp power connections are available, as are gasoline and diesel fuel. Some mechanical repairs can be arranged through independent contractors. A small ship's and variety store is just behind the docks, and Happy Days Restaurant is within a two-block walk.

**Island Harbor Marina
(919) 354-3106**

> Approach depth: 4½ feet (minimum at low
>     water)
> Dockside depth: 4-5 feet (low water)
> Accepts transients: yes
> Fixed wooden piers: yes
> Dockside power connections: 30 & 50 amps
> Dockside water connections: yes
> Gasoline: yes
> Diesel fuel: yes
> Mechanical repairs: limited (independent
>     technicians)
> Ship's & variety store: yes
> Restaurant: nearby

## Bogue Inlet (Standard Mile 226.5)

Just north of Swansboro, Bogue Inlet marks the southern foot of Bogue Sound. Shoaling at the intersection of the inlet and the ICW has been a common occurrence for time out of mind. Bogue Inlet is a capricious cut and should not be attempted without local knowledge. Fishermen in Swansboro use the inlet on a regular basis to cruise offshore for game fish. If you are lucky enough to spot one of these locals, you might try following him or her. Otherwise, it is best to pass Bogue Inlet by.

# BOGUE SOUND NAVIGATION

From the Atlantic Beach Bridge, the ICW follows Bogue Sound generally west for 17 nautical miles. The sound is a uniformly shallow body of water, with depths of 2 to 3 feet being the norm. For this reason, the sound's waters outside the Waterway cut are seldom used by cruising craft.

Fresh southwesterly winds can kick up an uncomfortable chop above flashing daybeacon #29; below #29, a series of barrier islands shelters the Waterway from all but the roughest weather. These same breezes can cause leeway, quickly pushing unwary navigators onto the channel's edge. Watch your stern carefully to avoid slippage.

West of the Atlantic Beach Bridge, there was once a wide basin of deep water, and passing cruisers did not have to be too careful about coming abeam of flashing daybeacon #3B by a proper distance to its northerly side. Now, however, the southerly side of the channel has shoaled, and boaters cannot be so lax about their passage. Once through the bridge, immediately begin curving your course a bit to the north, pointing to pass between flashing daybeacons #4A and #3B. Be *sure* to pass north of #3B. Very shoal water lies south of this marker.

During my latest on-the-water research, flashing daybeacon #4A was absent. It is uncertain whether it will be restored or whether it has been removed permanently.

Observe all markers carefully as you continue cruising west on the ICW. It is essential that you correctly identify all aids to navigation along the Waterway's passage through Bogue Sound. A navigational error will land you in less than 3 feet of water outside the channel. It's a good idea to keep your binoculars close at hand to help pick out the various daybeacons.

Boaters cruising past flashing daybeacon #6 may spot two floating markers to the southwest. Ignore these aids to navigation. They mark a channel leading to Pine Knoll Shores, an exclusive housing project on Bogue Banks. No facilities are available for transient boaters. As the channel calls for local knowledge, this side trip is not recommended for strangers.

Just east of unlighted daybeacon #7, the entrance to Peletier Creek opens out to the north.

*Peletier Creek*  The creek's entrance from the ICW is marked by four unlighted daybeacons. To enter, hold to the channel's mid-width as you pass between the first set of daybeacons. Continue on course, pointing to come abeam of unlighted daybeacon #3 fairly close to its easterly side. Immediately after passing #3, begin favoring the starboard side of the channel slightly. Soon, you will pass unlighted daybeacon #5 to your port side. Cruise back to the mid-width as you come abeam of #5 and continue holding to the centerline as you work your way upstream.

Eventually, the creek splits. Boaters seeking a well-sheltered anchorage may choose to anchor in the creek just short of the fork. Don't attempt to land by dinghy, however, as all the surrounding land is privately owned.

A cruise up the northeasterly arm will lead you to most of Peletier's facilities. The first facility to starboard is Wilde Boatworks, followed by Taylor Boat Works. Not far upstream is the Harbor Master repair yard, still to starboard. Finally, the creek

*Spooners Creek Yacht Harbor*

leads to 70 West Marina.

Peletier Creek's left-hand fork leads upstream to a series of private docks and Coral Bay Marina.

**Spooners Creek**    Not far west of Peletier Creek, the entrance to Spooners Creek lies north of flashing daybeacon #9. To enter, hold to the mid-width between all pairs of daybeacons. Once past the last pair, squeeze slightly to starboard for best depths. Soon, the creek swings 90 degrees to port. Shortly thereafter, the gas dock and marina office of Spooners Creek Yacht Harbor will come abeam, also to port.

**On the ICW**    From flashing daybeacon #9 to flashing daybeacon #41, a distance of 12 nautical miles, the Waterway continues well marked and reasonably easy to follow. There are no facilities or anchorages along this stretch. Near flashing daybeacon #13, a privately marked entrance channel leads north to a condominium dock complex, but these facilities do not offer any services for cruising boaters. West of flashing daybeacon #29, the ICW ducks behind a series of barrier islands that protects the route from most of the chop caused by

fresh southwesterly breezes.

After passing between unlighted daybeacon #40A and flashing daybeacon #41, the Waterway cuts west and begins its approach to the fixed, high-rise Emerald Isle Bridge. Before reaching this span, cruisers have access to the Island Harbor Marina channel between #41 and unlighted daybeacon #42.

**Island Harbor Marina**    To enter Island Harbor, watch to the south for the docks while cruising west from #41 toward #42. The entrance is between two small barrier islands directly abeam of the marina. Continue on the ICW until you can turn into the mid-width of the passage between the islands. Don't cut either corner or you will find shallow water. Once past the islands, continue straight into the marina. Two uncharted and unlighted navigational aids mark the sides of the channel just south of the passage between the two islands.

**On the ICW**    West of unlighted daybeacon #42, the ICW flows under the Emerald Isle Bridge. This modern high-rise has a vertical clearance of 65 feet. Soon after passing through, you will observe a No Wake sign near unlighted daybeacon #44. This sign marks the beginning of the Waterway's passage through the Swansboro area. It is a good idea to proceed at slow speed through this entire region.

West of flashing daybeacon #45, the Waterway soon meets up with the northeasterly reaches of Bogue Inlet. Shoaling on the southerly side of the ICW is a common problem. Favor the northerly side of the channel until you are well past the inlet. Keep a sharp watch for temporary buoys placed at the inlet intersection to warn of recent encroachments on the ICW channel. Be ready for strong currents as you pass the inlet's mouth.

***Bogue Inlet***   To the south, the Bogue Inlet channel is located west of flashing daybeacon #45. The inlet is subject to continual change and should not be attempted without local knowledge. Buoys and other aids to navigation are not charted.

For some inexplicable reason, several early editions of chart 11541 bear a note that Bogue Inlet is closed to navigation. This is an incorrect notation.

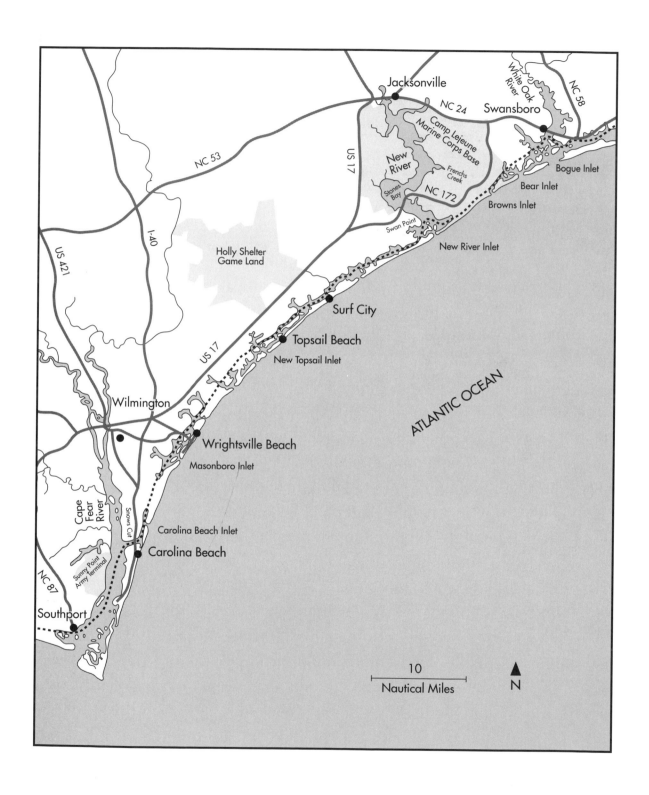

Jacksonville

White Oak River

NC 58

NC 24

Swansboro

Camp Lejeune Marine Corps Base

New River

Frenchs Creek

US 17

NC 53

Bogue Inlet

Bear Inlet

NC 172

Browns Inlet

Stones Bay

Swan Point

New River Inlet

I-40

Holly Shelter Game Land

US 421

Surf City

US 17

Topsail Beach

New Topsail Inlet

Wilmington

ATLANTIC OCEAN

Wrightsville Beach

Masonboro Inlet

Cape Fear River

Snows Cut

Carolina Beach Inlet

Sunny Point Army Terminal

Carolina Beach

NC 87

Southport

10
Nautical Miles

N

# Bogue Inlet to Cape Fear River

South of Bogue Inlet, the ICW is the only inland passage open to large cruising vessels. In fact, except for the New and Cape Fear Rivers, the Waterway is the only readily navigable inland body of water on the state's southeastern coastline.

The ICW here is quite different from the large, open sounds and rivers to the north. Cruising now becomes a matter of generally following one well-marked channel through canal-like sections with a very limited number of destinations and side trips. Tidal currents pick up markedly all the way to (and south of) the South Carolina border. The swiftly moving waters can be a real concern for single-screw trawlers and sailcraft. In spite of this difficulty, skippers who have weathered too many waves on the state's northern waters may welcome the mostly calm and protected cruising grounds to the southeast.

The Waterway's banks are mainly in their natural state. Passing cruisers can often observe saltwater marsh flats undisturbed by man's presence. The large number of fishermen often seen along this section bear witness to the region's fine angling.

The New River, which boasts its own inlet, is a large, consistently deep body of water. It is easily navigable far inland to the city of Jacksonville. The banks of the river are part of Camp Lejeune Marine Corps Base and are for the most part undeveloped.

**Charts**

You will need three NOAA charts for navigation of the ICW and the New River:

**11541** covers general navigation of the Waterway from Atlantic Beach to Wrightsville Beach

**11534** details the ICW from Masonboro Sound to the Cape Fear River and Southport

**11542** covers the New River from the ICW to Jacksonville

New River Inlet can only be rated as a fair possibility for strangers. Local knowledge is desirable, even if not absolutely necessary, for successful navigation of this seaward channel. The inlet is subject to shoaling, and most markers are not charted, as they are frequently shifted.

The facilities between Swansboro and Carolina Beach are excellent but concentrated. Good transient services are located in Swansboro, Swan Point, and Wrightsville Beach. Between these pleasure-boating centers, however, are long, isolated stretches that do not offer any haven for the cruising boater.

Reliable anchorages are scarce between Swansboro and the Cape Fear River. Even the few creeks that have sufficient depths are subject to rapid tidal currents.

The southeastern North Carolina coastline between Swansboro and Carolina Beach took the brunt of Hurricane Fran in 1996. Topsail Beach was all but laid waste by the storm. It appears that many of the homes and buildings on this fragile island will never be rebuilt, including Topsail Marina. The various marinas at Wrightsville Beach also suffered cruelly from the great storm, but repairs were well under way by the time of this writing. Chances are you will see little evidence of the hurricane by the time of your visit. Carolina Beach, too, was hard hit by Fran; this community's marina facilities are in the process of recovering as well.

Fortunately, and perhaps miraculously, the vast majority of Fran's damage was confined to the lands and waters north of Carolina Beach. Bald Head Island and Southport, lying 30 miles or so to the south, suffered only minor havoc.

## ICW TO NEW RIVER

From the charming coastal village of Swansboro, located opposite Bogue Inlet, the ICW flows through a series of small sounds and shallow sloughs until reaching the New River. This portion of the Waterway is sometimes used by the Marine Corps for artillery practice. Fortunately, such maneuvers are infrequent and are seldom a major problem.

### Swansboro (Standard Mile 229)

Swansboro is another North Carolina coastal community that has preserved the atmosphere of an earlier time. The town waterfront channel cuts sharply east-northeast from unlighted daybeacon #47. The marina facilities are adequate, and the colorful downtown business district is peppered with interesting gift and antique shops and more than a few memorable restaurants.

Hurricane Fran was not a welcome visitor to this quaint town. Damage along the town waterfront was severe. Casper's Marine Service lost all its docks, and the city pier—formerly useful for dinghy dockage—was still in a state of disrepair in January 1997. Fortunately, a new pier has just been constructed as this account was being penned.

Fran destroyed or heavily damaged a number of other buildings along the waterfront. I was shocked to see that there was nothing left of the building which once housed the old Snap Dragon

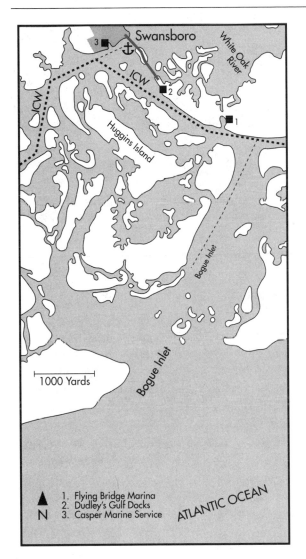

1. Flying Bridge Marina
2. Dudley's Gulf Docks
3. Casper Marine Service

Flying Bridge Marina, the northernmost of Swansboro's facilities, is tucked in its own dredged basin along the Waterway's northern shore east of flashing daybeacon #46. This marina is now composed mostly of "boataminiums," but a few transients are sometimes accepted for overnight dockage at the fixed wooden piers. Entrance and dockside depths run around 5 feet. All berths offer water and 30- and 50-amp power connections. There are some low-key shoreside showers. Gasoline and diesel fuel can be purchased.

Flying Bridge features three on-site restaurants: a deli/pizzeria (which is excellent for galley stocking), a seafood restaurant, and a raw bar with a large-screen television.

**Flying Bridge Marina
(919) 393-6677**

Approach depth: 5 feet
Dockside depth: 5 feet
Accepts transients: limited
Fixed wooden piers: yes
Dockside power connections: 30 & 50 amps
Dockside water connections: yes
Showers: yes
Gasoline: yes
Diesel fuel: yes
Restaurant: three on-site

Dudley's Gulf Docks lies northeast of the ICW near unlighted daybeacon #46A. This facility suffered fairly severe dock damage at the hands of Hurricane Fran, but virtually all had been repaired as this account went to press. Visiting cruisers can again coil their lines here with confidence.

Dudley's offers a large ship's and variety store, as well as expanded haul-out services. There is even a large, metal dry-stack storage building next

Restaurant. The Crabhouse Restaurant, located a bit farther northeast, was also heavily damaged, but repairs were in progress.

Three marinas, two of which cater to transient boaters, serve Swansboro mariners. These fine facilities make a visit practical as well as pleasant.

to the piers. Transient dockage is available at fixed wooden piers with all power and water connections. Typical dockside soundings at the outer piers range from 6 to 8 feet, while the innermost docks have a few 4½- to 5-foot depths at low water. Showers are available to wash away the day's salty accumulations. Gasoline, diesel fuel, and full mechanical repair services are offered. Haul-outs are accomplished by a marine railway. Dudley's even provides a courtesy car for those who want to tour downtown Swansboro or visit one of the local supermarkets without having to walk across the bridges. Transportation can also be arranged to many of downtown Swansboro's restaurants. All in all, Dudley's can lay claim to some of Swansboro's best services for transients and boaters in need of repairs.

**Dudley's Gulf Docks**
**(919) 393-2204**

Approach depth: 8–12 feet
Dockside depth: 6–8 feet at the outer slips,
   4½–5 feet at the innermost docks
Accepts transients: yes
Fixed wooden piers: yes
Dockside power connections: 30 & 50 amps
Dockside water connections: yes
Showers: yes
Gasoline: yes
Diesel fuel: yes
Mechanical repairs: extensive
Below-waterline repairs: yes
Ship's & variety store: yes
Restaurants: several nearby

Casper's Marine Service guards the southwestern foot of the Swansboro channel northeast of flashing daybeacon #46C. This facility lost all its docks as a result of Hurricane Fran. Nothing was left of these structures but pilings during my last visit to Swansboro. Fortunately, owners W. T. and Susan Casper had plans for rebuilding their fixed wooden piers. When finished in late 1997, these structures will be exclusively reserved for transients. Call ahead of time to be sure slip space is available.

The new docks will offer full power and water connections. Gasoline and diesel fuel are already in the offing, as are a portable waste pump-out system and new showers. Casper's also offers a large, state-of-the-art dry-stack storage building which can service power craft as large as 30 feet.

Be on guard against the incredibly strong tidal currents that sweep out of the White Oak River to the east-northeast as they approach Casper's docks. I suggest you employ your largest fenders.

Limited mechanical repairs are available for gasoline engines. The marina has a 20-ton travel-lift; according to the owners, however, haul-outs are becoming a less and less important part of their business.

Casper's Marine Service is in the heart of Swansboro's historic district. All the town's restaurants and antique shops are within a quick

*Swansboro waterfront*

step of the docks. A 1-mile walk through town to N.C. 24 will bring you to the nearest supermarket. Ask the marina staff for directions.

---

**Casper's Marine Service
(910) 326-4462**

Approach depth: 10–12 feet
Dockside depth: 8+ feet
Accepts transients: planned
Fixed wooden piers: planned
Dockside power connections: planned
Dockside water connections: planned
Showers: yes
Waste pump-out: yes
Gasoline: yes
Diesel fuel: yes
Mechanical repairs: limited
Below-waterline repairs: limited
Restaurants: several nearby

---

Many boaters, particularly those with sailcraft, choose to anchor in the Swansboro channel rather than berth at the marinas. Depths run 8 feet or better, and there is good cover from northern and southern winds. Strong blows from the east or west are another matter. Very strong tidal currents in and out of the White Oak River run through this anchorage. Be *sure* your anchor is holding before you head below for a well-earned toddy.

The small Swansboro city pier overlooks the village waterfront northwest of unlighted daybeacon #4. Now that repairs are complete (see above), it can once again serve as a ready dinghy stop. Cruisers anchored in the Swansboro channel now have easy access to the downtown business district.

The broad, beautiful waters of the White Oak River border Swansboro to the east and northeast. This stream was once deep and much-used

but is today shallow and quickly filling with silt. Some blame the construction of the causeway joining Cedar Point and Swansboro. Whatever the reason, the river is almost never entered today except by fishermen in small craft.

## Downtown Swansboro

Swansboro's main street, Front Street, runs through the enchanting historic district; it is lined with shops, some housed in historic buildings which speak of a simpler era. Take time to stroll the town's quiet lanes and sample the offerings of the various stores. Some deal strictly in antiques, while others have modern gifts, a wine selection, and fresh flowers.

Swansboro is blessed with a surprising collection of excellent restaurants. One, Captain Charlie's Seafood Paradise (106 Front Street, 910-326-4303), is my choice as the finest fried-seafood eatery in North Carolina and possibly the world. Open for the evening meal only, Charlie's begins serving at 5 P.M. every day of the week from Memorial Day through Labor Day. The restaurant is generally closed the entire month of January and remains closed on Mondays from February through Memorial Day. Charlie's serves a bowl of its down-east chowder with every meal. The restaurant also features clam fritters and deviled crab. Charlie's fried seafood is its greatest attraction. Prepared in some secret way, it has a rich taste that is unique.

If you happen to visit Swansboro during the breakfast or luncheon hour, consider the 1950s-style Yana's Ye Olde Drug Store (119 Front Street, 919-326-5501). The breakfast menu here features a full range of omelets and some gut-busting pancakes. The midday fare consists of excellent sandwiches and cold drinks, including a great milk shake. Boaters who have been lucky enough to grow up in a small Southern town will be reminded of the drugstore lunch counters which once graced almost every village south of the Mason-Dixon line.

If you seek the best cappuccino, espresso, or ice cream in town, find your way to the Church Street Coffee Company (105 Church Street, 910-326-6771). This quaint firm, housed in the 1888 James Moore House, is simply filled with Americana. During fair weather, patrons can sip their brew in an outside seating area with a good view of the waterfront and the ICW. Whole-bean coffee, coffee flavorings, and fine chocolates can also be purchased here. Don't miss this one!

Among a host of their compatriots, two downtown Swansboro gift shops are worth every visitor's attention.

Russell's Old Tyme Shoppe (116 Front Street, 910-326-3790) is a mammoth gift and home-furnishings store. The owner is an artist herself, and more than a few of her wares are on display. Russell's is housed in three renovated buildings which have been joined together. This shop has recently outgrown its already prodigious floor space and expanded into several satellite locations. Ask the staff of the Front Street shop for directions.

And be sure to visit the gift shop called Through the Looking Glass (101 Church Street, 910-326-3128), which offers eclectic gifts and a good selection of wines.

## Swansboro History

The Swansboro region has long been inhabited. Archaeological evidence indicates that Algonquin Indians occupied the surrounding countryside from about 500 A.D. to colonial times. Settlement of the surrounding lands by English colonists began around 1730, when Jonathan Green built a house at the mouth of the White Oak River. Green soon died, and his widow married Theophilus Weeks, who is credited with being the founder of Swansboro. Weeks was appointed inspector of Bogue Inlet and later operated a boardinghouse in the area. About 1770, he began to sell portions of his large property holdings, at which time the town's development began.

Swansboro was incorporated in 1783 and named in honor of Samuel Swann, former Speaker of the North Carolina legislature. Thanks to its proximity to Bogue Inlet and the White Oak River, which were quite navigable in those days, the town soon became an important port. During the Revolutionary War, a number of patriot privateers operated from the harbor, and several saltworks were built nearby. By 1786, Swansboro had assumed such importance that it was declared a separate customs district.

Captain Otway Burns, naval hero of the War of 1812, was born and grew up in Swansboro. In 1818, Burns brought national attention to the port town by constructing the first steamship to float in North Carolina waters. Today, a small park overlooking the water just northeast of Captain Charlie's commemorates this historical figure. The park's star attraction is a bronze statue of Burns.

Swansboro continued to prosper until the Civil War. Shipbuilding and the export of naval stores were the mainstays of the local economy. The Civil War brought an end to the port's boom days. Swansboro was twice occupied by Union forces, in 1862 and 1864. After the war, the naval-stores trade fell off. Eventually, the town's sole industry was commercial fishing.

## ICW to New River

The 17-statute-mile run from Swansboro to the New River is one of the loneliest sections of the North Carolina ICW. Facilities are nonexistent, and the available anchorages run from doubtful to borderline dangerous. Tidal currents continue to make their presence felt. When maneuvering, be aware of potentially rapid water movement.

## Hammocks Beach State Park (Standard Mile 231.5)

Southwest of unlighted daybeacon #51, a marked channel leads southeast to Hammocks Beach State Park, one of the few wilderness parks in North Carolina. The uncrowded beaches and surrounding dunes are spectacular, but the same claim cannot be made for the approach cut. Low-tide depths of 3½ feet grace portions of the park channel. Some years ago, I spent the better part of an afternoon reflecting on the channel's problems while aground on a sand shoal. The situation has not improved.

As matters now stand, Hammocks Beach State Park must be left to shallow, outboard-powered craft and the state-operated pontoon ferry leaving from Swansboro. Others enter at their own peril.

## Chris Craft Creek (Standard Mile 233.5)

Northeast of flashing daybeacon #55, a small creek striking northwest was once the home of a Chris Craft yacht-manufacturing facility. This plant is now closed, but the creek can serve as an anchorage for boats drawing less than 4 feet. Low-water depths at the creek's entrance run 4½ feet. The waters deepen to 5 and 6 feet on the stream's interior reaches.

The best spot to anchor is on the broad northwesterly section of the stream. Try pitching the hook abeam of the old brick office building along the northeasterly shore. There is enough swinging room for craft up to 36 feet. Low-tide depths in the anchorage run 5 to 6 feet. This spot offers excellent sanctuary from all but exceptionally strong southeasterly winds blowing straight up the creek. The surrounding shores contain a private home or two. The old yacht plant is visible in the distance; its abandoned docks are prominent on the rear shores of the creek.

## Warning!

Southwest of flashing daybeacon #59, the ICW runs through a portion of the huge Camp Lejeune Marine Corps Base. The marines sometimes use the Waterway's eastern shore for a target range. There is a sign warning of intermittent shelling near #59. These artillery maneuvers do not often present a problem, as they are infrequent and generally last only a few hours. When practice is under way, the Marine Corps posts warning boats at either end of the shelling area. Occasionally, more extensive maneuvers close the ICW for several days. Notices of such activity are always displayed at marinas above and below the affected portion of the Waterway.

## Banks Channel (Standard Mile 237.5)

Different portions of the loop-shaped creek known as Banks Channel intersect the ICW northeast and southwest of flashing daybeacon #61 (incorrectly charted as flashing daybeacon #64 on the May 11, 1996, edition of chart 11541). This current-plagued stream is a fair overnight stop *in good weather only* for skippers who can keep their anchor from dragging. Trust me, you'll have to see the tidal current to believe it.

Minimum depths of 6 to 7 feet hold on Banks Channel's northeasterly entrance from the ICW to within 100 yards of the creek's charted southwesterly turn. Thereafter, low-water soundings rise to 4½ feet in places. Northwest of these shallows, there is enough swinging room for vessels as large as 36 feet. The surrounding shores are undeveloped marsh and do not afford the best protection in foul weather.

Banks Channel's southwesterly intersection with the ICW lies just northeast of unlighted daybeacon #63. Minimum 8-foot depths hold for 100 yards southeast of the stream's junction with the Waterway. Again, the tidal currents are fierce, but there is enough room for a 36-footer. The shoreline is similar to that along the stream's northeasterly entrance.

## Mile Hammock Bay (Standard Mile 244.5)

At flashing daybeacon #65A, the ICW turns sharply west and begins its approach to the New River and New River Inlet. Short of this confusing intersection, passing cruisers who pilot craft drawing less than 4 feet can anchor on charted Mile Hammock Bay.

Unfortunately, the marked entrance, which cuts northeast between flashing daybeacons #66 and #68, has shoaled to low-water soundings of only 4 to 4½ feet. Depths on the marked interior waters run between 5½ and 8 feet as long as you

stay between the markers. First-timers should be *sure* to read the navigational information on Mile Hammock Bay before attempting entry.

Mile Hammock Bay is part of Camp Lejeune. Fortunately, the marines do not object to pleasure craft anchoring in these waters. You should not attempt to dinghy ashore under any circumstances!

If a Marine Corps artillery practice is in the offing, you will be wise to continue south to the marina facilities at Swan Point. Cruisers who believe they can sleep under these circumstances should think again.

Mile Hammock Bay offers fair to good protection from all winds. This is not the place to ride out a full gale, but otherwise, you should be comfortable during the night.

## New River Inlet (Standard Mile 246)

Unlighted nun buoy #72A marks a strategic intersection. New River Inlet flows south-southeast, while the main body of the New River lies to the northwest. The ICW continues south and southwest and soon approaches the facilities at Swan Point.

New River Inlet is used by local boaters on a regular basis without mishap. Though it is more reliable than any other inlet between Beaufort and Wrightsville Beach, the channel can still be treacherous. The cut is fairly well marked, but local knowledge is certainly desirable. Buoys are not charted, since they are frequently shifted to follow the ever-changing sands.

Before attempting to run New River Inlet, consider a stop at Swan Point Marina to check on current conditions. You might also watch for a local craft and follow it out to sea.

# ICW TO NEW RIVER NAVIGATION

While not as open as the state's northerly waters, this section of the North Carolina coastline still provides enjoyable cruising and a reliable channel. Tidal currents do pick up, however, so be on guard against lateral leeway.

**Swansboro**   Soon after you pass Bogue Inlet south of the Waterway, the entrance to Flying Bridge Marina will come abeam to the north just east of flashing daybeacon #46. Dudley's Gulf Docks lies northeast of unlighted daybeacon #46A.

As you approach unlighted daybeacon #47, the Swansboro waterfront channel will be sighted in the distance. Don't enter the cut until you are well northwest of #47. Cruisers bound for the Swansboro waterfront channel can cut sharply east-northeast and cruise into the cut 100 yards northwest of #47.

While cruising on the Swansboro channel, stay north and northwest of unlighted nun buoy #2 and unlighted daybeacon #4. Very shallow water flanks the passage south and southeast of these markers.

Casper's Marine Service, the third and final Swansboro marina, will come abeam to the north just as you turn into the waterfront passage.

Many boats, particularly sailcraft, choose to anchor in the Swansboro channel rather than berth at the marina facilities. By staying north of #2 and #4, you can cruise all the way to White Oak Bridge in 8 to 13 feet of water. Practice good anchoring techniques when dropping the hook, as the tidal currents draining from the White Oak River are absolutely fierce.

**South on the ICW**   South of Swansboro, the ICW continues through shallow sounds and sloughs to the New River Inlet intersection. This stretch of the Waterway is sheltered, and chop is almost never a problem.

After passing unlighted daybeacon #47, point to come abeam of flashing daybeacon #46C to its south-southeasterly side. Past #46C, the Waterway turns sharply west-southwest. Two small, unlighted floating buoys, #47A and #47B, outline the southerly side of the ICW channel. Floating markers are rather unusual along the North Carolina segment of the ICW, so their presence here leads me to conclude that this section is subject to change. Be sure to identify all markers correctly before continuing on your way.

After passing between flashing daybeacon #49 and unlighted nun buoy #50, the ICW swings back to the southwest. The Waterway holds this general direction until the approach to New River Inlet.

Southwest of unlighted daybeacon #51, you will observe the Hammocks Beach State Park channel making off to the south-southeast. Don't attempt to enter unless your boat draws less than 3 feet.

**Chris Craft Creek**   Southwest of the state-park channel, just northeast of flashing daybeacon #55, the creek that once played host to a Chris Craft manufacturing facility opens out northwest of the ICW.

Skippers piloting craft that can stand a few 4½-foot low-tide soundings can enter this stream by slightly favoring the northeastern (starboard-side) banks. Continue upstream, favoring this shoreline slightly, until you spot the old red-brick Chris Craft office building peeping out over the northeastern shore. Drop anchor as this structure comes abeam.

The old yacht plant's docks will be visible to the north.

**On the ICW**    Immediately opposite the entrance to Chris Craft Creek, Sanders Creek strikes off to the south. Chart 11541 correctly notes 4-foot depths in this stream. Large cruising vessels should bypass Sanders Creek.

**Shacklefoot Channel**    I no longer recommend exploration or anchorage on Shacklefoot Channel, located northeast of flashing daybeacon #59. Depths have now shoaled to 4½ feet or less! The creek is attended by the strong tidal currents so typical of this region. Even small, shallow-draft craft should probably continue past Shacklefoot Channel.

**On the ICW**    Southwest of flashing daybeacon #59, the Waterway flows to flashing daybeacon #61 (incorrectly charted as #64 on the May 11, 1996, edition of chart 11541). Northeast of #61, the wide northeasterly mouth of Banks Channel opens out on the southeasterly shores.

The southwesterly entrance into Banks Channel makes into the Waterway's southeasterly banks immediately northeast of unlighted daybeacon #63, the next aid to navigation on the ICW.

**Banks Channel**    Favor the southwesterly (starboard-side) banks when entering the northeasterly mouth of Banks Channel. After cruising upstream for 75 yards, cut back to the creek's mid-width. Cease your exploration well before reaching the stream's southwesterly turn. Depths decline approaching this bend. Instead, anchor well northwest of the shallows. Be *sure* your anchor is well set and not dragging before you go below!

Successful entry into the southwesterly mouth of Banks Channel also calls for favoring the southwesterly banks. Continue favoring this shoreline until you cruise to within 300 yards of the stream's sharp northeasterly turn. Stop before passing through this bend. Very shallow water lies to the east and northeast.

Consider anchoring 200 yards short of the turn. The same stricture against dragging anchor holds for these waters as well.

**On the ICW**    Southwest of unlighted daybeacon #63, the ICW follows a straight canal-like channel to the Onslow Beach Bridge. This span is subject to mechanical breakdowns. Fortunately, it opens on demand. Its closed vertical clearance is 12 feet.

The ICW takes a turn to the west at flashing daybeacon #65A and begins its approach to a three-way intersection with the New River and New River Inlet. Before reaching this rather confusing juncture, passing cruisers have access to the anchorage on Mile Hammock Bay immediately west of flashing daybeacon #66.

**Mile Hammock Bay**    Remember that low-water entrance depths into Mile Hammock Bay have shoaled to 4 and 4½ feet. To enter, pass between unlighted daybeacons #1 and #2, then between #3 and #4. For best depths, favor the starboard (southeasterly) quarter of the entrance by passing closer to #2 and #4 than to #1 and #3. Once inside the bay's mouth, be sure to stay well west of unlighted daybeacon #6. Shallows lie east and northeast of this aid. There is also a smaller section of shoals southwest of #6. To avoid this hazard, stay at least 250 yards off the bay's southerly shoreline.

**On to New River**    West of Mile Hammock Bay, the ICW soon begins its approach to the New River junction. Don't be in a hurry! Take the time to study chart 11541 carefully and sort out the various markers. Three channels converge at unlighted nun buoy #72A, and the large collection of markers can be monumentally confusing. Be prepared to find different aids to navigation than those shown on chart 11541 or discussed below. These are changeable waters. The Corps of Engineers makes frequent alterations in the scheme of the various buoys and daybeacons.

The ICW, which always looks to me to be the smallest of the three channels, cuts west-southwest from #72A and follows an outlined track to flashing daybeacon #2. Notice that the numbering scheme of the Waterway markers begins anew at this point.

Southeast of #72A, boaters can follow the channel leading to New River Inlet. The initial portion of the passage is deep, but soundings become questionable as you approach the cut's seaward entrance. Markers are not charted, as they are frequently shifted. Seek local knowledge at one of the Swan Point marinas. Or better yet, follow in the wake of a local vessel.

At #2, the Waterway swings almost due south and soon approaches the marina facilities at Swan Point just north of unlighted daybeacon #4.

This discussion now turns to the New River. The account of the ICW and the facilities at Swan Point will resume later in the chapter.

## NEW RIVER

The New River (Standard Mile 246) is a large, generally deep, well-marked body of water. It extends inland for 17 nautical miles from the ICW to Jacksonville. Until recently, pleasure craft have not frequented this formidable stream. Now, thanks to improved marina facilities, there is good reason to change this long-standing practice.

The New River is thoroughly undeveloped. Except for a small area near Pollock's Point Bridge, the entire shoreline is part of the Camp Lejeune Marine Corps Base and is for the most part in its natural state. Don't attempt to land along the river, as the Marine Corps property is restricted. Sheer earthen cliffs line some sections of the banks, giving the stream a wild, primeval look.

You may be struck by the lack of protected anchorage on a body of water this size. To be sure, some bays and creeks are a good spot to drop the hook, but most of the river's waters are so open that you must be careful to anchor where the shore will provide an effective lee from the prevailing wind.

One well-protected marina, friendly to transients, is available to cruising craft on the New River south of Jacksonville. A few federally sponsored marinas catering primarily to military personnel lie along the river's track. Passing cruisers can sometimes purchase gasoline at these havens, but little else is available. Jacksonville boasts two marinas which accept transients and a restaurant which provides dockage for its patrons.

Navigation of the New River is relatively simple. You should not have any difficulty in cruising all the way to Jacksonville. Some boaters may enjoy the New River for its wild natural scenery; others may find it boring for its lack of development.

## Sneads Ferry

The fixed, high-rise Pollock's Point Bridge crosses the river about 3 nautical miles from its mouth. This bridge is the modern replacement for a ferry that for many years operated on the lower New River and eventually gave its name to the whole region. According to an article by Dave Owens in *The State* magazine, Edmund Ennett began operating a ferry at a spot known as "Lower Ferry" in 1759. In 1760, Robert Snead opened a tavern on the river's southern shore. He may have piloted the ferry himself for a time. After the Civil War, a former slave, Caroline Pearson, managed the ferry until her death at the age of 110. Pearson was followed by Kitt Brown, a Primitive Baptist preacher, who was in turn succeeded by James Owens, the father of the author of the article.

For many years, the ferry was poled by hand. James Owens improved upon this method by pulling the ferry along a steel cable. When not in use, the cable lay on the river bottom so as not to obstruct traffic. Finally, the old ferry was replaced by a wooden bridge in 1938.

Today, the entire southern shore of the lower New River is known as Sneads Ferry. As Owens put it, "Although the ferry is gone . . . it lives on in the name of our community as well as in fond memories of older residents."

## Old Ferry Marina

Skippers who have cruised the New River in the past and been shackled by the absence of pleasure-craft facilities on the stream's lower reaches will be glad to learn that a new facility, Old Ferry Marina, has solved this problem. Old Ferry flanks the river's southwesterly banks southwest of flashing daybeacon #23 (just downstream, or southeast of, the Sneads Ferry high-rise bridge).

Actually, Old Ferry Marina is a modern incarnation of a forgettable, poorly maintained facility that occupied this location many years ago. The current version is, thankfully, nothing like its predecessor.

Old Ferry Marina's scantily marked, PVC-pipe-lined entrance channel carries 5 feet of water at low tide. Captains piloting craft that draw 4 feet or better should probably call the dockmaster ahead of time to get the latest entry-cut instructions. Depths in the marina's protected dockage basin run 5 to 6 feet at mean low water. Berths are provided at modern, fixed wooden piers with full power and water connections. Waste pump-out service is available, as are shoreside showers, but no fuel or laundromat facilities are offered. Minimal repair services are in the offing. For heavier work, the dockmaster will be glad to call in local independent mechanics. A large dry-stack storage building for small power craft is also located on the marina grounds. The dockmaster's office doubles as a boaters' lounge.

Skippers in search of provisions will discover a convenience store 1.5 miles down the road. The marina staff can usually be relied upon for a complimentary ride. Closer by, visitors will find the Saratoga Restaurant. This low-key dining spot is open evenings every day except Sunday during the spring, summer, and fall. In winter, the restaurant is open Thursday through Saturday evenings. Cruisers who have access to automobile transportation can visit the excellent Riverview Restaurant, located nearby.

All in all, I highly recommend that my fellow cruisers give Old Ferry Marina their most serious consideration, particularly if bad weather is in the offing. Just watch out for that entrance cut.

## Old Ferry Marina
## (910) 327-2258

Approach depth: 5 feet (minimum at
low water)
Dockside depth: 5-6 feet (minimum at
low water)
Accepts transients: yes
Fixed wooden piers: yes
Dockside power connections: 30 & 50 amps
Dockside water connections: yes
Showers: yes
Waste pump-out: yes
Mechanical repairs: limited, also available
through independent technicians
Restaurants: nearby

## Other Anchorages and Facilities

Most anchorages on the New River offer only partial protection. Two unnamed coves of Morgan Bay on the river's western shore west of flashing daybeacon #46 and unlighted daybeacon #47, respectively, offer 6-foot depths and shelter from western and southwestern winds. The shoreline of both anchorages is in its natural state.

Wallace Creek, one of the best anchorages on the New River, cuts into the southeastern corner of Morgan Bay. The stream's entrance is marked by flashing daybeacon #2. Stiff western breezes can create an unwelcome chop, but there is adequate sanctuary from other airs. Minimum depths are 6 feet. The stream's shore has some residential development. Gasoline is available from a military marina on the southern shore, but no dockage or diesel fuel is offered.

Southwest Creek, located on the river's southwestern shore between flashing daybeacons #50 and #52, is a possible anchorage for most any craft in light to moderate winds, particularly from the southwest. Due to its large size, however, the

creek does not render adequate protection in heavy weather. Entrance depths are 7 feet, but soundings soon deteriorate to 4 or 5 feet on the creek's upper reaches. Most of the shoreline is untouched, though a small portion has been developed as a recreation park for Marine Corps personnel. Gasoline is available at a military marina on the northern shore, but no diesel fuel or overnight berths are offered.

Northeast Creek cuts into the New River's northeastern banks near flashing daybeacon #50. Again, because of its large size, the creek does not provide good protection. Southwestern winds can blow up the entire length of Southwest Creek, located across the river, and stir up a nasty chop in Northeast Creek. Most of the shoreline is in its natural state, though there is a house here and there. Part of the southeastern banks borders a Marine Corps golf course.

In spite of soundings shown on chart 11542, you will encounter 4- and 5-foot depths as Northeast Creek swings to the east. Entrance depths are 7 or 8 feet.

## Jacksonville

The thriving city of Jacksonville is just the sort of community you might expect to find near a large Marine Corps base. The main highway is dotted with fast-food restaurants, used-car lots, and shops of every description. While Jacksonville is not always pleasing to the eye, there is no denying that a great variety of goods and services is available within a short walk of the waterfront.

The marina scene in Jacksonville has undergone a welcome change for the better during the past several years. First up is Kerr Street Marina.

This facility flanks the river's easterly shore north of flashing daybeacon #61, on the old site of Tideline Marine (see below). Most of Kerr Street's slips are covered, but a few are open and are appropriate for use by sailcraft. Most of the available dockage is taken up by month-to-month renters, but the marina owner informed me that transients are gladly accepted if they make it this far upriver. Depths alongside range from an impressive 10-plus feet in the outer slips to as little as 4 feet for berths closest to shore. Power connections in the 15- to 30-amp range are offered, as are water connections. A small ship's store is located on the premises. Several restaurants and convenience stores along U.S. 17 can be accessed via a 4- to 5-block walk.

As of this writing, Kerr Street Marina was in the process of repairing the roofs of its covered slips, which were heavily damaged during Hurricane Fran. This work should be completed by the summer of 1997. The owners hope to add gasoline sales by that time as well.

### Kerr Street Marina
### (910) 455-8995

Approach depth: 8+ feet
Dockside depth: 4-12+ feet
Accepts transients: yes
Fixed wooden piers: yes
Dockside power connections: 15 & 30 amps
Dockside water connections: yes
Ship's store: yes
Restaurants: several nearby

Jacksonville's latest facility is the new incarnation of Tideline Marine, co-owned by an old friend and classmate of this writer's. In 1994, Tideline moved to a new location flanking the river's westerly shoreline a short hop upstream from Kerr Street Marina. The energetic husband-wife owner team undertook the renovation of an old icehouse and have received a local award for their restoration efforts.

Visiting cruisers with shallow-draft vessels are welcomed to a well-protected harbor with new, fixed wooden slips and full power and water connections. The entrance channel's depth of 3 to 3½ feet will be the limiting factor for many large cruising vessels. Depths in the harbor range from 6 to as little as 3 feet. There are a limited number of slips available for visitors. To be on the safe side, call ahead of time to check on berth availability.

Shoreside, you will discover an ultranice ship's store offering charts, marine publications, clothing, and a full line of marine hardware. Gasoline can be purchased dockside. Sales of small powerboats are in the offing, as are repairs for outboards, I/O's, and some gasoline inboards. Several restaurants and a convenience store are within easy walking distance.

If your craft can stand the skinny depths, I highly recommend a visit to Tideline's new location. You won't find a warmer welcome anywhere.

### Tideline Marine
### (910) 455-2979

Approach depth: 3-3½ feet
Dockside depth: 3-6 feet
Accepts transients: yes (call ahead)
Fixed wooden slips: yes
Dockside power connections: 20 & 30 amps
Dockside water connections: yes
Gasoline: yes
Ship's store: yes
Mechanical repairs: outboards, I/O's, and some light inboard gas-engine work
Restaurant: nearby

Boats that can clear a 13-foot fixed bridge can cruise north and northeast of Tideline and take advantage of the fixed wooden pier adjacent to Fisherman's Wharf Restaurant. Dockage is provided for restaurant patrons only. Depths alongside run 3 to 4 feet.

# NEW RIVER NAVIGATION

To enter the New River, cruising boaters must follow an improved, well-marked channel upriver to Pollock's Point Bridge. Depths in the cut run 7 to 10 feet. Observe all markers carefully and watch for leeway, as depths quickly decline outside the dredged area.

*Old Ferry Marina*  Between unlighted daybeacon #21 and flashing daybeacon #23, watch to the southwest for a few white PVC pipes outlining the channel to Old Ferry Marina. Once abeam of this cut, turn sharply to port and point to pass all the pipes to your starboard side. Eventually, the marked passage leads to a protected dockage basin. You will spy most of the marina's docks and the dockmaster's office to starboard.

*On New River*  From flashing daybeacon #23, the channel cuts west and soon flows under Pollock's Point Bridge, a fixed high-rise span with a vertical clearance of 65 feet.

Once past the bridge, set a new course to come abeam of flashing daybeacons #25 and #27 to their fairly immediate northern sides. At #27, the channel swings sharply northwest, then northeast. Pass #28 to its southwestern side and come abeam of #28A to its southwestern quarter. Once abeam of #28A, swing northeast and point to pass #29 to its fairly immediate eastern side. Past #29, the river becomes deeper and is easily navigated to Jacksonville.

*Stones Bay*  North and northeast of unlighted daybeacon #29, the New River channel flows through the broad waters of Stones Bay. The main body of the bay lies northwest of the marked cut. Though most of the waters are deep, a substantial shelf of shallows extends out from the shoreline. Stones Bay is so large that it affords little protection from any breeze. It is not recommended as an overnight anchorage.

*On the New*  After Stones Bay, no further sidewaters are encountered until flashing daybeacon #46. French Creek makes into the New River's easterly banks well east of unlighted daybeacon #39. Do not attempt to explore this wayward stream. Depths of 2 or 3 feet render it useless to cruising boaters.

*Morgan Bay*  From #46, the two unnamed coves of Morgan Bay are visible on the river's western shore. The first body of water is located between Town and Holmes Points and the second between Holmes and Ragged Points. If you choose to enter, don't be in a hurry. In spite of charted soundings, you will encounter 6-foot depths in the coves. Don't cruise near the shoreline, as depths deteriorate further.

*Wallace Creek*  The marked entry channel into Wallace Creek lies northeast of flashing daybeacon #46 on the southeastern corner of Morgan Bay. Depths shown on chart 11542 are incorrect. When entering, you can expect 7- or 8-foot soundings between #46 and flashing daybeacon #2. Past #2, you will encounter 6-foot depths in the creek's channel.

To enter, set course from #46 to come abeam of flashing daybeacon #2 by 25 to 30 yards to its northern side. Once abeam of #2, set a new course to come abeam of unlighted daybeacon #4 to its immediate northern side. Don't hurry, watch your depth sounder, and don't let leeway ease you to starboard onto the shallows extending out from the creek's southern shore.

A Marine Corps pleasure-craft facility flanks the southern shore just past #4. Depths from #4 to the marina run 5 to 6 feet. Consider anchoring near #4. Farther upstream, soundings of 4 feet wait to bar your path.

**On the New**   From flashing daybeacon #46, it is a straightforward run to flashing daybeacon #50. From #50, visiting cruisers have access to two large sidewaters, both of which are possible anchorages.

**Southwest Creek**   Southwest Creek, located on the river's southwestern shore, has depths of 7 feet at its entrance. Soundings deteriorate to 4 or 5 feet on the creek's upper reaches. If you choose to enter, set course from #50 to come abeam of unlighted daybeacon #1 by 200 yards to its northern side. Don't approach Ragged Point, located south of your course, as it is surrounded by shoal water.

Once past #1, turn to the southwest and point to come abeam of unlighted daybeacon #2 by 50 yards to its southeasterly side. You should hold 7-foot depths before passing #2. The Marine Corps marina lies northwest of #2. Gasoline is available here, but be warned that approach depths fall off to 4 feet.

*Tideland Marina–New River*

If your craft draws more than 3½ feet, you should probably not cruise upstream from #2. Depths decline to 4 or 5 feet in spite of soundings noted on chart 11542. For craft that draw 3 to 3½ feet, the best bet for anchorage is south of #2. Don't attempt to venture where the creek narrows to a small stream. Depths fall off to 4 feet or less.

**Northeast Creek**   Northeast Creek strikes into the river's banks northeast of flashing daybeacon #50. Minimum 6-foot depths can be held to within 100 yards of the charted sharp point of land on the creek's northern shore southwest of the "Tank" designation. To enter, strike a course from flashing daybeacon #50 for the entrance's mid-width. Continue following the centerline through the creek's first turn to the east. The most protected anchorage is 200 yards short of the sharp point of land described above. You should be safe and secure in this haven unless winds exceed 15 knots.

**On the New**   From flashing daybeacon #50, cruisers can follow a well-marked, improved channel that holds 8-foot minimum depths to Jacksonville. Observe all markers carefully; the bottom quickly rises outside the dredged channel. The river begins to narrow past unlighted daybeacon #53. Rough water should not be any problem in this section.

*Jacksonville* North of flashing daybeacon #61, Kerr Street Marina abuts the river's eastern shore.

The new headquarters of Tideline Marine will come abeam to the west after another 300 yards.

Not far upriver, two fixed bridges, the first with 13 feet and the second with 15 feet of vertical clearance, cross the river. If you can clear these, you will see Fisherman's Wharf Restaurant to port.

## ICW TO WRIGHTSVILLE BEACH

Below the New River, the ICW follows a narrow, canal-like passage until it flows to Wrightsville Beach. South of Swan Point, the Waterway's shoreline begins to rise from the level of the saltwater marshes to the north. Trees become more numerous along the mainland banks, and the cut is often lined with fine homes, some with private docks.

One of this region's most striking characteristics is its tidal nature. Swift currents flow into and out of the many shallow seaward cuts along the eastern shore. Anchorages are unreliable, since bottom configurations can change quickly in the rapidly flowing water. The creek that provided a safe harbor just a few months ago may now have shoaled to grounding depths.

For these reasons, only a few isolated waters are recommended for anchorage between Swan Point and Wrightsville Beach. If you choose to enter any sidewaters, sound your way in carefully. Watch your depth sounder at all times to catch any recent depth changes before they catch you. Also, watch for leeway slippage caused by the

swift currents. This is not a stretch of the ICW to be casually traversed.

Marina facilities are sparse along this stretch. Swan Point is home to a popular and well-respected marina recommended by this writer. In the aftermath of Hurricane Fran, the ICW passage south of Swan Point to Wrightsville Beach can now claim only a single facility that caters to cruising craft. The old Topsail Beach Marina was all but destroyed by Fran and will apparently not be rebuilt.

Alert navigators can enjoy this section of the ICW, but unwary skippers may find themselves contemplating the value of good coastal navigation from a sandbar.

### Swan Point (Standard Mile 247)

South of the ICW–New River intersection, charted Swan Point offers a good marina and a fine restaurant. Swan Point Marina overlooks the Waterway's western banks near unlighted daybeacon #4. This is a superior marina with full-service repairs and a genuine "can-do" attitude.

On more than one occasion, the people at Swan Point have helped me and my assistants extricate ourselves from jams brought on by faulty marine hardware. No one will ever complain about the service they receive at Swan Point Marina.

Hurricane Fran wreaked havoc on Swan Point Marina's outer dock. That structure is now undergoing repair and should be finished by late 1997. In the meantime, virtually any visiting craft can be accommodated on the inner harbor slips.

Swan Point Marina welcomes transient boaters at overnight berths. Its fixed wooden-decked piers feature full power and water connections. Approach depths run 8 feet and soundings alongside in the protected dockage basin are 5 to 6 feet. Gasoline, diesel fuel, extensive mechanical repairs, and haul-out service via a 40-ton travel-lift are available. A large, well-stocked parts, ship's, and variety store overlooks the harbor. Showers and a laundromat are located just behind the retail store. A courtesy car is available for a run to the grocery store located several miles up the road. Swan Point Marina is the only sure refuge directly on the ICW between Swansboro and Harbour Village Marina, so don't pass its location lightly!

Located a short distance from Swan Point Marina, Bayview Restaurant (910-327-3311) offers a delectable sampling of beef and seafood dishes. The restaurant provides courtesy transportation to and from Swan Point.

A second facility, New River Marina (910-327-9691), is located just south of Swan Point Marina. New River Marina is primarily a small-craft facility. Visiting cruisers can purchase gasoline and diesel fuel. Depths alongside run around 6 feet. A medium-size ship's and variety store is adjacent to the docks.

### Surf City (Standard Mile 260.5)

Southwest of unlighted daybeacon #69, a small canal cuts to the southeast just northeast of the Surf City swing bridge. The channel used to serve Surf City Marina, but that facility was laid low by Hurricane Fran, and its future (if any) is far from certain. The entrance cut's low-water depths of 3 feet severely limited access to this facility even before the storm.

### Topsail Beach (Standard Mile 264)

You'd have to see it to believe it. Take my word for it, that describes the destruction on Topsail in the wake of Hurricane Fran. This writer and his first mate had the rare opportunity to photograph some of the devastation a few days after the great storm's passage. If an entire squadron of B-52 bombers had overflown Topsail and unloaded full payloads onto this fragile strand of sand and

**Swan Point Marina**
**(910) 327-1081**

Approach depth: 8 feet
Dockside depth: 5–6 feet
Accepts transients: yes
Fixed wooden piers: yes
Dockside power connections: 30 & 50
    amps
Dockside water connections: yes
Showers: yes
Laundromat: yes
Gasoline: yes
Diesel fuel: yes
Mechanical repairs: extensive
Below-waterline repairs: yes
Ship's & variety store: yes
Restaurant: nearby

sea grass, they could scarcely have caused greater damage.

Topsail Beach Marina was all but destroyed and, according to the best available information, will probably not be rebuilt. A new, small inlet was opened across the banks. Just what effect this petite seaward cut will have on the Topsail channel and its associated tides remains to be seen.

For at least a year or two following the great storm, until the channel is firmly reestablished (or not), visiting cruisers would be wise to avoid this side trip and the anchorage I used to recommend on these waters. Matters are just too uncertain at this time. I will keep a check on this situation and provide an update in the next edition of this guide.

## Harbour Village Marina (Standard Mile 266)

A modern pleasure-craft facility graces the Waterway's northwestern shore about halfway between flashing daybeacons #93 and #96. Harbour Village Marina is located adjacent to a huge country-club, golf, tennis, and housing project but is a separate entity.

Harbour Village's well-protected harbor basin, cut out of the mainland, features interior depths of 6 to 8 feet. With periodic dredging, the entrance channel now has low-water soundings of 6 feet. Cruising boaters should feel fortunate indeed that Harbour Village accepts transients. Overnight berths are provided at concrete-decked floating docks featuring the latest power and water connections. Shoreside, visitors will find first-class showers, a laundromat, a boaters' lounge, and a snack bar. Gasoline, diesel fuel, and free waste pump-out are available. Cruising guests have golf and tennis privileges at the nearby clubhouse. Skippers who enjoy resort-style marinas will want to make every effort to coil their lines at Harbour Village for an extended stay.

**Harbour Village Marina
(910) 270-4017**

Approach depth: 8 feet
Dockside depth: 6–8 feet
Accepts transients: yes
Floating concrete piers: yes
Dockside power connections: 30 & 50 amps
Dockside water connections: yes
Showers: yes
Laundromat: yes
Waste pump-out: yes
Gasoline: yes
Diesel fuel: yes
Mechanical repairs: independent contractors
Variety store: yes

## Pages Creek (Standard Mile 279)

Some 0.7 nautical mile southwest of the Figure Eight Island swing bridge, which is itself southwest of unlighted daybeacon #120, Pages Creek opens out on the Waterway's northwestern banks. Two facilities make their home on this stream. Low-water entrance depths run as little as 4½ feet in the scantily marked channel. If you draw 4 feet or more, it would be best to enter at either high tide or midtide. Be sure to read the navigational information below before attempting your first entry into Pages Creek.

One of Pages Creek's facilities, Waterway Marine Service (910-686-0284), specializes in below-the-waterline haul-out repairs. The yard uses a large crane for hauling purposes. Canadys Marina sells gasoline and maintains a small, quaint ship's and variety store but offers no other services for transients.

*Clamming on Stump Sound*

### T-Shaped Creek (Standard Mile 280)

Study chart 11541 and notice the T-shaped creek making into the northwestern banks northeast of flashing daybeacon #122. Chart 11541 notes a boating-services designation #38 on this stream. Two facilities are located on the creek, but one of them, Oak Winds Marina (910-686-7319), has no facilities for visitors.

Coastal Carolina Yacht Yard (910-686-0004) overlooks the northwesterly tip of the creek. Full mechanical repairs for gas and diesel engines are offered, as are below-the-waterline repairs. Haul-outs are accomplished by a 15-ton travel-lift, a 30-ton crane, and a 100-ton marine railway. Obviously, this yard is *serious* about hauling pleasure craft.

Neither transient dockage nor fuel is available from either of the stream's nautical establishments.

Low-tide entrance depths on the T-shaped creek run in the 4½- to 5-foot range. If your draft exceeds 3½ feet, it might be a good idea to wait for high tide.

## ICW TO WRIGHTSVILLE BEACH NAVIGATION

Back on the ICW at flashing daybeacon #2, where the discussion of the New River area began, the Waterway flows south past the facilities at Swan Point. Be sure to cruise along at idle speed until you are well south of unlighted daybeacon #4.

**Swan Point**   Swan Point Marina lines the western bank immediately north of unlighted daybeacon #4. West of unlighted daybeacon #6, passing cruisers may note a marked channel leading to Bayview Restaurant. Don't try it; depths have shoaled to 3 feet.

**On the ICW**   From unlighted daybeacon #4, the ICW runs generally southwest for 12 nautical miles to the Surf City Bridge. This stretch of the Waterway does not offer any viable sidewater opportunities.

West-southwest of unlighted daybeacon #25, you will pass through a fixed bridge with a vertical clearance of 65 feet.

At flashing daybeacon #27, the ICW begins to knife through the shallow reaches of Stump Sound. Passing boaters may spot oyster fishermen wading in the shallows surrounding the sound. Large power craft will do well to reduce their wake when passing these salty workmen. Don't attempt to explore any section of the sound off the Waterway! Depths quickly decline outside the marked channel.

Soon after passing unlighted daybeacon #69, you will approach the Surf City Bridge.

**Surf City**    Just northeast of the Surf City Bridge, the shallow Surf City channel opens out from the ICW's southeastern shoreline. Considering the cut's lack of depth and the absence of any operational pleasure-craft facilities, wise cruisers will just keep on trucking down the ICW.

**On the ICW**    The Surf City swing bridge has a closed vertical clearance of 12 feet. It opens on the hour from 7 A.M. to 7 P.M. year-round and opens on demand during nighttime and early-morning hours. Plan your itinerary around these restrictive times to avoid long delays.

Southwest of Surf City, the Waterway flows into the shallow waters of Topsail Sound. Again, the bottom rises quickly outside the ICW channel. No accessible sidewaters are to be found until unlighted daybeacon #86.

**Topsail Beach Channel**    As described above, the Topsail Beach channel is a highly speculative proposition in the wake of Hurricane Fran. Couple this navigational difficulty with the lack of any operational pleasure-craft facilities on the Topsail Beach channel and you have good reason to simply wave from the Waterway as you continue south to the marinas at Wrightsville Beach.

**On the ICW**    From unlighted daybeacon #86, the ICW continues to the southwest. Boaters bound for Harbour Village Marina will spy the entrance making into the northwestern banks between flashing daybeacons #93 and #96.

Watch for unusually strong side-setting currents as you pass the errant New Topsail Inlet channel near flashing daybeacon #98. At times, the waters simply boil through this cut. Don't even think about entering this shoal-plagued channel!

Some 0.6 nautical mile southwest of unlighted daybeacon #120, you will pass through the Figure Eight Island swing bridge. This span has a closed vertical clearance of 20 feet but opens on demand. Take care to leave plenty of maneuvering room between yourself, the bridge, and any other waiting vessels while the bridge is opening. As usual along this stretch of the ICW, the tidal flow is noteworthy.

Just southwest of the swing bridge, Figure Eight Island Marina guards the southeasterly banks. Do not enter. This facility is ultraprivate.

**Pages Creek**    Some 0.7 nautical mile southwest of the Figure Eight Island swing bridge, a single set of floating markers denotes the northward-running channel into Pages Creek, home of Waterway Marine Service and Canadys Marina. Low-tide depths in this indifferently marked cut run as little as 4½ feet. After leaving the marked entrance behind, favor the western (port-side) banks heavily. Eventually, the docks will come abeam to port.

On the northwestern shore just past the entrance to Pages Creek, a shallow cut leads to Johnson Marine Service. This is a small-craft facility. The entrance holds only 3-foot depths.

**T-Shaped Creek**    A short hop northeast of flashing daybeacon #122, the charted T-shaped creek cuts northwest to Coastal Carolina Yacht Yard and Oak Winds Marina. Enter on the creek's mid-width.

**On the ICW**    Southwest of flashing daybeacon #122, the Waterway continues down a canal-like passage to Wrightsville Beach. Just northeast of flashing daybeacon #125, a creek with a marked entrance channel intersects the ICW along the southeastern shore. This stream is too narrow for anchorage and leads to a series of private docks. There is little to interest visitors.

The Wrightsville Beach bascule bridge crosses the ICW 1.0 nautical mile southwest of flashing daybeacon #125. This infamous span has a very restrictive opening schedule. And just to make matters more interesting, the tidal currents flowing under the bridge have to be seen to be believed. I have piloted a 35-foot sailcraft with the diesel aux-iliary at its maximum safe setting and barely been able to make headway against the current. Approach this bridge with extreme caution and leave yourself plenty of maneuvering room.

The Wrightsville Beach bascule bridge has a closed vertical clearance of 20 feet. It opens on the hour only from 7 A.M. to 7 P.M. Southwest of the bridge, cruising boaters have access to the many facilities lying about Wrightsville Beach.

# WRIGHTSVILLE BEACH

Wrightsville Beach (Standard Mile 280) is one of North Carolina's major pleasure-boating centers. There are many marinas in the immediate vicinity that offer not only overnight berths but just about any service a cruising boater might ever require. Wrightsville Beach also boasts several excellent restaurants within walking distance of the waterfront. Cuisine ranging from fried seafood to continental fare is readily available for famished cruisers.

Wrightsville Beach suffered through Hurricanes Bertha and Fran, the latter storm causing much more damage. Dockside Marina and Restaurant lost all its docks, and Seapath Yacht Club's outer pier was savaged.

I'm happy to report that all this devastation had virtually disappeared by the time of my last visit, during February 1997. Seapath was in the process of replacing its outer docks, now complete. Otherwise, almost everyone was back in full operation. This quick action is a testament to the resiliency of the North Carolina marine community.

Motts Channel (see below), a victim of shoaling even prior to the storms, was adversely affected by the two hurricanes. However, visiting mariners will be pleased to know the channel has just been dredged to a depth of 8 to 12 feet and they can cruise this useful link with confidence.

The town of Wrightsville Beach, located southeast of the ICW, is a vacation community composed of beach homes, condominiums, restaurants, and motels. Unfortunately, the area has succumbed to extensive commercial development that is not always pleasing to the eye. There is no denying, however, that the beach's popularity is well deserved. With its excellent shoreside accommodations, Wrightsville Beach can justly lay claim to being one of North Carolina's most popular resorts.

Visiting mariners in search of marine supplies, charts, or publications will be glad to learn that the West Marine store (910-256-7878) is within easy walking distance of the waterfront. Ask any of the various marina staff for directions.

Should you want to sharpen your sailing skills, I highly recommend Waterways Sailing School (800-562-7245) in Wrightsville Beach. I do not normally recommend sailing schools, but I feel so strongly about master sailor Jerry Outlaw's quality operation that I simply must mention it.

For taxi service in the Wrightsville Beach–Wilmington region, call Lett's Taxi Service (910-458-3999), Port City Taxi (910-762-1165), or Yellow Cab (910-762-3322). For car rentals, call Thrifty Car Rental (910-343-1411) or Triangle Rental (910-251-9812).

### Wrightsville Beach Marinas

Southwest of the Wrightsville Beach bascule bridge, you will immediately encounter a host of marinas on both sides of the Waterway. One of the region's largest facilities, Wrightsville Marina Yacht Club, is located along the ICW's southeastern shore just past the bridge. This sumptuous facility can justly lay claim to one of the biggest collections of luxury power yachts on the North Carolina coast. Overnight transient berths are available at the facility's ultramodern wooden-decked floating docks. Depths at the outer slips top 12 feet, and you can expect at least 8 feet of water at the inner berths. The piers are equipped with the latest power, water, telephone, and cable-television connections. The adjacent showers and laundromat are climate-controlled and some of the nicest I have ever used. Gasoline, diesel fuel, and mechanical repairs through independent contractors are all available. An adjacent indoor/outdoor swimming pool is open to transient dockers.

Wrightsville Marina Yacht Club has recovered from all its hurricane damage as this account is being tapped out on the keyboard. Even the waste pump-out system is now back in operation.

A Redix store, which carries a *few* basic food items, supplies and clothing, and the Wrightsville Beach post office are only a few paces away. A supermarket is located 0.75 mile from the docks. For those who aren't up to the hike, courtesy transportation can sometimes be arranged through the marina.

The large, on-site restaurant hitherto known as Wally's has been sold to the Pusser's Rum folks and is renamed "Pusser's Landing at Wally's." The new owners have done extensive remodeling and a complete revamping of the menu. If this new dining attraction bears any resemblance to the Pusser's at City Marina in Charleston, South Carolina, passing cruisers are in for a *real* treat!

Come breakfast or lunch, the Causeway Café (910-256-3730), located a quick step to the southeast (toward the beach), is a popular choice. I can tell you from experience that the breakfasts are memorable.

---

**Wrightsville Marina Yacht Club
(910) 256-6666**

Approach depth: 12+ feet
Dockside depth: 8–12+ feet
Accepts transients: yes
Floating wooden piers: yes
Dockside power connections: 30 & 50 amps
Dockside water connections: yes
Showers: yes
Laundromat: yes
Waste pump-out: yes
Gasoline: yes
Diesel fuel: yes
Mechanical repairs: independent contractors
Restaurant: on-site, with several nearby

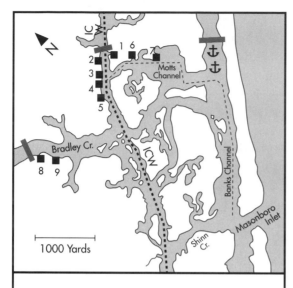

## WRIGHTSVILLE BEACH

1. Wrightsville Marina Yacht Club
2. Bridge Tender Marina
3. Airlie Marina
4. Crocker's Landing
5. Dockside Marina
6. Atlantic Marine
7. Seapath Yacht Club
8. Bradley Creek Marina
9. Boat House Marina

Just across the ICW from Wrightsville Marina Yacht Club, the combination fixed and floating wooden outer docks of Bridge Tender Marina and Restaurant wait to greet passing visitors. This facility is back up and running after its "Fran" damage. Transient dockage is once again available at the outer pier. The inner slips are in good shape as well.

The Bridge Tender is glad to accept transients for overnight or temporary dockage. Depths alongside are 10 feet or better. All berths feature water and 30- and 50-amp power connections. Gasoline and diesel fuel are available at the outer

pier. The dockmaster maintains a nice ship's and variety store overlooking the piers.

The adjacent Bridge Tender Restaurant (910-256-4519) has long been popular with Waterway cruisers. This dining spot, open in the evenings and for Saturday lunch, features a variety of seafood, beef, and chicken entrées.

The nearby Fish House Grille (910-256-3693), a much less fancy eatery, is open for lunch and dinner. Give the fried oyster sandwich a try.

For provisioning, your best bet is to take a taxi to the supermarket at Wrightsville Beach.

### Bridge Tender Marina
### (910) 256-6550

Approach depth: 12+ feet
Dockside depth: 10+ feet at the outer pier,
   6–7½ feet at the inner pier
Accepts transients: yes
Fixed & floating wooden piers: yes
Dockside power connections: 30 & 50 amps
Dockside water connections: yes
Gasoline: yes
Diesel fuel: yes
Mechanical repairs: independent contractors
Ship's & variety store: yes
Restaurant: on-site

The single pier of Airlie Marina is just past the Bridge Tender complex. This facility offers no transient services, and the rude dockage attendant made it clear to me that the management is not even interested in discussing the matter.

Just next door to Airlie Marina is Crockers Landing (910-256-3661), which is also the headquarters for Mid-Atlantic Yacht Sales (910-256-4342), dealers in larger power yachts. This facility is now entirely engaged in boat sales and no longer offers any services for transients.

Dockside Marina's floating wooden-decked

piers gaze out over the ICW's northwesterly banks a stone's throw southwest of Crockers Landing. Three days after Hurricane Fran, I had occasion to visit Dockside. There was nary a pier in sight. Yet when I next cruised through in early February 1997, not only were new, modern floating docks in place, but the on-site restaurant had been expanded. Gasoline and diesel-fuel sales are slated to begin anew by May 1997. Bravo!

Depths at Dockside Marina run from 8 feet to better than 10 feet. The friendly dockmaster here is eager to greet visiting cruisers. All slips feature water and 30-amp power hookups. Mechanical repairs can sometimes be arranged through local technicians. There is a small ship's and variety store just beside the docks. As with all the Wrightsville Beach marinas, provisions are only a short taxi ride away.

The cold and hot seafood sandwiches and the excellent seafood entrées at Dockside Restaurant (910-256-2752) are becoming legendary. The post-Fran incarnation of this dining attraction boasts a new upstairs and a climate-controlled dining room with an excellent view of the Waterway. During fair weather, you may also choose open-air dining overlooking the water.

**Dockside Marina
(910) 256-3579**

Approach depth: 12+ feet
Dockside depth: 8–10 feet
Accepts transients: yes
Floating wooden piers: yes
Dockside power connections: 30 amps
Dockside water connections: yes
Gasoline: yes
Diesel fuel: yes
Mechanical repairs: private contractors
Ship's & variety store: small
Restaurant: on-site

## Motts Channel and Associated Facilities (Standard Mile 283)

Northeast of flashing daybeacon #127, a marked cut known as Motts Channel strikes southeast and eventually intersects the so-called Banks Channel. Banks Channel, in turn, maintains excellent depths as it runs southwest to Masonboro Inlet.

Thanks to ongoing shoaling and the effects of Hurricane Fran, Motts Channel was recently dredged to between 8 and 12 feet. Skippers who have encountered this previously shallow cut will appreciate the new depths. Still, proceed with caution and a weather eye on the sounder because this area is susceptible to shoaling in the aftermath of storms.

Several facilities are located along Motts Channel, one of which is of great interest to cruising skippers. One of the few good anchorages near Wrightsville Beach is found along Banks Channel.

The large dry-stack storage building of Atlantic Marine (910-256-9911) overlooks the northeasterly bank of Motts Channel near its northwesterly intersection with the ICW. No services are available for visiting captains.

Northwest of unlighted daybeacon #21, the huge Seapath Yacht Club complex is visible immediately northeast of Motts Channel. If by some chance you are blind enough to miss the docks, the condos towering over the slips are sure to catch your attention. Most of the considerable dockage here is taken up by craft belonging to condo owners and members of the yacht club. Fortunately, transients are accommodated along the southwesternmost (outer) dock, and occasionally on the inner harbor berths as well.

*Wrightsville Marina Yacht Club*

**Seapath Yacht Club
(910) 256-3747**

Approach depth: 8–10 feet
Dockside depth: 8 feet (minimum)
Accepts transients: yes
Floating wooden piers: yes
Dockside power connections: 30 & 50 amps
Dockside water connections: yes
Showers: yes
Laundromat: yes
Waste pump-out: yes
Gasoline: yes
Diesel fuel: yes
Mechanical repairs: independent technicians
Ship's & variety store: yes
Restaurants: several nearby

As mentioned above, Seapath lost its outer dock to Hurricane Fran, but construction of a new, state-of-the-art wooden-decked floating replacement pier is now complete. Transients are once again readily accommodated here.

Seapath has minimum 8-foot dockside depths, which should be enough for even long-legged, fixed-keel sailcraft. Power and water connections are at hand, and the shoreside showers, laundromat, and ship's and variety store (all freshly rebuilt since Fran) are quite nice. Gasoline and diesel fuel can be purchased just beside the ship's store. Seapath also offers modern waste pump-out service. The friendly dockmasters will be glad to arrange for mechanical repairs with local independents.

Several restaurants are within a healthy walk of Seapath, including Causeway Café and the new Pusser's Landing at Wally's, both discussed above. The supermarket on Wrightsville Beach, mentioned above, is within an easy taxi ride. The local post office and the Redix store are also located nearby.

Southeast of unlighted daybeacon #14, Motts Channel intersects Banks Channel; unlighted daybeacon #14 was absent during this writer's last visit but may be back in place by the time you arrive. At #14, the marked route turns southwest on Banks Channel as it makes its way to Masonboro Inlet. To the northeast, good depths of 8 to 10 feet hold upstream to the charted 8-foot fixed bridge. These waters are a popular anchorage. Happily, there are not yet any anchoring restrictions beyond those dictated by good sense and common courtesy. There is superior cover from all but strong southwesterly winds. The surrounding shores are lined by a dense collection of private homes, condos, hotels, and other resort-type development.

Some skippers also anchor southwest of #14 on the charted bubble of deep water. Though this is acceptable in fair weather, I suggest the better-sheltered northeasterly waters unless overcrowding forces you southwest of #14.

The Banks Channel anchorages are plagued during summer weekends by the traffic of numerous small power craft and Jet-Skis. During these times, you may be awakened a bit earlier than what you had in mind.

Boaters anchoring in Banks Channel can make use of a small dinghy dock along the southeastern banks just southwest of the 8-foot fixed bridge. This pier is convenient for a visit to the beach or the many restaurants and retail shops in the immediate area.

### Bradley Creek (Standard Mile 284)

This account now returns to the ICW. The entrance to charted Bradley Creek is located along the northwestern shore 0.7 nautical mile southwest of the Wrightsville bridge. The marked entrance channel runs well upstream and holds 5½-foot depths at low tide.

In marked contrast to previous times, none of the three facilities on this stream now offers any dockage for transient craft. Cruising southeast to northwest, boaters traversing the Bradley Creek channel will first pass some docks along the southwestern banks associated with a private condo development. Next up is Boat House Marina (910-350-0023), also along the southwestern shoreline. This firm's primary business is the dry storage of small power craft, as evidenced by the large stack buildings just behind the docks. Visitors can purchase gasoline and visit the marina's ship's and variety store. Finally, the "boataminiums" of Bradley Creek Marina (910-350-0029) guard the creek's southwestern shore just short of the low-level fixed bridge. This large complex has extensive dockage, including some covered slips, but offers no facilities for cruising visitors.

*Bridge Tender Marina–Wrightsville Beach*

### Masonboro Inlet (Standard Mile 285, Shinn Creek Entrance)

Masonboro Inlet boasts one of the most reliable seaward channels along the North Carolina coastline. The cut is deep and very well marked. Twin stone jetties help give the channel a stable bottom. Though most of this seaward channel was unaffected by Hurricane Fran, I did note a large, new sand shoal building into the inlet's northeastern flank southeast of correctly charted flashing daybeacon #1. Some of the inlet's aids to navigation appear on chart 11541, but others are not shown, as they are shifted from time to time to reflect changes in the channel.

There are two routes from the ICW to Masonboro Inlet.

The more popular passage runs first southeast, then southwest via Motts and Banks Channels from the principal Wrightsville Beach waterfront.

Masonboro Inlet can also be approached via Shinn Creek, which makes into the ICW's southeastern flank between flashing daybeacons #128 and #129A. Though this stream is subject to shoaling, cruisers can currently expect minimum 7-foot soundings. To be on the safe side, check at one of Wrightsville Beach's many marinas for current depths on Shinn Creek.

Thanks to Masonboro Inlet's good depths, stable channel, and twin stone jetties, cruising boaters can put out to sea or enter from the open ocean with about as much confidence as is possible when navigating the sometimes tenuous routes between inland and offshore waters. Just watch out for the new, flanking sand shoal (see below).

*Seapath Yacht Club–Wrightsville Beach*

# WRIGHTSVILLE BEACH NAVIGATION

Northeast of flashing daybeacon #127, Motts Channel opens out southeast of the Waterway. This cut eventually intersects Banks Channel. Along the way, you will pass Atlantic Marine and Seapath Yacht Club, both on the northeastern bank.

Pass all red beacons to your port side and green markers to starboard as you cruise southeast on Motts Channel. The initial northwestern portion of the channel had shoaled after Hurricane Fran and, shallow prior to the storm, was in dire need of dredging. Happily the problem has been addressed and current depths are 8 to 12 feet. Pass between unlighted daybeacon #25 and a small, unlighted floating nun buoy designated as #24. This course will run you hard by the channel's southwestern flank.

From this point, the channel shifts eastward. Point to pass unlighted daybeacon #23 to its northeasterly side. Between #23 and the charted position of unlighted daybeacon #14, hold to the mid-width.

During my last on-site observations, in February 1997, unlighted daybeacon #14 was absent from its position at the intersection of Motts and Banks Channels. It is to be hoped that it will be back in place soon. In any case, pass northeast of #14 (or its charted position) and continue cruising southeast into the deep water of Banks Channel. At this point, you can turn northeast into the popular Banks Channel anchorage or swing southwest on your way to Masonboro Inlet.

The marked passage swings southwest toward Masonboro Inlet. Favor the southeasterly shore as you track your way southwest to the inlet. Shoal water abuts the northwesterly shoreline along this stretch.

Banks Channel intersects Masonboro Inlet southwest of unlighted daybeacon #10. Point to pass (correctly charted) unlighted junction daybeacon #WC to its southeasterly side. Cruise into the main body of the inlet channel, then turn southeast toward the open sea.

Immediately after making this turn, begin watching to the northeast for a large sand shoal building into the inlet's northeasterly flank from the southwesterly tip of Wrightsville Beach. Currently, two unlighted nun buoys, #8 and #8A, mark this potential obstruction. Be sure to pass well southwest of #8 and #8A. Be prepared to discover new aids to navigation placed in the channel to mark fresh incursions by this pesky shoal. Otherwise, simply pass all red, even-numbered aids to your port side and take green markers to starboard. The well-marked path will eventually lead you out to sea between the twin stone breakwaters. Next stop, Bermuda?

***On the ICW***  The ICW scoots past the entrance to Bradley Creek south of flashing daybeacon #127. If you decide to enter, be sure to stay strictly between the various markers. Low-water depths outside the channel are nil.

At flashing daybeacon #128, the ICW shifts slightly to the southwest and soon approaches the intersection with Shinn Creek, another route to Masonboro Inlet.

If you are simply passing by on the Waterway, stay well northwest of unlighted can buoy #129. Be on guard against strong currents as you pass the creek's mouth.

Should you be following Shinn Creek to Masonboro Inlet, abandon the ICW and pass northeast of #129. Yes, it may look wrong on the water, but trust me, this is the way to go. Shallow water lies southwest of #129. Continue following all the other markers through Shinn Creek until you intersect the principal Masonboro Inlet channel by passing between correctly charted flashing daybeacon #1 and unlighted junction daybeacon #WC.

## ICW TO CAPE FEAR RIVER

South of Wrightsville Beach, the Waterway knifes its way along a dredged channel through Masonboro Sound on its way to Snows Cut, which in turn leads to the Cape Fear River. A side channel leads south from the eastern entrance of Snows Cut to the popular resort community of Carolina Beach.

Hurricanes Fran and Bertha seem to have initiated some shoaling along the Waterway's flanks through Masonboro Sound. Savvy mariners will stick strictly to the ICW's centerline between Shinn Creek and Snows Cut.

This section of the North Carolina coastline was also hard hit by Hurricane Fran. Carolina Beach suffered severe beachside damage. One popular marina and boatyard just to the north was devastated but it has now been revived.

Marina facilities at Carolina Beach are now much reduced, not so much due to the hurricanes as to the changes made to one of the existing facilities. Consequently, with the exception of Masonboro Boatyard (see below), facilities for visiting cruisers between Wrightsville Beach and Southport are now rather scarce.

Only a single anchorage along this stretch is appropriate for large cruising craft. Located hard by Carolina Beach, it will serve your purposes well in all but very stormy conditions.

This section of the ICW is fairly sheltered. Unless strong winds are in the offing, cruisers should be able to enjoy the view as they head down the Waterway. Be sure to check out the many beautiful homes along the mainland shore. A good number have their own private docks, and you will most likely discover that many of these structures still exhibit hurricane damage.

All in all, this is an eye-pleasing portion of the run through the waters of southeastern North Carolina. But it is also one that requires caution and attention to navigational business. Unless winds happen to be light, you will find it a far smoother passage than your trek down the Cape Fear River to Southport.

## Masonboro Boatyard and Marina (Standard Mile 287)

Southwest of unlighted daybeacon #135, one of the most interesting boating facilities on the North Carolina coast will come abeam on the northwestern banks. Masonboro Boatyard and Marina welcomes not only transients, but live-aboards as well (though live-aboard pets are no longer allowed). The boatyard has the kind of down-home, almost carefree attitude which is so sadly lacking in many modern marinas and yards. The attitude here is laid-back, and the staff is ultrafriendly.

No live-aboard or boat owner at Masonboro Boatyard will soon forget Hurricane Fran. The storm surge piled straight into the harbor, destroyed most of the docks, and deposited many of the moored vessels in a heap at one corner of the dockage basin. Fortunately, as this account was being tapped out on the keyboard, dredging is complete on the marina approach channel.

Low-water depths now run 6 feet or better, though if history is any judge, this cut will be subject to future shoaling. Three ranks of ultra-modern concrete-decked floating piers are now in place, and more are planned for the future.. Masonboro Boatyard is most certainly back in business.

Transients are once again gladly accepted. The new slips feature full power and water connections. The first-rate shoreside showers, laundromat, and boaters' lounge are indicative of this facility's warm and salty attitude. Waste pump-out service is planned for the future.

Masonboro Boatyard specializes in mechanical repairs to sailcraft diesel auxiliaries, but service is available for all sorts of power plants. Haul-outs are accomplished by a crane with a rated capacity of 19 tons. Bottom work can be performed by the yard's professional staff or do-it-yourself boat owners. Service patrons may not hire outside contractors to do their bottom, shaft, or prop work.

A large parts store is located on the grounds. The marina provides a courtesy van that may be used for a limited period of time to visit local supermarkets or restaurants. The Trails End Steak House (910-791-2034) is within walking distance of the marina and reportedly serves excellent food.

All in all, I cannot speak too highly of Masonboro Boatyard and Marina as a haven for cruising people. If your plans call for you to spend a night between Wrightsville Beach and Southport, this is the spot.

## Masonboro Sound History

The history of Masonboro Sound is filled with

**Masonboro Boatyard and Marina
(910) 791-1893**

Approach depth: 6 feet
Dockside depth: 6 feet
Accepts transients: yes
Floating concrete piers: yes
Dockside power connections: 30 & 50 amps
Dockside water connections: yes
Showers: yes
Laundromat: yes
Waste pump-out: planned
Mechanical repairs: yes
Below-waterline repairs: yes
Ship's store: yes
Restaurant: nearby

romantic tales. In colonial times, there apparently was a Masonic meeting house near the sound's shore, one of the first such lodges in the Southern colonies. The years have clouded the location of the meeting house and the date it was constructed. Some believe that William Hooper, one of the state's signers of the Declaration of Independence, founded the chapter. Others disagree. But it seems certain that it was from this secret order that the sound derived its name.

Before 1700, the region was generally unoccupied. Many are the tales of pirates landing on the shores of Masonboro Sound to bury their ill-gotten booty. Captain Kidd, Blackbeard, and Stede Bonnet were all reported to have put in here from time to time.

In later colonial days and even after the Revolutionary War, Masonboro Sound was considered an ideal spot for a summer retreat. Many prominent citizens built homes along the banks to take advantage of the pleasant surroundings and cool ocean breezes.

In 1762, Thomas Godfrey was so taken with Masonboro's beauty that he wrote a poem about

the sound. The last stanza runs thus:

The Queen of Beauty, all divine,
Here spreads her gentle reign,
See, all around, the graces shine
Like Cynthia's silver train.

### Carolina Inlet Marina (Standard Mile 294)

Carolina Inlet Marina (910-392-0580) guards the westerly banks of the ICW between unlighted can buoys #155 and #155A. This facility lies west of Carolina Beach Inlet and is the last marina north of Snows Cut. Inlet Watch Yacht Club now manages the wet slips and dry-stack storage. Carolina Inlet Marina oversees the fuel dock, mechanical repairs, and boat sales. At the current time, nothing besides gasoline and diesel fuel is available for transients in this dockage basin.

### Carolina Beach Inlet (Standard Mile 294)

The unstable seaward cut known as Carolina Beach Inlet lies east of the gap between the ICW's unlighted can buoys #155 and #155A. Markers in the inlet are not charted, as they are frequently shifted, added to, and deleted. This is most definitely not one of North Carolina's reliable passages to and from the open sea. Visitors are advised to make use of Masonboro Inlet to the north or the Cape Fear River inlet to the south.

### Snows Cut (Standard Mile 295)

At flashing daybeacon #161, the ICW strikes west by way of an artificial canal known as Snows Cut. This passage leads Waterway cruisers to the Cape Fear River.

Tidal currents on Snows Cut are infamous. Captains piloting sailcraft or single-screw trawlers may want to consult the tidal tables and synchronize their passage with a fair-setting current. This little cut often reminds me of Wappoo Creek, just south of Charleston, South Carolina. On both canals, you almost have to see the rapidly moving water to believe it.

### Carolina Beach (Standard Mile 295)

South of Snows Cut's easterly entrance, a deep and well-marked channel, abandoned by the ICW, continues to Carolina Beach. Another popular resort community, Carolina Beach is a crazy-quilt collection of beach homes, condominiums, and motels. It is a miniature version of South Carolina's Grand Strand.

Since the last edition of this guide, major changes have come about in the Carolina Beach marina scene. By the summer of 1997, transient slips and other facilities for visiting craft are going to be hard to come by.

Just a short hop from Snows Cut, a marina of the same name lines the channel's western shore between unlighted daybeacons #2 and #4. Snows Cut Marina (910-458-7400) has been sold and will soon be the site of a townhouse development. The adjacent boatyard is being shut down, and fueling services will eventually be discontinued as well. This writer was not able to make an accurate assessment as to whether the new incarnation of this facility will accept visiting craft.

Should the new regime accept transients, visitors will discover first-class wooden-decked floating piers that survived Hurricane Fran in remarkably good shape. Apparently, full power and water connections will also be available.

My best advice at this point is to call ahead and see what services, if any, are available for transients.

Coquina Harbour at Carolina Beach lies almost opposite Snows Cut Marina on the easterly banks. This facility boasts a harbor partially enclosed by a breakwater and offers all-new wooden floating piers. Depths alongside run 5 to 6 feet at low tide. Water and 30- and 50-amp power connections are available. Showers, a laundromat, and a swimming pool are just behind the dockage complex in the adjoining condo development. Transients are supposedly accepted, but I found the docks unattended during my on-site research.

---

**Coquina Harbour at Carolina Beach (910) 458-5053**

Approach depth: 10+ feet
Dockside depth: 5–6 feet (low water)
Accepts transients: yes
Fixed wooden piers: yes
Dockside power connections: 30 & 50 amps
Dockside water connections: yes

---

Carolina Beach Municipal Marina occupies both shores of the channel's southerly terminus. The docks at this facility are no longer attended, and most of the slip space is taken up by local charter-fishing craft. Transients may be able to tie temporarily to a single, fixed, wooden visitors' pier along the westerly shores. No other facilities for cruising visitors are currently available.

Cruisers in search of overnight anchorage will find a good haven adjacent to the Carolina Beach channel. Depths of 7 to 19 feet line the cut's easterly flank from a position just south of unlighted daybeacon #5 to a point just north of unlighted daybeacon #6. Protection is good except in strong northerly blows. The entire area is surrounded by heavy development, so this is not exactly an isolated haven. Be sure to show a bright anchor light!

# ICW TO CAPE FEAR RIVER NAVIGATION

South of its intersection with Shinn Creek, the ICW runs generally south and southwest for 8.5 nautical miles through Masonboro Sound to Snows Cut. This man-made canal leads from the southerly tip of the sound to the Cape Fear River and has a rather heavy current.

The Waterway channel through Masonboro Sound is well marked but seems to be shoaling along its edges. Pay careful attention to all markers. For best depths, stick conscientiously to the Waterway's centerline.

### Masonboro Boatyard and Marina

Southwest of unlighted daybeacon #135, the newly dredged and marked entrance channel to Masonboro Boatyard is now in place. Minimum depths are currently 6 feet.

### On the ICW

At unlighted daybeacon #141, the ICW leaves chart 11541. Have 11534 ready at hand.

South-southwest of unlighted can buoy #155, you will spy the entrance to Carolina Inlet Marina and Inlet Watch Yacht Club to the west-northwest.

The channel leading to Carolina Beach Inlet lies east of the gap between #155 and unlighted can buoy #155A. Don't attempt this seaward cut! The markers are not charted, and the inlet is subject to continual change.

Be alert for strong side-setting currents on the ICW as you pass the inlet channel's mouth. Don't let the tide push you onto the channel's edge.

### Snows Cut

South of unlighted daybeacon #159, the Waterway takes a sharp turn to the west and enters Snows Cut. This man-made canal links the ICW to the Cape Fear River.

To enter Snows Cut, come abeam of flashing daybeacon #161 by 50 yards to its westerly side, then turn sharply west into the mid-width of the cut. There are no markers on the canal, but it is consistently deep. You should not have any shallow-water difficulty if you keep to the middle. The stream is spanned by one fixed bridge with a vertical clearance of 65 feet. Currents run very swiftly through the cut. Sailcraft and single-screw trawlers should be particularly alert.

At flashing daybeacon #163, the Waterway enters the eastern reaches of the Cape Fear River. This chapter's account of the ICW ends here. To pick up the route's southward trek, refer to chapter 10.

### Carolina Beach

South of Snows Cut, a deep channel leads to Carolina Beach. To enter, leave the ICW at flashing daybeacon #161 and set course to pass unlighted daybeacons #2 and #4 to their fairly immediate eastern sides. At #4, Snows Cut Marina will come abeam on the channel's western shore. The breakwater-enclosed basin of Coquina Harbour at Carolina Beach is on the opposite bank.

As you continue south on the Carolina Beach channel, pass all red beacons to your starboard side and green markers to port.

South of unlighted daybeacon #5, good water abuts the channel's easterly side. Cruisers seeking overnight anchorage can cruise into these ample depths and drop the hook on the waters north of unlighted daybeacon #6. For best depths, don't approach the easterly shoreline too closely. Be sure to anchor well off the main channel and show an anchor light.

South of unlighted daybeacon #7, the southernmost marker on the Carolina Beach channel, hold to the passage's mid-width. Just before the stream's southern terminus, the single transient pier of Carolina Beach Municipal Marina is accessible to starboard.

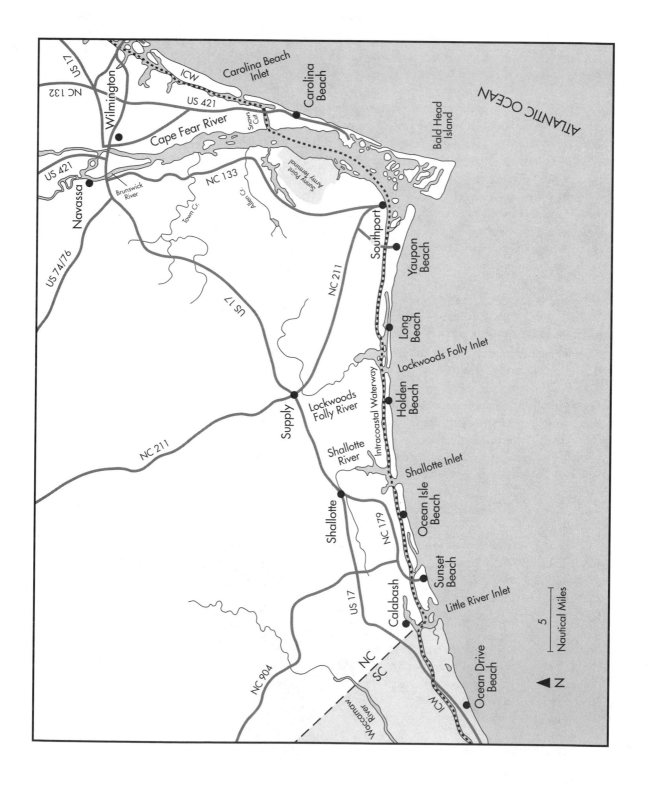

# Cape Fear River
# to South Carolina

## Charts

You will need two NOAA charts for navigating the waters of southeastern North Carolina:

**11537** covers the Cape Fear River from its inlet to Wilmington

**11534** follows the ICW from Snows Cut to South Carolina

The navigable waters of southeastern North Carolina consist of the Cape Fear River and the ICW. Most pleasure boaters hurry past and see only the Waterway. However, additional cruising opportunities are available which should not be dismissed lightly.

The Cape Fear River is North Carolina's most commercially important stream. The port city of Wilmington, perched on the northerly portion of the river's easterly shore, hosts the state's largest waterborne freight terminal. The Cape Fear is the only Tar Heel river to empty directly into the open sea. A wide, very deep, well-marked channel leads past the awesome offshore Frying Pan Shoals. Huge freighters, tankers, and containerized cargo ships regularly ply the stream to Wilmington.

For pleasure boaters, the Cape Fear offers reliable passage to the open sea and interesting cruising in the Wilmington area. Wilmington's reasonably good public dockage is soon to be augmented, which will at last give visiting cruisers the ready means to visit this fascinating city. There are a few anchorages along the way, but one of the havens I used to recommend is now a bit difficult.

The ICW enters the Cape Fear River from Snows Cut and follows the great stream south for 10 nautical miles. The Waterway then ducks into a narrow, canal-like passage that leads past the old town of Southport. First-class facilities are available to cruising boaters in this utterly charming port of call.

Visiting cruisers should know that virtually all aids to navigation on the Cape Fear River have recently been renumbered. The NOAA charting folks have not yet caught onto this new scheme of aids to navigation. Be *sure* to carefully study the navigational information in this chapter, or you may end up cruising past Southport or Snows Cut.

South of Southport, the ICW follows a mostly man-made cut all the way to South Carolina. Along the way, marinas are located hard by Lockwoods Folly and Shallotte Inlets.

The famed seafood town of Calabash marks the southernmost limits of North Carolina cruising. It is actually necessary to enter South Carolina before cruising back to the north to visit Calabash. The village offers a good marina and a host of generally mediocre seafood restaurants.

The waters of southeastern North Carolina, while limited, still offer cruising ground where pleasure boaters have seldom been. Don't be in such a hurry to complete your passage of Tar Heel waters that you overlook this region's considerable charms.

## Cape Fear History

E. Lawrence Lee, one of the leading authorities on the history of southeastern North Carolina, has called the Cape Fear River "the lifeblood of the land through which it runs." Strangely enough, this vital river remained a veritable wilderness throughout much of the state's early colonial period.

Spaniards exploring the Carolina coast in the 16th century discovered the stream and named it the Jordan. The great beauty of the River Jordan became a matter of legend among the Spaniards, but reality was much harsher.

In 1526, a Spanish expedition attempted to establish a colony on the Cape Fear, but the effort ended in failure after much suffering. This venture was followed by an abortive colonization attempt by settlers from Barbados and New England. Hoping to concentrate the colony's population, the Lords Proprietors closed the Cape Fear region to settlement for the next 50 years. The river became a haven for pirates. The surrounding lands remained a wilderness and became an unofficial border between North and South Carolina.

A pitched battle took place on the Cape Fear River in 1718 between the famous pirate Stede Bonnet and forces from South Carolina. Bonnet was defeated and carried back to Charleston, where he was subsequently tried and hanged.

In the early 18th century, Major Maurice Moore traveled north from South Carolina to help his neighboring state in the Tuscarora Indian wars. He was impressed with what he saw of the Cape Fear region as he passed through. He correctly foresaw the surrounding land's vast potential for the production of naval stores. He and his family established a large plantation along the river. Through his considerable influence, he enticed others of his class to immigrate. Thus, the Cape Fear region came to be settled by wealthy planters holding large tracts. This was very different from early settlement in other parts of North Carolina, where the first residents were generally refugees or those seeking religious freedom.

Seeing the need for a commercial center, Major Moore laid out the town of Brunswick in 1725. The village was located near the main channel of the river, so deep-draft ocean vessels could easily use the port. Brisk trade soon developed. Between 1773 and 1776, more than 300 cargo vessels entered and cleared the town wharves. Several Royal governors resided in Brunswick, and the assembly sometimes met there.

By 1773, a new village had sprung up at the fork of the Cape Fear River north of Brunswick. First known as Dram Tree and later called Newton and New Liverpool, it was advantageously situated at the confluence of the two streams that brought traffic from vast sections of the state's interior.

As time passed, a bitter trade rivalry developed between the two towns. Finally, Royal Governor Gabriel Johnston cast his lot with the newer village, possibly because of an ongoing feud with the powerful Moore family of Brunswick. In 1740, the community of Newton was incorporated as Wilmington. From that time on, it was the center of commerce for the lower Cape Fear.

Brunswick survived until the late 18th century simply because deep-draft vessels could not negotiate the river shoals to Wilmington. The old town was attacked on several occasions during the Revolutionary War and was finally burned by the British in 1781. Today, nothing of this once-vital commercial center can be seen from the river.

For many a year following the Revolutionary War, tar, pitch, and turpentine—naval stores—continued to be briskly exported from Wilmington. Several Civil War battles were fought along the Cape Fear River between Union naval forces and strong Confederate forts guarding the stream. Wilmington was the last major city of coastal North Carolina to fall to Federal troops.

As the postwar years passed, the large plantations were broken up. Most disappeared entirely. One of the largest, Orton Plantation, remains. Located near the site of Brunswick, its grounds are open year-round to visitors. Boaters will find it necessary to rent a car to visit this lovely site.

Wilmington survived Reconstruction and again began to expand. It was the site of major shipbuilding activities during both world wars. After World War II, North Carolina began to construct modern port facilities at Wilmington. Today, visiting boaters cruising the upper Cape Fear can see cargo and commercial ships from all the world docked at the extensive wharves.

After a slow beginning, the Cape Fear River and Wilmington assumed great commercial importance. Today's thriving trade seems to assure a prosperous future.

## UPPER CAPE FEAR RIVER

North of Snows Cut, the Cape Fear continues well marked and easy to navigate. The Brunswick River, just south of Wilmington, provides some opportunities for overnight anchorage, but shoaling at its entrance calls for extra navigational caution. Public docks with minimal power and water connections are available on the Wilmington waterfront. These facilities will soon be augmented by a new "Riverfront Park" slated to contain a whole collection of floating piers.

The Wilmington portion of the Cape Fear River offers interesting sightseeing as you cruise past the many large commercial craft usually docked there. North of Wilmington, the Cape Fear splits. The northwesterly branch offers some additional opportunities to anchor.

The city of Wilmington has undergone a tasteful renaissance during the last several years. The colorful waterfront bristles with wonderful restaurants and interesting places to see and shop and dozens and dozens of beautifully restored historic homeplaces. I suggest that every cruiser put a red circle around Wilmington on his or her chart. Those who miss the many attractions of this seagoing community will be less for the omission.

## Wilmington Marine Center

East of flashing daybeacon #59 (noted on the July 9, 1994, edition of chart 11537 as #53), one of the most exciting private facilities developed in the Wilmington region in many years stands ready to greet visiting cruisers. Wilmington Marine Center is a huge, 50-acre marine-oriented development which will eventually house many related firms servicing both commercial and pleasure craft.

Transient pleasure craft are accepted at both fixed and floating wooden-decked piers. The complex includes 73 wet slips, a few of which are covered, and two long face docks partially reserved for transients. Mean low-water entrance and dockside depths are 6 feet. The helpful and

friendly management has warned me that river conditions may lower the soundings just a bit, but this is a relatively rare occurrence. All slips feature water and 30- and 50-amp power connections. Gasoline and diesel fuel can be purchased, and showers are on the premises. A short taxi ride allows cruisers to sample downtown Wilmington's many restaurants.

Below-the-waterline (haul-out) repairs are performed by the on-site Baker Marine Service Company (910-395-5008). This firm boasts a 100-ton marine railway and a 70-ton travel-lift. Mechanical repairs were being farmed out to independent technicians at the time of this writing, but the yard will probably have its own mechanics by the time you read this account.

Thanks to this facility and the Wilmington waterfront docks, cruising boaters now have more reason than ever to track their way north on the Cape Fear River from Snows Cut.

---

**Wilmington Marine Center
(910) 395-5055**

Approach depth: 6 feet (low water)
Dockside depth: 6 feet (low water)
Accepts transients: yes
Fixed and floating wooden piers: yes
Dockside power connections: 30 & 50 amps
Dockside water connections: yes
Showers: yes
Gasoline: yes
Diesel fuel: yes
Mechanical repairs: yes
Below-waterline repairs: extensive
Restaurants: accessible by taxi

## Brunswick River

The Brunswick River, once called an "errant arm" of the Cape Fear, was for many years the home of a large, mothballed merchant fleet. The old craft are gone now, and the Brunswick can serve as an anchorage for craft drawing 5 feet or preferably less.

The river's southerly entrance makes into the Cape Fear's westerly bank north of flashing daybeacon #59 (currently charted as #53). A large, unmarked shoal has built out from the entrance's southerly point. Navigators must take extra care to avoid this obstruction. Otherwise, entrance depths run as much as 6 to 20 feet.

Beyond its tricky entrance, the Brunswick River swings sharply north. Drop anchor along the stream's centerline at any spot that strikes your fancy well short of the low-level fixed bridge spanning the river upstream. Avoid both shorelines. Shallows extend outward from both banks.

Protection is adequate for all but the heaviest weather. The stream is a bit wide for effective shelter in gale winds. Otherwise, most any pleasure craft can drop the hook here with confidence.

*Cape Fear Lift Bridge–Wilmington*

## Wilmington

Wilmington is a vital, active city. Since the completion of Interstate 40 in 1992, the town has been growing geometrically. The downtown historic district adjacent to the Cape Fear River has undergone major redevelopment and restoration during the last two decades. What was at times a fitful and uncertain march toward success has at last seemingly met its goal. Within the past five years, visitors have been discovering the charms of downtown Wilmington in ever-increasing numbers. New and expanded restaurants and retail shops of all descriptions have opened in response to this influx of business. What is so encouraging, though, is that all this development has been carefully managed to enhance the city's historical heritage. You won't find any fast-food restaurants with garish neon signs in Wilmington's historic district.

As further witness to Wilmington's respect for its past, many enchanting private homes, some dating back to the 19th century, have been lovingly restored throughout the district. Some of the best of these can be observed by walking along South Front and Second Streets. If you admire houses whose roots stretch back into the early history of our nation, don't miss the dreamlike walk down these quiet lanes.

If you are in need of taxi service in Wilmington, call Lett's Taxi Service (910-458-3999), Port City Taxi (910-762-1165), or Yellow Cab (910-762-3322). If you'd like to rent a car to explore the city, call Thrifty Car Rental (910-343-1411), Triangle Rental (910-251-9812), or Enterprise Car Rentals (910-799-4042).

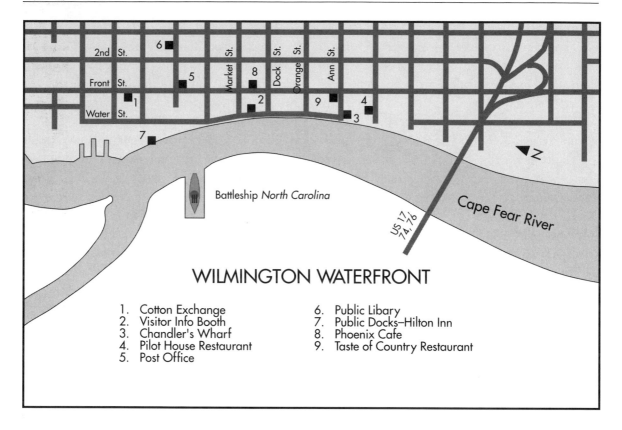

## WILMINGTON WATERFRONT

1. Cotton Exchange
2. Visitor Info Booth
3. Chandler's Wharf
4. Pilot House Restaurant
5. Post Office
6. Public Libary
7. Public Docks–Hilton Inn
8. Phoenix Cafe
9. Taste of Country Restaurant

### Wilmington Facilities

The 400-foot Wilmington municipal face dock lines the Cape Fear's eastern bank from a point north of the charted position of the Battleship *North Carolina* battleship memorial to the Hilton Inn.

Just south of the pleasure-craft facilities, a series of commercial docks lines the eastern banks. Often, naval and Coast Guard vessels are moored to these wharves for public view and visitation. The *Henrietta II*, a paddle-wheel tour boat that plies the river, is also docked along this stretch. Presumably, all these piers will eventually be incorporated into the ongoing "Riverfront Park" project (see below).

Pleasure craft are welcome to berth at the Wilmington public docks. Your best bet is to tie up abeam of the Hilton. Two (and only two) 30- and 50-amp power boxes and water hookups are available along this portion of the fixed wooden-faced dock. To register for power and water, make arrangements through the adjacent Hilton Inn (910-763-5900). Though general dockage is free along the whole downtown waterfront, the Hilton charges a significant fee for use of the power and water connections. Visiting cruisers should also be aware that the city imposes a 72-hour free dockage limit.

It's a bit of a crawl from your cockpit up to the piers, as the docks are quite tall. Boaters also

*Wilmington waterfront tulips–Battleship* North Carolina *in background*

have to negotiate a wooden railing atop the docks, but several hinged sections of the top railing help alleviate this problem. Depths are in the 8- to 12-foot-plus range.

Boaters docked at the Wilmington waterfront facilities should be on guard against the river and tidal currents that flow by the piers at astonishing speeds. Be ready for this swift water movement as you approach the docks. Have all hands stand by with fenders just to be on the safe side.

From the boater's point of view, the most exciting development in downtown Wilmington is the scheduled completion within the next year or two of an extensive "Riverfront Park" along the Cape Fear's easterly bank from the Coast Line Convention Center to the Castle Street boat ramp. As part of this project, a collection of piers and perhaps even some floating docks will be constructed, all of which should be open to visiting cruisers. Upon the completion of the "Riverfront Park," downtown Wilmington should be a premier pleasure-craft port of call.

As this guide went to press, construction was poised to begin on a new marina/repair yard likely to be called Bennett Brothers Yachts Marina. This facility will line the eastern bank of the Northeast Cape Fear River (see below) a short hop upstream of the Hilton Inn. This new marina/repair yard will be under the ownership of the estimable folks who manufacture those wonderful Bennett Brothers yachts. Early discussions between this writer and some of the principals indicated that the marina will be a first-class facility which will accept transients. A travel-lift and full mechanical repair capabilities are planned for the yard portion of the operation. When complete, this facility will add immeasurably to downtown Wilmington's appeal for visiting cruisers.

## Downtown Wilmington
## Restaurants and Shopping

It would take a separate book to describe all the things to see and do and the various places to eat in downtown Wilmington. Only a few of my favorites can be mentioned here. You are encouraged to strike out on your own. You never know when you may come upon a new and intimate dining spot or a beautifully restored homeplace which speaks eloquently of a far-removed era.

Any visit to downtown Wilmington should begin at Chandler's Wharf, a combination dining and shopping complex overlooking the waterfront at the southerly terminus of Water Street.

Here, you will find the Pilot House Restaurant (2 Ann Street, 910-343-0200), the premier dining establishment in all of Wilmington, at least according to this writer's palate. The dining room has large plate-glass windows gazing directly out over the Cape Fear River. Outside dining is also available. Both options offer a wonderful setting to watch the day's light fade from the waters. The restaurant's fare is imaginatively prepared and totally delicious. I highly recommend the Carolina Seafood Bisque as an appetizer. It may just be the best seafood soup I've ever had. The evening entrées are all noteworthy.

Next door is Elijah's Restaurant (2½ Ann Street, 910-343-1448). This is a more informal dining spot than the Pilot House. Elijah's specializes in fresh seafood. Open-air dining overlooking the river is very popular here during fair weather.

The principal Chandler's Wharf shopping complex is housed in a building a short step north on Water Street. A whole raft of retail shops is located under the roof of this converted warehouse.

Another dining spot of note is the Phoenix Cafe (9 South Front Street, 910-343-1395). Set in a converted store, the Phoenix is the gathering place for the local arts crowd. The cappuccino is wonderful, and the sandwiches are all that any famished appetite could desire. The unique nighttime entrées are prepared with unusual care, and the desserts—well, words just fail me. If you can

stand the noisy and sometimes smoky atmosphere, the Phoenix ranks with the Pilot House among Wilmington's most outstanding dining choices.

The Cotton Exchange shopping and office center overlooks the northern end of Water Street close by the Hilton Inn. This conglomeration of interesting shops and restaurants is housed in an old cotton warehouse. The gift and clothing shops alone can occupy many happy hours of your time. Come dinnertime, you will want to make the acquaintance of Nuss Strasse (910-763-5523), a German restaurant located in the complex. This establishment serves authentic Prussian cuisine prepared with meticulous care.

The Taste of Country Restaurant (226 South Front Street, 910-343-9888) offers an all-you-can-eat Southern-style buffet. The atmosphere is of the "horse trough" variety, but the food is quite good and noticeably prolific.

## Wilmington Attractions

First-time visitors to the old port city should begin their tour at the Cape Fear Coast Convention and Visitor's Bureau (24 North Third Street, 910-341-4030), located in the 1892 courthouse. Patrons will discover pamphlets and brochures for all the local and nearby attractions. During the summer months, the center is open seven days a week, but during the winter, hours are generally restricted to weekends.

Horse-drawn tours of downtown Wilmington's historic district depart regularly from the western foot of Market Street, within a stone's throw of the public docks. The ever-so-charming half-hour tours are offered Tuesday through Sunday from 10 A.M. to 10 P.M. For information, call 910-251-8889.

*Carriage tours–Wilmington Historic District*

The Battleship *North Carolina* (910-251-5797) makes its permanent home in a small bay just across the river from Wilmington. This colossal attraction is a bit too far for walking. Cruising visitors can take a land taxi or catch the water taxi from the foot of Market Street.

If you are interested in colonial history, don't miss the Burgwin-Wright House (224 Market Street, 910-762-0570). This historic homeplace served as the temporary headquarters of British general Charles Cornwallis after what another writer has described as his "strange victory" at the Battle of Guilford Courthouse. The house has a deep underground basement—almost a dungeon—where it is reported that patriot prisoners of war were held during the English occupation of Wilmington. There is also a mysterious underground tunnel leading to the banks of the Cape Fear River. Some whisper that it was once used to smuggle pirate treasure. The Burgwin-Wright House has been magnificently restored and is open to the public Tuesday through Saturday from 10 A.M. to 4 P.M. An admission fee is charged.

Don't miss the Cape Fear Museum (814 Market Street, 910-341-4350). There is no better place to become acquainted with the natural character and history of the entire Cape Fear River basin. I

*Restored homes in Wilmington Historic District*

have always been taken with the re-creation of the Civil War battle that took place at nearby Fort Fisher. In a more modern vein, there is a display dedicated to basketball superstar Michael Jordan, who grew up in Wilmington.

Second only to my love of boats and cruising is my interest in early American railroads. That's why you'll find this writer checking out the Wilmington Railroad Museum (501 Nutt Street, 910-763-2634) at every opportunity. If you share my passion for the iron rails, don't miss this attraction.

If by now it is dawning on you that there is much to see, do, and eat along the Wilmington waterfront, you are beginning to realize the many and varied charms of this revitalized coastal city. Go quietly and perhaps you may be able to hear the old cotton carts carrying their fleecy loads to the waterfront amid the call of pilots and the smell of produce waiting to be loaded aboard sailing schooners. For the sensitive and knowledgeable visitor, historic Wilmington seldom fails in its reward.

## Wilmington Special Events

Downtown Wilmington hosts several annual events. The fabulous Azalea Festival, held in mid-April, is an extravaganza of food, entertainment, and arts. It is the largest of Wilmington's annual events. If you happen to be cruising by at the appropriate time, do yourself a big favor and make every effort to attend.

The Wilmington Riverfest usually takes place the first weekend in October. This is a typical fall festival with a heavy emphasis on crafts and live street entertainment.

For winter fun, the well-heeled among us might try the Connoisseurs' Wine and Art Auction, held in February at the elegant Graystone Inn. Who knows, you may actually have the chance to bid on that 1983 Château Margaux you've always dreamed about.

That same month, music fans can check out the North Carolina Jazz Festival. Held at the Hilton Inn on Saturday and Sunday evenings, this is a must for all who enjoy jazz. For information, call 910-763-8585.

## Northeast Cape Fear River

The Cape Fear River divides just above the public docking facilities at the Hilton Inn. The easterly branch is known as the Northeast Cape Fear River. The initial stretch of this stream is very commercial. This guide's coverage of the Northeast Cape Fear River ends at the charted 26-foot bascule bridge. Good depths continue upriver for quite some distance but begin to fall off as the river leaves all development behind. Exploration of this extreme upriver region is best left to small power craft and canoes.

## Cape Fear River to Navassa

The main northwesterly branch of the Cape Fear (which retains that name) cuts under a 55-foot fixed bridge and abruptly leaves the 20th century behind. It's hard to believe how quickly you can find yourself cruising between untouched shorelines when just a minute ago the commercial piers of Wilmington were close at hand.

Minimum 8-foot depths continue upstream to an intersection with the northerly reaches of the Brunswick River just below the industrial center at Navassa. Craft up to 32 feet can cut south on the Brunswick River in 8-foot minimum depths and drop anchor in a truly remote region. The surrounding shores are undeveloped marsh. If it were not for the Navassa buildings, visible in the distance, you could believe yourself anchored in the wilds of South Carolina's Cape Romain.

# UPPER CAPE FEAR NAVIGATION

Be sure you have chart 11537 in your navigational arsenal before committing to a cruise of the upper Cape Fear River to Wilmington. You will need this cartographical aid to chart your progress along the great river and keep out of trouble.

Flashing daybeacon #163 marks the western exit of Snows Cut. Two marked channels lead southwest and northwest, respectively, into the Cape Fear River. The Waterway follows the southwestern cut, while the northwestern channel provides easy access to the upper Cape Fear and the Wilmington area.

During 1996, virtually all the aids to navigation on the large ships'–Cape Fear River channel were changed. This was apparently part of a project to move the inlet's sea buoy a bit farther out into the briny blue. Incidentally, the Cape Fear River inlet sea buoy has now been renumbered #CF.

The charting folks at NOAA have not yet caught onto these significant changes, which has led to monumental confusion. In the account below, I will do my best to make sense of this mess. It is to be hoped that new editions of charts 11534 and 11537 will soon put this confusion to rest.

**North from Snows Cut**   The markers on the actual ICW–Snows Cut channel (east of the main Cape Fear River channel) have *not* changed. Charts 11534 and 11537 still reflect the correct configuration of aids to navigation.

Those boaters who choose to cruise north on the Cape Fear River from Snows Cut should set course from flashing daybeacon #163 to pass unlighted daybeacon #1 to its immediate northeasterly side, then come between flashing daybeacon #B and unlighted daybeacon #3. Don't cut the Snows Cut northerly entrance point too closely. Shallows seem to be building out from the promontory.

After passing between #3 and #B, take all subsequent red markers to your starboard side and green beacons to port as far as the intersection with the main Cape Fear River channel at unlighted daybeacon #12. From a position between #3 and #B, continue on the same course, pointing to pass unlighted daybeacon #4 to its southwesterly side. Come abeam of flashing daybeacon #5 to its immediate easterly side.

At #5, the channel takes a sharp turn to the north. Set a new course to come abeam of and pass unlighted daybeacons #7 and #9 to their fairly immediate easterly sides. Come abeam of flashing daybeacon #10 to its westerly quarter.

From #10, it is a quick run to the main Cape Fear River channel. Cut to the northwest and point to pass unlighted daybeacon #12 to its southwesterly side.

Charted flashing daybeacon #37, which used to mark the western flank of the main Cape Fear River channel opposite Snows Cut's northern entrance, has apparently been removed. In the absence of this aid, continue cruising northwest on the same course for 75 yards past unlighted daybeacon #12, then swing north on the main Cape Fear channel, point-ing to come abeam of flashing buoy #42 (currently charted as flashing buoy #38) by 25 to 50 yards to its western quarter.

North of #42, the Cape Fear channel contin-ues well marked, deep, and easy to follow for sev-eral miles upstream to flashing buoy #58 (currently charted as #52). No sidewaters are to be found between #42 and #58.

The river channel cuts a bit to the north-northeast at #58 and flows toward Wilmington's port facilities. Large piers, warehouses, and pe-troleum tanks line the eastern shore. Mammoth freighters and tankers are often visible here.

The marked channel leading to Wilmington Marine Center strikes east abeam of flashing daybeacon #59 (currently charted as #53). Sim-ply cruise between the various markers into the dockage basin, passing red markers to your star-board side and green markers to port.

The southerly mouth of the Brunswick River cuts into the Cape Fear's westerly shore north of #58.

**Brunswick River**   Cruise into the mouth of the Brunswick River from the Cape Fear by favoring the entrance's northerly shores. Study chart 11537 and note the correctly depicted shoal bulging out from the southerly point. Take extra care to bypass these 3-foot waters.

Don't attempt to anchor in the stream's en-trance, as it is crossed by an oil pipeline. A sign on the southern shore warns of this hazard.

Continue upstream by sticking strictly to the mid-width. Soon, the river passes through a sharp turn to the north. A large shelf of shallow water ex-tends well outward from both banks past this turn.

Though it is possible to anchor almost anywhere along the stream's centerline, most boaters will not

want to cruise too far north. The river is eventu-ally blocked by a fixed bridge and a patch of shoal water.

**On the Cape Fear**   Hold to the mid-width and it is a simple matter to travel north to Wilmington. You will pass commercial wharves and warehouses on both shores. Take the time to fully enjoy this unique op-portunity to view large numbers of commercial craft at close quarters.

Eventually, you will encounter the Cape Fear Bridge, which has a closed vertical clearance of 65 feet. Past the span, the city of Wilmington will come abeam on the eastern shore.

**Wilmington**   After passing through the Cape Fear Bridge, look east and you will see a portion of Chandler's Wharf and the Pilot House Restaurant.

North of Chandler's Wharf, the Battleship *North Carolina* will be more than obvious to port. Don't attempt to enter the small bay in which the ship rests. It is guarded by an underwater chain.

Soon after passing the battleship, you will spot the Wilmington public docks adjacent to the Hilton Inn on the eastern shore. If you wish to berth here, tie up, then check at the hotel desk about power and water connections.

**The Cape Fear Splits**   North of the Hilton, the Cape Fear soon splits. The easterly cut is known as the Northeast Cape Fear River. The stream soon leads to a second bridge. This guide's coverage of the Northeast Cape Fear ends here. North of the bridge, the river remains deep for some distance, but it soon leaves chart 11537 and is therefore not recommended for cruising boaters.

**Northern Cape Fear**   The stream's northwesterly

fork retains the name Cape Fear River. If you are following this arm, you will pass under a 55-foot fixed bridge soon after cruising through the south-easterly mouth. Suddenly, you will be plunged into an area that is mostly undeveloped. This comes as a shock so soon after leaving the urbanized Wilmington area. Depths on the northerly Cape Fear are quite deep, typically 15 to 30 feet.

Eventually, the river leads to a railroad bridge at the Navassa industrial center. Just short of the span, the upper reaches of the Brunswick River intersect the Cape Fear along the southern shore.

**Upper Brunswick River**   The northerly portion of the Brunswick River can serve as a very sheltered anchorage for craft under 35 feet. Simply enter the creek on its mid-width and select a likely spot. Discontinue your explorations well short of the charted 3-foot shoal south of Sturgeon Creek.

**North of Navassa**   This guide's coverage of the Cape Fear River ends at the Navassa railroad bridge. Good depths continue upstream, but the stream soon leaves chart 11537, as is the case with the north-eastern branch. Cruising boaters are strongly advised to discontinue their northward trek at Navassa.

# ICW AND LOWER CAPE FEAR RIVER

South of Snows Cut, the ICW follows the lower reaches of the Cape Fear River for almost 10 nautical miles until the Waterway takes a sharp cut to the west near the village of Southport. South of the ICW landcut, the Cape Fear flows toward its wide and deep inlet. This seaward cut provides reliable access to the open sea.

Bald Head Island, which borders the inlet's eastern shore, is one of the great ecological show-places in North Carolina. The island has undergone careful development during the last decade and now boasts a marina that accepts transients.

As mentioned above, virtually all the markers on the Cape Fear River channel have been renumbered. Be *sure* to read the navigational information in the next section of this chapter to learn about the new numbering scheme before venturing onto this mighty river.

## Cape Fear Anchorage (Standard Mile 305)

Study chart 11534 and notice the deepwater channel cutting to the northwest immediately northeast of flashing buoy #23 (currently charted as #19). This stream is actually part of the cooling canal for the nearby Brunswick nuclear power plant. In years past, this channel was outlined by informal pilings, but these indifferent aids to navigation have now been removed. Additionally, a portion of Snow Marsh has seemingly disappeared. Depths outside the channel rise quickly to grounding levels. In view of such unfortunate characteristics, this anchorage is no longer recommended for large cruising vessels.

## Bald Head Island

Bald Head Island, also known as Smith Island and Cape Fear Island, is a unique ecological entity. The small landmass is the most tropical spot in North Carolina. Such warm-weather plants as Spanish bayonets, palmettos, and palm trees grow here. Tradition claims that frost has never touched the island.

During the 1960s, Bald Head Island was the subject of intense controversy. A group of private investors was determined to commercially exploit the land, while an armada of environmentalists was equally determined to maintain the island's natural state.

Fortunately, this problem has been largely solved. Extensive homesites and townhouses have been developed along the southwestern beaches and in the interior maritime forests. Many other portions of the island have been carefully preserved in their natural state. Visitors will be delighted by the island's narrow paved streets, along which residents travel in electric golf carts. Through voluntary cooperation, these vehicles are now the main motorized transportation on the island. It is impossible to visit Bald Head without coming away with the idea that this is how a maritime island should be developed. Nature and the island's residents truly live in harmony. It is to be hoped that this desirable state will continue for many years to come.

Bald Head Island offers beautiful beaches and some great hiking, particularly in the undeveloped areas. Visitors can also visit the venerable lighthouse known as "Old Baldy." This sentinel of the sea is now ornamentally lit by island residents.

The management of Bald Head has dredged a harbor and marina on the island's western shore not far from the charted lighthouse. The marina channel lies east-southeast of flashing daybeacon #13 (currently charted as #11). Minimum low-water entrance depths run in the 5- to 7-foot range. There is 6 to 9 feet of water in the dockage ba-

**Bald Head Island Marina
(910) 457-7380**

Approach depth: 5–7 feet
Dockside depth: 6–9 feet
Accepts transients: yes
Fixed wooden and floating concrete piers: yes
Dockside power connections: 30 amp & some 50 amp
Dockside water connections: yes
Showers: yes
Laundromat: yes
Waste pump-out: yes
Gasoline: yes
Diesel fuel: yes
Ship's & variety store: yes
Restaurant: nearby

sin. Transients are accepted at the floating concrete and fixed wooden piers. Water and 30-amp power connections are available at each berth; some slips also have 50-amp hookups. Expanded showers (two per bathroom) and a laundromat are located shoreside. Gas, diesel fuel, and waste pump-out service are available. Cruisers can replenish their galleys and marine supplies at the Island Chandlery store, which overlooks the harbor's southern tip. The marina staff will be glad to arrange transportation to the dining room at the nearby Bald Head Island Club (910-457-7300). The wine list here is noteworthy. By all accounts, don't miss the summer buffets.

Boaters should be aware that Bald Head Island Marina suffers from a considerable tidal-surge problem courtesy of the nearby Cape Fear Inlet. Boats lying at the docks are subject to a goodly amount of vertical bobbing. While many boaters take this motion in stride, others find it quite annoying.

In spite of the surge problem, this writer encourages you to visit Bald Head. I think you will discover that the island's delightfully harmonious development will be well worth your time. With its excellent marina facilities, Bald Head Island should be on every passing cruiser's list of overnight stops.

## Cape Fear Inlet

The extraordinarily well-buoyed Cape Fear Inlet is one of only three stable seaward channels on the entire North Carolina coastline; Beaufort and Masonboro Inlets are the others. Cape Fear Inlet is used regularly by a host of oceangoing, deep-draft commercial vessels. Cruisers can make use of this inlet with confidence.

# ICW AND LOWER CAPE FEAR NAVIGATION

During 1996, virtually all the aids to navigation on the Cape Fear River channel were changed. This was apparently part of a project to move the inlet's sea buoy a bit farther out into the ocean. Incidentally, the Cape Fear River inlet sea buoy has now been renumbered #CF.

Since the charting folks at NOAA have not yet caught onto these significant changes, confusion has been the result. This writer has received a number of letters from northbound ICW cruisers who passed the channel leading from the Cape Fear to Snows Cut because they were looking for flashing buoy #29. It has been renumbered #33!

In the account below, I will do my best to make sense out of this mess. It is to be hoped that new editions of charts 11534 and 11537 will soon put the matter to rest.

Fortunately, the various markers on the southerly ICW portion of the Snows Cut channel east of the large ships'–Cape Fear River channel have *not* been renumbered. Charts 11534 and 11537 still give an accurate account of this.

When departing Snows Cut at flashing daybeacon #163, turn west-southwest and point to pass unlighted daybeacon #165 to its fairly immediate northwesterly side. The charted range

markers will prove helpful in keeping you to the channel. Some 50 yards short of the forward range marker, flashing daybeacon #A, the Waterway cuts sharply southwest. Set a new course to pass unlighted daybeacon #167 to its northwesterly side.

From #167, it is a straight shot southwest into the Cape Fear channel. Set course to pass unlighted daybeacons #170, #172, #174, and #176 by 10 yards to their southeasterly sides. Continue on course, pointing to come abeam of flashing daybeacon #177 to its westerly side. At #177, slow down and take a moment to sort out the various aids. The ICW continues southwest, then south, passing flashing buoy #33 (currently charted as #29) to its easterly side.

South of #33, the color scheme on the Cape Fear's system of navigational aids take precedence. As you are now going downriver, pass all red, even-numbered markers to your port side and green aids to starboard.

From #33, set course to eventually pass flashing daybeacon #30 (currently charted as #26) to its westerly quarter. Though the channel is quite broad between #33 and #30, be aware of the correctly charted shallows to the west.

An alternate channel leads west from #33 to a

series of wharves on the western shore. Boaters should not enter this channel. The docks are part of the Sunny Point Marine Base and are off-limits to pleasure craft.

From #30, the ICW follows the main channel south for 6 nautical miles to flashing buoy #18 (currently charted as #14A). The channel is deep and well marked. Keep chart 11534 handy to resolve any questions about the river's many markers.

**Cape Fear Inlet**    West-northwest of flashing buoy #18, the Waterway turns sharply west and leaves the Cape Fear. For those interested in putting to sea or visiting Bald Head Island, a navigational account of Cape Fear Inlet is now presented.

From #18, set course to come abeam of flashing buoy #16 (currently charted as #14) to its westerly side. Southwest of #16, you will see a series of daymarks leading to the west. These aids mark an improved channel leading to Oak Island's Coast Guard station. This cut is for the exclusive use of the Coast Guard and should not be entered.

To proceed seaward, turn southeast and set a new course from #16 to come abeam of flashing buoy #15 (currently charted as #13) to its easterly side. It is a fairly long run of 1 nautical mile between the two aids. Shallow water lies well to the north and northeast.

West of #15, an unmarked cut known as Western Bar Channel leads to the ocean. Don't try this treacherous passage. The channel lacks any markings, and bottom configurations shift constantly.

From #15, set course to pass flashing daybeacon #13 (currently charted as #11) to its easterly side, then come abeam of flashing buoy #11 (currently charted as #9) to its southeasterly quarter. Do not drift west or northwest of #13 or #11 into the 2- and 3-foot waters of Jay Bird Shoal.

Once abeam of #13, use your binoculars to look east-southeast. You will spy the twin wooden breakwaters of Bald Head Island on the western shore. These structures flank the entrance channel to Bald Head Island Marina.

**Bald Head Island**    If you choose to enter Bald Head Island Harbor, head directly for the mid-width between the twin breakwaters. Approach depths are quite deep, typically 18 to 25 feet. Inside the small cut, the bottom quickly rises to 5-foot minimum depths. Be prepared to compensate for strong tidal currents when entering the harbor through the breakwaters. Nighttime entry is quite tricky and is not recommended except for those with local knowledge.

Once through the entrance, swing to starboard and inquire at the fuel dock about slip space.

**Seaward on the Cape Fear**    From flashing buoy #11 (currently charted as #9), the well-marked (but renumbered) channel leads seaward. Observe all markers carefully, and remember that, like most inlets, the Cape Fear cut can produce a menacing swell. The outermost sea buoy on this channel has now been renumbered #CF.

# ICW TO SOUTH CAROLINA

As the ICW turns west from the Cape Fear River, it darts past the charming river village of Southport. This community has surprisingly good facilities for cruising boaters, good restaurants, and a down-home atmosphere which beckons visitors to linger and rest from their travels.

Not far to the south, Dutchman Creek provides reasonably good overnight anchorage for craft drawing 5 feet or less. This stream is often used by local boaters to ride out heavy weather.

The next facilities to the south are at Lockwoods Folly Inlet, 9 nautical miles west of Southport. Shallotte Inlet, 8 nautical miles beyond Lockwoods Folly, has a marina that welcomes cruisers. Another marina just north of the South Carolina line accepts transients and provides fueling services.

South of Shallotte, the ICW soon passes into South Carolina. However, a deep, well-marked creek leads back to the village of Calabash in extreme southeastern North Carolina. There is now a full-service marina in Calabash, which greatly facilitates visits to the village's seafood restaurants by us seafaring folks.

## Southport (Standard Mile 309)

For many, many years, Southport has been one of the most peaceful spots on the Southern coast. I spent many a happy summer as a boy walking its lovely lanes, living aboard my father's boat, and fishing the waters of Frying Pan Shoals. On one remarkable day—before there were limits, you understand—three of us caught 78 Spanish mackerel.

Today, Southport stands ready to greet cruising visitors with one good marina, a surprising collection of sophisticated restaurants, and a raft of interesting parks and antique shops. I suggest that first-timers spend at least one day off the water getting to know this gem of the southeastern North Carolina coastline.

## Southport Marina (Standard Mile 309)

Two harbors serve the village of Southport.

The easternmost is located a short hop west of flashing daybeacon #1. It was here that I spent many a summer evening dreaming of cruising beyond the horizon. Now, this basin is primarily a commercial facility and offers few services for cruising craft.

The western basin's southern entrance sits hard by flashing daybeacon #2A. Here, passing cruisers will discover one of the largest marinas in North Carolina. Built by the state as a model but now privately leased, Southport Marina is run by a responsive management team looking to attract visiting boaters. In times past, others who leased this facility did not have nearly so upstanding a reputation. Thankfully, as long as the current management is in place, this problem is forgotten.

Southport Marina offers extensive transient dockage at fixed wooden docks and at floating wooden-decked finger docks set out from fixed concrete piers. Depths run 5 to 8 feet, the deeper soundings found along the outer docks. Every slip features full power and water connections. Extensive showers and a full laundromat are housed in the large building overlooking the basin. Recently, a sandwich shop has taken up residence on the second floor.

Gasoline, diesel fuel, waste pump-out service, and a ship's store which sells nautical charts are available to cruisers. Mechanical repairs can be arranged through local contractors. Haul-outs are accomplished by a 75-ton travel-lift. Do-it-yourself bottom work is allowed.

For those ready to take a break from the liveaboard routine, the Sea Captain Lodge (910-457-5263) stands guard over the northerly banks of the dockage basin. This is a large, modern, conveniently located motel with a swimming pool.

When lunchtime or dinnertime rolls around, cruisers will be glad to know they are within easy walking distance of many of Southport's excellent restaurants (see below).

Just across the street from Southport Marina, my good friends at Southport Harbor Marine Repair (614 W. West Street, 910-457-9164) offer a well-supplied ship's and parts store. Extensive mechanical repairs are available for outboards, I/O's, and small diesel power plants. Trust me, these people are great. Please stop by and tell Gene and Rina I sent you.

## Southport Restaurants

Within the last several years, the restaurant situation in Southport has taken a decided turn for the better. If you want good fried seafood or burgers, they're here for the taking. On the other hand, if your taste runs towards sophisticated or even exotic fare, you've also come to the right place. What's really great is that all the restaurants reviewed below (and several others) are within easy walking distance of Southport Marina. Ask any of the marina staff or a local for walking directions.

Soon after leaving the Cape Fear River and passing the ICW's flashing daybeacon #1, you will

---

**Southport Marina
(910) 457-9900**

Approach depth: 8–10 feet
Dockside depth: 5–8 feet (low water)
Accepts transients: yes
Floating wooden, fixed wooden, and
    fixed concrete piers: yes
Dockside power connections: 30 & 50 amps
Dockside water connections: yes
Showers: yes
Laundromat: yes
Waste pump-out: yes
Gasoline: yes
Diesel fuel: yes
Mechanical repairs: independent contractors
Below-waterline repairs: yes
Ship's & variety store: yes
Snack bar: yes
Restaurants: several nearby

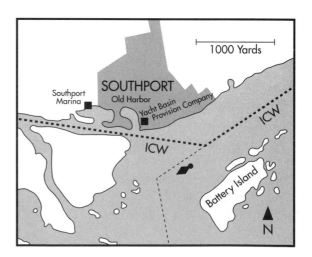

spy the Ship's Chandler Restaurant (910-457-6595) along the northerly banks, followed by Port Charlie's Restaurant (910-457-4395). The Ship's Chandler serves down-home fried seafood. Port Charlie's has a more extensive menu featuring steaks, pasta, and even some Cajun dishes. While neither of these establishments is this writer's personal favorite, the food is more than acceptable.

If the weather is warm and you are up for a truly funky dining experience, find your way to the Yacht Basin Provision Company (130 Yacht Basin Drive, 910-457-0654). Frankly, there are few establishments like this one left. Virtually all dining is outside overlooking the Southport commercial dockage basin. Drinks are acquired on the "honor system," and the atmosphere is decidedly bohemian. And let's not forget the food. The burgers are awesome, and both the grouper and crab cake sandwiches are enough to make the staunchest skeptic a believer. There are even a few fixed wooden slips "out back" which cruising patrons may use while dining. If space is available, cruisers taking their evening meal here can remain tied up overnight at no additional charge. Water and 30-amp power hookups are available. Boats as large as 45 feet can usually be accommodated. Depths alongside run around 5½ to 6 feet at low tide. The Yacht Basin Provision Company is open for business from the middle of March through December 1.

Want to wake up the old taste buds? If so, make your way to Thai Peppers (115 East Moore Street, 910-457-0095). The menu is an eclectic combination of Chinese, Indian, and Thai dishes ranging from mild to downright fiery.

If it's time to dig out your last clean shirt and take your cruising companion out for a really nice evening, find your way to Mr. P's Bistro (309 North Howe Street, 910-457-0832). Recently featured in several Southern magazines, Mr. P's serves a quality selection of veal, lamb, steaks, and seafood. The seafood gumbo is quickly becoming a local legend. Hang onto your wallet, as Mr. P's can be a bit expensive, but the reward is undoubtedly worth it. Mr. P's is open Monday through Saturday in the evening only.

## Southport Attractions

Southport has many old homes that have weathered the years quite well. Quite a few feature plaques with the date of construction and the family name of the builder. Many of the local streets are lined by lovely, old oak trees twisted by the ever-present coastal winds. A stroll through Southport can truly ease the tensions of the modern world.

The downtown business district has an impressive collection of antique and gift shops. Things haven't changed much since the 1950s in downtown Southport. It is fortunate that "modern improvements" have never overtaken the village.

*Southport Marina*

Pause a few moments in your cruising travels to explore the downtown streets. You won't regret taking an up-close look at a small-town America that has all but vanished elsewhere.

If you want to experience the shoreside charms of Southport, turn east from the marina and walk down Brunswick Street past the old commercial harbor. Soon, you will run into North Caswell Avenue. Turn right, then left on West Moore Street. This lane will lead you directly into the downtown district.

After sampling the shops, walk north for two blocks on N.C. 211/Howe Street (Southport-Supply Road) and watch to the right for Franklin Square Park. This restful, shady park is graced by many of the town's stately oaks. If you have fought too many waves, take a moment to pause here. The park's recuperative influence is most impressive.

Next, you should visit the Southport Visitor's Center (107 East Nash Street, 910-457-7927). During summer, the center is open Monday through Saturday from 10 A.M. to 5 P.M. Here, you can acquire all sorts of information about Southport and surrounding Brunswick County. Ask for the pamphlet describing the mile-long Southport Trail. This stroll will introduce you to many of the village's historic points of interest.

Another good spot to check out is the Southport Maritime Museum (166 North Howe Street, 910-457-0003). There is no better place to get in touch with the region's rich maritime heritage, which stretches back to the days when only Native Americans wandered the watery path of the Cape Fear. The museum is open Monday through Saturday from 10 A.M. to 4 P.M.

Finally, if you enjoy reading the always-in-teresting, sometimes-quirky inscriptions on old grave markers, plan a visit to the Old Smithville Burial Ground at the corner of East Moore and South Rhett Streets. Here, you will find many markers dedicated to seafaring families, some of whose descendants still live and work in Southport.

### Indigo Plantation Marina (Standard Mile 309.5)

Along the Waterway's northern shore between Southport Marina and Dutchman Creek, the owners and management of Bald Head Island have constructed a large residential development and marina known as Indigo Plantation. The mainland depot for the Bald Head Island ferry has also been moved to this harbor.

Though the original plan was to accept transients at Indigo Plantation Marina, all the available slips have been rented to resident craft. While this marina may look good from the water, passing cruisers need enter only for a closer look.

### Dutchman Creek (Standard Mile 310)

Guarding the Waterway's northern shore just west of unlighted daybeacon #5, Dutchman Creek provides the only sheltered anchorage between Southport and Calabash. Minimum depths of 5 feet can be held in the unmarked entry channel, but a navigational mistake could land you in 3 feet of water. Depths temporarily improve to 6 feet or better between the entrance and the stream's first turn to the northwest. Craft drawing no more than 5 feet can anchor with good protection on the initial stretch of the creek just north of its mouth. There should be enough swinging room for boats up to 35 feet in length. Both shores are composed of saltwater marsh in its natural state. On calm summer nights, the creek is usually a haven for bloodthirsty mosquitoes and other winged pests. The scenery is not as attractive as that on some other anchorages along the North Carolina portion of the ICW.

## Blue Water Point Marina (Standard Mile 320)

West of unlighted daybeacon #32, the ICW begins its approach to an intersection with the Lockwoods Folly River, then treks across the northerly reaches of Lockwoods Folly Inlet. Blue Water Point Marina (formerly Sportsman's Marina) is located south of unlighted daybeacon #36. This facility is under new management which encourages transient business. The marked entry channel has one lump near its intersection with the ICW which carries only 4 to 4½ feet at low water, but the remainder of the channel has 6 to 7 feet of water. Depths alongside range from 5 to 6 feet. All dockage is at floating wooden-decked piers featuring full power and water connections. Gasoline and diesel fuel are ready for pumping dockside. There is also an on-site ship's store with a few basic variety items including sandwiches.

Just behind the dockage basin, visitors will discover The Fish House Restaurant (910-278-1230). I have not had the chance to sample the fare here, but it seems likely that the seafood is fresh. There is also an adjacent motel.

While a few showers and other amenities would be nice, Blue Water Point can now claim to provide adequate transient services. In fact, it is probably the best-equipped marina between Southport and Holden Beach (see below). If you aren't in desperate need of a shower, consider stopping for an evening. Tell Larry I sent you.

**Blue Water Point Marina
(910) 278-1230**

Approach depth: 4–7 feet
Dockside depth: 5-6 feet
Accepts transients: yes
Floating wooden piers: yes
Dockside power connections: 30 & 50
   amps
Dockside water connections: yes
Gasoline: yes
Diesel fuel: yes
Ship's and variety store: yes
Restaurant: on-site

## Lockwoods Folly River (Standard Mile 320)

Northwest of unlighted daybeacon #36, a marked channel strikes north up the Lockwoods Folly River to a commercial fishing-craft dockage basin. The various flats on either side of the cut are rich with oysters, and gatherers can often be spotted bending to their task.

With its minimum 5-foot depths, the channel is certainly deep enough for many pleasure craft, but it is quite narrow and does not offer any possibilities for anchorage.

## Lockwoods Folly Tale

Boaters often wonder how the inlet, river, and surrounding lands acquired the unique name of Lockwoods Folly. It seems that a Mr. Lockwood lived near the inlet many years ago. He decided to build his dream boat on the nearby river. Though no definite information is available on the craft, the times would seem to dictate that it was a sailing vessel of some sort. Tradition claims that the ship was made of the finest materials and that Lockwood looked forward to many years of reliable service.

Much to his dismay, Lockwood discovered that he had built the boat with too deep a draft to clear the inlet's outer bar. Whether from a broken heart or a broken pocketbook, he left his dream boat to rot in the river. The old derelict came to be called Lockwood's Folly. Though the ship is now long gone, the name stuck.

## Holden Beach Marina (Standard Mile 323.5)

What must surely be one of the friendliest marinas in southeastern North Carolina guards the Waterway's northern banks between flashing daybeacon #51 and the 65-foot fixed Holden Beach highway bridge. Holden Beach Marina offers transient dockage at floating wooden piers with water and 30-amp power connections. Minimum depths alongside are 5 feet. Showers are on the premises. Gasoline, diesel fuel, and mechanical repairs are all available, though diesel service is limited. Dry-stack storage for small power craft is also offered. Holden Beach Marina maintains a well-stocked ship's and variety store. A grocery store is within walking distance, as are several good restaurants. The marina management recommended Captain Willies Restaurant, the Barn Restaurant, and the Beach Cafe to this writer, but I have not yet had the chance to check them out.

The piers at Holden Beach Marina are quite sheltered, though tidal currents are much in evidence, as is usual for this portion of the coastline. Slip space is limited at this facility, so advance dockage arrangements are highly recommended.

**Holden Beach Marina**
**(910) 842-5447**

Approach depth: 10+ feet
Dockside depth: 5 feet (minimum)
Accepts transients: yes
Floating wooden piers: yes
Dockside power connections: 30 amps
Dockside water connections: yes
Showers: yes
Gasoline: yes
Diesel fuel: yes
Mechanical repairs: yes (limited diesel service)
Ship's & variety store: yes
Restaurants: several nearby

## Hughes Marina (Standard Mile 330)

West-northwest of flashing daybeacon #71A, the ICW begins its often-scary passage across the intersection of the Shallotte River and Shallotte Inlet. Currents here can be awesome, and frequent dredging is required.

The two low-level ranks of Hughes Marina's concrete floating docks jut out from Bowen Point, located at the Shallotte River's west-side entrance point between unlighted daybeacon #75 and flashing daybeacon #77. Hughes offers limited transient dockage. The available slips have water hookups, but the only power to be had requires a long power cable stretched up the docks to connections on top of the hill overlooking the piers. The current that sweeps past these docks has to be seen to be believed. Entrance depths run 5 to 6 feet. There are minimum 5-foot soundings dockside.

Gasoline is available, and the marina management hopes to offer diesel fuel in the future. Showers can be arranged at a small, rather funky motel just in back of the marina. Mechanical repairs are available through independent con-

*Oyster gathering on Lockwoods Folly River*

tractors. The on-site restaurant is rather small, but it serves ultrafresh fried seafood.

All in all, Hughes Marina can only be rated a fair possibility for large cruising craft. The low-level piers, the intense currents, and the lack of ready power connections are all significant disadvantages.

**Hughes Marina**
**(910) 754-6233**

Approach depth: 5–6 feet (low water)
Dockside depth: 5 feet (low water)
Accepts transients: yes
Floating concrete piers: yes (very low-level)
Dockside power connections: limited
Dockside water connections: yes
Showers: yes
Gasoline: yes
Mechanical repairs: independent contractors
Restaurant: on-site

### Shallotte Inlet (Standard Mile 330)

Shallotte Inlet, lying west-southwest of unlighted daybeacon #80, is shoal and changeable and should not be attempted. The intersection of the inlet and the ICW is subject to frequent shoaling and is one of the trickiest portions of the entire North Carolina portion of the Waterway.

### Shallotte Legend

Since earliest colonial times, the waters of Shallotte Inlet have had a reputation for remarkable healing powers. According to Charles Harry Whedbee, many local residents claim the inlet is the famous stream of Indian legend "where infections, fevers, and vapors were cured simply by bathing in its magical waters."

Apparently, miraculous cures are so numerous that men of modern medicine do not doubt the waters' healing qualities. Many longtime residents can tell of several family members who were cured after bathing in the inlet.

Whedbee states that a reed peculiar to Shallotte Inlet may well hold the answer to the waters' curative qualities. A breadlike substance in the center of the reed seems to grow a penicillin-like mold when wetted by salt water. The next incoming tide washes the mold off. The resulting "milky water" seems to have been present during most of the miraculous cures.

The healing powers of Shallotte Inlet are seemingly as much a matter of fact as of legend. If you have been looking for a personal Fountain of Youth, try the waters of Shallotte Inlet.

### Pelican Point Marina (Standard Mile 335.5)

West of flashing daybeacon #98, the docks of Pelican Point Marina front the Waterway's northern shore. This facility offers transient dockage at its fixed wooden outer dock. Water, some 20-amp power connections, and a small number of 50-amp hookups are available. Depths alongside are 7 to 8 feet or better. There are also some small, inner floating wooden piers, but these are often used by local craft. Depths are not as good at these inner slips, with low-water soundings raging from 4 to 6 feet. Gasoline and diesel fuel are available, as are full mechanical repairs and drystack storage. The marina can usually arrange transportation to restaurants and grocery stores. Again, strong tidal currents are sometimes in evidence at the docks. Skippers of sailcraft and single-screw powerboats should be mindful of these conditions.

*Holden Beach Marina*

**Pelican Point Marina
(910) 579-6440**

Approach depth: 10+ feet
Dockside depth: 7–8 feet at outer dock,
   4½–6 feet at inner slips
Accepts transients: yes
Fixed wooden (outer) and floating
   wooden (inner) piers: yes
Dockside power connections: 20-amp
   & minimal 50-amp service
Dockside water connections: yes
Gasoline: yes
Diesel fuel: yes
Mechanical repairs: extensive
Ship's & variety store: yes
Restaurants: transportation usually available

## Pontoon Bridge (Standard Mile 338)

West of unlighted daybeacon #105, boaters will encounter the last remaining pontoon bridge in North Carolina. A pontoon bridge is an interesting structure to watch in operation. The center of the bridge actually floats on pontoons. When it comes time for the span to open, the center is pulled back by a cable on one side. When the traffic has passed, the center is pulled back into position by a cable on the opposite side.

Unfortunately, this fascinating structure has been slated for replacement by the North Carolina Department of Transportation. The residents of nearby Sunset Beach are fighting this plan, not only to preserve the historic bridge but to help lessen automobile traffic coming onto the beach. I wish the island residents well in their efforts.

On the negative side, the pontoon span (which has 0 feet of closed vertical clearance) follows a restricted opening schedule much of the year. From April 1 through October 30, it opens only on the hour from 7 A.M. to 7 P.M.

## Calabash, Calabash Creek, and Associated Facilities (Standard Mile 342)

Calabash Creek, lying just northeast of the Waterway's intersection with Little River Inlet, provides the first (and one of the few) opportunities for overnight anchorage on this section of the ICW. Shoaling not noted on the latest edition of chart 11534 has occurred at the creek's southwesterly mouth northeast of the ICW's unlighted daybeacon #2. Boaters can now expect typical low-water depths of 5½ to 6 feet over the entrance bar. Similarly, the channel farther upstream between flashing daybeacon #4 and unlighted daybeacon #6 has shoaled along its easterly flank. Local reports indicate that these waters may be slated for dredging in 1998.

Good anchorage is to be found along lower Calabash Creek's eastern and northeastern shores between the creek's unlighted daybeacon #2 (not to be confused with unlighted daybeacon #2 on the ICW) and flashing daybeacon #4. Low-water depths of 5½ to 9 feet run within 30 yards or so of shore between #2 and unlighted daybeacon #3. Similar depths are found between #3 and the creek's sharp swing to the north near flashing daybeacon #4. Swinging room should be sufficient for boats as large as 40 feet. Shelter is excellent from all but strong southern and southwestern winds, which blow straight in from the creek's mouth. A few attractive homes overlook the eastern and northeastern banks. The marsh island to the west is undeveloped.

Calabash Creek leads north and northeast to the village of Calabash, located barely within the borders of North Carolina. A marked channel holding minimum 6- to 8-foot depths is, for the most part, easily followed to the village waterfront. There are no marinas on the Calabash waterfront, but diplomatic boaters may be able to negotiate dockage for the night at one of the many commercial docks.

Fortunately, the longtime problem of finding a slip in or near Calabash has been solved by the addition of a fine facility, Marsh Harbour Marina. A well-sheltered dockage basin sporting 120 slips has been dredged northwest of the creek's unlighted daybeacon #8. Entrance depths in the marina channel run 7 to 9 feet, and boaters will find 8 to 17 feet of water dockside. Marsh Harbour also holds the distinction of being the closest marina to Little River Inlet.

Transients are accepted for overnight or temporary dockage at concrete-decked floating docks with water connections and power connections up to 50 amps. Gasoline, diesel fuel, waste pumpout service, and shoreside showers are readily available. Mechanical repairs can be arranged through local independent contractors. It's a quick walk into downtown Calabash, where you will find a host of restaurants. Some of the local dining establishments offer free dockside pickup and delivery for visiting cruisers. Ask the dockmaster for advice.

Marsh Harbour has completed three condo units and a large clubhouse overlooking the northwestern corner of the dockage basin. More condos are planned. For a small fee, boaters may use the heated pool and exercise room in the clubhouse. Those who would like to take a break from the live-aboard routine will discover that luxury condos are usually available for rent and that an attractive discount is offered to those who arrive by water.

*Oak Island Lighthouse*

### Marsh Harbour Marina
### (910) 579-3500

Approach depth: 5½-9 feet
Dockside depth: 8-17 feet
Accepts transients: yes
Concrete floating docks: yes
Dockside power connections: up to 50 amps
Dockside water connections: yes
Showers: yes
Waste pump-out: yes
Gasoline: yes
Diesel fuel: yes
Mechanical repairs: independent contractors
Restaurants: many nearby

The village of Calabash has long been famous for its fried seafood. You may want to step ashore and test its reputation for yourself. Frankly, I've always found the seafood here a bit ordinary. My taste buds must be in the minority, though, as hundreds of thousands make the trek to Calabash's restaurants year after year.

# ICW TO SOUTH CAROLINA NAVIGATION

To enter the ICW landcut from the Cape Fear River, set course from a position abeam of flashing buoy #18 (currently charted as #14A) to come abeam of flashing daybeacon #1 to its northerly side. Just before reaching #1, you will pass unlighted daybeacon #2 to its southerly side.

The color configuration returns to its usual ICW pattern west of #1. Past #1, the village of Southport will come abeam along the northerly shore.

West of flashing daybeacon #1, you will catch sight of a long wooden pier abutting the northerly banks. This structure is part of a local park and is not meant for dockage by any size craft.

*Southport*    Just west of flashing daybeacon #1, the first of Southport's harbors will come abeam to the north. Most pleasure-craft skippers will want to continue west to Southport Marina. The marina entrance opens out on the northern shore a short hop east of flashing daybeacon #2A.

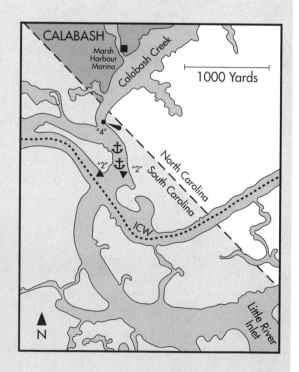

**On the ICW**   The ICW run between Southport and Lockwoods Folly Inlet consists of a canal that is mostly man-made and offers only one sidewater possibility. While the Waterway is quite straightforward in this section, don't become casual about navigation. Most of the shoreline between Southport and South Carolina is quite shoal. Stick strictly to the mid-width.

**Dutchman Creek**   Dutchman Creek lies on the Waterway's northern shore immediately west of unlighted daybeacon #5. Enter on the centerline and drop anchor before cruising through the stream's first sharp turn to the northwest. Farther upstream, 4-foot depths wait to trap the unwary.

**On the ICW**   West of unlighted daybeacon #9, the Waterway ducks under the Oak Island fixed bridge, which has a vertical clearance of 65 feet. Between flashing daybeacon #16 and unlighted daybeacon #28, you will spot many vacation homes along the southern shore. These are part of the extensive resort community of Long Beach.

Take care when passing flashing daybeacon #18. The northern side of the channel is subject to shoaling from the small, charted, unnamed creek. To avoid this potential hazard, favor the southern side of the channel, but don't approach the southern bank too closely.

The Waterway turns southwest at flashing daybeacon #24, then swings sharply back west at flashing daybeacon #29. A shoal seems to be building out from the northern shore at this bend. For best depths, pass #29 close by its northern side.

West-northwest of flashing daybeacon #33, the ICW begins its entry into the waters lying about Lockwoods Folly. As is always true when the Waterway passes close to an inlet, the channel is subject to shoaling. Observe all markers carefully. Be on the alert for small, floating markers placed along the channel's edge to mark new incursions by the surrounding shallows.

**Blue Water Point Marina**   South of unlighted daybeacon #36, a marked channel leads south to Blue Water Point Marina. Remember that low-tide depths in this cut run as little as 4½ feet.

**Lockwoods Folly River**   You will sight the marked passage up the Lockwoods Folly River along the ICW's northern flank between unlighted daybeacons #36 and #39. The first aid to navigation on this channel is unlighted daybeacon #1. Should you decide to explore the river, pass all red markers to your starboard side and take green beacons to port. As you are now going upriver, this color scheme is to be expected.

**Lockwoods Folly Inlet**   Between unlighted daybeacon #46 and flashing daybeacon #48A, the ICW darts past the northern reaches of Lockwoods Folly Inlet. Cruisers should pass green can buoys #47 and #47A to their northern sides and point to pass unlighted nun buoy #48 to its fairly immediate southern quarter. This area is subject to shoaling and strong tidal currents. Caution should be exercised by all skippers, particularly those who pilot slow-moving power craft and sailcraft. Watch carefully for leeway. If you are under sail, have the auxiliary on standby.

Avoid the inlet itself. It is subject to continual change, and aids to navigation are not charted.

**On the ICW**   West of flashing daybeacon #48A, the ICW continues its narrow way south. It is bordered by an ever-thickening band of private homes

*Anchoring on Calabash Creek*

along this stretch, some with their own private docks fronting the Waterway. Watch for several official no-wake zones. Remember, even on unrestricted portions of the Waterway, you are legally responsible for any damage caused by your wake.

West of flashing daybeacon #51, the Waterway passes under a fixed high-rise bridge with 65 feet of vertical clearance. Just before reaching the bridge, you will spy Holden Beach Marina on the northern shore.

**Shallotte River and Shallotte Inlet**   The ICW channel remains straightforward and easy to follow until flashing daybeacon #71A. Here, the ICW begins to

enter the Shallotte River–Saucepan Creek–Shallotte Inlet area. This treacherous portion of the Waterway is subject to continual shoaling and strong currents. Cruise along at "red alert." Detail one crew member to do nothing but watch the sounder. Be ready to discover different markers than those pictured on chart 11534 or covered below.

It would be foolish to discuss the several shoals currently impinging on the ICW channel between flashing daybeacons #71A and #83. By the time of your arrival, they will have changed several dozen times. In general, though, favor the southern (ocean) side of the Waterway channel when passing the mouth of the Shallotte River between #71A and flashing daybeacon #77.

Past flashing daybeacon #77, the Waterway twists west-southwest and enters Saucepan Creek. Just before entering the creek, you will pass Hughes Marina to the north at charted Bowen Point.

From unlighted daybeacon #80 to flashing daybeacon #83, the Waterway skirts the inner (northerly) reaches of Shallotte Inlet. Here again, shoals appear and disappear overnight. Over the years, I have observed more dredging along this portion of the ICW than on any other section of the Waterway from North Carolina to Florida. In general, favor the northerly (mainland) side of the channel slightly. The worst shoals seem to lie southeast of unlighted can buoy #81. Of course, this situation will probably change by the time you visit.

Flashing daybeacon #83 marks the Waterway's return to a sheltered, stable landcut. The channel remains easy to follow to South Carolina waters. You will encounter no further sidewaters until reaching Calabash Creek.

West of unlighted daybeacon #91, the Waterway passes through a fixed high-rise bridge with 65 feet of vertical clearance. Some 0.6 nautical mile west of unlighted daybeacon #105, you will encounter the Sunset Beach pontoon bridge. Approach the bridge slowly. Before cruising through, wait for the pull-back cable to drop to the bottom after the span is open. If you have the time, pause on the opposite side to watch the center span being drawn back into place.

Southwest of unlighted daybeacon #115, the ICW leaves North Carolina. However, by using Calabash Creek, it is possible to reenter the state at the village of Calabash.

*Marsh Harbour Marina*

**Calabash**   To enter Calabash Creek, leave the Waterway just before reaching the ICW's unlighted daybeacon #2 by turning 90 degrees to the northeast. This maneuver is complicated by the presence of another unlighted daybeacon #2, which acts as the first marker on the Calabash Creek channel. Don't be confused by the numbering similarity of these two aids to navigation.

Favor the eastern shore as you enter the creek. As you would expect, pass all red markers to your starboard side and green beacons to port as you head upstream to Calabash. The shallowest portion of the channel is between the creek's entrance and Calabash Creek's unlighted daybeacon #2. Cruisers can currently expect some 5½-foot depths at low water.

After Calabash Creek's unlighted daybeacon #2, the channel begins a lazy turn to the northwest. Avoid the port-side banks between #2 and flashing daybeacon #4. Shallow water abuts the western and southwestern banks along this stretch.

As mentioned earlier, a popular anchorage lies along the creek's eastern and northeastern banks between #2 and #4. Simply feel your way a short distance off the channel, drop the hook, and settle down for an undisturbed evening.

Northwest of unlighted daybeacon #3, Calabash Creek forks. Avoid the branch leading to the west, as depths here are more than suspect. Instead, follow the northern fork past flashing daybeacon #4.

A new shoal known locally as "the Parking Lot" has built up along the channel's southeastern flank between flashing daybeacon #4 and unlighted daybeacon #6. Favor the western and northwestern sides of the cut between #4 and #6 to avoid this hazard.

You will spy the entrance to Marsh Harbour Marina along the northwestern banks hard by unlighted daybeacon #8. The channel is marked by two small, unlighted spar-type buoys.

A series of markers leads farther upstream on the main creek through depths of 8 to 10 feet to Calabash. East-northeast of unlighted daybeacon #9, Calabash's waterfront opens out on the port shore. If you continue upstream, be sure to pass flashing daybeacon #10 to your starboard side.

The first dock you will encounter is a long pier owned by Calabash Fishing Fleet.

Currently, there is little in the way of dockage for pleasure craft on the Calabash waterfront. Most cruising boats would do better to berth at Marsh Harbour Marina, just downstream, and then walk into the village.

Don't attempt to continue upstream on Calabash Creek past the village waterfront. Depths soon rise to grounding levels.

**On to South Carolina**   This guide's account of the ICW's southward trek ends at Calabash Creek. For a continuing account of the Waterway, please consult this writer's *Cruising Guide to Coastal South Carolina and Georgia.*

I hope you have enjoyed your trek through North Carolina's varied and fascinating waters. If you've had only half the fun that I've enjoyed in bringing this material to you, my purpose has been more than satisfied. Good luck and good cruising wherever your travels take you!

*Quiet Southport*

# INDEX